Barbara Ann L

12/10/10

2/1/11

THE
DARK
GAZE

THE
DARK
GAZE

MAURICE BLANCHOT AND THE SACRED

KEVIN HART

THE UNIVERSITY OF CHICAGO PRESS, CHICAGO AND LONDON

Kevin Hart is professor of English at the University of Notre Dame.
He is the author of numerous works, including *The Trespass of the Sign:
Deconstruction, Theology, and Philosophy* and *Samuel Johnson
and the Culture of Property.* He is also the author of several volumes
of poetry, including *Flame Tree: Selected Poems.*

The University of Chicago Press, Chicago 60637
The University of Chicago Press, Ltd., London
© 2004 by Kevin Hart
All rights reserved. Published 2004
Printed in the United States of America

13 12 11 10 09 08 07 06 05 04   1 2 3 4 5

ISBN: 0-226-31810-9 (cloth)
ISBN: 0-226-31811-7 (paper)

The University of Chicago Press gratefully acknowledges the support of the
Institute for Scholarship in the Liberal Arts of the College of Arts
and Letters of the University of Notre Dame
in the publication of this book.

Library of Congress Cataloging-in-Publication Data

Hart, Kevin, 1954–
The dark gaze : Maurice Blanchot and the sacred / Kevin Hart.
    p. cm. — (Religion and postmodernism)
Includes bibliographical references and index.
ISBN 0-226-31810-9 (cloth : alk. paper) —
ISBN 0-226-31811-7 (pbk. : alk. paper)
1. Blanchot, Maurice—Philosophy. I. Title. II. Series.
PQ2603.L3343Z674 2004
843′.912—dc22

2004009445

CONTENTS

ACKNOWLEDGMENTS

In two decades of reading Blanchot, I have chalked up many debts, and it is a pleasure to acknowledge them now. Harold Bloom, Yves Bonnefoy, Mark Brett, Jacques Derrida, Geoffrey Hartman, Michael Holland, Tony Kelly, Leslie Hill, John Milbank, Jean-Luc Marion, Emmanuel Mosès, David Odell, Cyril O'Regan, Jill Robbins, Mark C. Taylor, and David Tracy have offered advice or information or posed questions I have found useful. Paul Kane and Regina Schwartz have never ceased to encourage me in this project, as in all my academic work. Walter Veit kindly checked my translations from the German where necessary, while conversations with Kate Rigby about German literature and philosophy invariably made me see further than I could have done otherwise.

A much earlier version of chapters 1 and 2 was read at "Australian Divagations: Mallarmé and the Twentieth Century," a conference held in 1998 at the University of Melbourne. I also read parts of later versions to the Department of French at Monash University in Melbourne and in the research colloquium of the Department of Religious Studies at the University of California, Santa Barbara. I read sections of chapters 2 and 3 in the research colloquium of the Center for Comparative Literature and Cultural Studies at Monash University. Another part of chapter 3 was read in the Department of Religious Studies at Temple University, Philadelphia. Different sections of chapter 4 were read in the Comparative Literature colloquium at Northwestern University, Evanston, and to the Department of Philosophy at Villanova University. A portion of chapter 5 was read at the Humanities Colloquium at Deakin University in Geelong, Australia. A very early version of chapters 1 and 2 appeared in *Australian Divagations: Mallarmé and the Twentieth Century*, edited by Jill Anderson (Peter Lang, 2002). Part of a draft of chapter 2 was published in *Transcendence*, edited by Regina Schwartz (Routledge, 2004). A section of chapter 3, now heavily revised and expanded, appeared in *Religion, Modernity, and Postmodernity*, edited by Paul Heelas with the assistance of David Martin and Paul Morris (Basil Blackwell, 1998). A version of chapter 4 appeared in the *Oxford Literary Review* 22 (2000). A passage from chapter 6 was published in the *Journal of Philosophy and Scripture* (2004). Finally, an earlier version of chapter 3 appeared as a small-press booklet entitled *The Impossible* (Vagabond Press, 2003). My thanks to all editors and publishers. I wish to thank the anonymous readers for the University of Chicago Press and Randy Petilos and Alan Thomas, not least of all for their patience in waiting several years for the typescript of this book to arrive at their office. Last but not least, I would like to thank Tommy Davis and J. P. Shortall for considerable help in checking citations, Susan Tarcov for her meticulous copyediting, and Scott Moringiello for assistance in correcting the proof.

I taught graduate seminars on Blanchot, usually twinned with Bataille, Kafka, or Lévinas, at Monash University over the period from 1992 to 2001, and I would like to pay tribute to my students for their attention and their astute questions over the years. In particular, I would like to thank Robyn Horner and Clive Madder, who worked as my research assistants at different times. In the fall of 2001 I was invited to Villanova University to be visiting professor of Christian philosophy. I taught a doctoral seminar there entitled "Maurice Blanchot and the Sacred," and the students in that class will find traces of our lively conversations in these pages. I am thankful to John D. Caputo for inviting me to Villanova and for participating in the seminar.

It is with deep gratitude that I thank my wife, Rita, and my daughters, Sarah and Claire, for sustaining me while I was writing this book, both in Australia and in the United States. My daughters grew up with their father never very far from at least one pale yellow Gallimard volume by Blanchot. I remember how Claire would come into my study to kiss me goodnight while I was writing these chapters, and how she would sometimes say as a farewell, "Happy Blanchot dreams!" I recall telling the story to Jacques Derrida who said, smiling, "But there are no happy Blanchot dreams!" Perhaps so; but he was the first person to set me thinking about Blanchot, and it is with profound thanks for that and for everything else that I dedicate this study to him.

ABBREVIATIONS

All references to the writings of Blanchot, Bataille, and Lévinas are given first to their translations in English, whenever available, and then to the French original. When only the French original is available, I have made a translation myself and cited the French edition. The following abbreviations are used.

BATAILLE

LÉVINAS

INTRODUCTION: THE DARK GAZE

1

At the end of his contribution to the *Nouvelle Revue Française* for May 1963, Maurice Blanchot reflects on setting down one of the two books he had been considering. On closing this book, he tells us, he felt as though "the very history of criticism and culture closed."[1] The act was accompanied by a "melancholy serenity," and he considered himself sent forth and authorized "to enter a new space." "What space?" he asks himself, and then develops a bold metaphor by way of answer:

> It is nearly understood that the Universe is curved, and it has often been supposed that this curvature has to be positive: hence the image of a finite and limited sphere. But nothing permits one to exclude the hypothesis of an unfigurable Universe (a term henceforth deceptive); a Universe escaping every optical exigency and also escaping consideration of the whole—essentially non-finite, disunited, discontinuous. What about such a Universe? Let us leave this question here and instead ask another: what about man the day he accepts confronting the idea that the curvature of the world, and even of his world, is to be assigned a negative sign? But will he ever be ready to receive such a thought, a thought that, freeing him from the fascination with unity, for the first time risks summoning him to take the measure of an exteriority that is not divine, of a space entirely in question, and even excluding the possibility of an answer, since every response would necessarily fall anew under the jurisdiction of the figure of figures? This amounts perhaps to asking ourselves: is man capable of a radical interrogation? That is, finally, is he capable of literature, if literature turns aside and toward the absence of a book? (350; 513–14)

The book that Blanchot had closed is Georges Poulet's *Les Métamorphoses du cercle* (1961), a copious and brilliant study of the ways in which an influential definition of God is variously recast in literature as an image of being human.

Deus est spaera cujus centrum ubique: so runs a definition of the deity that goes back to the twelfth century. Its familiarity in modern European languages goes beyond the doctrine of God in theology and beyond the practice of holy contemplation: "God is the sphere of which the center is everywhere and the circumference is nowhere."[2] If we recognize the phrasing from Pascal, we see the image most sharply and memorably in the final canto of the *Commedia* where Dante, finally allowed to enjoy all that he can of the beatific vision, represents the deity as a fixed point, a *nunc stans*, that consists of three circles:

> Nella profonda e chiara sussistenza
>> dell'alto lume parvemi tre giri
>>> di tre colori e d'una contenenza;
> e l'un dall'altro come iri da iri
>> parea reflesso, e'l terzo parea foco
>>> che quinci equindi igualmente si spiri.[3]

The Italian philosopher Giordano Bruno (1548–1600) was one of the first to dislodge this theology, not by explicitly disputing it but by following one of its consequences. If God reveals himself at every point in the universe, then human beings can stand anywhere and contemplate the divine glory. Once that move has been made, a dialectical response can be given. And so it was: "The soul is a kind of center," Bruno proclaimed (Poulet, *Metamorphoses*, xxvi).[4] Poulet admirably summarizes the shift in perspective: "Everywhere is the center of the divine activity. Everywhere too is the center of the activity inherent to the soul" (xxvii). So Tommaso Campanella can rightly exclaim, "The soul will become an immense sphere," and Thomas Traherne will echo him, "My soul is an infinite sphere in a center" (xxvii). Again, Poulet reflects on the change: "The infinite sphere has now become the symbol, not only of God, but of man. The infinite sphere is nothing now but the field encompassed by human consciousness" (xxvii). Far from being a casual choice, "consciousness" is one of Poulet's signature words. Especially in the United States, he was described as a "critic of consciousness" because he argued that when we read we reconstitute in our innermost selves the consciousness associated with the text: we think the thoughts of another person, not quite the author but a "sort of human being" that lives in the reader while the book is being read.[5] In reading, two consciousnesses become one, and the reader's "I" becomes more and more fully realized.

When Blanchot senses the closure of an era on laying aside *Les Métamorphoses du cercle* he is not dismissing either Poulet or his study.[6] On the contrary, he acknowledges that the book recapitulates "the very history of criticism and culture" and that this history still retains value. Blanchot and Poulet admire many of the same figures in French literature—Mallarmé and Rimbaud, Flaubert and Proust, among them—and both draw deeply, if rather differently, from phenomenology. Poulet dedicated the chapter on the Swiss diarist Henri Frédéric Amiel (1821–81) to Blanchot, and we read there that "consciousness without an object is a thought which forbids itself to think, at least to think explicitly, and which consequently ceaselessly searches and flies from itself in an endless movement, of which Maurice Blanchot many times has given an unforgettable description."[7] This insight into *Thomas l'obscur* (1941), among other works, is not the sole reason for the dedication, however. In a letter to Marcel Raymond on January 2, 1962, Poulet wonders whether all Blanchot's writing is not, in effect, "the portrait of an existence no different from that which rules Amiel after getting away from . . . the divine center."[8] Amiel "only knows the immensity of absence," Poulet notes in *Les Métamorphoses du cercle* (209). A little over a year before, Poulet wrote to Raymond that one sees in Blanchot, as in several others of his generation, "*the experience* [expérience] *of the absence of God*," and that this "is perhaps one of the distinctive traits of our epoch" (Raymond and Poulet, *Correspondance,* 57). Absence and transcendence are very close in meaning, Poulet observed, and the frequency with which one finds affirmations of the absence of God indicates a relation with "other epochs where Christianity is vibrant, the times of Augustine, Calvin, Pascal and Kierkegaard" (57).

Poulet is right: the experience of the absence of God has been a distinctive trait of his generation and those that have followed. Yet in one way or another it has broadly informed French intellectual culture since the Enlightenment, and we might take the execution of Louis XVI on January 21, 1793, to introduce a new register in French consciousness. Pierre Klossowski once observed that "At the moment the blade severs the head of Louis XVI," people as different as the marquis de Sade and Joseph de Maistre see "the representative of God dying."[9] He went further: "It is the blood of the temporal representative of God and, in a deeper sense, the blood of God that falls on the heads of the insurgent people" (226). The execution of Louis XVI meant that religious authority was to be sundered from civil government in the republic and that there was to be no place for clerics. The calendar itself was to be revised in order to remove Christian associations, and a cult of Reason was instituted. No sooner was this process in motion, however, than there was talk of "l'unité sacrée"; and Robespierre argued forcefully to the National Convention that God did indeed exist and that the soul was immortal. This is the God of Jean-Jacques Rousseau, infinitely distant from us, not the God of Saint Augustine, *interior intimo meo et superior summo meo*;[10] and this *Être Suprême* was celebrated at a festival orchestrated by Robespierre on June 8, 1794. An atheism that countenanced talk of the sacred with respect to society, and an absent God who is revealed in the mind rather than in Scripture: we can take these two positions as vanishing points between which much French intellectual life would be played over the following centuries. It has been a rich and varied performance, featuring in recent decades the "mystique athée" of Georges Bataille and René Char and the "Dieu qui vient à l'idée" of Emmanuel Lévinas and the advocates of *la religion sans religion*.[11]

Before the Revolution, the king embodied divine authority in both his body natural and his body politic.[12] Yet one consequence of the execution of Louis XVI was a willingness to regard the sacred as dispersed throughout the republic, not concentrated in the figure of the king. Jules Michelet noted how the sacred passed from the king to the people, who were wrapped in "a mystical cloak" ("une enveloppe mystique") until they could grow strong.[13] Louis XVI had sacrificed himself, he thought (along with many others), and now the French people, like others before them, must take on lives of self-sacrifice. Such lives would raise them, along with France, to a higher spiritual level.[14] If the National Convention thought that the death of the king would bring about a thoroughgoing desacralization in French society, they were very much mistaken. Within decades, the myth of the Martyr-King had led some people back to the churches. Michelet indignantly remarked on the reconciliation of church and royalty brought about by the "passion" of Louis XVI in his *Histoire de la Révolution française* (1847–53).[15] A swelling of attendance at mass was only one reaction to the regicide. Other signs of re-sacralization appeared in France in the nineteenth and twentieth centuries, some of them bizarre (Bataille's Madame Edwarda) and others perplexing (Blanchot's Outside).

One sign that is neither bizarre nor perplexing, at least for us, appears when we pass forward half a century from Jules Michelet to Émile Durkheim. In his late work *Les Formes élémentaires de la vie religieuse* (1912), the great sociologist insisted on an absolute dualism of all social phenomena as either profane or sacred. It is a division more heterogeneous than that between good and evil, he thought, for it concerns everything, not simply ethics. A resolute supporter of the republic, Durkheim saw the sacred as "nothing other than society hypostasized and transfigured," a view that allowed him "to interpret ritual life in secular and social terms" and, we might add, to discern impulses toward the sacred in secular society.[16] Georges Bataille inherits richly from Durkheim, and nowhere more clearly than when he imagines people watching a ritual execution. "The victim dies and the spectators share in what his death reveals": the sacred.[17] Equally, he differs from Durkheim in extending the range of the sacred. It is more than communication between human beings; it is communication between reality and us.

Bataille identifies "that which mystical experience apprehends with that which the rites and myths of the community bring into play."[18] Blanchot receives this tradition partly from Durkheim, Marcel Mauss, and Roger Caillois, and partly by way of Bataille's interpretation of them.

We can glimpse what Blanchot takes from this tradition and what he does with it by reflecting on Durkheim's definition of "religion." *"A religion,"* he writes, *"is a unified system of beliefs and practices relative to sacred things, that is to say, things set apart and forbidden—beliefs and practices which unite into one single moral community called a Church, all those who adhere to them"* (*Formes,* 44). Blanchot will not interest himself in the positivism of Durkheim's definition, and will talk of the sacred more than of religion (and never of the profane). Keeping an association of the sacred and community, he will argue that community is dispersed by what holds it together. If he urges us to think a new community, one that cannot be avowed by a sovereign individual because it is grounded in the death of the other person, he also invites us to abandon all hope that it can be unified or perpetuated. By way of what he calls the Outside, or the Impossible, or the Imaginary, he will try to refigure the sacred, to separate it from the God of the positive religions and their theologians.[19] He will do so not with overt reference to French sociology but, more often than not, by way of reading French and German literature and philosophy. Yet references to sociological investigations do occur, and nowhere more suggestively than when, following Caillois, he talks of expiating the sacred character of limit experience.[20]

But, as I said, Poulet *is* right: Blanchot, like others of his generation, testifies to an experience of the absence of God. Heidegger warned us decades ago that the absence of God is "not nothing" but on the contrary is the fullness of a vast and complex heritage, and even earlier he had said that "The flight of the gods must be experienced [*erfahren*] and endured."[21] If Blanchot interprets this experience by way of atheism, he acknowledges that the deity returns as a ghost in the assumptions of philosophy and in the reserve on which literature calls. More than that, Blanchot is exemplary in his understanding and treatment of this experience.[22] He indicates more fully and more rigorously than others of his generation what it means to experience the absence of God. And he attends more carefully than they do to the complexity of the experience. To deny God is not thereby to eliminate transcendence; it is to see how that question is transformed and where it takes up its new abodes.[23] To lose faith that life has an overarching meaning is not to dismiss mystery; it is to recognize that the human relation is mysterious, that the legitimate processes of demystification cannot find traction there. Blanchot would like to declare himself an atheist, yet the discipline of his thought drives him to conclude that no one can rightly say "*I* am an atheist": the "I" and "God" are homologous.[24] As with Nietzsche, there can be no quick or easy passage from atheism to modern secularism.[25] The idea of God returns in attenuated or grotesque forms, and even the view of community Blanchot affirms ultimately derives from a model of prayer. Besides, Poulet is not without reason in associating him with a "religious horror," one that is caused by the "presence of the sacred" (*Metamorphoses*, 86). It would have been impossible for Poulet to see Blanchot steadily and evenly on this issue, let alone formulate the matter sharply in a letter to a friend. Blanchot's ideas were in flux at the time, and he was at variance with some fundamental assumptions on which Poulet depends. Literature as consciousness is a notion that must be called into question, Blanchot thinks, and along with it the assumption that literature is associated with an interior life. The unity of an "I," and the unity presupposed by the notion of the metamorphoses of the circle, are to be challenged, as is the idea of a human subject turning an author, or a "sort of human being," into a correlate of one's consciousness.

Blanchot's contribution to the *Nouvelle Revue Française* for May 1963 was entitled "Ars Nova." Shorter than many of his critical pieces of the time, it nonetheless refers to an unusually wide range of authors and questions, gathering them into a single meditation that was long intently focused on the relations of art and philosophy—or, better, the philosophical assumptions that covertly regulate what it is to be human. The other book under review, the French translation of Theodor W. Adorno's *Philosophie der neuen Musik* (1949), provides Blanchot with a basis for arguing that literature is not wholly suborned by the politics of culture but is essentially "postcultural" (348; 511). There is a link between culture and humanism, he points out, and behind it there is a presumption that everything, including culture and the very project of being human, is organized by an appeal to "unity, totality or continuity" (348; 510). Since literature is "radical interrogation" (350; 514) or "pure question" (349; 512), it leads us to contest culture and humanism; it elaborates itself in terms of fragmentary writing, not complete and polished books, and in doing so it indicates a change of epoch. We are slowly moving away from the cultural world so richly described by Poulet's *Les Métamorphoses du cercle*, and exposing ourselves to new and unsettling ways of living with one another.

The metaphor that Blanchot advances for understanding what these new ways of living will mean is drawn from Albert Einstein's application of the general theory of relativity to cosmology. In earlier centuries people believed that material reality was formed into a universe, a profound unity. Their faith was supported by a metaphysical and theological affirmation of a God who is Himself one.

But now we must slowly come to terms with the thought that the universe has no such underlying unity. Such is Blanchot's understanding of the shift in scientific paradigms. What attracts him to the new view, here as elsewhere, is Einstein's reliance on the non-Euclidian geometry developed by Georg Riemann (1826–66).[26] The general theory of relativity construes space-time as a four-dimensional Riemannian space, and Blanchot is very taken with the idea of a Riemannian manifold with negative curvature, one that forms a hyperbolic rather than a spherical space.[27] Its consequence is a vision of a universe with insufficient mass ever to halt its expansion. This open universe is what excites Blanchot, although he is perhaps hasty to suggest that our new intelligence of the cosmos implies that it has no unity and that we must therefore be chary of the word "*universe*." The thought of a reality that is "essentially non-finite, disunited, discontinuous" evokes the lexicon of general topology rather than that of Riemannian geometry. And we should not forget that Einstein was the one who brought space and time into a unity and that, beginning with him, cosmologists have been in quest of a unified theory of the universe rather than being at ease in appreciating its plurality.

In affirming this new sense of reality, Blanchot says, we are summoned "to take the measure of an exteriority that is not divine" (350; 514). Yet if we accept Einsteinian cosmology it does not thereby follow that there is no God. Certainly Einstein himself saw no reason to abandon belief in the deity, although, as a loyal follower of Spinoza, he did not cling to a personal deity. "My religion," he once said, "consists of a humble admiration of the illimitable superior Spirit who reveals himself in the slight details we are able to perceive with our frail and feeble minds."[28] As it happens, the very time Blanchot was writing "Ars Nova" was a period of intense philosophical and theological speculation about divine providence in the age of modern science.[29] In *Process and Reality* (1929) Alfred North Whitehead had presented a fresh understanding of the deity that was taken by his admirers to square religion with the insights of cosmology, and his ideas were extended, ramified, and debated in the 1950s and early 1960s.[30] The God of process theology is not omnipotent and omniscient but nevertheless guides creation. "He is not *before* all creation but *with* all creation," as Whitehead crisply puts it.[31] Later theologians, including those of a more orthodox stripe than Whitehead, have found reason to see a convergence between belief in God and the discoveries of modern science. Some invite us to see in Einstein's cosmology a place for mystery that was denied in the earlier Newtonian worldview, while others find inspiration there for reforming theology itself. As one thoughtful Protestant voice puts it, the older dogmatics, "devoted to positive knowledge of God grounded in and informed by divine revelation," should be replaced by "a dogmatics operating with fluid axioms in the modern style instead of with fixed axioms or principles in the static style of the past."[32]

Explicit analogies drawn from mathematics and cosmology are rare in Blanchot, the only other one directly signaled occurring in "L'Interruption (*comme sur une surface de Riemann*)" (1964), and thankfully so. French intellectuals of his age and younger, people as different as Jacques Lacan and Alain Badiou, have a penchant for appealing to mathematical models, though rarely with sufficient justification or with the degree of convincing detail that would satisfy a mathematician. Blanchot's analogies with the hard sciences cause fewer flickers of concern than those entertained by his countrymen, and yet the metaphors they generate are never entirely satisfactory. Besides, his questioning uncovers a more radical vision of being human than is implied by his ruminations on Einstein. What he calls "the space of literature" is the place or, better, nonplace where discontinuity reigns and everything we encounter is strange, and it is in questioning literature and approaching this space that we are led to figure being human by way of the impossible as well as the possible. We can best approach this space or this interval—the French *espace* allows for both—by considering one of the things that Blanchot applauds in the new cosmology, the idea of "a Universe escaping every optical exigency" ("Ars Nova," 350; 514); and this will also serve to help explain the metaphor I have chosen as a guide in this study, "the dark gaze." Before leaving cosmology, however, I need to draw on it just one more time.

The theory of general relativity proposes that light always travels along the shortest path between two points. Even if space is negatively curved, light never wanders, and yet it is exactly this quality of detour or errancy that Blanchot wishes to affirm in the "new space" that beckoned to him after closing *Les Métamorphoses du cercle*. To do so he must speak against the light and prize speech over seeing. In one of his dialogues, "Parler, ce n'est pas voir" (1960), one of his unnamed speakers suggests that "to see is to experience [*l'expérience*] the continuous and to celebrate the sun, that is, beyond the sun: the One";[33] and the two speakers find themselves opposing to sight not just any speech but only "the one in which 'error' speaks: the speech of detour" (29; 40) or, as it is named a little later, "writing" (29; 41). It is characteristic of Blanchot that one of his speakers observes that this wandering speech discloses what the author of "Ars Nova" called "an exteriority that is not divine" (350; 514) that is held here in the dialogue to be "before any *fiat lux*" (31; 43). The omnipotent God who created the world out of nothing by commanding "Let there be light" is imagined not to have absolute mastery of reality, for there is an exteriority that was prior to creation and that remains forever outside it. This exteriority is not what the Bible calls the darkness "upon the face of the deep," the *tohu vabohu* of Genesis 1:2, but what Blanchot calls the Outside, a stultifying space composed entirely of images that tolerates no gods or God because it disrupts all unity. It is a neutral space, not neutralized: being perpetually generates nonbeing there. In responding to this statement the other speaker immediately refers to "sacred speech" (31; 44). Shortly after, the first speaker adds that no allusion is being made to "the superior Word of which our human words would be but an imperfect imitation" (32; 45); and yet the theme of the sacred has been announced, and not for the first or last time.

The chapters to come are an attempt to read Blanchot as a thinker whose meditations on literature, philosophy, and society are crossed by a thought of the sacred and who seeks to rethink religious faith, specifically the faith of the Jews, without any confession of God, in the register of ethics. Also, because I take Blanchot to be an exemplary figure, the chapters take several soundings of the religious thought of his generation and our times. I have already taken one preliminary sounding, the affirmation of the sacred at work (but without working) in community. There are three more that need to be noted:

1. *The displacement of the mystical.* In the twentieth century we find a revival of interest in the mystical, which had been out of favor, even among theologians, since Pierre de Bérulle and the "French School" had started to lose their influence at the end of the seventeenth century.[34] Attention has been mainly focused on a mysticism of spirituality rather than on a mysticism of exegesis. (In France the importance of Lucie Christine's *Journal spirituel* [1910] and the story of Madeleine Sémer's conversion and mystical experiences [1923] can stand as indices of this new concern.)[35] And it has been partly framed by philosophical concerns about the limits of experience inherited from Immanuel Kant.[36] Bataille observes that he and Blanchot represent *la nouvelle théologie mystique*, which he glosses as an encounter with the unknown. Whether knowingly or not, he alludes to *la nouvelle théologie*, a movement in European Catholicism in the middle decades of his century, best known for its rethinking of grace and for its interest in *réssourcement*: the exploration of the full heritage of the Catholic faith, beginning with the Church Fathers. Bataille and Blanchot are equally concerned with reaching the limits of experience, although they adopt different ways of attaining it. Like Bataille, Blanchot rejects the notion of a transcendent being (or being as transcendent, Saint Augustine's *idipsum*) with which one can merge, and seeks instead an obscure point beneath the world, as it were, rather than above it, which withdraws as one approaches. To feel the attraction of this point is to experience nonexperience; it is a phased counterpart of the ecstasies to which some

Christian mystics have testified. Blanchot develops not a mysticism of exegesis so much as a displaced mysticism of writing: to write is to transform the instant into an imaginary space, to pass from a time in which death could occur to an endless interval of dying. I take this movement to illuminate the "atheistical mysticism" that one variously finds in the poetry of René Char, Rainer Maria Rilke, Paul Celan, Edmond Jabès, and Roberto Juarroz and the fascination with dying or other states that one finds in the fiction of Samuel Beckett, Hermann Brock, Franz Kafka, and Robert Musil. In its linking of creation and fall, it bears witness to the return of Valentinian gnosticism in modern times, while also partly clarifying the more formal meditations on the alterity of *la différance* that preoccupy Jacques Derrida and the figures associated with him.[37]

2. *The philosophy of the neuter.* Emmanuel Lévinas convicted Martin Heidegger of developing a philosophy of the neuter, a thinking of impersonal being that occludes ethics, and congratulated Blanchot on having exposed this tendency in the master's writings.[38] Heidegger can be seen as the most recent major contributor to a philosophical style that began with Parmenides. Looking more closely at western thought than Lévinas does, we can see a shorter sequence that is cued into this history. It begins with the Latin Averroists, features Duns Scotus and Francisco Suárez, and passes into modern thought by way of René Descartes. It was Henri de Lubac and others associated with *la nouvelle théologie* who identified this sequence in the late 1930s, although it entered general discussion some two decades later. Hans Urs von Balthasar showed how this subtradition adduces a concept of neutral, indeterminate being that is prior to the distinction between infinite and finite being, that is, between God and creation.[39] This neutral being becomes the object of metaphysics in the modern age, and—as Balthasar and Jean-Luc Marion show in their own ways—radically skews our understanding of the deity.[40] Blanchot's thought of the neutral Outside contests the philosophy of the neuter. The Outside interrupts being. In its earlier form it denotes the sacred in its malign form (it is identified with Hades) and can be seen to anticipate the more affirmative postmodern absorption with reality as constituted by images; while in its later form (which does not replace the earlier), the infernal dimension is forgotten and it opens a postmetaphysical ethics of the other person. Yet Blanchot takes the Outside to dispel any possibility of belief in God: no unity and light are possible there. We can see Blanchot, then, standing at the juncture of two important positions: exposing the philosophy of the neuter (Parmenides and Heidegger), and affirming the thought of the neutral (Heraclitus and Char). The one bypasses infinity, while the other restores infinity at the level of ethics while maintaining it as a resource of an atheism that cannot quite be affirmed.

3. *Religion without religion.* Blanchot argues that a postmetaphysical ethics, based on the human relation, can be derived from a reading of the Hebrew Bible. The prophets engaged in dialogue with the Almighty, yet Israel's most enduring legacy is not the vision of the One Lord but the hope of holding oneself and the Other in relation by dialogue. It is the other *person* who is the Wholly Other, Blanchot affirms; and Israel must continue in its painful passage from the particularity of revelation to the universality of ethics.[41] Prophecy, revelation, and transcendence, as well as the mystical and the sacred, are to be reset in the context of the human relation, an exposure to the Outside by way of the other person. The sacred is inscribed in community where it is expiated, for the community is dispersed by what gathers it together. I take this general move to be not only Blanchot's response to the sociological studies of Durkheim, Mauss, and Caillois but also his inflection of a venerable approach to religion by way of naturalizing the supernatural, often with a reduction to ethics. Doubtless it can be traced back to Avicenna. It can easily be found in Feuerbach and his progeny, although it surfaces in many places.[42] It meets Blanchot, however, mainly in the formulations of Kant and Lévinas. The general approach has been carefully reworked by Derrida, who in *Donner la mort* gathers together Hegel and Kierkegaard, Heidegger and Ricoeur, Patočka and Marion, as thinking the possibility of religion without revelation. To this list others might be added, not least of all the Wallace Stevens who evokes a "dimension in which / We believe without belief, beyond belief."[43] Not all of this tribe figures the possibility of religion mainly by way of ethics, and not even Blanchot (whom Derrida does not mention in *Donner la mort*) is entirely happy with the word *ethics.*[44] Yet, in English translation, Derrida's words appear as a homage to Blanchot for they use the unsettling syntax he favors: "religion without religion."[45] Like others before him, Blanchot wishes to retain the sacred and to leave religion. He refigures what "sacred" means in dialogue with Heidegger and Bataille, and his position might be suggested by coining the expression "the sacred without the sacred." It is a position that does not eliminate faith but rephrases it in the context of the human relation. There is no God, but I must have faith in the God who appears in the other person when he or she talks with me.

2

When Poulet praised Blanchot in *Les Métamorphoses du cercle* for describing so well the state of "consciousness without an object" he was surely thinking of his friend's first novel, *Thomas l'obscur,* and especially of the remarkable passage where Thomas's eye becomes useless for sight; it sees nothing yet apprehends something: "It saw as object that which prevented it from seeing. Its own glance [*regard*] entered into it as an image, just when this glance seemed the death of all image."[46] The dark that floods into Thomas's eye at once stops him from seeing in his usual manner and enables him to see the night as it truly is. The night allows Thomas to glimpse its mystery with what I call a dark gaze.

I find this dark gaze throughout Blanchot's writing, although its significance can vary considerably from work to work. In the early novel *Aminadab* (1942), when Thomas meets Barbe's eyes, he encounters "a pure and candid gaze [*un regard*] from which all light had faded away."[47] Almost forty years later, in *L'Écriture du désastre* (1980), the "suffering of our time" is captured in an old man with "gaze extinguished" ("sans regard") (81; 129). Nothing is made of either remark, chilling though they are. Nor, about the same period as *Aminadab*, is anything special made to weigh on the description in *Faux pas* (1943) of anguish as "a gaze [*regard*] that veils itself."[48] Yet the notion takes on significance when Blanchot also in *Faux pas* ponders one of Marcel Jouhandeau's novels about the country town of Chaminadour. When pondering the novelist's "gaze" (*regard*) he observes that "He sees clearly what is present only by making it absent or by grasping it in an image that makes it seem imaginary" (231; 265).[49] Here we see the first reliable instance of the dark gaze: it is the vision of an artist who sees being as image, already separated from the phenomenal world and yet not belonging to a separate order of being. Later, in *Celui qui ne m'accompagnait pas* (1953), we will witness a look that does not link up with its object, "a gaze that is perhaps connected to the word 'write'" (75; 141).

Several years after the reflections on Jouhandeau, in "La Littérature et le droit à la mort" (1947–48), we find Blanchot brooding on a "metamorphosis"[50] in which language is transformed into matter. Having turned language into no more than the shape and weight of words, literature has not vanquished meaning but repositioned it: meaning is now outside the human mind. "Literature is that experience [*expérience*] through which the consciousness discovers its being in its inability to lose consciousness, in the movement whereby, as it disappears, as it tears itself away from the meticulousness of an I, it is re-created beyond unconsciousness as an impersonal spontaneity, the desperate eagerness of a haggard knowledge [*savoir*] which knows nothing, which no one knows, and which ignorance always discovers behind itself as its own shadow changed into a gaze [*changée en regard*]" (331–32; 320).[51] This consciousness now set in writing and unable to escape existence is a shadow that looks at us without being either truly alive or dead. We have passed from a subject's gaze at an object to an object's gaze at a subject, and we will find that Blanchot keeps both in play in his mature writing. The dark gaze will recur as a "dead gaze" ("regard mort") that fixes us in states of fascination, like Rilke's contemplative look that comes from the heart of death, and in *L'Arrêt de mort* like death's stare at the narrator, "the most terrible look" ("le regard le plus terrible").[52] It is the gaze of fascination in which "blindness is vision still, vision which is no longer the possibility of seeing, but the impossibility of not seeing, the impossibility that becomes seeing, which perseveres—always and always—in a vision that never comes to an end: a dead gaze, a gaze become the ghost of an eternal vision."[53] What is most disturbing about the gaze, as we shall see in the first chapter, is that it abolishes the distance between subject and object and indicates that the distance inheres within reality: an anterior reality infects reality as we usually conceive it.[54] One can be led to that disaster from the subject pole or from the object pole. And yet the disaster can be received affirmatively so that the gaze appears bittersweet, as though one were finally released from all care. I think of *Thomas l'obscur* where, right at the end of the *récit*, the people perceive "a glance [*regard*] whose immensity and sweetness awoke in them unbearable desires" (117; 137), and *Celui qui ne m'accompagnait pas* where, again at the end, we hear of a "tranquil smile of no one, intended for no one, and near which one could not dwell near oneself" (90; 167).[55]

L'Arrêt de mort, like a good deal of Blanchot's fiction, beginning with *Thomas l'obscur*, involves a creative reworking of the story of Eurydice and Orpheus.[56] Blanchot interprets the old story in a beautiful meditation, "Le Regard d'Orphée" (1953), which he points out is the elusive center of *L'Espace littéraire* (1955), and which we might see as organizing without ever fully unifying everything he has written.[57] Certainly Blanchot does not forget the story. "Let us once again recall Orpheus and Eurydice," a speaker in another of Blanchot's dialogues invites us in 1962, almost ten years after "Le Regard d'Orphée" appeared. "Eurydice is the strangeness of the extreme distance that is *autrui* at the moment of a face-to-face confrontation; and when Orpheus looks back, ceasing to speak in order to see, his gaze [*regard*] reveals itself to be the violence that brings death, the dreadful blow."[58] Orpheus's gaze is not his first look into the shades, which seeks to take the beloved from the darkness back into the light, but his second look, which consigns Eurydice to death forever. Eurydice is the one who resists being seen, who does not come into the light, and in this she is utterly unlike Dante's Beatrice who, as Blanchot says in a late piece, has "her being wholly in the vision one has of her, a vision that presupposes the full scale of the seeable, from the physical sight that strikes one like lightning to the absolute visibility where she is no longer distinguishable from the Absolute itself: God, and the *theos*, theory, the ultimate of what can be seen."[59] Although Greek, Eurydice is not associated with a thematics of vision; if anything, she belongs to that part of the Greek heritage that opens toward the world of the Hebrew Bible where sight is not especially prized.[60]

I will return to Orpheus and Eurydice in a moment, but before I do I wish to forestall a possible confusion by pointing out how the dark gaze differs from the phenomenological conversion of perception. For Husserl, the *epochē* and the transcendental reduction allow one to be finely aware of one's intentional relations with the world, and the subject is affirmed as the center of experience. The dark gaze, however, contests the primacy of the subject and construes experience as precisely that which exposes the "I" to a loss of mastery and power. Does this mean that the dark gaze is the same as what Jean-Paul Sartre called "the gaze"? Not quite, although it is worth taking a moment to explore the similarity between them. The look of the other has always disturbed Blanchot. As early as "Des diverses façons de mourir" (1944), one of his many literary columns for the *Journal des Débats*, he argued that one dies a little merely by being seen by others and that death would consist in being seen completely.[61] Sartre's analysis of being-looked-at in *L'Être et le néant* (1942) certainly comes to mind, and indeed Blanchot alludes to Sartre's book in his article. "Death is the triumph of the point of view of the Other over me," says Sartre; "it transforms life into destiny." Blanchot quotes the sentence and then goes on to cite another: "The unique characteristic of a dead life is that it is a life of which the Other makes himself the guardian."[62] Anyone who has read more than a page or two by Blanchot will know how important Heidegger's account of death is to him. It comes as no surprise then to find him citing Sartre's arguments with Heidegger over death. Even so, it would be a mistake to see the two Frenchmen converging in their interests. Sartre is careful to distinguish being-looked-at from empirical vision, and yet his entire analysis of the gaze presumes a rapport with visibility. A dissident phenomenologist, like all the most influential ones, Sartre at least remains faithful to one of the grounding metaphors of the original movement in his emphasis upon the light of intelligibility.

With appropriate modifications, the same could be said of Martin Heidegger. Swerve as he might from Husserl in passing from epistemological to ontological concerns, he nonetheless prized the metaphor of light. Recall, for instance, his lectures at Freiburg in the winter semester of 1942–43 ventured under the title "Parmenides." There Heidegger told his students that θεάομαι (looking) does not mean representing. There is no question here of seizing an object through sight, for θεάομαι denotes the way in which the one who looks shows himself. "Looking, even human looking, is, originally experienced, not the grasping of something but the self-showing in view of which there first becomes possible a looking that grasps something."[63] Not a function of the subject, looking is a provision of sight made by Being itself. "Through such looking, man is distinguished,"

Heidegger told his students, "and he can be distinguished by it only because the looking which shows Being itself is not something human but belongs to the essence of Being itself as belonging to appearance in the unconcealed" (104). The Blanchot fascinated by what I call the dark gaze would surely be drawn to the idea of this looking that has nothing human about it. For all his admiration of Heidegger, though, he differs fundamentally from the thinker of Todnauberg because, at heart, he is not a proponent of θεάομαι (looking); he does not have any ambition to determine the presence of things, let alone to do so by way of sight. Although often cited by advocates of literary theory, Blanchot keeps his distance from the discipline. "You theoreticians, know that you are mortal," he declaims in *L'Écriture du désastre* (1980), "and that theory is already death in you."[64] In the same spirit, Blanchot cannot agree with Edmund Husserl's emphasis on insight (*Einsehen*) as essential for the phenomenological gaze. Following Lévinas, he sees this stress on sight—"no mere form of speaking," Husserl assures us—as turning a human relation into an intentional correlate.[65]

Not only does Blanchot reject the light of presence and representation but also the light of consciousness. In one of his columns for the *Journal des Débats* he values the "new novel" for its ability to "put out the light of understanding," and decades later in *L'Entretien infini* he questions the light cast by Descartes's *cogito*, "I think therefore I am."[66] To write, he says, is to be detached from the day.[67] More generally, he distances himself from the theology of light that runs through the Bible, the Church Fathers, the medieval scholastics, right down to his own days. This theology of light is nothing if not comprehensive. It begins by associating life and light (Ps. 36:9), truth and light (John 3:21), and God and light (1 John 1:5). It is warmly elaborated by Saint Augustine when he extols God as *intelligibiliter lucent* (intelligible light) and then as *lucem incommutabilem* (immutable light) "higher than my mind—not the light of every day, obvious to anyone, nor a larger version of the same kind."[68] Later, when Saint Augustine reflects on Tobias, Isaac, and Jacob (by way of Plotinus), he declares, "ipsa est lux, una est et unum omnes, qui vident et amant eam" (This light itself is one, and all those are one who see it).[69] Centuries later, Saint Thomas Aquinas suggests that "the very actuality of a thing is, in a certain way, its light," while his contemporary, Saint Bonaventure, starting from James 1:17, speaks of the *Patre luminum*, the *lumen sacrae Scripturae*, and the *lumen cognitionis philosophicae*, the Father of lights, the light of holy Scripture, and the light of philosophical knowledge.[70] Even as a Catholic boy, Blanchot will turn sharply away from the *lumen fidei*, the light of faith in God, and yet, as we shall see, his ethics relies on what Saint Thomas calls credence, and he speaks of the strange clarity of the Outside, of a light associated with reading, and of a light that comes from the dark disaster.[71] He will come to link the face of the other person with light, and in another context will affirm a "fire without light," a passion that burns life without illuminating it.[72]

Religion is widely held to have two sources in faith and the sacred, and over the course of his writing life Blanchot responds to each source. Like Rudolf Otto, he separates the sacred from revealed faith, although, unlike him, he reinstates faith at the level of the human relation.[73] Also, following Durkheim, he distinguishes the sacred from the positive religions: the sacred has a social existence, in terms of a tension with the profane, and is not necessarily derived from personal belief in God or a pantheon of gods.[74] He does this chiefly because, like Lactantius in the *Divinae Institutiones* (305–13), he tacitly accepts that the Latin word *religio* has its root in *religare*, meaning "to bind"; and so he regards religion as bespeaking a deep unity.[75] He has good reason to do so, of course, although it is worth noting that he nowhere considers the rival etymology, that *religio* ultimately comes from *relegere*, meaning "to read again and again," the interpretation favored by Cicero and approved by Saint Augustine, and the one that best fits his practice as a literary critic.[76] So when Blanchot speaks of the sacred, he does not imply any confessional adhesion on his part or even a firm conceptual link to the positive religions. There is a historical reference, one that goes back to the Jews, but no more than that.

His willingness to preserve sacrifice and the sacred, not to mention a tight relation between them, is evident when we return to the story of Orpheus and Eurydice. "All the glory of his work," Blanchot writes of Orpheus, "all the power of his art, and even the desire for a happy life in the lovely, clear light of day are sacrificed [*sacrifiés*] to this sole aim: to look in the night at what night hides, the *other night*, the dissimulation that appears."[77] To see Orpheus's transgression by way of sacrifice is to see through lenses ground by Georges Bataille. And to think of sacrifice with Bataille is to look back to nineteenth-century understandings of the notion as supplying a single ground on which all religion was based.[78] Whether Blanchot thinks, as Bataille seems to, that "sacrifice" has just the one meaning in all situations is not clear. It is plain, however, that he is heavily indebted to his friend's understanding of the notion and consequently to the writings of Henri Hubert and Marcel Mauss as well as Durkheim. Without Hubert and Mauss's *Essai sur le sacrifice* (1899) there could be no theory of "communication" in Bataille or Laure, and no Blanchot as we know him today.[79]

Blanchot is chiefly influenced by several of Bataille's emphases with regard to the sacred: that it both attracts and repels, that there is a passage from the individual to the community, and that the essence of sacrifice is immolation to death without return. With regard to each line of influence, Blanchot maintains his originality. To begin with, on his understanding, worked out primarily with regard to Hölderlin and Heidegger, the sacred is always anterior to the act of composition. Orpheus descends to Hades in order to save Eurydice and yet, in the end, abandons her to a second death. Why? Because he becomes attracted to the *"other night,"* the ghostly image of night, disconnected from and prior to the meaningful alternation of night and day, that nonetheless impresses itself upon consciousness as a vacant and obsessive repetition. Consider this paragraph from his meditation on the myth: "His gaze [*Le regard d'Orphée*] is thus the extreme moment of liberty, the moment when he frees himself from himself and, still more important, frees the work from his concern, frees the sacred contained in the work, *gives* the sacred to itself, to the freedom of its essence, to its essence which is freedom."[80] Orpheus sacrifices twice in the one movement: in singing his lyric he yields the sovereignty of his "I" and becomes a "he" or a "one"; and accordingly the poem is abandoned as a possible whole and enters the realm of the fragmentary which is also, Blanchot will argue, the space of community.

Unlike Bataille and Durkheim, though, Blanchot does not regard the sacred as unifying a community or as doing any positive work at all. On the contrary, the sacred holds the self and the other person at a distance from one another, in a relation that is doubly dissymmetric. In Sophocles' *Antigone* the chorus tells us that nothing is more "wondrous and strange" (δεινότερον) than man; Blanchot subtly revises the insight to read that nothing is more strange than the human relation.[81] Any way we look at it, we are taken from the promised land of being and wholeness, a place that phenomenology as much as Christianity has tried to describe.[82] Bataille will tell us that sacrifice indicates a continuous realm from which we have been exiled by life itself, but Blanchot will say that it points us to a nonworld of nihilism, one that we cannot quite enter because, long after the death of God, we still cling to theological assumptions such as the primacy of light and the inevitability of unity. To become nihilists, as Blanchot thinks we should (even if the word itself is not to be trusted), we must recognize that no value has intrinsic value, that there is no *univer*se, and that ethics presumes difference, not identity.[83]

In talking of sacrifice and nihilism we have come a long way from the analogy with the Einsteinian cosmos with which I started, but, in doing so, we have entered more surely into Blanchot's world. And in fact Blanchot never quite leaves cosmology. As late as *L'Écriture du désastre* (1980), we find him pondering it anew, this time in the context of the sacred:

Is the cosmic the way the sacred, disguising itself as transcendence, seeks to become immanent? Is the cosmic thus the temptation to melt into the fiction of the universe, and thereby become indifferent to the tormenting vicissitudes of the near at hand (the neighboring)? Would the cosmic be a little heaven in which to survive, or with which to die universally, in stoic serenity? A "whole" which shelters us, even as we dissolve therein, and which would be natural repose—as if there were a nature outside of concepts and names? (75; 121)

In these questions Blanchot distances himself from a Greek heritage that comes to us from Anaximander and Anaximenes, from Plato and Aristotle: the assumption that the cosmos is a natural and perfect unity. In the cosmos everything is one "by virtue of the immanent norm which integrates the individual things into a totality."[84] Against this view, Blanchot sets the thought of the disaster, the "break with the star, break with every form of totality" (75; 121) that has always and already occurred. The sacred, if it is to play any role in Blanchot's writing, is to be associated with the ceaseless dispersal of the Outside, not with Unity. It is to be associated with nihilism, not with religion. And this is not simply because Blanchot adopts a negative attitude toward the ontology of totality. As the passage I have just quoted implies, the thought of the Greek cosmos quietly turns us away from facing our responsibility to our neighbors. So, in a curious way, Blanchot finds a convergence of Einsteinian cosmology, nihilism, and Hebraic ethics.

3

Anyone who writes about Blanchot will readily testify that it is not the easiest of tasks. Rather than speak of the perplexing temporality of the narratives or the obliquity of the criticism, I would like to draw attention to something else. The main difficulty I have encountered in writing this book has been establishing the appropriate level at which to engage with Blanchot's writing. Here we have an author with strong philosophical interests but who writes meditative essays, fragments, and narratives, not academic studies. Fragmentary or not, those essays are often as complex and as dense as the genres can tolerate, let alone the readership of journals like *Critique* and the *Nouvelle Revue Française*, and when they are revised, especially in *L'Espace littéraire* and *L'Entretien infini*, they can place even more intellectual demands upon the reader. Never, though, do the texts change genre; they do not become research papers or treatises, styles of writing from which Blanchot explicitly distances himself, and consequently there is little point in looking for technical arguments or close attention to examples and counterexamples, or even in expecting that he discuss all the writers who are important to him.[85] To read his essays and reviews with tact, to open oneself to learning from them, requires that the principle of charity be extended, and kept open at full stretch, more often than is usual when reading work of philosophical interest. Among modern thinkers, only Kierkegaard and Nietzsche are usually accorded this sort of special treatment, and they fall more readily into a philosophical canon than Blanchot does.

Not simply philosophical in orientation, Blanchot is also drawn to what he calls "the 'spiritual' life."[86] The scare quotes alert us, if we needed reminding, that he is not endorsing any spirituality that directly derives from the positive religions. We have lost the divine, he realizes, at least in all the forms officially recognized in the Judeo-Christian West, and he accounts it a disaster not just for human hopes of immortality but for art. "What will become now of art, now that the gods and even their absence are gone, and now that man's presence offers no support? . . . And where will art find, elsewhere than in the divine, elsewhere than in the world, the space in which to base and to withhold itself?"[87] The answer comes by way of "'spiritual' life," which, for him, is not an endorsement of the life of the mind or an inner life or an integrated approach to life but a commitment to the radical interrogation that literature calls us to pursue. Sometimes it seems to be a peculiar twist of the Platonic dialectic that leads us from the phenomenal world to the world of ideas: by incessant questioning we pass from the world about us to the nonworld of the imaginary, from the world of Hegelian Spirit to the nonworld of counterspirit. At other times there is no questioning at all but a revelation of the Outside.

Always, "the 'spiritual' life" is a question of experience: not an encounter in the present that yields positive knowledge but rather a peculiar passage from time to place. Blanchot situates it in terms of the rival visions of Mallarmé and Rilke concerning death.[88] Mallarmé celebrates the instant that annihilates while Rilke apprehends a place without temporal vector. In the eighth of the Duino elegies he calls it *Nirgends ohne Nicht*, "nowhere without no." Let us listen to a passage of that elegy:

> Wir *haben nie, nicht einen einzigen Tag,*
> *den reinen Raum vor uns, in den die Blumen*
> *unendlich aufgehn. Immer ist es Welt*
> *und niemals Nirgends ohne Nicht: das Reine,*
> *Unüberwachte, das man atmet und*
> *unendlich weiß und nicht begehrt. Als Kind*

verliert sich eins im Stilln an dies und wird
gerüttelt. Oder jener stirbt und ists.
Denn nah am Tod sieht man den Tod nicht mehr
Und starrt hinaus, vielleicht mit großem Tierblick.[89]

"'Spiritual' life" would involve passing from the world we know to a place that is untouched by negation. It would be "nowhere" but not conditioned by "no." It would be a "pure space" unmotivated by desire, a space that children know and that the dying approach and perhaps become. Blanchot does not hesitate to respond to this "nowhere without no" as the form of the sacred that is given to us today. Equally, he does not associate this space with any hope. It is not even a space but rather the *approach* of a space that exiles us from ourselves and condemns us to an endless wandering.[90] It is never a place that one can call home.

No one can read Blanchot at all closely and fail to see how central the category of experience is for him. The passage from the instant of time to the strange space of "nowhere without no" is what he sometimes calls "the experience of non-experience"; and this, I take it, is a part of what Poulet had in mind when he wrote to Raymond about Blanchot's experience of the absence of God.[91] *The Dark Gaze* begins by considering the ways in which "non-experience" resembles mystical experience: I have in mind an author facing the ordeal of the neutral Outside to which the imaginary points in *L'Espace littéraire* (1955), a little boy's revelation of a dark and empty heaven in "(Une scène primitive?)" (1980), and a man's sense of elation when almost shot by an impromptu firing squad in *L'Instant de ma mort* (1994). In all three places Blanchot remains close to the Bataille of *L'Expérience intérieure*. Although he never doubts that this is a work apart from all others, Blanchot comes to be drawn in his later writing to Lévinas's account of ethics as first philosophy. *The Dark Gaze* ends by considering the role of "non-experience" in affirming the infinite conversation between the self and the other person. What Blanchot calls "the human relation" remains close to what Lévinas calls, simply, "religion." I should say that I do not follow either Blanchot or Lévinas here: in the Christian religion, adoration and prayer precede and inform ethics.

I have not been tempted to stage a debate between my Catholic faith and Blanchot's atheism. Rather, I have wanted to listen carefully to his response to the sacred and his reformulation of faith. I have sought to understand his reservations about the sense and function of the "I" and his notion of experience, and to see what he has learned from the Bible. Throughout, I have wanted to trace the ways in which his notions of faith and the sacred pass through the notion of the dark gaze: the faith I must have in the other person comes to me by way of the

Outside, he says, and the Outside is all we have of the sacred. In doing this I have wanted to take Blanchot's atheism very seriously as a striking expression of contemporary *homo humanus*. At the same time I have sought to value this atheism as a rigorous expression of a counterspirituality from which we can all learn, even if we fold it into confessional practices that are very far from Blanchot's commitments.

1
.

ART OR THE MYSTICAL?

1

       In its most general form, the question I would like to pose in this chapter was raised, then quickly dropped by Stéphane Mallarmé. I am thinking of a lyric from *Parnasse contemporain* (1866), "Les Fenêtres," and in particular of the moment when the speaker of that poem sees himself reflected in a hospital window and cries out, "Je me mire et me vois ange! et je meurs, et j'aim / —Que la vitre soit l'art, soit la mysticité— / À renaître" (I see myself and see an angel! and I die, and long / —Whether the window be art or the mystical— / To be reborn).[1] No ordinary window, this, for it separates two worlds, one that is "triste" and "fétide," and another characterized by a "ciel antérieur où fleurit la Beauté" (former sky where Beauty flowers).[2] This dualism of the real and the ideal recalls the world of *Les Fleurs du mal* (1857), yet the young Mallarmé is already distancing himself from his master, Charles Baudelaire. He elects the ideal, even though he is not sure whether it is art or a vision that enables him to grasp it. Is it possible to know? At the very least the question should be posed. And so I ask on his behalf: Is the window "art" or "the mystical"?

       I will be returning to an anteriority, even to a "ciel antérieur," in the chapters to come, and to Mallarmé as well, but not to the young man who wrote "Les Fenêtres." The speaker of that poem links the ideal with his death ("je meurs"), and indeed in 1866 and again in 1867 Mallarmé himself testified in letters to friends that, after a dreadful religious crisis, he had died—"je suis mort," "je suis parfaitement mort"—and it is the spiritual being who writes these words who will accompany us in what follows, even if we may not hear him speak very often in his own voice.[3] For Mallarmé passes the death he experienced in his anguished nights at Tournon to French writers of the twentieth century, for whom it was situated with respect to other influences and took on different though not completely unrelated senses. It was what will become known as the "death of the author" and the "limit-experience." As Blanchot represents Mallarmé position, the experience of writing marks the suspension of beings and lets us glimpse being in all its brilliance.[4]

For Georges Bataille, this limit- or negative experience is to be understood as sacred: it is the revelation of the continuous through the sacrificial death of a discontinuous being. Indeed, for Bataille the distinction between art and the mystical is subtended by the sacred in this precise sense of the word, and in consequence the young Mallarmé's question—art or the mystical?—has to be rephrased.[5] Blanchot agrees that the distinction between art and the mystical is misleading and that both terms rely on a prior sense of the sacred. Unlike Bataille, however, he declines to think of the sacred in terms of fusion and integrity.[6] For him, the sacred is the effulgence not of a transcendent point to which all things aspire but rather of an illusory point below the earth, as it were, which comes into being as one writes and attracts as it withdraws. One approaches that point by an endless contestation of concepts and words. Where Saint Augustine would seek to ascend to the light of God's face by strict meditation, Blanchot descends to a dark gaze by the fierce contestation involved in literature, a sacrifice of both the author and his words.

2

Let us begin with Bataille's *L'Expérience intérieure*, a febrile meditation that, among other things, responds to and displaces *Le Livre de l'expérience des vrais fidèles* by the thirteenth-century Umbrian mystic Angela of Foligno.[7] Bataille begins by affirming inner experience at the expense of mystical ecstasy; even so, Jean-Paul Sartre believed himself justified to dub the author "a new mystic."[8] He has been sharply criticized for the expression, although since Bataille called the fourth part of his book "Post-Scriptum au Supplice (ou la nouvelle théologie mystique)," the philosopher was not without reason for his choice of words.[9] Equally, Bataille has a solid ground for objecting to the description: he does not believe in the Judeo-Christian God. "Inner experience" is an experimental attempt to touch the indefinite reality that abides outside the self; when the attempt succeeds it is intensely pleasurable but also anguished (a taboo is violated) and strictly pointless (no knowledge of this Outside can be distilled). It is hardly the mysticism of Saint Augustine, Saint Bernard of Clairvaux, Dame Julian of Norwich, or Angela herself. And yet, as Bataille freely admitted years after *L'Expérience intérieure*, from a certain angle he can be seen to stand "in the line of mystics of all times."[10]

Keeping that equivocation between mysticism and atheism in mind, I turn to a passage near the beginning of "Post-Scriptum au Supplice (ou la nouvelle théologie mystique)." It is a rare anecdote by Bataille, or anyone, about Maurice Blanchot:

> Outside of the notes of this volume, I only know of *Thomas the Obscure* where the questions of the new theology [*la nouvelle théologie*] (which has only the unknown [*l'inconnu*] as object) are pressing, although they remain hidden. In a way which is completely independent from his book—orally, yet in such a way that he in no respect lacked the feeling of discretion which demands that, close to him, I thirst for silence—I heard the author set out the foundation for all "spiritual" life, which can only:
> —have its principle and its end in the absence of salvation, in the renunciation of all hope,
> —affirm of inner experience that it is authority (but all authority expiates itself),
> —be contestation of itself and non-knowledge [*non-savoir*].[11]

The Blanchot introduced in this short passage is a writer, to be sure, though not quite the reclusive author whose name we know today. His first novel, *Thomas l'obscur* (1941), is commended not so much for its literary value as for its theological insight, and, as the scene develops, the young novelist is presented as a severe, if somewhat perverse, theologian and as something of a mentor to his older friend.

The "new theology . . . has only the unknown as object," Bataille tells us. Even before we ask what the "unknown" is, we must recognize that what makes this theology *new* is that it is centered on the sacred, rather than on faith or a harmony of faith and reason. It is experiential rather than dogmatic. If it can be called a new *mystical* theology, it is new mainly because it construes the mystical as grounded in a notion of the sacred: mystical experience (or "negative experience" or "inner experience") places us in continuity with reality.[12] I quote from *L'Érotisme* (1957) because Bataille moves too quickly in *L'Expérience intérieure* to make the point clearly and mires us in distinctions that perplex as much as they illuminate. We are expected to recall that, for him, "God differs from the unknown" (5; 5:17). But how? When we speak of God we are touched by "a profound emotion, coming from the depths of childhood," while the unknown "leaves one cold, does not elicit our love until it overturns everything within us like a violent wind" (5; 5:17).

It is a curiously drawn distinction. In the first place, it does not adduce different traits that God and the unknown might have but sketches the effects they have on us. And in the second place, once we have been thoroughly shaken by the unknown, we become disposed to love it—and this can only compromise the clarity of the distinction. If we love the unknown, then it can no longer be completely unknown.[13] Without giving us an opportunity to object, Bataille goes on to mark the difference between God and the unknown in quite another way. Our apprehension of the divine is like our experience of poetry. "The poetic is the familiar dissolving into the strange, and ourselves with it. It never dispossesses us entirely, for the words, the images (once dissolved) are charged with emotions already experienced [*éprouvées*], attached to objects which link them to the known [*connu*]" (5; 5:17). And he concludes, "We are only totally laid bare by proceeding without trickery to the unknown [*l'inconnu*]. It is the measure of the unknown which lends to the experience [*expérience*] of God—or of the poetic—their great authority. But the unknown demands in the end sovereignty without partition [*partage*]" (5; 5:17). Christian mystics fall short of inner experience, it would seem, because they refer their raptures to what they have been told of God instead of entrusting themselves entirely to their transports. And poets do not fully achieve inner experience because they cling, at least in part, to events they have already lived.

By contrast, Blanchot is to be prized because he attends to the unknown, and for Bataille this makes *Thomas l'obscur* neither mystical nor poetic. Before and after Bataille turns to the novel, however, he gives us reason to doubt that there is a clear distinction between the mystical and the poetic in his senses of the words. For most writers, composition is regulated by the sovereignty of the imagination or by appeals to craft. Yet for a few others, Blanchot included, writing exceeds all project and leads to the unknown; it involves the sacrifice of words and, in the same gesture, of the author himself.[14] And so *Thomas l'obscur* is sacred speech. Just before he relates the anecdote about his friend, Bataille quotes two passages from the novel. The first is by far the more interesting, and it is easy to see why it appeals to the author of *Histoire de l'oeil* (1928):

Night soon appeared to him to be darker, more terrible than any other night whatsoever, as if it had really emerged from a wound of thought which could no longer think itself, of thought captured ironically as object by something other than thought. This was night itself. Images which created its darkness flooded into him, and his body transformed into a demoniacal mind sought to represent them to himself. He saw nothing and, far from being overcome, he made from this absence of visions the culminating point of his glance. His eye, useless for sight, took on extraordinary proportions, began to develop in an inordinate fashion and, dwelling on the horizon, allowed night to penetrate into its centre in order to create an iris for itself. Through this void, therefore, it was his glance and the object of his glance [le regard et l'objet du regard] which were mingled. This eye, which saw nothing, did not simply grasp the source of its vision. It saw as would an object, which meant that it did not see. His own glance [regard] entered into him in the form of an image at the tragic moment when this glance [regard] was regarded [considéré] as the death of all image.[15]

The "wound of thought" evoked here can be satisfactorily explained only with reference to the central philosophical contention in the novel, that Descartes's Cogito, "I think therefore I am," is ultimately self-refuting and that the proposition we should affirm is "I think therefore I am not." And Thomas's relationship with the darkness, intimate if deeply unsettling, can be grasped only in and through the revelation that this living Thomas is inescapably tied to an obscure twin who does not have the gift of consciousness yet nonetheless haunts the living Thomas under the complex sign of "reality and death."[16] This argument and this drama will concern us in the fourth chapter when we turn to Blanchot's account of selfhood. Suffice it to say for now that Thomas encounters a night that precedes the usual alternation of day and night.

He does not suffer a dark night of the soul, what Saint John of the Cross calls a "cruel spiritual death," the anguish of being convinced that God has turned His back on the beloved.[17] That night is at heart a "passive purgation" (303) and eventually it opens onto a morning of joy. On the contrary, Thomas's dark night suffocates any thought of the divine and has no beginning or end. The saint is concerned with a "wound of love" (117); Blanchot reworks that image as a "wound of thought." To emerge from the "dark contemplation" is to participate in the divine life, and the saint explains this in an image that the young Mallarmé would have appreciated: "If the window is totally clean and pure, the sunlight will so transform and illumine it that to all appearances the window will be identical with the ray of sunlight and shine just like the sun's ray" (117). Yet for Blanchot there is no light to come. The dark gaze that enters Thomas denies the possibility of seeing and frustrates the possibility of experience; and yet, at the same time, it gives Thomas an opportunity to view the night as it essentially is—a darkness without enduring essence—and allows him to have experience in its radical sense: the peril of passing from a moment in time to the space of images. It is, if you like, an experience *of* experience, for Thomas slides from "sense experience" to "experience without sense," from that which yields positive knowledge to that which, in not offering itself to the senses, cannot enter the order of knowledge. This is what Bataille urges us to see when he speaks of the new theology as having "only the unknown as object."

We have to be careful in talking of the unknown as an object since, if Blanchot is correct, the distance between subject and object collapses in inner experience to reveal, at the last possible moment, a distance in being itself: a fissure that allows for the production of images. This distance (as Blanchot insists on calling it) cannot be traversed by a gaze but "is" a dark gaze that cannot be borne.[18] To have appeared before it is already no longer to be an "I." We can speak of the unknown as object only before an experience of it begins. That said, if the unknown can be a provisional object—the space of images, say—the new theology must be concerned with *docta ignorantia* and not *indocta ignorantia*, the known unknown and not the unknown unknown.[19] Someone might desire inner experience and might regard that desire and its possible fulfillment in religious terms. A reflection, systematic or not, on entering the unknown might be called "the new theology," and it would have as a legitimate aim a statement of how inner experience can be achieved. *L'Expérience intérieure* is itself partly a memorial of the new mysticism and partly a volume of the new theology, one that contains formal propositions such as "Principle of inner experience: to emerge through project from the realm of project" (46; 5:60). In fact this principle is central to the new theology. One has to meditate on something familiar in order to slide toward the unknown where the subject-object distinction will be dissolved. A believer might choose a crucifix, for example. Bataille sometimes used a photograph of a Chinese man being tortured.

Bataille alludes to the *Spiritual Exercises* of Saint Ignatius Loyola, and doubtless the passage from the five senses to the spiritual senses described there appealed to him.[20] Also, the fact that Bataille started to practice yoga in 1938 carries weight in determining the sort of discipline that he took upon himself.[21] It marks a new way of approaching the sacred after the rituals of Acéphale earlier in the decade. Another discipline, mystical theology, also guides us on the path of spiritual enlightenment; and one might expect "the new mystical theology" to do the same. For Bataille, the very act of writing *Thomas l'obscur* or *L'Expérience intérieure* can help to characterize the experience of the unknown. We should be careful, though, not to assume that Bataille and Blanchot approach the unknown in the same ways. There is no reason to think that Blanchot ever meditated in order to glide toward a limit, but good reason to think that over the course of his life he was granted feelings of "ravaging joy," "a feeling of extraordinary lightness, a sort of beatitude."[22]

3

The anecdote in *L'Expérience intérieure* records a conversation that took place sometime between the end of 1940, when Pierre Prévost introduced Bataille to Blanchot, and the summer of 1942 when the book was completed.[23] The two friends had talked about Bataille's quest to go to the end of the possible in man, and they had come to share the expression "inner experience."[24] One thing that agitated Bataille was the thought that because his experiences challenged all authority they could not themselves be justified. What would happen, he thought, were "God, knowledge, the suppression of pain to cease to be in my eyes convincing objectives, if the pleasure to be drawn from a rapture were to annoy me, even shock me, must inner experience from that moment seem empty to me, henceforth impossible, without justification?" (7; 5:19). He asked the question of several friends, but only Blanchot's answer satisfied and calmed him. We have already heard it: "experience itself is authority" and "authority expiates itself" (7; 5:19). It is a remarkable formulation, and to make sense of it we have to recall Roger Caillois's words in *L'Homme et le sacré* (1939): "Expiation is the act that permits the criminal to resume his normal activity and his place in the profane community, by ridding him of his sacred character."[25] Inner experience would at once render its practitioner sacred and then remove that quality from him or her. It would remain only as a trace. As I have said, *L'Expérience intérieure* is partly a work of the new mysticism and partly a work of the new theology. Yet when Blanchot appears there it is as "new theologian" to Bataille's "new mystic," and the novelist seems comfortable with the role, for he adopts it in his own writings.

Blanchot's review of Bataille's book appeared on May 4, 1943, in "Chronique de la vie intellectuelle," the weekly column he wrote for the *Journal des Débats*. Religion has taught us to question our immediate interests and easy consolations, he reminds us, before observing of man that "there is a demand in him that nothing in this life answers."[26] He explores the thought. "To go beyond, beyond what he desires, what he knows, what he is—that is what he finds at the bottom of every desire, of every knowing, and of his own being" (37–38; 48). History shows us, he believes, that this endless unrest gives rise to the thought of "an absolute beyond," an unearthly world, and so the principle of questioning everything meets its limit. To realize that the principle has reversed itself in the hope of heaven is to reaffirm that everything can be put in question, including oneself, and so "man meets unknowing as the expressing of this supreme calling into play," and—perhaps with a backward glance to *Thomas l'obscur*—he adds, "Unknowing throws back into the night what a man knows about himself" (38; 48). The old question "What is it to be human?" no longer appears within the reassuring horizon of the possible; rather, it is to be witnessed by way of the impossible. It is a question no longer simply of understanding how we live but of dealing with existence itself.

"The dialectics of anguish carries to the utmost the calling into question of the one who exists," Blanchot tells us. "It withdraws from him any possibility of saving the least piece of himself. It casts him into an endless fall in which he loses himself by the increasingly vertiginous fear of losing himself" (39; 49). These lines replay in another key themes associated with the dark night of the soul, impressively so, yet for Bataille and Blanchot illumination is to be gained otherwise and in terms of a different thematic. For them, following Alexandre Kojève's intensely Heideggerian reading of Hegel, history is already over, more or less: only the *dénouement,* world revolution, remains. The negativity that made history a chronicle of conflict no longer has an outlet, with the consequence that humans must investigate the meaning and value of the *nothing* that is left for them to accomplish.[27] "We enter with a leap into a situation that is no longer defined by useful operations or by knowing [*savoir*] . . . but one that opens up onto a loss of knowledge [*connaissance*]" (39; 49). For Bataille, when one is at this extreme limit it is not self-contradictory to say, as Mallarmé did, "I am already dead" (44; 5:58). It is this limit-experience that deeply interests Blanchot: "This state, a state of violence, of tearing apart, of abduction, of ravishing, would in every respect be similar to mystical ecstasy if it were disengaged from all the religious presuppositions that often [*souvent*] change it and, by giving it a meaning, determine it. The ecstatic 'loss of knowledge [*connaissance*]' is properly inner experience" (39; 49–50). Religious presuppositions *often* change the character of ecstasy, Blanchot says. A student of mysticism would query his assumption that there is only one sort of ecstasy: union and rapture should be distinguished.[28] And a close reader of the passage would note that Blanchot's phrasing implies that religious presuppositions do not *always* change the experience and that he leaves open the possibility that one or more mystics meet with his approval.

Such mystics would be unusual, even among ecstatics and visionaries. For inner experience has no meaning, no value; it provides no answers and offers no reassurances. The authority it confers does not last because the subject has not escaped the condition of being put in question. But there is communication: not a linking of two distinct beings but a dissolving of the self into the continuity of the unknown. "Rapture is not a window looking out on the outside, on the beyond," Bataille tells us, "but a mirror" (54; 5:69). And we recall the young man in "Les Fenêtres" seeing himself transfigured in the hospital window ("Je me mire . . ."). In calling rapture a mirror rather than a window, Bataille stresses that inner experience is transgressive: no transcendence is offered. An important consequence follows. A mystical ecstasy might be entirely personal, a secret relation between God and the soul. Not so with inner experience: because it transgresses publicly identifiable norms it can never be the preserve of an individual with no reference whatsoever to others.[29] It is an insight that Blanchot will take much further in his later work.

Bataille insists that mystical ecstasy is a limiting of inner experience: the quest for the unknown is subjugated to what is already known. Even Saint John of the Cross and Saint Teresa of Ávila, both of whom valued intellectual visions over the more consoling sensuous visions, fall short of inner experience (4–5; 5:17).[30] At no time, however, does Bataille reflect that in affirming the nothingness outside the self he has already determined that there is no God: if mystical ecstasy is limited by clinging to existential judgments about the deity, so too is inner experience. The problem is not raised by Blanchot, who presents his friend's position sympathetically, although this is not significant in itself. Early and late, his criticism tends to begin by paraphrasing the position under consideration, making the logic of the text quite clear before, if need be, exposing it to prior considerations that require the position to be adjusted or abandoned. As it happens, Blanchot agrees with the Bataille who asserts that "religious presuppositions" skew a radical calling into question of the self and its horizons. He readily concedes that communication with God presumes "the bursting of limits, the loss of self" (40; 50); and yet since this God cannot put Himself into question, the mystic entertains the hope of returning to that infinite being. No matter how devastating the experience of the divine might be, the mystic is not usually asked to give up belief in ultimate meaning or unity. There is no complete and utter abandonment that signifies "naked loss in the night" (40; 51), and the new mystical theology reflects on that extreme experience.

That said, the new theology also draws from currents of the old. It recalls the mystical theology of the Pseudo-Denys, of course, but the Areopagite is not the highest name in the western mystical pantheon, at least not for Blanchot. On November 4, 1942, only six months before reviewing L'Expérience intérieure, Blanchot reflected on two new translations of Meister Eckhart.[31] He began by deploring the "gross curiosity that our time exhibits about any mystical movement" and alluded to "the kinship that brings together the great themes of Eckhartian mysticism with certain tendencies of present-day ways of thinking."[32] He named Kierkegaard and Jaspers, writers for whom "in the intensity of immanence absolute transcendence is grasped" (27; 35), though perhaps he also had Bataille's recent meditations on transgression in mind. Blanchot spoke in his column of the "I" that, "by deepening itself beyond all determination, is confused with the divine 'Thou' in a union that breaks the structures proper to subject and object" (26; 34). He did not chastise Eckhart with a failure to affirm inner experience in all its purity; in fact, he said, "This experience is properly that of the fact of existing" (26; 34). He appreciated, it seems, the Meister's insistence that the affirmation of life requires no appeal to a ground other than life itself.[33] Like inner experience, life is its own authority. Similarly, the primordial unity of the Godhead and the soul caused no critical response, no flicker of concern, not even after we are told that for Eckhart, "The beyond is inside us in a way that separates us forever from ourselves, and our nobility rests in this secret that causes us to reject ourselves absolutely in order to find ourselves absolutely" (26; 35). And in his concluding paragraph, when reservations about the Meister would be expected, we hear that "faith's supreme experience" is "beyond all measure and all end" (27; 36), and that "A kind of triumph . . . emerges from Eckhart's ascent through nothingness and despair. A noble and magnanimous assurance persists in the torments of the night" (27; 35).

Anyone who knows Eckhart's homilies and tractates and the criticism that Blanchot was soon to be writing will not be surprised that the Frenchman finds the Thuringian to be a congenial spirit. Eckhart's understanding of detachment must also have been appealing to the Blanchot who was to argue for a doublet of engagement and disengagement in the literary life.[34] All the same, it is puzzling to find Blanchot not wanting to distance himself from Eckhart's vision of the soul's unity with the Godhead and of the nobility of the inner man, and one half expects him to revise his estimation of Eckhart's mysticism after he has weighed L'Expérience intérieure in his weekly column.[35] That does not happen, and in fact it is several months after his review of Bataille's irruptive book that he accounts for his admiration for Eckhart. It occurs in a column devoted to the seventeenth-century German mystic Angelus Silesius. He asks what the expression "knowledge [connaissance] of God" signifies. "One only knows that to which one becomes identical," he says. "And to become identical to God demands of man not only that he lose all that which makes him man, but, still more, that he annul all that which makes him believe that he knows God. To lose oneself in all the senses of the word, to find death and to kill what one has and what one is; this is the only path of knowledge."[36]

These remarks become more clear when we recall Eckhart's distinction between God and the Godhead. Before the world was made, the deity was "absolutely undetermined," as Blanchot phrases a teaching he rightly regards as common to Silesius and Eckhart, and the act of creation not only brings creatures into being but also causes "the deity [to create] himself as God."[37] Only the poorest in spirit, those who are free from God's will as well as their own, can be unified with the Godhead, for one must first divest oneself of all images, all attachment to anything that is not truly divine. When a man joins himself with the Godhead "he is more dead than death, he is exactly this dead God, to which Christ has been given as the model; he is the one who is refused everything, even the ecstasy where love is united with love in a preliminary duality." Eckhart's God puts Himself in question, Blanchot thinks; and the Godhead, that absolute no-thing-ness, can be known only in unknowing.[38] For Blanchot's Eckhart, "notions of salvation, hope and bliss no longer count."[39] To be one with the Godhead is for Blanchot to be able to say "I am already dead" with Bataille and Mallarmé. It is to have touched the continuous, the realm of being without beings, pure no-thing-ness.

When "Maître Eckhart" was reprinted in *Faux pas* (1943), the third paragraph was omitted. In the lines he consigned to oblivion Blanchot had rehearsed what little we know of the Dominican's life and noted that "we know nothing of the inner experience [*expérience intérieure*] of which his doctrines are only the speculative fruits."[40] He does not doubt that Eckhart enjoyed an extremely rich "spiritual experience," and nowhere does he distinguish inner experience from mystical ecstasy. Here then is a mystic whose "religious presuppositions" do not distort inner experience. The second paragraph was also altered: references to Schelling, Hegel, and Novalis were dropped, as was an allusion to the fifteenth-century cardinal and mystic Nicholas de Cusa. On January 6, 1943, however, Blanchot dedicated his column to the author of *De docta ignorantia*. He agrees with Maurice de Gandillac that the Cusanus's theology resembles Eckhart's while still finding reason to distinguish them:

> the cardinal remains foreign to all inner experience [*expérience intérieure*] in the strict sense. The non-knowledge [*non-savoir*] which he leads us to is not, as with Meister Eckhart, the result of the complete deprivation of the soul; it does not signify the anguished death by which it renounces everything, even God, and throws itself in an abyss where it

is ready to lose itself. Non-knowledge [*non-savoir*], "learned ignorance" of Master Cusa is the term of a dialectical process where discursive knowledge [*connaissance*], having been affirmed, denied, then reunited in a synthesized affirmation and negation, and finally this synthesis suspended in order to overcome it, comes naturally to the Unknowable. The interest of this thought is that while pretending to safeguard absolute transcendence it seeks to determine the channels of access which remain open in order to attain it; it wants spirit, through the activity which is proper to it, to have the same experience of God for which the mystics assign a total passivity to the soul; it substitutes non-knowledge [*non-savoir*] which is rupture with discourse and sacrifice of all thought with a discursive non-knowledge [*non-savoir*] which is the crowning of progress and the expression of a continued development.[41]

There are, then, two sorts of nonknowledge: one breaks decisively with discourse, while the other is discursive, conceived within the realm of the possible. We find the former in Eckhart, the latter in the Cusanus who construes the Creator as *Possest*, the possible that is actual (*posse-est*). What ultimately distinguishes the two mystics is that the Cusanus does not affirm the total passivity of the soul in its painful and joyous exposure to the deity.

The distinction is not without difficulties. If the nonknowledge we associate with Eckhart breaks with discourse and sacrifices all thought, how do we learn of it? The question is not considered in "Maître Eckhart" but is raised at the end of Blanchot's review of *L'Expérience intérieure* several months later. There we learn that discourse "is not forbidden to try to account for that which escapes discourse" (41; 52). Not at all: that attempt is necessary, "since translation, although never being satisfying, still keeps an essential part of authenticity insofar as it imitates the movement of challenge that it borrows, and, by denouncing itself as unfaithful guardian, doubles its text with another that supports it and erases it by a kind of permanent half-refutation" (41; 52). Bataille's writing, like Eckhart's, contests itself, perpetually calls its authority into question. As Bataille says in *L'Expérience intérieure*, shortly after evoking Saint John of the Cross's fall "into the night of non-knowledge," and with Blanchot's calming advice in mind: "Experience, its authority, its method, do not distinguish themselves from the contestation" (12; 5:24). Inner experience for Bataille is neither art nor the mystical, as we have seen, and yet Blanchot's way of determining how we can learn of nonknowledge indicates a slightly different attitude to it. For all his affirmation of living inner experience to the full, as though one were the last man, he remains intrigued by the relation between this experience and the texts that present it. Consider "Réflexions sur la jeune poésie," his column for May 27, 1942. To write is to exclude "any preliminary agreement with an already expressed spiritual form," but writing can rediscover this form "as its own invention." Religious poetry, if it is truly *poetry*, "is not necessarily heretical in its expression, but it is always so in its origins."[42]

When reading the Christian mystics Blanchot rules a rather sharp line. On the one side he places Eckhart and Saint John of the Cross, in both of whom he detects to a greater or lesser extent the idea "that man must necessarily seek God through non-knowledge."[43] And on the other side he places Angelus Silesius and Nicholas of Cusa, both of whom he suspects of literary or philosophical ambition. A close study of both sides of the line would cast doubt on the confidence with which it is drawn, although to be fair it must be said that the genre of the weekly literary column invites the bold remark and that Blanchot's columns are unusually nuanced and patient for literary journalism. Nonetheless, when a selection of his reviews was gathered together for publication Blanchot acknowledged the dangers of decisive judgments in his choice of title, *Faux pas*. Of more importance here and now, however, is that he recognized that not all mystical experiences occur in the realm of the possible; a spirituality like Eckhart's can be grasped by way of inner experience or the impossible. When such experience is presented it inevitably runs the risk of passing through the codes and conventions of representation. It happens with Angelus Silesius, of whom Blanchot reflects, "the mystical substance is itself altered by the literary spirit and intellectual subtleties," and he even goes so far as to declare that "Art corrupts the élan that it wants to transmit." The column ends with his saying that Silesius "appears as a mystic without profound and binding mystical experiences, and like William Blake, asking of speculation and poetry the movement towards the heights which his time, then, would not know how to confirm" (3).

How could he know what Silesius had or had not experienced? Besides, given that Blanchot has already established a relation between experience and text, it seems strange that he comes down so hard on Silesius. It must be that, for him, the poetry of the *Cherubinischer Wandersman* (1657) does not bear witness to a radical self-contestation. Certainly Silesius reworks motifs from Eckhart (most likely by way of John Tauler) and John Ruysbroeck; some of his verses rephrase well-known epigrams by Daniel Czepko von Reigersfeld; and there is an emphasis on affirming antitheses that can be neatly resolved. It all suggests a sensibility with one eye focused on literature, and that is enough for Blanchot to be cautious in his assessment of the mystic and poet. Earlier in the year, on June 9, 1943, he observed that inner experience can find its way into poems. Reflecting on Dominique Aury's *Anthologie de la poésie religieuse française* he noted,

> The path which leads from Maurice Scève to Rimbaud is marked by works which are religious through the inner experience [*expérience intérieure*] they seek to communicate, but are also characterized by their escape from religion. It is less a matter of deistic or philosophical reverie than texts where the poet, turning the illumination which he has received or provoked into utterances, makes himself his own sacrificer and enters into the secrets which only have their sense in poetry itself . . . The true mystical poems of our language, those that are born of an inner discovery, of a ravishing, of a revelatory anxiety, have been construed outside religious traditions.[44]

Orthodox religious meditations and petitions question little or nothing, Blanchot thinks, and only those poems that contest their authority can be regarded as conducting inner experience. As Blanchot said on May 27, 1942, when reflecting on the "new poetry," "One can make out continual slips in these relationships between poetic experience and inner experience."[45] The very ordering of *Faux pas* itself bears this out: the review of *L'Expérience intérieure* follows four essays on religious thinkers and is in turn followed by reflections on Proust and Rilke, each of whom, as we are told, has sometimes been interpreted from the perspective of the mystical.[46]

Bataille regards inner experience as neither mystical nor poetic, as that which is always to come, and to begin with Blanchot appears to agree completely with him.[47] Literature, he said on November 11, 1942, with André Gide in mind, is "an actual experience [*expérience*] whose results . . . cannot be measured in advance"; it "must be followed to the end to know where it leads its author, in what transformations of the self it culminates."[48] He may not believe in metaphysical or religious transcendence, but he plainly endorses a form of self-transcendence. At first, listening to Blanchot talk about literature is like hearing Bataille urging us to value poetry as a means of illumination, but within a sentence Blanchot moves to speak about literature as existing in its own right, even though the writer remains clearly in view. We must admit, he says, "that the art that is most submissive to the artist, that least breaks with rules and disciplines, whose use demands a constant attention, precisely the art that is made under perfect dependence on the one who makes it, is also the one most likely to transform the creator profoundly, to carry him beyond where he thought he would be. Literature . . . has an absolute existence" (298; 340).

While Blanchot vigorously defends Bataille's raptures, his personal interest is otherwise than in fusion with the unknown. He does not want to affirm that inner experience is neither mystical nor poetic but something slightly different: that the art and mysticism of value to him contest their authority without end. Unlike Bataille, then, Blanchot focuses on the relations of experience and literature, experience and mystical writing. Those relations require him to employ the traditional vocabulary of imitation and translation but also to introduce talk of "inner discovery" and sacrifice. The poet "makes himself his own sacrificer," we have heard him say, and the notion will interest us in the third chapter. Certainly Blanchot can distinguish the mystical from art and thought when it suits him to do so, for he has no desire to affirm immediate experience of a "'central' point."[49] By and large, though, he attends to something anterior to that distinction: the power of contestation, a ceaseless questioning that undoes its own claims to authority and indeed to power.

4

Announcements of "the new theology" are teasingly familiar to historians of theology. Bataille, who attended the seminary at Saint-Flour in 1917–18, visited the Benedictines at Quarr Abbey on the Isle of Wight in 1920, and worked at the Bibliothèque Nationale where he borrowed books by the mystics, would have known that well.[50] Indeed, it could be argued that in the heat of polemic in the twelfth century, the very word *theologia* can be construed as "new theology." William of St. Thierry says sarcastically of Peter Abelard, "Haec est nova novi theologi theologia" (Here is the new theology of a new theologian), while Saint Bernard of Clairvaux begins his letter to Innocent II on Abelard by saying, "Habemus in Francia novum de veteri magistro theologum" (In France we have a new theologian from an old master).[51] What infuriated Bernard was the presumption of Abelard's students in daring to talk about the sacred mysteries on the flimsy basis of a knowledge of dialectic and not, as he had, a profound knowledge of the Scriptures.[52] The *via moderna* was not to be trusted. When Abelard and Bernard were entering the lists against one another, *theologia* was beginning to change its meaning, from the practice of holy contemplation to an academic discipline; and Bernard was not the only one to be disturbed by the shift in meaning, not to mention the greater and more worrying cultural transformation that it bespoke.

To modern ears the expression "*la nouvelle théologie*" refers to a diffuse movement whose most intense moment was in the 1940s. It denotes the work of historians and theologians in the Jesuit House of Studies in Fourvière, near Lyons, and several others—Dominicans, an Oratorian, and a lay philosopher—

whose work was heading in the same broad direction. Almost always those three French words are encased in quotation marks or set in italics. For the critics of the movement, who chose the term, the scare quotes supplied the necessary hint of derision they were after: no authentic Catholic theology could be new. And for the theologians of Fourvière and their allies quotation marks were needed in order to keep the expression at a distance, for in their minds their project was a *réssource-ment*, a return to the Church Fathers and the scholasticism of the twelfth and thirteenth centuries. In 1942 Henri de Lubac and Jean Daniélou co-founded the important edition of patristic texts *Sources chrétiennes*, the very year, as it happens, that Bataille and Daniélou started to exchange ideas.[53] Around that time also Marie-Dominique Chenu, Étienne Gilson, and Lubac helped to refocus attention on what Saint Thomas Aquinas actually wrote, rather than on what Counter-Reformation commentaries had said he had written. It is understandable that Lubac and his confrères could not recognize themselves as rejecting the old theology in favor of a new one. On the contrary, in their eyes they were affirming the old theology as a corrective of long-standing yet modern deviations.

In its contemporary theological sense, the expression "new theology" was first used by Pietro Parente, who had influence in the Holy Office, in an article on Chenu and Louis Charlier for *L'Osservatore romano* of February 9–10, 1942. And the old-new name entered the debate with a double flourish: in French and in italics. These "two excellent Fathers have made themselves the knights-errant" of "this *nouvelle théologie*," Parente says; they have been "rudely demolishing the heretofore-classical system of our schools" while not presenting "any reliable material or sound criteria for a reconstruction in harmony with the indefeasible demands of a perfect orthodoxy."[54] With the publication of Lubac's *Surnaturel* (1946), the expression became increasingly charged with polemical force, and it was Lubac himself who came to be the main object of Roman displeasure.[55] An influential Thomist teaching at the Angelicum in Rome, the formidable Réginald Garrigou-Lagrange, published an aggressive essay, "La Nouvelle Théologie où va-t-elle?" (1946), and answered the question he had posed by darkly saying that *la nouvelle théologie* was no more than a return to theological modernism.[56] On September 16, 1946, Lubac and several of his fellow Jesuits were called before Pius XII at Castelgandolfo. "There has been much talk, but not enough reasoning in depth about a 'new theology,' perpetually evolving as everything else evolves, perpetually on the move but never getting anywhere," the pope complained (Lubac, *At the Service*, 248), and the voice of Garrigou-Lagrange could be heard in those words. The pope's address appeared the following day on the front page of *L'Osservatore romano*. Reflecting on this papal admonition and a similar one directed at the Dominicans, Father T. M. Bochenski in *La Liberté* for February 8, 1947, evoked the specter of "a disturbing movement, strangely connected with modernism," which "has been developing in several countries, particularly in France, where a number of books, articles and mimeographed courses have come out, propagating an erroneous irrationalist doctrine" (Lubac, *At the Service*, 249).

It is as though what Garrigou-Lagrange and other old-style Thomists called *"la nouvelle théologie"* had grown from the same soil as *la nouvelle théologie* that was being urged at the same time by Bataille and Blanchot. They had not, of course—or not in any straightforward way. All the same, a little historical reflection can help us bring the Bataille and Blanchot of the early 1940s into sharper focus. There is nowhere better to begin than with the observation that modernism in theology came as varied reactions to the rigid scholasticism widely taught in seminaries after Vatican I (1869–70) and to the somewhat wooden Thomism often presented to students after Leo XIII's call in *Aeterni Patris* (1879) for theology to be centered in the *summae* of Saint Thomas Aquinas. (Blanchot captures the flavor of those years and those institutions when he characterizes the *Summa theologiae* by saying that Thomas's "mode of questioning . . . is actually a mode of answering.")[57] Like all movements that gain their impetus by reacting against a state of affairs, theological modernism had more centrifugal force than internal cohesion. Friedrich von Hügel sought to determine an experience of transcendence and set his jaw against immanentism, George Tyrrell desired a stronger stress on the divine immanence without giving up transcendence, while Alfred Loisy appears to have fluctuated between a thoroughgoing immanentism and a belief in transcendence.[58] When Pius X vigorously condemned modernism in the encyclical *Pascendi dominici gregis* (1907), Loisy could only shake his head at the Vatican's assumption that the modernists were "a homogenous and united group."[59] In theory, modernism can be approached "from below," by patiently reading Maurice Blondel, Ernesto Buonaiuti, and Lucien Laberthonnière, along with those I have already named, and in doing so one can gain a sense of a loose and sometimes conflicting group of writers; and it can be approached "from above," by adopting the viewpoint of *Pascendi*, namely, that modernism is a closely interconnected series of doctrines.[60] But the alternatives have not been received as equally balanced. Within ecclesial politics for the three decades after the encyclical, *Pascendi* had the effect of annihilating individual writers and turning them into representatives of a movement.

With hindsight, and succumbing a little to its inevitable temptation *post hoc ergo propter hoc*, it would be all too easy to see Bataille and Blanchot as taking theological modernism to a strange extreme. Modernism would have been rife when they were young, so much so that Pius X had called it the *mal francese* of the Church.[61] Where the modernists prized experience over doctrine, the two Frenchmen jettisoned all doctrine and focused on inner experience. Where some modernists, at least according to *Pascendi*, associated faith and the unknowable, the Frenchmen were fascinated with nonknowing.[62] Where the modernists were attracted by a soft-focus mysticism, the Frenchmen admired the more severe mystics while castigating some of them for their lack of rigor in the last analysis. There are of course better reasons to see Bataille and Blanchot distinguishing themselves from cultural modernism, especially surrealism.[63] On December 28, 1948, Bataille had written to Gaston Gallimard to announce that he was preparing two new books, one of which was *Philosophie et religion surréalistes*.[64] An essay he had composed earlier in the year, "La Religion surréaliste," was doubtless in his mind. There he argues that while it is fiercely opposed to institutional religion, surrealism is nonetheless informed by a profound spiritual concern, one that is displayed in an interest in myth and its ritual enactments. It is the towering achievement of surrealism "to find in ritual the most incisive and tangible forms of poetic life."[65] Yet it is just here that surrealism founders, for while ritual presumes a material value for the community, surrealism is "the most complete negation of material interest" (77; 7:388). Unless surrealism adds to itself a concrete thinking of community, its poetry can only be frivolous. Or, in other words, surrealism will be ineffectual unless it recognizes that the images with which it works are manifestations not of art but of the sacred, that they are products not of individual unconsciousnesses but of the community, that they abide at the level not of representation but of communication.

The other book that Bataille proposed to Gallimard was *Maurice Blanchot et l'existentialisme*. Neither this nor the other title was ever written, although from what we know of Bataille's thought at the time it is likely that he would have distinguished his friend from the new and fashionable philosophy, arguing, as he was to do in another abandoned work several years later, that Blanchot is "the most original mind of the day," that he "has revealed the strangest, the most unexpected, perspectives on human existence."[66] Sartre is not an academic philosopher, Bataille readily conceded, but what is wrong with existentialism is precisely its intellectualism, and in particular its conversion of passion to the themes of individual choice and responsibility. At least the surrealists see well beyond the individual, their abiding interest being to reach past the self, and this gives them "a *spiritual authority* in whose name it is possible to speak."[67] Wholly of a piece with this, they maintain that liberty precedes the individual. Freedom is to be discovered *in* the world, in seizing the instant for its own sake, and not by setting oneself *against* the world in order to create a self. The true name for this authentic freedom is none other than ecstasy, Bataille tells us while adding the rider that this freedom is all there is to ecstasy, *"despite* the concerns of the mystics."[68] For his part, Blanchot observes that surrealism is at once wedded to the idea of the Cogito—it is an attempt to establish an immediate relationship with oneself—and equally caught up in the discovery that language is independent of the human subject. Surrealism has always dreamed of man's being able to "turn round on himself and seize a gaze [*saisir d'un regard*] that is no longer his own."[69] And we recall Blanchot's first novel where Thomas engages with the night: "His own glance entered into him in the form of an image at the tragic moment when this glance was regarded as the death of all image" (15; 18).

More pertinent than the influence of artistic modernism on Bataille, I think, is that of the theological antimodernists. As a convert and seminarian, he would have been introduced to the Thomism of the day. He would have been shown the *Summa theologiae* and the *Summa contra gentiles* through the lens of Counter-Reformation commentaries on the great works. The most influential of these was written by Tommaso de Vio Gaetani Cajetan (1469–1534), the authority of which was intensified when Leo XIII ordered it to be bound with the *Summa theologiae* in the authorized edition of his works, the "Leonine," volumes of which started to appear in 1882 and have continued to appear for over a century. What is called "antimodernism" in theology, as unfair a designation as "modernism," turns on the view that dogmatic propositions are unchanging because the truth itself does not change. Of particular interest here is the antimodernist emphasis on neoscholasticism, especially the view that there is a pure human nature, self-sufficient and therefore independent of grace. It had been mooted before Cardinal Cajetan taught the idea, in the writings of Denys the Carthusian (1402–71), which had perhaps been directly influenced by the Cusanus; but it was in Cajetan's commentaries that this notion was first presented as the teaching of Thomas.[70] His position was endorsed by Domingo Bañez (1528–1604) and John of St. Thomas (1589–1644), among others. It did not pass without comment. No less an eminence than Francisco Suárez (1548–1617) noted that Cajetan's thesis is of the *moderniores*, although, since he made little of the difference between Thomas and Cajetan, the doctrine kept being taught by theologians, right up to and including Garrigou-Lagrange, and became the staple fare of the dogmatics manuals.

Overwhelmingly committed to the doctrine of God's transcendence, the average Catholic theology that ran from the late seventeenth to the early twentieth century in effect removed the deity from the daily lives of men and women. God's existence could be proven by the light of natural reason, but fundamentally the order of divine grace is above the order of nature: such in outline is the *duplex ordo* theory that Lubac sought to expose and replace. He did so by patient historical analysis rather than by bold theological speculation, pointing out that the view that grace has merely extrinsic relations with nature cannot be traced to Aquinas but can be found in his Counter-Reformation Spanish commentators. There is simply no doctrine of "pure nature" in Aquinas, he argued; on the contrary, the traditional Catholic teaching is that we are created in the substantial image of God and thereby constituted so that we desire God. We do not *have* desire for God, Lubac maintained, we *are* that desire: it is imprinted on our created nature.[71] Not that God is in any way coerced by our longing for Him, for saving grace is only and ever freely given and is in no way dependent on God's act of creation.

It is one thing to honor the transcendence of God, quite another to remove God from the world; and for the theologians of Fourvière the *duplex ordo* had unwittingly achieved the latter through the former. In effect the Church had separated itself from the world, leaving social and political life without the guidance of those entrusted to preach the gospel. If secularism was growing so quickly, Lubac and all thought, it was partly because the Church showed so little interest in secular culture and society. The supernatural order was held by ecclesial authorities to be "so apart" from the natural order, Lubac noted, "that it was forbidden to have recourse to it in any of the great human debates of our time."[72] Against this state of affairs Lubac argued for what one commentator calls an "original experience," a longing for the divine whose substantial image we are.[73] From this perspective, transcendence is a movement within immanence; it marks human affect as well as intellect, it orients action in the social and political sphere as well as at the prie-dieu and before the altar. This is not a *new* theology, its proponents maintained, it is the one true Catholic teaching.[74] And it comes to light only as a consequence of discovering anew the Thomas of the *summae*, a Thomas who, though never obscure, was long obscured by commentators.

Bataille was not at all interested in retrieving an authentic Thomist teaching, but he was intent on displacing and parodying the Thomism to which he had been exposed. The Christian God, for him, is an absolutely transcendent being, "the sovereign form *par excellence*," remote from men and women.[75] This God is no more than the confusion of reason and the sacred, he thought, and once we realize with Pascal and Kierkegaard that He is not the ground of reason we are left with the ambiguity of the sacred.[76] The Latin adjective *sacer* can mean "holy" or "soiled," Bataille reminds us, and he refuses to resolve the ambiguity as Durkheim did by distinguishing the sacred from the profane.[77] Christianity blandly accepts that distinction, he thinks, and poses a supreme being, "distinct and limited like a thing" which in effect reduces the divine world to the terms of the profane world.[78] God would be a discontinuous being, like the humans he created, and since for Bataille religion is nothing less than a quest for a lost intimacy with the continuous, any religion that posits a supreme being is in danger of losing its religiosity. The believer would foreclose on sovereignty in favor of servitude. And such is the case with Christianity, "the least religious" of the major world faiths.[79] How can this be? Because Christianity fails to recognize the sanctity of transgression and thereby reduces the scope and strength of religion. Acknowledging only the beneficent side of the sacred, Christianity hastily identifies its dark, malefic side with natural man and the profane world. The violence associated with transgression is thereby reversed in favor of divine love that attempts to transform this world of discontinuity into a holy world of continuity.

Bataille's rejection of Christianity is not deeply motivated by skepticism caused by the higher criticism, or by finding the doctrine of atonement morally repugnant, or by objections to the ethics of Jesus. It is intensely centered on the doctrine of God. Christianity, as he describes it, is structured by his inflection of the *duplex ordo*, and he associates it with the Thomism he was taught. *L'Expérience intérieure* was the first of several volumes he called *La Somme athéologique*, and earlier he had signed the pornographic story *Madame Edwarda* "Pierre Angélique," literally "angelic stone" or "angelic Peter" but also a pun on "Père Angélique," Angelic Father.[80] Any Catholic of the day would be likely to think: Saint Thomas Aquinas, *doctoris angelici*, "angelic doctor." Now *Madame Edwarda* and the second part of *L'Expérience intérieure* ("Le Supplice") were conceived as a unity, Bataille informs us, and of the two the story expresses his views the better.[81] When it was uncoupled from "Le Supplice," *Madame Edwarda* was to be the first of a trilogy, *Divinus Deus*, in which the debauchery of Pierre Angélique was to be explored further.[82] Madame Edwarda, the main character of the story, is indeed a "madam" in a Parisian brothel, and the story turns on the revelation she gives to the drunken Pierre. On being shown her vagina, Pierre stammers, "Why . . . why are you doing that?" only to receive the astonishing reply, "You can see that for yourself . . . I'm GOD."[83] Edwarda puts on a black domino hood and runs outside, followed by Pierre. "She was entirely black, simply there, as distressing as an emptiness, a hole. I realized she wasn't frolicking, wasn't joking, and indeed, that, beneath the garment enfolding her, she was mindless: rapt, absent. Then all the drunken exhilaration drained out of me, then I knew that She had not lied, that She was GOD" (152; 3:24).

Just as Aquinas enjoyed ecstatic experiences over the course of his priestly life, including a final *raptus* that made all he had written seem like straw, so Bataille affirms an inner experience whose best expression is the erotic excess evoked in *Madame Edwarda*. Bataille was to be not so much a "new mystic" as a "new Thomas." Transcendence was not on the agenda for this atheistic Thomas, his concern was to be with transgression. Even so, *La Somme athéologique* parallels the Aquinas of Lubac, if only for a short stretch, in that it has no truck with extrinsicism or intellectualism. Bataille may not affirm transcendence in immanence, but, in his own way, he advocates a temporary overcoming of the self through transgression, an event marked by the dark pleasures of violating a taboo. He may not believe in a natural longing for God, but he affirms a "principle of insufficiency" at the heart of being human that bespeaks "the blind and impotent flight of all life toward an indefinable summit."[84] The *duplex ordo* of Cajetan and Suárez might never be made into a theme for Bataille, yet it was to be known in its contemporary effects. Existentialism was to be criticized for its intellectualism and surrealism for its extrinsicism. The latter complaint is signaled in an early essay, "La 'Vieille Taupe' et le préfix *sur* dans les mots *surhomme* et *surréaliste*" (1929–30?). The surrealists desire another order above the natural, as the prefix *sur* suggests, but in seeking that higher realm they make all that is earthly into a value. "All claims from below have been scurrilously disguised as claims from above: and the surrealists, having become the laughing-stock of those who have seen close up a sorry and shabby failure, obstinately hold on to their magnificent Icarian pose."[85] It is hardly an incisive criticism, and it is one that Bataille would never repeat when writing on surrealism.

In the *Second Manifeste* (1930) Breton had announced, "Everything tends to make us believe that there exists a certain point of the mind at which life and death, the real and the imagined, past and future, the communicable and the incommunicable, high and low, cease to be perceived as contradictions."[86] Bataille agreed, but not wholly: "I shall add: Good and Evil, pain and joy." And he went further: "This point is indicated both by violent literature and by the violence of a mystical experience: only the point matters."[87] Breton's flourish about a point that transcends all contradictions shows evidence of his recent, admiring reading of Hegel; and one can only surmise whether if Breton and Bataille had discussed this point in any detail they would have agreed for very long. The point that attracts Bataille is approached by way of transgression, not transcendence; and while the line between the two is sometimes ambiguous in Bataille's essays his intent is to keep it distinct. He could not be more plain in *L'Expérience intérieure* when he associates the point with "a pure inner fall into a void" (122; 5:142). Blanchot also approved Breton's longing for this point, seeing there, as has been noted, the desire for "man to turn round on himself and seize a gaze that is no longer his own."[88] It is something he had imagined in *Thomas l'obscur,* although he will come to see it in terms of depth rather than height, miasma rather than transcendence: "the lowest *point,* the furthest removed from lucidity and the moment in which lucidity, piercing this point, finds itself again and frees itself."[89] By the time of *L'Espace littéraire* (1955), he will come to call it an "original experience."[90] In its unfettered desire to oppose all art and reach a point transcending opposition, surrealism was a prime instance of what Blanchot had already come to call "terror." That is not a criticism as much as an index of its seriousness, although, for his part, Blanchot would come to see literature and mysticism as answering instead to "the lowest *point,* " the center of the night that endlessly withdraws before the endless movement of contestation.

5

"Terror" is the word that Jean Paulhan used in *Les Fleurs de Tarbes* (1941) to evoke the project of those writers for whom thought or feeling took precedence over language and form.[91] Blanchot was greatly excited by the book, and in his column for October 21, 1941, he hailed it as "one of the most important works of contemporary literary criticism."[92] He added two further reflections on the book and presented a reduced version of this long review as his first critical study, *Comment la littérature est-elle possible?* (1942).[93]

From the romantics to the surrealists, Paulhan argued, writers have prized originality, purity, or rupture as the enabling condition of literature, while downplaying language as an imperfect medium and a purveyor of cliché. But these "terrorists" are mistaken, he contended, for one can never tell for sure whether an arresting line represents an original thought or is a function of an exotic trope. Our only hope of apprehending reality is by acknowledging the inevitability of rhetoric and agreeing to treat tropes as tropes. In his dashing début as a critic, Blanchot reads *Les Fleurs de Tarbes* beyond its apparent meaning, suggesting that its author does far more than commend a purified rhetoric.[94] Paulhan also writes a "secret book" that is contained between the lines of the one offered to the public, and in that hidden work he reveals himself to be a revolutionary of a Copernican or Kantian kind. As we have seen, on May 4, 1943, Blanchot will praise *L'Expérience intérieure* for attempting to translate Bataille's raptures, which evade the strictures of discourse, into a discursive language that denounces itself at every opportunity. Here, though, many months before Bataille's book appeared, Blanchot proposes the idea of one text hiding another in the same work.

Blanchot does not claim to be original in finding two texts in the one piece.

In a later essay on *Les Fleurs de Tarbes*, "Le Mystère dans les lettres" (1946), he quietly acknowledges the influence of Mallarmé who wrote an essay of the same title and who argued that an obscure text might have a very clear meaning hidden deep within.[95] More particularly, he directs us to Pierre Nicole's *Traité de la grâce générale* (1715) for the germ of the idea. A Jansenist, Nicole had long been embroiled in the debate over nature and grace. Cornelius Jansen, bishop of Ypres, had strongly argued in his *Augustinus* (1641) against the scholastic view that in theory men and women could have been created in a state of pure nature. Supernatural grace was essential, he thought. Most Jansenists maintained that while God gave sufficient grace to all, He did not also provide efficacious grace to everyone; and without the latter salvation was practically impossible. For his part, Nicole argued that a general, sufficient grace genuinely offers men and women a way of getting to heaven. There are parts of the *Traité* that Lubac could have read with all the warmth of fellow feeling. His contemporary, Bataille, would have found Nicole less congenial, if only because elsewhere Nicole approaches mystical experience with a lively skepticism.[96] Blanchot, however, is less taken with Nicole's thoughts on grace and mystical prayer than with his observation on the doubleness of books:

> Books being only masses of thoughts, each book is in some way double, and imprints two kinds of ideas in the mind. For there is a mass of formed thoughts, expressed and conceived distinctly, imprinted in it; besides that, there is another compound imprinted in it, of indistinct views and thoughts, that one feels but would have difficulty expressing, and it is ordinarily in these views thus excited though unexpressed that the beauty of books and written works consists.[97]

What interests Blanchot are those thoughts "excited though unexpressed" that give rise to the sense of mystery in literature. Looking back from the vantage point of Jacques Derrida's *De la grammatologie* (1967), one could be forgiven for finding in Nicole an adumbration of what is called there "the dangerous supplement" and what others sometimes call the problematic of double inscription.

According to Blanchot, if one follows the surface of Paulhan's book, it appears that he reaches the following conclusion. An author who admits that rhetoric is unavoidable, who follows the rules of poetics and therefore uses form and meter, rhymes and the unities, will discover exactly what was being sought by the methods of terror, an "impersonal and innocent language" that will put him or her in "contact with the virginal newness of things" (78; 94). Far from being opposed to terror, rhetoric turns out to be "perfected terror."[98] For the terrorist has always desired, Blanchot (paraphrasing Paulhan) tells us, nothing less than access to an "inaccessible purity" (81; 98) and has wanted to place the reader "in a direct relationship with the veiled world . . . the pure religion" (80; 97). Blanchot is not being unfaithful to *Les Fleurs de Tarbes*. And if one knows Paulhan at all well, this language should not come as a surprise. Earlier he suggested that "One must return to the mystics. Of all the philosophers, only they openly put their philosophy to the test and *realize* it."[99] And he hinted of experiences or thoughts he had enjoyed or suffered, "which one achieves in a flash and which one cannot sustain, but from which, once they have appeared, infinitely unfold the apparent world with its brightness and darkness, its joys and filthinesses."[100] Nothing in *Les Fleurs de Tarbes* contradicts this kind of event. Indeed, Paulhan seems to have entertained the idea that his book gave some insight into the divine Word.[101]

It is the secret book and its revolution with which Blanchot wishes to be associated, and his entire review is devoted to disclosing it. And when he calls the secret book an "infernal machine," we might well suppose that it is not designed to reveal "the pure religion." Even in titling his piece "Comment la littérature est-elle possible?" he sides with the revolution, since he invites us to recall the guiding question of the first *Critique*, "How is experience possible?"[102] Kant showed that the categories of the understanding are the only means by which a person can legitimately claim to have experience. And if we credit the references to Paulhan's Copernican or Kantian revolution, Blanchot is suggesting that the secret book argues that thought turns around language and not vice versa. Authors may believe themselves to be terrorists, but without commonplaces and conventions they would not know how to write a page. What seems to render literature impossible turns out to be its condition of possibility. Doubtless this sounds like a second-order reflection on literature. For Blanchot, however, there is no insulation between first- and second-order levels, between "literature" and "criticism." No argument is being launched to the effect that a poem or a story elaborates itself in a space protected by the knowledge that literature is produced by following conventions: that would amount to no more than a caricature of *la littérature classique*. Instead, we are being urged to see that poetry and stories are produced not by meticulously following the laws of poetics but by railing against them while nevertheless having recourse to them: recombining some and rejecting others, needless to say, yet never escaping them altogether.

In Blanchot's recasting of Kant's question, then, "literature" does not simply replace "experience." Literature is itself always tied to the writer's experience, not because it answers to a particular psychological state but because it comes into existence by a relentless questioning of what enables it. Terrorists pride themselves on the authenticity and vitality of their experiences and deride conventions because, as Blanchot puts it, these are nothing but "much-used rules, the rules themselves being the result of former experiences and, as such, remaining necessarily foreign to the personal secret whose revelation they are supposed to help."[103] Authenticity, individuality, *Erlebnis* or "lived experience": all these are compromised by an author's inevitable negotiations with form and convention. What must be pointed out to the terrorists, Blanchot thinks, is that the writer's situation is always a negotiation between experience and nonexperience. Of course, a writer must have tasted life, as Rilke's Malte Laurids Brigge said so memorably, and will bring to the blank page a wealth of experience, but once pen is put to paper one is required to engage with conventions, nonexperience: the act of writing opens up experience in the sense of *Erfahrung*, a journey to be taken, the end of which is unknown and which will surely change the one who travels.[104] As Blanchot said in his column for November 11, 1942, literature is "an actual experience" ("une véritable expérience"),[105] and it is the art "that least breaks with rules and disciplines" that is most likely "to transform the creator profoundly, to carry him beyond where he thought he would be" (298; 340).

Understood in this way, writing is an experience enabled by the nonexperience afforded by genre and the unities, form and meter, rhetoric and rhyme. In the years to come Blanchot will explore that experience from different angles and talk about it by way of the "neuter," the "Outside," and the "disaster," words that will need to be explained at the right time. At the moment, though, it seems clear that where Bataille sought raptures occasioned by meditation, Blanchot opened himself to nonexperience by writing: the sacrifice of words and the author.[106] Both might be characterized as "experience of non-experience." I take the phrase from Blanchot's essay "L'Expérience-limite" (1962), written shortly after Bataille's death, in which he tries to analyze his friend's leitmotif. Bataille's ecstasies are limit-experiences, we are told, which Blanchot interprets to mean "the experience of non-experience." So important is the formulation, it is allocated a paragraph to itself, and one can see a great deal of Blanchot's writing condensed there. I have already touched on the senses of the expression that link it to literature and "the new mystical theology" and have suggested that Blanchot is primarily concerned with a movement of contestation that is anterior to the distinction between art and the mystical and that is coordinate with sacrifice. In the final chapter we will see that the expression formalizes part of what is at issue in ethics and political life for him. Now, however, I wish to explore something both close to and distant from Blanchot: a sense of the expression "experience of non-experience" that, while acknowledging its provenance in mystical writings, is in fact motivated by a skeptical attitude toward affective mysticism.

One of Henri de Lubac's most brilliant allies in overturning the *duplex ordo* theory of grace and nature was Hans Urs von Balthasar. Of particular interest here is not his theology of grace but his approach to faith in his theological aesthetics. Our faith does not open the way for new experiences, he says; on the contrary, it is "the surrender of one's own experience to the experience of Christ, and Christ's experience is one of kenotic humiliation and self-renunciation."[107] Such is his sense of how ordinary Christians are to live. It is in "mysticism," a word that Balthasar carefully wraps in quotation marks, that "every deeper experience (*Erfahrung*) of God will be a deeper entering into (*Einfahren*) the 'non-experience' of faith, into the loving renunciation of experience" (412). The allusion is to the dark nights of Saint John of the Cross, which are, he says, "precisely an '*experience* of non-experience,' or an experience of the negative, privative mode of experience, as a participation in the total archetypal experience of the Old and New Testaments" (413). Here mystical experience is regarded as extraordinary not because it falls under the rubric of a theological positivism, whose coordinates it ignores, but because it is Christian renunciation lived in a more rigorous and intense fashion than can be asked of the majority of the faithful. The ground of the *via negativa* is held to be biblical rather than existential.

Renunciation of experience can therefore be thought even within Christianity as a passage from the mystical, understood in terms of particular events, toward a faith that is to be lived every day. "For you have died, and your life is hidden with Christ in God," as Saint Paul said (Col. 3:3). Over the course of this study, I will argue that Blanchot, who rejects the Christian revelation as clearly and firmly as anyone can, follows the same movement: he passes from prizing remarkable experiences whether Bataille's or Proust's or Rilke's to affirming the everyday, although for him that avowal amounts to the most stringent denial of God that is humanly possible. Long before he becomes uncomfortable with the idea that only creative writers are privileged to brush against nonexperience, Blanchot returns to *Les Fleurs de Tarbes* to explore a passage from "the mystical" to "mystery" in literature. There is no transfiguration in mystery, no special event as there was for the narrator of "Les Fenêtres," nothing that is shown or hidden, no meaning or nonmeaning that is revealed. The mystery in literature is not the discovery of a secret but rather "a secret way of seeing," one that enables the reader to "distort the logical exactness of the first meaning" that the text offers to us.[108] Mystery will therefore allow the reader to discern two orders within a text, one public and one secret, and the word *text* here can mean "life" as well as "script." The way is opened for a displacement of the *duplex ordo* in which God does not appear and in terms of which the distinction between transcendence and transgression is not to be trusted. It is not a dualism, but it is a duality with which Blanchot will struggle all his life—calling it the possible and the impossible, the dialectical and the neutral, even death and dying—and it will be a constant concern from now on.

2

•

BLANCHOT'S PRIMAL SCENE

1

Before Blanchot became associated with
"the new mystical theology" proposed by Bataille in the early 1940s, he had re-
acted strongly against the "theological furor" of Jews and revolutionaries alike in
the mid- to late 1930s.[1] And yet these early political articles are themselves fiery
defenses of transcendence: the national transcendence of France.[2] His detesta-
tion of Léon Blum may not have led him to cry "Plutôt Hitler que le Front Popu-
laire," but in its own fashion his political journalism lent support to Charles
Mauras's call for *La France seule*.[3] Although personal redemption may not have
been anywhere on Blanchot's agenda, he went as far as to advocate terrorism as a
method of "public salvation."[4] Thinking about Blanchot's early identification of
terrorism and national transcendence, and his later *récits* and reflections on the
space of literature, Denis Hollier asks, "What about this scandal? It does not ba-
sically focus on the fact that the same hand could have written this but also that,
could have penned such words or signed such sentences. It focuses on a much
more primitive scene: Surprise! So he existed too! Literature does not completely
prevent existence! Blanchot is not transcendental! He too has—or at least had—a
'superfluous, harmful I.' (I even saw him once, pale but real, in a committee, in
May 1968.)"[5]

The humor turns, needless to say, on a deliberate confusion of "author" and
"agent" and makes the most of Blanchot's refusal to appear in public and of remarks like this: "before the work, the writer does not exist; after the work, he is
no longer there: which means that his existence is open to question—and we call

him an 'author'! It would be more correct to call him an 'actor,' the ephemeral character who is born and dies each evening in order to make himself extravagantly seen, killed by the performance that makes him visible—that is, without anything of his own or hiding anything in some secret place."[6] Hollier's criticism is directed not so much at the young Blanchot, contributor to *Combat* and other journals of the far right in the late 1930s, but at the older, left-wing Blanchot who argues that literature divides and disperses the writer's "I."[7] To point to Blanchot's very existence as a human being suffices to expose the folly of his theory of literature, it would seem. The gesture is more familiar in English than French literature. We recall the well-known scene in James Boswell's *The Life of Samuel Johnson, LL.D.* (1791) when the great moralist gives his judgment on Bishop Berkeley's doctrine of the nonexistence of matter. "I never shall forget the alacrity with which Johnson answered," Boswell says, "striking his foot with mighty force against a large stone, till he rebounded from it, 'I refute it *thus.*'"[8] For Hollier, the material existence of a writer constitutes "a primitive scene" of greater explanatory value for literature than any amount of talk about the death of the author.

Yet there is a more primitive scene available to us, one related by Blanchot himself several years before Hollier wrote his piece. It concerns a revelation of something more fundamental than history or even existence, although as we shall see later in this study Blanchot believes it to have indirect moral and political implications. I have in mind a late text originally and beguilingly entitled "Une scène primitive" (A Primal Scene) but whose title was slightly changed when Blanchot included it in *L'Écriture du désastre* (1980) so that it would read, perhaps quite differently, "(Une scène primitive?)":

> (A primal scene?) *You who live later, close to a heart that beats no more, suppose, suppose this: the child—is he seven years old, or eight perhaps?—standing by the window* [la vitre], *drawing the curtain and, through the pane, looking. What he sees: the garden, the wintry trees, the wall of a house. Though he sees, no doubt in a child's way, his play space, he grows weary and slowly looks up toward the ordinary sky, with clouds, grey light—pallid daylight without depth.*
>
> *What happens then: the sky, the* same *sky, suddenly open, absolutely black and absolutely empty, revealing (as though the pane* [la vitre] *had broken) such an absence that all has since always and forever more been lost therein—so lost that therein is affirmed and dissolved the vertiginous knowledge that nothing is what there is* [que rien est ce qu'il y a], *and first of all nothing beyond. The unexpected aspect of this scene (its interminable feature)*

is the feeling of happiness that straightway submerges the child, the ravaging joy to which he can bear witness only by tears, an endless flood of tears. He is thought to suffer a childish sorrow; attempts are made to console him. He says nothing. He will live henceforth in the secret. He will weep no more.[9]

2

"(Une scène primitive?)" determines and overdetermines a narrative space: between the dead and the living, writer and reader, child and adult, inner and outer, this world and a possible beyond. It tells of a vision, and therefore stages the old difficulty of presenting the unpresentable. This would not be the first time that one of Blanchot's characters has enjoyed or suffered a vision. In *Le Très-Haut* (1948), for example, Henri Sorge has "a kind of revelation": "Until very recently people were only fragments and they projected their dreams onto the sky . . . But now man exists. That's what I discovered."[10] Here, though, the vision is a child's; and while it may seem to be negative—to present a disaster, in fact—it is not taken so by the child. It is received as sublime, but not in the Kantian sense: no supersensuous destination is indicated.[11] On the contrary, religious consolation is explicitly denied. Yet the revelation is taken to be overwhelmingly affirmative, yielding "the feeling of happiness," and it forms the basis of a secret that is not so much covert information as a way of living and dying. (The little boy would perhaps agree with Agathe in Robert Musil's novel *The Man without Qualities* [1951] when she says to Ulrich, "You believe that mysticism is a secret through which we enter another world; but it is only, or even, the secret of living differently in our world.")[12] Blanchot's story about that little boy turns on a window. If what the text describes inclines us to regard it as "mystical" or "religious," albeit in a sense that would need to be clarified, the title makes us pause and sends us on a detour via psychoanalysis, with no guarantee of ever returning to those words. For the expression "primal scene" inevitably points us to Sigmund Freud's "From the History of an Infantile Neurosis" (1918 [1914]), better known as the Wolf-Man case, which also features a little boy and a window. Before anything else, then, let us look to Freud.

The Wolf-Man case centers on a dream that the patient had when "three, four, or at most five years old": "*I dreamt that it was night and that I was lying in bed . . . Suddenly the window opened of its own accord, and I was terrified to see that some white wolves were sitting on the big walnut tree in front of the window.*"[13] The Wolf-Man traces his dream back to a story related by his grandfather in which a wolf leaps through a window, surprises a tailor, and has his tail docked. A sense that this is not a fully satisfying basis for the dream leads the Wolf-Man to further interpretation. "He thought that the part of the dream which said that 'suddenly the window opened of its own accord' was not completely explained by its connection with the window at which the tailor was sitting and through which the wolf came into the room. 'It must mean: "My eyes suddenly opened." I was asleep, therefore, and suddenly woke up, and as I woke I saw something: the tree with the wolves.'" This points Freud beyond his provisional conclusions, "*A real occurrence—dating from a very early period—looking—immobility—sexual problems—castration—his father—something terrible*" (265). It leads, indeed, to a crucial stage in the analysis, one to which Blanchot alludes in the title, or lead line, of his text. Freud ventures a radical hypothesis about the basis of the Wolf-Man's neurosis: "He had been sleeping in his cot, then, in his parents' bedroom, and woke up, perhaps because of his rising fever, in the afternoon, possibly at five o'clock, the hour which was later marked out by depression. It harmonizes with our assumption that it was a hot summer's day, if we suppose that his parents had retired, half undressed, for an afternoon *siesta*. When he woke up, he witnessed a coitus *a tergo*, three times repeated; he was able to see his mother's genitals as well as his father's organ; and he understood the process as well as its significance" (268–69). This is Freud's "primal scene," supposedly witnessed by an infant one and a half years old.

What is called into question when Blanchot adds a question mark to "Une scène primitive"? For Hélène Cixous, who devotes part of a seminar to reading the text, nothing is denied, disclaimed, or disputed; the new punctuation simply serves to underline the nature of the event as limit-experience.[14] From one angle this explanation is perfectly judicious. No one can say with assurance that he or she has enjoyed or suffered a limit-experience; it is not something that one appropriates, remembers, and turns to knowledge: hence the question mark. But there are other possible interpretations that relate more closely to the words in the title. It could be the status of the scene that is threatened: is it a primal scene, an original fantasy, or a screen memory? Or could it be the psychoanalytic reference itself that is called into doubt or at least suspended? After all, Blanchot observes that in his judgment only those "for whom analysis is a risk, an extreme danger, a daily test" have the right to use a psychoanalytic lexicon, and the addition of parentheses around the title, which almost shelter the text from the psychoanalytic allusion and vice versa, could be taken as a sign of Blanchot's discretion.[15] Or is it perhaps the sexual basis of the primal scene that is at issue? The text speaks of *a*, not *the*, primal scene. Maybe there is for Blanchot a scene whose primal status is not related to parental coitus. "I wish," he says, "for a psychoanalyst to whom a sign would come, from the disaster" (9; 20).

Those words suggest that the best way to find an answer to our questions is to read "(Une scène primitive?)" in its final frame, *L'Écriture du désastre*. There we find that it is immediately preceded by a discussion of Donald W. Winnicott and Serge Leclaire on the early construction of selfhood. For Winnicott, the infant is shaken by agonies before a self is formed, and traces of these disturb the adult in later life, being transformed into acute fears of the loss of self in breakdown or death. "There are moments . . . when a patient needs to be told that the breakdown, a fear of which destroys his or her life, *has already been.* It is a fact that is carried round hidden away in the unconscious." The patient must remember the primitive trauma, "but it is not possible to remember something that has not yet happened, and this thing of the past has not happened yet because the patient was not there for it to happen to."[16] So the analyst must register those immemorial agonies in the analysand's memory by means of transference and thereby assure him or her that there is nothing to fear because, in a psychologically effective sense, breakdown or death has already taken place. While he concedes the therapeutic effectiveness of this technique, Blanchot objects to the fictive realization of an immemorial past, the linearity this imposes on the subject, and the individualization of that past. Taken together, Winnicott's treatment of the fear of death amounts to an endorsement that death is possible—it has a meaning and a truth—and accordingly it results in a steady refusal to accept death as the impossibility of dying, a notion that Blanchot explored years earlier in *Thomas l'obscur*.

A preferable report on the situation is offered, Blanchot thinks, by Leclaire in his case study "Pierre-Marie or the Child" (1975). Here Leclaire elaborates on the need to kill the *infans* in oneself. "Psychoanalytic practice is based upon bringing to the fore *the constant work of a power of death—the death of the wonderful (or terrifying) child who, from generation to generation, bears witness to parents' dreams and desires. There can be no life without killing that strange, original image in which everyone's birth is inscribed.*"[17] Unlike Winnicott, Leclaire will tolerate no confusion of this "first death" and our "second death," deep rooted though their conjunction is in our psyche. To allow those two deaths to become conflated is to fail to recognize "the most imperative summons of our bondage—to be born again and again to language and desire" and to yield to "the glorification of failure or the making of life into a sacred venture, the cult of despair or the defense of faith" (4). In psychoanalytic terms, the *infans* is a primary narcissistic representation whose task in each of us is to accomplish the work of death; and we can live and speak, Leclaire argues, only on the condition that it is forever consigned to death. Because the representation is primary it cannot become conscious, and the silent child can never be killed openly. Moreover, the child can never be destroyed once and for all, since it perpetuates itself with each murderous attack. Already dead, the *infans* is still condemned to suffer an interminable dying, like the Hunter Gracchus in Kafka's story. This "impossible, necessary death" functions as a primal scene for Blanchot, but plainly not in the classical Freudian sense, as the question mark indicates.

Let us circle back to "(Une scène primitive?)" with this renewed understanding of its title or lead line. We need to clarify what kind of text it is, whether it reports on a moment of transcendence (however negative or peculiar) or transgression, and whether we have the right to call it "mystical" or "religious" with appropriate qualifications. Cixous takes the text to be autobiographical, and even if one is skeptical about that word, especially with such a reserved man who, after all, writes of the young boy in the third person, it is easy enough to find other passages in Blanchot's writing that sit with this interpretation, not least of all a remark in *Le Pas au-delà* (1973) that the "'Self'" ("*Moi*") was "as if fissured, since the day when the sky opened upon its void."[18] Of course it is equally easy to find evidence for the view that the text is a tissue of literary allusions. The image of vacant skies is a commonplace for the absence of God, and there are sources other than Freud for the window motif, all of which would be familiar to Blanchot. I am thinking of Hölderlin "in his madness 'declaiming' at the window [*la fenêtre*]," Baudelaire intoning "Je ne vois qu'infini par toutes les fenêtres," Lautréamont's Maldoror speaking to the little boy sitting on a bench in the Tuileries, and, as we have seen, Mallarmé in "Les Fenêtres" pondering the alternative "Que la vitre soit l'art, soit la mysticité."[19] Autobiography, fiction, or faction: the pressing questions raised by "(Une scène primitive?)" cannot be contained within these tried and tested literary alternatives, as *L'Écriture du désastre* and in fact the whole of Blanchot's oeuvre helps to make clear. To a certain extent that body of work offers itself as a long commentary on "(Une scène primitive?)," even as that text seeks to read everything that Blanchot has written.

Those two short paragraphs about a boy by a window also recall another primal scene, this time by someone who has interested Freudians over the years.[20] I have in mind a passage in book 9 of *The Confessions* where Saint Augustine reports on a vision—or, more correctly, an audition—he enjoyed some six months after his baptism.[21] It could with justice be called a primal scene of Christian mysticism.[22] The event took place at Ostia, when he, his family, and some friends were resting on their return from Milan to North Africa where they would serve God by living in a contemplative community. In Blanchot's narrative, the little boy looks through a window into a garden, comes to understand "that nothing is what there is," and bursts into tears of happiness, which, being misunderstood, bring someone to comfort him, perhaps a mother or a father. The entire passage is spoken by a dead man—or, more accurately, by someone who imagines he is already dead. By contrast, a parent is intimately involved in the episode that Saint Augustine evokes, a mother who is soon to die, as the narrator knows, and the entire passage—indeed, the whole of the *Confessions*—is a prayer:

> The day was immanent when she was about to depart this life (the day which you knew and we did not). It came about, as I believe by your providence through your hidden ways, that she and I were standing leaning out of a window [*fenestram*] overlooking a garden . . . The conversation led us towards the conclusion that the pleasures of the bodily senses, however delightful in the radiant light of this physical world, is seen by comparison with the life of eternity to be not even worth considering. Our minds were lifted up by an ardent affection towards eternal being itself [*idipsum*]. Step by step we climbed beyond all corporeal objects and the heaven itself, where sun, moon, and stars shed light on the earth. We ascended even further by internal [*interius*] reflection and dialogue and wonder at your works, and we entered into our own minds. We moved up beyond them [*transcendimus eas*] so as to attain to the region of inexhaustible abundance where you feed Israel eternally with truth for food. There life is the wisdom by which all creatures come into being, both things which were and which will be. Furthermore, in this wisdom there is no past and future, but only being, since it is eternal. For to exist in the past or in the future is no property of the eternal. And while we talked and panted after it, we touched it in some small degree by a moment of total concentration of the heart. And we sighed and left behind us "the first fruits of the Spirit" (Rom. 8:23) bound to that higher world, as we returned to the noise of our human speech where a sentence has both a beginning and an ending.[23]

Then Augustine reflects on what has just happened and tells us, "even if in not just this way and with exactly these words," how the conversation reached this height. Were one to rid oneself of all images, quiet the soul and the imagination, bracket all language, and keep silent, then, at just that point, God would speak in an unmediated way. "We would hear his word, not through the tongue of the flesh, nor through the voice of an angel, nor through the sound of thunder, nor through the obscurity of a symbolic utterance." There would be no mediation whatever:

That is how it was when at that moment we extended our reach and in a flash of mental energy attained the eternal wisdom which abides beyond all things. If only it could last, and other visions of a vastly inferior kind could be withdrawn! Then this alone could ravish [rapiat] and absorb and enfold in inward joys [interiora gaudia] the person granted the vision. So too eternal life is of the quality of that moment of understanding after which we sighed. (9.10.25)

In several ways "(Une scène primitive?)" refigures the audition at Ostia. Where Augustine and Monica touch "eternal being itself," idipsum, the boy encounters the "there is," il y a, the eternal rustling of nothingness at the heart of being.[24] Neither being nor nonbeing, the il y a is an index of what Blanchot calls the neuter or the Outside: a stagnant void in which time has no direction and possibility has no hold. This is not a nonplace like Plato's khôra or Kant's noumenal realm; it does not subtend phenomenal reality in an unconditioned manner. Neither is it tohu va bohu, the formless waste before creation imagined in Genesis 1:2. Nor does Blanchot regard it as an illusion to which we are prey: he will tell us that it is neither subjective nor objective. Without examining the notion closely here, we can point to the horror the il y a evokes in Thomas at the beginning of Thomas l'obscur where the night neither gives itself to experience nor withdraws so that it cannot be experienced. It fascinates and frightens. Elsewhere Blanchot defines mystical ecstasy, like that enjoyed at Ostia, as "experience of what is not given in experience."[25] This would be the sheer "abundance" to which mother and son testify, not the "nothing" that the boy discovers.[26] Infinitesimally close in how they are described, the experience of God and of the il y a are also infinitely distant from each other.

Exactly how the two experiences differ can be charted more closely. Mother and son broach a life beyond this life, the boy by the window has his mortality absolutely confirmed. The Christians ascend beyond all created things and are finally touched by the eternal wisdom "beyond all things" (super omnia), while the boy appears to be passive throughout his revelation; it is the sky that is "suddenly open, absolutely black and absolutely empty." If the sky is empty, though, it cannot be active: mystery does abides not in the heavens but in a way of seeing, as Blanchot long ago explained with respect to Paulhan. So the boy receives the revelation by way of himself, by not quite coinciding with himself; he experiences the event as an image in the moment when the classical distinction between "reality" and "image" breaks down. In both scenes the participants enter a darkness, pass from external scenes to an inner world, yet Augustine and Monica transcend that interiority while the boy lives inside a secret that, as we are later told, *"is not linked to an 'I'"* (137; 208) and is therefore not interior. The episode in Ostia turns on conversation, while the event in France is solitary: however, conversation will become, for the mature Blanchot, that which forbids mystical fusion.[27] For all their differences, the passages conclude on a similar note: mother and son sigh, the little boy cries. Each of the participants is "ravaged" with joy.

All this can be deduced from a comparison of the two narratives when they are held at a little distance from their respective contexts. Once returned to their usual homes, the extent of the refiguring is more fully revealed, as is the complexity of specifying the relations between them. For one thing, just as Augustine reflects on the experience he has evoked, so too Blanchot meditates on his child's vision, directly in passages also called "(Une scène primitive?)" and indirectly in other fragments. At first one might think that Blanchot simply affirms an atheistic vision over and against Augustine's Christian ecstasy. If we examine both passages in their contexts, however, things are a little more complex. Is it so clear in the first place, people have asked, that Augustine reports a *Christian* experience?[28] Of course, the passage quotes from and extensively alludes to Scripture, and this testifies to the fact that he is interpreting his and Monica's experience in Christian terms.[29] Yet he has already reported a heightened experience of being after having studied the books of the Platonists in Milan in 386, and his Platonism is a medium of the audition at Ostia, one that remains in the *Confessions* even though it was composed some ten years after the event.[30]

As a young man, Augustine was strongly influenced by Cicero's exaltation in the now lost *Hortensius* to study philosophy, and, in doing so, to learn how to transcend mere earthly things and so gain happiness in contemplation. Readers of Plotinus will remember the tractate on beauty, especially the description of the ascent toward the Good in *Enneads* 1.6.7. At the same time, the episode runs counter to Plotinus who in *Enneads* 5.1.6 speaks of "leaning in soul towards Him by aspiration, alone towards the alone," something that does not happen when mother and son approach the deity in prayer.[31] To find traces of Platonism in Augustine's description of the audition at Ostia in no way compromises the claim that it was an experience of the God whom Christians adore. The borderlines between Christianity and Platonism were divided and at times unmarked in fourth-century Roman culture.[32] Perhaps it is best to say simply this. An audition was surely enjoyed at Ostia: it was pre-understood in terms of Christianity, and for Augustine this Christianity had itself been approached by way of Plotinus's *Enneads*, in part if not whole, and Porphyry's *De regressu animae*. Augustine's understanding after the fact is equally important: it is possible that the experience confirmed for the son the value of the mother's interpretation of Christianity. No philosopher herself, she nonetheless guided her son in and through her faith to the most intense spiritual moment of his life to date.[33]

Turning to Blanchot, there is reason to be cautious when saying that "(Une scène primitive?)" is atheistic. We are told, in the very book that houses the passage, that atheism does not simply erase God from one's concerns or one's vocabulary. "We carry on about atheism, which has always been a privileged way of talking about God" (92; 145). Indeed: there is the moral privilege claimed by protest atheism, the right to prosecute God for the sheer horror of exposing innocents to evil; and there is the methodological privilege, about which Heidegger speaks so firmly, that requires the philosopher not to invoke the deity precisely in order to philosophize freely about the event of being.[34] Blanchot makes it plain that a line runs between the experience evoked in "(Une scène primitive?)" and events such as Augustine's. "I call disaster," he says, "that which does not have the ultimate for a limit: it bears the ultimate away in the disaster" (28; 49). It needs to be underscored that he calls this loss of the divine a *disaster*: we are detached from all hope of heaven, left with the truth that there is no overarching meaning to life and the cosmos, and while this lack of final meaning is to be affirmed, its aspect as a catastrophe for humankind is to be acknowledged. His atheism is neither cold nor triumphalist. In fact it mimics the phrasings of the mystics, dangerously so, as Blanchot is the first to realize. Only once we are safely "well outside of mysticism" are we asked to recognize certain traits that associate the thought of the *il y a* or the neutral with the divine. We are invited to hear "the undemanding, the disastrous demand of the neutral" (74). The neutral is no divinity, of course, and certainly no ineffable Godhead beyond divinity. All the same, Blanchot cannot resist miming a prayer to it: "O neutral, free me from my weariness, lead me to that which, though preoccupying me to the point of occupying everything, does not concern me."[35]

As I have already mentioned, the main evidence for regarding "(Une scène primitive?)" as autobiographical is in *Le Pas au-delà*, not *L'Écriture du désastre*, and it makes those two paragraphs represent a moment when the "'Self'" ("*Moi*") was "as if fissured, since the day when the sky opened upon its void" (2; 9). What is striking here is that the import of the vision concerns not the reality of God but the construction of the subject. The child does not experience a sudden loss of self in ecstatic union with the deity but rather realizes that selfhood (and the identity, presence, and unity it assumes as form, ground, or horizon) has been immemorially lost, forever divided from itself. "'I' ['*Je*'] die before being born" (101; 157), we are told some pages after we read the story of the boy. Always and already fissured, the self has never been substantial. On the face of it, Blanchot might be taken to be arguing for a position much like David Hume's, namely, that there is no such entity as the self, only a bundle of affects and percepts; and in some respects his view of the self does converge with the Scottish philosopher's.[36] Hume would agree that the self is a *"canonic abbreviation of a rule of identity,"* as it is put in *Le Pas au-delà*, though he would not be sympathetic to Blanchot's affirmation of a neutral realm that is irreducible to the phenomenal world.[37] Descriptions of this nonplace as "where being ceaselessly perpetuates itself as nothingness" or "that which has never come, which is neither staunched nor spurting forth but coming back—the eternal lapping of return" would strike him as idle metaphysical speculation.[38] Exactly how Blanchot establishes the reality, if the word be allowed, of this strange realm will become more clear as we go on. In *L'Écriture du désastre*, though, it is starkly declared as a revelation, much as Friedrich Nietzsche told us of his sudden insight into the eternal return at Sils-Maria in August 1881.[39] Interestingly, the element of repetition is given not in the revelation itself but in the fragments that foreshadow and reflect on it. At issue in those passages is a way of being in relation "to the most ancient," the Outside, "to what would seem to come from furthest back in time immemorial without having ever been given" (3–4; 11).

If we take all this on credit, as we have to do if we confine ourselves to *L'Écriture du désastre*, we must say that the child's vision is, strictly speaking, not an event but the return of an event that has never actually occurred, that has never found a moment in which to present itself.[40] There can be no talk of a black-and-white contrast between the two events since for Augustine the self is always divided by competing desires, though it seeks unity. "What then am I? What is my nature?" he asks God in the *Confessions*, then says, "It is characterized by diversity, by life of many forms [*varia, multimoda vita*], utterly immeasurable."[41] More differences between the two passages can be drawn out. Augustine and Monica touch the eternal which has no past and no future; the young Blanchot encounters that which cannot lodge in the present but which is "always already past" and "yet to come" (1; 7). The black, empty sky that opens before the boy is not an invisible presence that the day has concealed until now; it is "un ciel antérieur," albeit of a somewhat different kind from that which Mallarmé evoked, and far removed from "la Beauté." It escapes representation. Elsewhere, Blanchot calls it "the *other* night," that eerie interruption of time when absence impinges on consciousness as though it were a mode of presence, that state of chronic insomnia when one is confronted by the impossibility of sleep. "It is not true night, it is night without truth, which does not lie, however—which is not false. It is not our bewilderment when our senses deceive us. It is no mystery, but it cannot be de-mystified."[42] In other words, "the *other* night" is neutral.

Two important and related things follow from Blanchot's account of the rev-elation that the child receives. First, the boy does not have what we could call, in all rigor, "an experience"; for how can one experience a return of what never hap-pened? From now on "experience" in this context must be rethought without di-rect reference to presence and, at the same time, without coding absence as neg-ative. Since this experience is not a "lived event" it is "already nonexperience," Blanchot concedes, before adding that it is "just an excess of experience" (51; 85). This enigma marks all Blanchot's later writing, helps to explain its paradox-ical flair and, more than that, its sheer difficulty; it calls for constant vigilance. This encounter with the neutral, neither an experience nor a nonexperience, "(falsely) imitates transcendence," Blanchot admits, and then adds, "transcen-dence . . . always wins out, even if only in a negative form."[43] It is easy to see what he has in mind. Augustine talked of the transcendent God as "Measure without measure" as "Number without number" and as "Weight without weight."[44] And Blanchot finds that the neutral imposes the same syntax on him but with a quite different sense: "death without death," "being *without* being," and "relation with-out relation."[45] Second, while the child "will live henceforth in the secret," he has no interiority to be sharply distinguished from an exteriority. "(Une scène prim-itive?)" shows that what Bataille calls an "inner experience" is neither interior nor an experience but rather communication with the Outside. Once that has been said, it should be palpable that the question mark in the title also puts at risk both "scene" (there is no representation) and "primal" (the event never took place).[46] Or, as Blanchot would have us say, the event was lived as an image: the child was neither free to choose a response nor able to remain disinterested.[47] The recognition that being is fissured and discloses the *il y a* or the Outside or the neutral is a matter of ontological attunement.

3

Let us begin again, once more with "(Une scène primitive?)," but this time I would like to recall another claim it has on us: its right to be regarded as literature. Now literature in Blanchot's sense of the word denotes a text that has "an underlying deceitfulness in it," which means that it denies what it represents.[48] So if "(Une scène primitive?)" is literature it can scarcely be taken as a belated report of an experience, as one might have been tempted to do on a first reading. More particularly, "(Une scène primitive?)" is an example of what has been known in France as a *récit*. The word can mean simply the act of telling something, and Pierre Corneille (1606–84) was one of the first to use it in that way. He also used it in a literary sense, as the narration of an event that has come to pass, and this is more relevant to our purposes. It was this meaning of the word that Ramon Fernandez had in mind when in the 1920s he distinguished *roman* and *récit* in an important essay on Honoré de Balzac.

It is instructive to see how Fernandez draws the distinction and, in particular, what he says about the récit. "*The novel is the representation of events which take place in time, a representation submitted to the conditions of apparition and development of these events.—The récit is the presentation of events which have taken place, and of which the reproduction is regulated by the narrator in conformity with the laws of exposition and persuasion.*"[49] So *Madame Bovary* is a novel, Fernandez says, while *Adolphe* is a récit: in the one, the event "*takes place*" while, in the other, it "*has taken place*" (63). In the former, characters are developed in space and time; in the latter, events are "withdrawn from the action of time and from an actual place in space" (64): they are made known, but by "abstract schemes which simplify them" (64). More precisely, the récit "*tends to the substitution of an order of conceptual exposition for the order of living production, and of rational proofs for aesthetic proofs*" (65). Not only will one find analyses in a récit but also they seem "*to determine and justify the action*" (66). The following passage is worth quoting in full. It will resonate with anyone who has read *Thomas l'obscur*, *L'Arrêt de mort*, or any of Blanchot's récits:

> A *récit* . . . is in direct relation with the life which it recounts, the painting of living reality, and the success of such painting remains after all its principal objective and the measure of its validity. The narrator has to reascend the slope of his first conception and to establish a relation of reciprocal justification between his ideas and the concrete representations which form the aesthetic part of the work. But a *récit* will always betray the modalities of its genesis and the intellectual work which has presided at its formation. However much the deceptive pieces of scenery [*les trompe-l'œil*] may be multiplied, the effects varied, and the narrator's emotions be justly and beautifully conveyed [*traduire*], it will be impossible to prevent the thing told from being *terminated* and its representation from having become independent and obeying only the laws of combination of the impersonal mind. (67)

Blanchot performs a remarkable twist on the récit as described by Fernandez. He remarks the inability of the text to be terminated by orienting it, insofar as possible, to what he calls "the interminable, the incessant": the neutral Outside to which writing leads us.[50] In figuring the récit in this way, he takes it to be not one literary genre among others but the hidden process of literary composition.[51]

For Blanchot, *récit* means several things: first, it relates just the one unusual event; second, it does not report an event but creates it in the process of narration; and third, it is a curious movement, "toward a point—one that is not only unknown, ignored, and foreign, but such that it seems, even before and outside of this movement, to have no kind of reality; yet one that is so imperious that it is from that point alone that the narrative draws its attraction [*le récit tire son attrait*], in such a way that it cannot even 'begin' before having reached it; but it is only the narrative [*récit*] and the unforeseeable movement of the narrative [*récit*] that provide the space where the point becomes real, powerful, and alluring."[52] It is this point to which Blanchot attends in preference to the transcendent point that Breton extols in the *Second Manifeste*. To get a better fix on it, I turn to Blanchot's remarks on Freud's primal scene in *L'Entretien infini* (1969). The primal scene is rendered there as a "primary 'event'" ("'événement' premier") that is "individual and proper to each history, a scene constituting something important and overwhelming, but also such that the one who experiences it can neither master nor determine it, and with which he has essential relations of insufficiency."[53] From here Blanchot departs from the classical Freudian account.

The primary event is a beginning to the extent it is singular and unique for each person, yet it cannot function as a beginning because once named it becomes enmeshed in a set of differential relations and is therefore "always ready to open onto a prior scene, and each conflict is not only itself but the beginning again of an older conflict it revives and at whose level it tends to resituate itself" (231; 346). The origin cannot be touched, although the limit can be transgressed. Not only is the primal scene unable to be recalled to consciousness but also it retreats from being named through deferred action. "Every time," Blanchot says, "this experience has been one of a fundamental insufficiency; each of us experiences the self as being insufficient" (231; 346). This conclusion can lead to a thinking of the community, and Blanchot does just that in his *La Communauté inavouable* (1983). Here, though, in *L'Entretien infini*, he follows another path that takes him to the newborn child for whom "everything is exterior, and he himself is scarcely anything but this exterior: the outside, a radical exteriority without unity, a dispersion without anything dispersing" (231–32; 346).

If we substitute "récit" for "self" Blanchot's view of narration becomes more distinct, not because narrative is one of the ways in which psychoanalysis is performed but because each "récit" and "self" strives to find its own kind of primal scene. Freud searches for the event that will connect everything, Blanchot for the point that will inaugurate the artwork and render it interminable, at least in principle; the one isolates a past that was never present to a consciousness, the other a past unpresentable to any consciousness.[54] The movement toward the unknown and unknowable origin must be true of all récits, Blanchot thinks, although there will be some narrations that thematize this structural truth. Samuel Beckett's *L'Innommable* (1953) is one of these. "Aesthetic feelings are no longer appropriate here. We may be in the presence not of a book but rather something much more than a book: the pure approach of the impulse from which all books come, of that original point where the work [*l'œuvre*] is lost, which always ruins the work, which restores the endless pointlessness [*désœuvrement*] in it, but with which it must also maintain a relationship that is always beginning again, under the risk of being nothing."[55] The same can be said of his own récits. They are errant quests for an inaccessible point outside literature but having no existence before the act of writing, and the approach to which is what makes them literature. In other words, Blanchot's narrations and some of his essays are attempts to uncover a primal scene while indicating that both "primal" and "scene" are themselves to be contested by the movement of discovery. The primal scene withdraws as it attracts.

In *L'Espace littéraire* Blanchot calls this movement of attraction and withdrawal "the original experience" ("l'expérience originelle") and makes a crucial move in linking it to a "radical reversal" ("renversement"). This reversal has quietly echoed throughout *L'Espace littéraire*, beginning with the essay on Mallarmé: "Writing appears as an extreme situation which presupposes a radical reversal" (38; 37). To write poetry, *le maître* found, is not to find being or the deity but nothingness and the absence of God. Now, though, we are to find a wider sense of "radical reversal" in which even Mallarmé can be placed, albeit in a position of high honor. Let us play back the meditation "La littérature et l'expérience originelle" near its end when Blanchot is rapidly reviewing his argument in order to forge the link:

> But what is art, and what can we say of literature? The question returns now with a particular violence. If we have art—which is exile from truth, which is the risk of an inoffensive game, which affirms man's belonging to the limitless outside where intimacy is unknown, where he is banished from his capability and from all forms of possibility—how does this come about? How, if he is altogether possibility, can man allow himself anything resembling art? If he has art, does this not mean that, con-

trary to his apparently authentic definition—the requirement which is in harmony with the law of the day—he entertains with death a relation which is not that of possibility, which does not lead to mastery or to an understanding or to the progressive achievements of time, but exposes him to a radical reversal?[56]

Earlier in *L'Espace littéraire*, Blanchot identified Hegel, Nietzsche, and Heidegger as philosophers who, for all their many differences, concur in thinking of death by way of the possible.[57] Human being is to be approached, they agree, starting from death. This is not simply the familiar claim that modern philosophy rejects religious transcendence and correspondingly affirms immanence and finitude. Rather, it is suggested that modern thought is a concerted attempt to render death possible: to find in death a meaning and a truth that will orient our understanding of life. Now these three philosophers also make high claims for the importance of art. For Hegel, art has been the sensuous manifestation of *Geist*; and for Heidegger it is what lets the truth of beings come to us. That art is supremely valuable is also Nietzsche's view—art is "'more divine' than truth," he declares—though in no sense does he think that art reveals a higher or more profound truth.[58] "*Honesty* would lead to nausea and suicide," we are told elsewhere. "But now there is a counterforce against our honesty that helps us to avoid such consequences: art as the good will to appearance."[59] In other words, art's value consists in its ability to deceive in the interest of affirming life. It is this sentiment that animates the dramatic sentence of 1888 that Blanchot quotes admiringly and that he thinks serves to disengage Nietzsche from Hegel and Heidegger: "We possess *art* lest we *perish of the truth.*"[60] Unlike Heidegger, Blanchot does not take this aphorism to indicate the main ways in which the will to power holds sway with regard to human beings.[61] Nor does he interpret it to mean that art is of use merely in distracting us from serious philosophizing we might do or from the horrors to which life can lead us. Rather, Blanchot thinks, art takes us to the abyss where truth can find no traction.

Blanchot's gloss on Nietzsche can be grasped only when one sees that for him all artistic creation is a fall, what he called a "disaster" some thirty-five years before the appearance of *L'Écriture du désastre*.[62] As we have seen, literature is a quest for a point, an obscure origin that comes into being only once the journey has commenced and that withdraws when approached. This quest begins as a necessary movement of negativity: an image is formed of a thing (an object, a tableau, a situation), and this image bears the meaning and the truth of the thing. Such is the traditional understanding of the image; the representation is held at a distance from what is being represented. To remain at this level of understanding, however, is to allow the classical image to occlude the relationship of resemblance in being. For, like Lévinas, Blanchot insists that an event or a thing resembles itself;[63] it is doubled in its appearing, being both itself and its image. It is this doubling that Blanchot calls the relationship of resemblance. We cannot grasp it because it has always and already happened, and it does not reassure us with a meaning and a truth as the image, classically understood, does. Rather than consoling us with the thought that the real and the image are distinct and stable orders, that we can measure the truth of an image against the reality it represents, it tells us that the imaginary is within a thing or, as Blanchot likes to put it, that the distance *between* a thing and its image is always and already *within* the thing. It is none other than being that subverts any attempt to compare the real and the imaginary.[64]

Negativity generates ambiguity: on the one hand, an image that is subsequent to the thing; while, on the other hand, a relationship of resemblance that suggests the imaginary cannot be separated from being. "Yes, at that time, everything becomes image," Blanchot says of the moment when one discerns the relationship of resemblance, "and the essence of the image is to be entirely outside, without intimacy, and yet more inaccessible and more mysterious than the innermost thought."[65] Fascinated as one is by the dark gaze of the imaginary at the heart of being, no one can remain before it: the ambiguity between image and the imaginary cannot be resolved. An image gives us a grip on reality; the imaginary makes us lose that grip. We pass from meaning to nonmeaning, from truth to nontruth. An artwork "makes what disappears in the object appear": the statue makes us alive to the marble, the poem alerts us to the words on the page or in the air.[66] The marble does not retreat before its function, as in a building, nor do the words become transparent, as in a report; rather, the materials are disconnected from being, they are appearances only, with no work to do, or, if you like, their work *is* nothing other than an idling in the artwork. To the extent that we can read a poem and make decent sense of it, the poem answers to the negativity of the concept and the image as usually understood. Yet the poem also opens onto the imaginary where we lose a positive relation with present being. The first aspect of the work is the realm of the possible: it remains in relation with the world and names it. The second aspect yields to the impossible: there is no relation with the world as constituted by consciousness, for the imaginary is always fixed in a past that never occurred and has no place in which it may abide.[67] Here one encounters the ghostly image of language, of words without being. It is an anonymous and impersonal abyss, a neutral space, and one is mesmerized by an empty repetition, the eternal return of what never truly begins and never remains itself.

Art shows us, Blanchot thinks, that human being is linked to the neutral Outside, the space of impossibility; it does so not by aesthetic or formal effects but because being is always and already doubled. Because a thing resembles itself, being is riven and perpetuates itself as nothingness in a poem or a sculpture. There is no question then of bringing an aesthetic attitude to bear on being and thereby generating a neutral realm.[68] Instead, being gives rise to the absence of being as well as to its presence. Even so, art can be summoned to judge those philosophies that construe death as a possibility. Nietzsche helps us to criticize Hegel and Heidegger, and we must try to read Nietzsche against himself. Where modern philosophers and artists have established a metaphysics, an epistemology, or an ethics and then worked out the consequences for art, Blanchot examines the nature of art based on a phenomenological consideration of being and uses the insights gained there to criticize modern thought *en bloc* as a philosophy of possibility. It may be that Hegel magisterially reveals to us that life is in truth the animation of death.[69] And it may be that Heidegger brilliantly establishes that death is "the possibility of the absolute impossibility of Dasein."[70] But the sheer fact that we have art suffices, Blanchot thinks, to cast doubt on the confidence with which Hegel orchestrates the dialectic, Nietzsche pronounces on the right time to die, and Heidegger regards the impossible as within a dying man's power, as the last possibility that he can realize. Art involves us in a "radical reversal," a turn that points us to the impossible rather than the possible.

Notice that Blanchot does not simply reject the Hegelian dialectic, Nietzsche's injunction to die at the right time, or Heidegger's claim about *Dasein*'s demise, for there is a clear sense in which death remains linked to possibility. His concern is otherwise: to disclose an aspect of death that opens onto impossibility, and he calls this "dying." The image fascinates us with the absence of being, and because it offers us no end it can be regarded as the very space of dying. Lévinas puts it well: "In *dying*, the horizon of the future is given, but the future as a promise of a new present is refused; one is in the interval, forever an interval."[71] Yet the question of how death and dying are related is very far from new. One of the most significant discussions takes place in *The City of God* (completed in 426), which is well known because of Saint Augustine's insistence that death is an evil even for the man or woman who dies in the odor of sanctity. What agitates is not death but dying:

> For as there are three times, before death, in death, after death, so there
> are three states corresponding, living, dying, dead. And it is very hard to

define which is before death, nor dead, which is after death, but dying, which is in death. For so long as the soul is in the body, especially if consciousness remain, the man certainly lives; for body and soul constitute the man. And thus, before death, he cannot be said to be in death; but when, on the other hand, the soul has departed, and all bodily sensation is extinct, death is past, and the man is dead. Between these two states the dying condition finds no place; for if a man still lives, death has not arrived; if he has ceased to live, death is past. Never, then, is he dying, that is, comprehended in the state of death [*Numquam ergo moriens, id est in morte, esse conprehenditur*].[72]

Faced with these difficulties, we should submit to common usage and talk of "before death" and "after death," Augustine adds, while conceding that "no words can explain how either the dying are said to live, or how the dead are said, even after death, to be in death" (4.21). Certainly the dead cannot be said to be dying, even though they are "in death"; and Augustine points out that the Latin *moritur*, "he is dying," cannot be declined in the perfect tense.

Augustine correctly sees that dying cannot be incorporated into an economy of life and death: for him, the dying die and pass into the next life where they will be judged. Had Augustine not been bound to the dogma of immortality, Blanchot would perhaps say, he could have teased out his fundamental insight that dying opens onto a neutral state. Where the saint develops a dualism of life and death, the writer explores the duality of death and dying. *L'Écriture du désastre* may not tell us what we have already heard from *The City of God*, that "two cities have been formed by two loves: the earthly by the love of self, even to the contempt of God; the heavenly by the love of God, even to the contempt of self" (14.28), but it does speak of "two languages . . . one dialectical, the other not; one where negativity is the task, the other where the neutral remains apart, cut off both from being and from not-being" (20; 38). And Blanchot adds in a rare moment of advice, "In the same way each of us ought both to be a free and speaking subject, and to disappear as passive, patient—the patient [*le patient-passif*] whom dying traverses and who does not show himself" (20; 38).

Blanchot is committed to the possible and the impossible as phased counterparts, not to a dualism of the earthly and the heavenly. Indeed, his second novel, *Aminadab* (1942), expressly rejects the metaphor of ascent. The main character, Thomas, has been slowly making his way up to the highest floor of a strange boarding house he entered at the start of the story. On the verge of his goal, meeting the girl whose face he perhaps glimpsed from the street, he comes across a young man who censures his ambition "to reach the heights, to pass from one floor to another, to advance inch by inch" while suffering privation and disease (185; 211). All this time he has been following the wrong path. Instead of ascending, he should have descended, and in the beautiful caves beneath the earth he would have truly found himself. It is too late, however, and Thomas continues with his quest. A young girl tells him that in the final room, right at the top of the house, night will unfold completely, she will become truly beautiful, and the lamps will be turned so that their inscriptions which he has wanted to read will be facing him. And yet the girl also says that if the night covers Thomas he will not experience it, he will not be able to see her, and the lamps will not be lit to illuminate the inscriptions: "Everything will be covered in darkness." And she goes on: "But in a moment we will be permanently united. I will stretch out my open arms; I will embrace you; I will roll with you through great secrets. We will lose each other and find each other again. There will never be anything to separate us. What a shame you will not be able to witness this good fortune!" (196, 197; 224, 225).

Strangely enough, it is the novel's enigmatic title that illuminates these two meetings. "Aminadab" names several persons in the Hebrew Bible, but the most relevant source is Canticles 6:12, "Or ever I was aware, my soul made me like the chariots of Amminadib," a particularly vexing *crux interpretum*, the details of which need not concern us. In this verse Aminadab (to use the Romance spelling) has been taken to stand for both Christ and Antichrist, and in the reading that is of most interest to us, that of Saint John of the Cross, it is plainly the latter.[73] I quote the final stanza of "The Spiritual Canticle" in English translation:

No one looked at her,
Nor did Aminadab appear;
The siege was still;
And the cavalry,
At the sight of the waters, descended.[74]

And here is John of the Cross's commentary on the second line of that stanza:

In Sacred Scripture [Cant. 6:11], Aminadab, speaking spiritually, symbolizes the devil, the soul's adversary. He endlessly combated and disturbed her with the countless ammunition of his artillery to prevent her entry into this fort and hiding place of interior recollection with the Bridegroom. But in this place where she now dwells, she is so favored, strong, and victorious with the virtues, and with God's embrace, that the devil dares not come, but with immense fear flees and does not venture to appear. Also because of the practice of virtue and the state of perfection, the soul has so conquered and routed him that he no longer appears before her. And thus, Aminadab did not appear with any right to hinder this blessing I am after. (564)

Aminadab does not and can not appear in the mystic marriage. What we see in the final scenes of Blanchot's novel is not a perfect union of spiritual Bride and Bridegroom but inner experience. It should come as no surprise that Bataille quotes the *Aminadab* passage at length in *Le Coupable*.[75]

What if Thomas had chosen the better path, the one commended by the young man, and descended into the cool and beautiful caves beneath the earth? Then he would have encountered Blanchot's Aminadab who guards the way into the underground. A new Orpheus, he would have sought another woman—or is she the one glimpsed from the road?—Eurydice, "the profoundly dark point towards which art, desire, death, and the night all seem to lead."[76] She is not the transcendent point dreamed of by the surrealists but a point beneath the world that attracts and withdraws. She is the object of a vigilant and hopeless quest, yet her passivity exercises a certain power, no less conventional than the situation in which she is placed, for she fascinates Orpheus in her impossibility. We shall encounter her again.

4

After we have observed that the little boy in "(Une scène primitive?)" is spoken of in the third person, that all the assertions in that story are preceded by the incantation "suppose, suppose this," and that the entire passage is framed, from within and without, as autothanatography, the thought nonetheless persists that we must also consider it as a testimony. If "(Une scène primitive?)" is autobiographical, among other things, the event related there would have occurred around the beginning of the First World War. *L'Écriture du désastre*, the collection of fragments in which it figures prominently, broods not only on the "impossible, necessary death" that disperses the "I" but on the unspeakable disaster, the Holocaust. It is the Holocaust that makes the Second World War the most horrific of all wars, horrific not because of the scale of the conflict, which was already more tragic than could be borne, but because of what passed for so long under its cover. Here "disaster" means not only being cut adrift from a star—from guidance and hope—but also, in a cruel paradox, being given a star to wear in the death camps. One sharp fragment recalls "that young prisoner of Auschwitz":

(he had suffered the worst, led his family to the crematorium, hanged himself: after being saved at the last moment—how can one say that: *saved?*—he was exempted from contact with dead bodies, but when the SS shot someone, he was obliged to hold the victim's head so that the bullet could be more easily lodged in the neck.) When asked how he could bear this, he is supposed to have answered that he "observed the comportment of men before death." I will not believe it . . . Saved at the last minute [*le dernier instant*], the young man of whom I speak was forced to live that last instant again and each time to live it once more, frustrated every time of his own death and made to exchange it every time for the death of all [*chaque fois frustré de sa mort, l'échangeant contre la mort de tous*]. (82; 130–31)

How this passage offers itself to be read changed significantly in 1994, fourteen years after it was published, with the appearance of *L'Instant de ma mort*.[77] Blanchot's last récit, if it is one, tells of a young man, presumably Blanchot himself, who is taken by force from his house ("le Château") by a Nazi lieutenant. He leaves "in an almost priestly [*sacerdotale*] manner," is put before an impromptu firing squad, and then saved at the last moment.[78] The lieutenant is distracted, leaving time for a soldier to say, "'We're not Germans, Russians' . . . 'Vlassov army'" (5; 4). He makes a sign for the young man to disappear, and he does. "I think he moved away," the narrator says, capturing the dreamlike state of the moment while also associating himself all the more tightly with the character. The young man retains "the feeling of lightness" and eventually finds himself "in a distant forest, named the 'Bois des bruyères' where he remained sheltered by trees he knew well" (5; 4). The récit ends with the narrator evoking "the instant of my death henceforth always in abeyance" ("l'instant de ma mort désormais toujours en instance") (11; 10).

The young prisoner in Auschwitz and the young Blanchot taken from the Château are both placed before firing squads: the one time and again, the other only once. The prisoner relives his death each time he is made to perform his repugnant task; the writer finds that he has survived death and that, from then on, death no longer frightens him. In Auschwitz, the young prisoner exchanges his death for the deaths of others; in the French countryside, the young writer discovers to his horror that he has inadvertently done the same. He has worked with the Resistance; and the man he will become, who will write about that young prisoner, will declare that in the camps "resistance is spiritual."[79] He will meditate endlessly on Auschwitz: not by way of reparation for indirectly supporting a culture of anti-Semitism by contributing to *Combat*, *Aux Écoutes*, and other journals of the far right—he knows all too well that there can be no atonement: the dead cannot forgive—but by way of keeping the memory of horror alive and testifying that it is irreducible to the order of knowledge. One index of this can be found in a letter of 1989, replying to a query about his involvement in drafting the *Manifeste de 121* (1960) and his public intervention in politics at precisely that time. In his answer Blanchot ignores the request for information and speaks instead about the issue of the day, the hotly debated erection of a Carmelite monastery at Auschwitz. At one point he addresses the murdered directly, "You who are now dead, you who died for us and often because of us (because of our shortcomings), you must not be allowed to die a second time, and silence must not mean that you sink into oblivion."[80] In no sense are the dead of Auschwitz to be represented by way of Eurydice.

"Know what has happened, do not forget," Blanchot says when ending his fragment on the young prisoner in Auschwitz, "and at the same time never will you know" (82; 131). It is with this in mind that I would like to read a few lines of *L'Instant de ma mort*:

> I know—do I know it [*le sais-je*]—that the one at whom the Germans were already aiming, awaiting but the final order, experienced [*éprouva*] then a feeling of extraordinary lightness, a sort of beatitude (nothing happy, however)—sovereign elation? The encounter of death with death?
>
> In his place, I will not try to analyze. He was perhaps suddenly invincible. Dead—immortal. Perhaps ecstasy. Rather the feeling of compassion for suffering humanity, the happiness of not being immortal or eternal. Henceforth, he was bound to death by a surreptitious friendship. (5; 4)

"I know," the narrator tells us, and immediately the statement becomes perplexed. The lack of a question mark at the end of "do I know it" renders the expression ambiguous: it is both a question (do I know it?) and a redoubling of the claim to knowledge (I know it all too well). Yet there is reason to believe the event actually occurred. We can cite a letter from Blanchot to that effect, and we can also turn to *La Folie du jour* (1947): "I was made to stand against the wall like many others. Why? For no reason. The guns did not go off."[81] At the same time there is reason to doubt that the event entered into the order of knowledge. We recall Blanchot's strictures about the possibility of recalling ecstasy: "there is evidence—overpowering evidence—," he says (and he is thinking of Eckhart), "that ecstasy is without object, just as it is without a why, just as it challenges certainty. One can write that word (ecstasy) only by putting it carefully between quotation marks, because nobody can know what it is about, and, above all, whether it took place: going beyond knowledge, implying un-knowledge, it refuses to be stated other than though random words that cannot guarantee it."[82] That something happened is certain, as is the feeling of lightness, although what sort of event it was can never be known with any certainty. "Perhaps ecstasy" is the most that the narrator will risk.

Inevitably, we recall the event that occurred in the earlier war, "(Une scène primitive?)." The later récit uses the vocabulary of mysticism more freely than the earlier one, although once again it is impossible to decide firmly what is being affirmed or questioned. It is "a sort of beatitude": does "sort" serve to distance us from the claim that it is beatitude, or does it specify that it is a species of beatitude? It is "sovereign elation": are we to think of the elation of the mystics, or Bataille telling us "Sovereignty is NOTHING," or both?[83] It is "Perhaps ecstasy": does the ad-verb express reserve with respect to the claim that it is ecstasy, or reinforce that even authentic ecstasies cannot be retained by an individual? "(Une scène primi-tive?)" tells us that in understanding that "nothing is what there is," the boy is straightaway submerged by "the feeling of happiness," and that this is the scene's "interminable feature," the element that could be discussed endlessly in *the order of conceptual exposition*" as Fernandez says when describing the nature of the récit. In the later scene, however, the narrator explicitly tells us that the young man's feeling has "nothing happy" ("rien heureux") about it. The anteriority of death, which forms the burden of *L'Écriture du désastre*, takes away the fear of death con-sidered as the breakdown of personal identity and thereby leads to happiness. But the child of "(Une scène primitive?)" is not about to die. Awaiting execution, the young man outside the Château becomes a site where anterior death can collide with empirical death, where the death "within" might touch the death "without." Very quickly, the parenthetical assurance "nothing happy, however" is revised, for we are told the young man feels "the happiness [le bonheur] of not being immortal or eternal." In fact the feeling is double: happiness to be mortal and "compassion for suffering humanity," and this complex emotion carries more weight for the narrator than the possibility that his younger self experienced ecstasy ("Rather the feeling of compassion. . . . "). Whatever foldings of Christian mysticism occur in the first of the two paragraphs I have quoted are made even more complex by a vo-cabulary that recalls the Buddha. It is not the first time that Blanchot's language draws near to the language of the great oriental religions.[84]

Let us stay close to the strange experience or nonexperience that crosses the young man as he faces the firing squad. It takes hold in two distinct registers: with regard to the self (it is mortal) and with regard to justice (one must show compassion). In the paragraphs that follow, it is the latter that is explored, for when the young man who has been hiding in the "Bois des bruyères" returns to the world, he discovers that the farms are burning and three sons of local farmers have been slaughtered, but that the Château has only been looted: the young writer has lost a manuscript. "No doubt what then began for the young man was the torment of injustice. No more ecstasy; the feeling that he was only living because, even in the eyes of the Russians, he belonged to a noble class" (7; 6). It is as though Blanchot quietly indicates a basis of his political shift from right-wing monarchism to left-wing radicalism.[85] Saved at the last minute, only because of his class, he has been made to exchange his death for the deaths of the young farmers. The contrast with the young prisoner of Auschwitz is sharp: the young writer has been able to observe only his own comportment before death, and that experience has made death into a friend.

"No more ecstasy," he says: whatever inner experience had been enjoyed has been firmly replaced by a moral outrage directed partly against the invading army, partly against the injustice of class (and hence partly against himself: recall the words he addressed to the dead, "you who died for us"). But the temporal pattern that would allow "no more" its scope and strength has long since been disrupted: "There remained, however, at the moment when the shooting was no longer but to come, the feeling of lightness that I would not know how to translate [*traduire*]: freed from life? the infinite opening up? Neither happiness, nor unhappiness. Nor the absence of fear and perhaps already the step beyond [*le pas au-delà*]" (7–9; 6–7). The allusion to the intractable difficulty of translating inner experience into a written text recalls the closing passage of Blanchot's review of *L'Expérience intérieure* where we learn that "translation, although never being satisfying, still keeps an essential part of authenticity insofar as it imitates the movement of challenge that it borrows" (41; 52). Here, though, the experience is not represented by way of fragments but roughly translated into two questions, an evocation of the neutral, and a qualified affirmation of *le pas au-delà*.

To understand what is at risk in that strange expression, I turn to the book to which it lends itself as a title. "The circle of the law is this: there must be a crossing in order for there to be a limit, but only the limit, in as much as uncrossable, summons to cross, affirms the desire (the false step [*le faux pas*]) that has always already, through an unforeseeable movement, crossed the line."[86] No transgression without limit, then, and no limit without transgression: the logic is very well known. More arresting is Blanchot's claim that death wears "the face of the law" (24; 38) and that it is dying that is transgressive because, as we saw with Augustine, it is neutral. A later fragment, mostly consisting of a dialogue between two unidentified voices, considers what follows from this transgression. The law says that "it is forbidden to die *in the present*," observes one voice. To which comes the distorted echo: "there is no present for dying." The final exchange is perhaps the most interesting: "Thus a time without present would be 'affirmed,' according to the demand of the return," says the one, and "This is why even transgression does not accomplish itself," adds the other (107–8; 148).

The eternal return, a vision of which was vouchsafed to Nietzsche at Sils-Maria, is not to be grasped as having to live one's life over and over again. Rather, what eternally returns is the Outside, and it does so neutrally, as the ghost of what has never actually taken place. It was Pierre Klossowski who raised this question with regard to Nietzsche, Blanchot thinks, and thereby determined "a change so radical that we are incapable of mastering it, even of undergoing it [*le subir*]."[87] The change imagined here is thinking of time as forever and always divided by the neutral, and so yielding a present without presence. Granted, we live in time, but every moment opens onto a neutral realm, a time with no arrow, that we cannot master because no dialectic can get a foothold there, and that we cannot undergo because with respect to it there is no "I." Perhaps the "primal scene" can explain much about life, then, but unlike Freud's primal scene it does not reduce life to the realm of the possible. Blanchot's questions—"freed from life?" "the infinite opening up?"—are hardly rhetorical, yet the freedom and the infinity at issue are scarcely consoling.

3

•

THE IMPOSSIBLE

1

We recollect the scene: a book is published, a review appears, and both are elevated by the reviewer's authoritative judgment, "We thus find ourselves once again at the heart of the most serious debate, where perhaps our destiny is at stake."[1] It is a debate over poetry and the sacred, a sufficiently well worn topic one might think, although this treatment of it will prove to be extraordinary in both complexity and scope. We are used to discussions where art and religion engage one another, where the aim is to show that the one grounds, illuminates, refigures or supersedes the other, or that, taken together, they generate something new, like philosophy or romanticism. So this particular debate begins on recognizable territory with the first speaker condemning a divine poetry that detaches itself from the material world and endorsing a mortal poetry that is earthed in the here and now, a poetry that nonetheless affirms the sacred nature of what is. Once the second speaker begins, though, we are quietly led in another direction. For he asks us to consider that those eminent human possibilities, art and religion, both respond to an obscure dimension that precedes all gods and most certainly the God of the monotheistic faiths. This realm is impossible to name since it is neither phenomenon nor noumenon, and perhaps the best we can do is dub it "the impossible."

Who are the speakers in this debate? The first is Yves Bonnefoy. In 1959, when this exchange takes place, he is the author of two powerful collections of poems and, more recently, a volume of essays, *L'Improbable* (1959), that has prompted the review already mentioned, a commentary over two numbers of the

Nouvelle Revue Française. This brings us to the second participant. Speaking for the negative is Maurice Blanchot who has already brooded on the relations of art and religion in "La Parole 'sacrée' de Hölderlin" (1946), "La Folie par excellence" (1951), "La Bête de Lascaux" (1953), and the closing pages of *L'Espace littéraire* (1955) and who testifies to an admiration for Bonnefoy's poetry.[2] Over the forties and fifties he has become an important if somewhat mysterious figure in French literature, something that Bonnefoy had been trying to explain to English readers no more than a year before. And to that end he paraphrased the argument of Blanchot's most recent critical volume, *L'Espace littéraire*: "The essence of literature is not to be found in what it explicitly asserts but in its continual annihilation of the meanings which language forces it to compound with, in its flight toward its goal of silence. The poem exists in an 'essential solitude,' an eternal separation . . . something which tends to break down any kind of structure, because it is man's relation with nothingness and death."[3]

In reading Blanchot's "Le Grand Refus" and especially "Comment découvrir l'obscur?" Bonnefoy would doubtless find himself having to revise those words: poetry is shown there not to be a flight to silence but to have the double task of "*naming* the possible, *responding* to the impossible" (48; 68) precisely because man has a relation not only with nothingness and death but also with the neutral and dying. Even so, as he explained his countryman's ideas to the English, Bonnefoy could not have been in complete accord with them, or at least could not have regarded them as telling the full story about poetry. Blanchot and Bonnefoy often speak from contrary, though seldom from contradictory, quarters.[4] Neither endorses art as *mimesis*: Blanchot because being is ontologically unstable, Bonnefoy because art constitutes a denial of being.[5] Both affirm the impossible, but where Blanchot takes that word to denote dispersal in the nonworld of the imaginary, Bonnefoy regards it as indicating transcendent Unity.[6] And both invoke the "*other* dimension": for Blanchot the Outside, for Bonnefoy *la présence*.[7] For all that, at a distance they might seem akin, as "philosophical" or even "existential" writers. On closer inspection those descriptions seem too loose to wear. Besides, there are clear divergences of stance and style.

Over surrealism, for one thing: where Bonnefoy is attracted to surrealism for its affirmation of the underlying unity of the world, Blanchot values the same movement for its rigorous dissociation of language and the human subject.[8] Over philosophy, for another thing: where Bonnefoy regards the elevation of the intelligible over the sensible with dismay and draws only occasionally from Hegel and Heidegger, Blanchot reflects perpetually on the interlacing of philosophy and literature; passages from the *Phänomenologie des Geistes* partly frame the long meditation "La Littérature et le droit à la mort" (1947–48), while the importance of an early encounter with *Sein und Zeit* is everywhere apparent.[9] And finally, once they pass beyond a general conception of poetry as struggle, the two writers differ over the proper valences of poetry: while Mallarmé is an exemplary poet for Blanchot, the one who saw in and through the writing of verse that God is dead, for Bonnefoy, despite his high admiration for poems like "Le vierge, le vivace et le bel aujourd'hui," Mallarmé marks a dangerous temptation. To be sure, he came to see that "the only angel that appears at the windows of the Ideal is the reflection of the approaching seeker."[10] Yet he is the inescapable modern poet who seeks "la notion pure," not by dismissing this world in search of another but more subtly by following a tradition of rhetoric to the point of identifying reality and language (64).[11] Mallarmé denies poetry's essential finitude and erases the speaking subject, Bonnefoy tells us, and we cannot doubt that the poet who envisioned *Le Livre*, the man who was fascinated by the abyss and believed that absence is creative, remained blind to the truth that God is still to be born.[12]

2

As he crosses the vestibule of hell, Dante recognizes "The coward spirit of the man who made / The great refusal [*il gran rifiuto*]."[13] It is most likely Pietro di Murrone, the pious Benedictine hermit who lived on Mount Majella in the Abruzzi but who, against all expectation, was elected pope in 1294 at eighty-four years of age, took the name Celestine V, and abdicated after just five months. Unworldly and utterly inexperienced in the affairs of church and state, Celestine V both caused confusion in the Curia and was taken advantage of by King Charles of Naples and those seeking ecclesial power of one kind or another. For his part, Celestine V feared that exposure to the chiaroscuro of diplomacy and the many demands of high office left him insufficient time for prayer: he believed his soul to be in danger. Could he yield the papacy to another? The question had never arisen, though now both the pontiff and the cardinals hoped for an answer in the affirmative. It was agreed that the Holy Father could abdicate, and on December 13, 1294, Celestine V resigned the papacy, became a hermit once more (though this time closely confined in the castle of Fumone), and the sacred college soon elected Cardinal Benedetto Gaetani, Dante's enemy, who styled himself Boniface VIII.

No believer in heaven or hell, Bonnefoy also speaks of a "*great refusal*": a denial of death, implicitly made by poetry like Ronsard's, Racine's, Valéry's, and Claudel's, that is in its own way an abdication of the poet's responsibility to speak truly of life and death. "One kind of poetry will always seek to detach itself from the world, the better to grasp what it loves"; it may be called "divine," but it is "chimerical and untrue and fatal."[14] It requires a separation of "a concept [idée] of itself that it thus knows or feels to be its essence, its divine part, from the degradations of lived experience [vécu]" (102). The fault originates, however, not in poetry or piety but in a trust as old as Greece that the concept is neatly fitted to reality. "Doubtless the concept [concept], this almost unique instrument of our philosophy, is a profound refusal of death everywhere it bestows itself."[15] Only art resists the concept's gaze and heals the wounds it makes.[16] So it is possible, at least in principle, for there to be another kind of poetry, one that freely acknowledges finitude, celebrates the here and now, and therefore frustrates the rule of the concept. In this respect, Baudelaire is deemed exemplary in French literature, as is Rimbaud. It is this sense of poetry that guides the piercing lyrics of *Du Mouvement et l'immobilité de Douve* (1953) and *Hier régnant désert* (1958), the collections Bonnefoy published before the appearance of *L'Improbable* (1959).

We have already heard Bonnefoy use the word *divine*, and I have said that he speaks of a God to come. These are not isolated quotations. A theological vocabulary can be found everywhere in his writing, sometimes overtly and sometimes covertly, although the pressure of individual poems or essays will frequently change or even reverse the received meaning of a word. For instance, poetry is held to offer salvation precisely when it points us to an imperfect and mortal life; where mortality is traditionally regarded as a direct consequence of the Fall, Bonnefoy understands a fall to have occurred whenever death is denied; and far from being a *felix culpa* this refusal thwarts redemption.[17] Poetry suffers when it yields to the blandishments of the concept: it may transcend the here and now and eloquently testify to a universal order but only at the cost of losing touch with sensuous particulars. This is the movement of "excarnation," as Bonnefoy calls it, an inevitable process whenever there is writing and one that can easily go unchecked by dint of its strong, if aberrant, religious appeal. To explain that appeal, we are referred to the gnostic syndrome, that fuzzy set of beliefs in absolute dualism that places a transcendent deity beyond the reach of any positive theology and that regards the earth with suspicion if not downright contempt. For the gnostic there is a sharp difference between God, who remains distant and veiled, and the Creator, who has fabricated the universe through evil. In order not to remain immured in the lower orders of existence, the gnostic adept must see through the illusions of creation, including the *psyche*, and attain a saving knowledge of the *pneuma*, the uncreated spark hidden in each one of us. Since gnostic dualism is both irreducible and conflictual, only the most rigorous negative theologies can help in uncovering that divine spark in us. The adept must vigilantly strip away all the predicates conventionally attached to the divinity, for if taken literally or even figurally they will fatally mislead.

One need not read the volumes of Saint Irenaeus's *Adversus Haereses* or the *Excerpta ex Theodoto*, associated with Saint Clement of Alexandria, in order to find fragments of *gnosis*, and one does not have to delve into the exotic *Acts of Thomas* or ponder Valentinus's *The Gospel of Truth* to gain a sense of gnostic cosmology. For gnosticism is alive and vibrant in the twentieth century.[18] In the *Second manifeste* (1930), as we saw in the first chapter, André Breton memorably describes surrealism as a quest for "a certain point of the mind at which life and death, the real and the imagined, past and future, the communicable and the incommunicable, high and low, cease to be perceived as contradictions."[19] How to interpret this? One can say, as the young Bonnefoy did, that the romance of surrealism lies in its affirmation of the fundamental unity of the world, that when Paul Éluard writes of "aigles d'eau pure," the metaphor spans the gulf between appearance and reality. Such are the poetics of *Le Cœur-espace* (1945), especially in lines such as these:

> J'ai vu les chiens de vent déchirer les falaises
> Le linge massif roulant dans ma gorge (mais j'ai vécu dans cette maison
>   poreuse)
> J'ai vu le vent creuser les poutres de six heures la terre errer dans ses tombes
>   d'espace
> Il y avait un cimetière d'orties les preuves sourdes du vent se groupaient autour
>   des pierres
> J'ai vu le jour craquer j'ai vécu ces journées de déchirement du site.[20]

Or one can say, as Bonnefoy came to think, that idealism was tacitly assumed in this vision and that the "certain point" became the haunt of gnostic fantasies that seduce one away from the body and the material world. It is a view that Breton was to confirm in 1953, after Bonnefoy had left his circle.

Surrealism has finally identified the essence of poetic intuition, the master says, and now it seeks "not only to assimilate all known forms but also boldly to create new forms—that is to say, to be in a position to embrace all the structures of the world, manifested or not. It alone provides the thread that can put us back on the road of Gnosis as knowledge of suprasensible Reality, 'invisibly visible in an eternal mystery.'"[21] Breton had sharply attacked Georges Bataille in the *Second manifeste* as a defector from the camp of truth. And yet the Bataille of *L'Expérience intérieure* (1943) and *Le Coupable* (1944) was important for Bonnefoy who found there a passionate critique of the western presumption that systems of representation are capable of recovering presence. Once again, though, this critique can be variously understood. One can see Bataille as attempting, through a paroxysm of ecstasy, to transgress received limits in order to touch the unknown original plenitude. Like Rimbaud, Bataille would be attempting to expose a pact between language and reason, a complicity to value convention over essence, appearance over reality.[22] It is a vision that could not fail to attract Bonnefoy. However, one can read Bataille another way, as trying to communicate through death with a frightening "indefinite reality" that cannot be reduced to self or world.[23] And this is indeed how Bataille interprets his raptures. Inner experience turns out to be a burning of life rather than an illumination of it; it eschews any deep interiority in favor of the wholly unconditioned, that inhuman and godless continuum from which we are exiled by life itself. If this is gnosticism, it is a system that Valentinus and Basilides would not have recognized, for it is without a *pneuma*, without gnosis, without hope of salvation, and is obscurely rooted in community rather than in the individual.

What alerted Bonnefoy to this propensity to excarnation in Bataille and Breton was, ironically, the discovery of a secondhand copy of Lev Chestov's unconventional theological work *Potestas Clavium* (1923) in one of the little bookstalls dotted along the Seine.[24] I say it is ironic because it was Chestov whose friendship and writings influenced Bataille greatly in the early 1920s, especially by helping the Frenchman to read Plato with the right emphases in mind.[25] "Ordinary people seem not to realize that those who really apply themselves in the right way to philosophy are directly and of their own accord preparing themselves for death and dying," says Socrates in *Phaedo* 64a.[26] In *Potestas Clavium* Chestov points out that, for Socrates, this linking of philosophy and death is "a secret" for those who have not been initiated into the love of wisdom. "And the most extraordinary thing is that the secret has remained a secret to this day, even though it was revealed to men twenty-five hundred years ago and even though the *Phaedo* (64a), where the quoted words appear, is one of the best known and most admired of Plato's dialogues."[27] Far from being a scientific discourse, as Kant and the post-Kantians would have it, philosophy is an education in death and dying. Such was Chestov's conviction in book after book, and Bataille drew deeply from it when developing his notion of nonknowing, before and after he wrote *L'Expérience intérieure* (1943).

It was in 1944, several years before his break with the surrealists over the occultist tendencies of *Rupture inaugurale* (1947), that Bonnefoy found a copy of *Potestas Clavium*, although the Russian's affirmation of presence over essence, his dismissal of universal norms and his prizing of the individual, began to work on the young poet before he and Breton parted ways.[28] Those values must have been prized also by Bonnefoy's Russian friend, the music critic Boris de Schloezer, who helped to translate Chestov's philosophy, as well as the fiction of Dostoyevsky and Tolstoy, into French.[29] Like Chestov, Schloezer was a devout believer, and when Bonnefoy came to remember him in a passage of "Le Fleuve," the opening poem of *Dans le leurre du seuil* (1975), he imagined his dying friend hearing an earthly music reserved for him alone:

> *Et Boris de Schloezer, quand il est mort*
> *Entendant sur l'appontement une musique*
> *Dont ses proches ne savaient rien (était-elle, déjà,*
> *La flûte de la délivrance révélée*
> *Ou un ultime bien de la terre perdue,*
> *'Oeuvre', transfigurée?)—derrière soi*
> *N'a laissé que ces eaux brûlées d'énigme.*[30]

If reading Chestov could not make Bonnefoy look for the deliverance promised by the Christian revelation, at least it helped him to diagnose a gnostic longing in himself, a feeling that had found form through a reading of an early essay by Bataille on materialism and gnosticism.[31] But this longing was different from that of the ancient gnostics, and it outlasted any enthusiasm for Bataillian ecstasy. It is an ache for another country, a feeling that true life can be lived only elsewhere. Bonnefoy will use Virgil's eclogues or Poussin's landscapes to evoke that *arrière-pays*, as he calls it, though it must be stressed that the longed-for country is a place where one lives, grows old, and dies. "Yes indeed our country is beautiful, I cannot imagine anything else," he writes; "all the same, if the true life is over there, in a placeless elsewhere, that alone is enough for this place to seem like a desert."[32] Living here, in the keen awareness of another place, we feel a lack "whose grandeur is desire and whose frequentation is an exile." And so this ache is, in its way, a gnostic refusal. The recognition that living in a "placeless elsewhere" can be dreamed, not lived, is the painful burden of many of Bonnefoy's poems and essays, and it forces him to seek the plenitude of being in the here and now. Like concepts, dreams reveal only by concealing, and the task is to overcome both dreams and concepts in a quest for what is already here, if only we would see it. "The incarnation, that outside of the dream, is a nearby good," we are told.[33] And the gaze of the artist and the poet will be the means to achieve that end.[34]

Poetry is *ancilla theologiae*, then, although of course we are dealing with a "theology of the earth."[35] Reading and writing poetry will lead to the One, the plenum of being at the heart of the material world: such is Bonnefoy's confession of faith. And yet there must be further clauses in his *credo*, since language, even poetic language, is incapable of simply expressing that sacred presence. The situation is dialectical, and so a counterthesis appears: "To write, yes,—who has ever not done so? But to *unwrite* as well, by way of an experience [*expérience*] complementary to the poem."[36] Art brings experience into the light, though never completely; and the poem must be tested against experience: not so much to revise it (although that happens) but to offer what has thus far remained in shadow as the material for another poem. Without this interplay one would produce books that merely confirm each other, but with it one can slowly make a life that bespeaks "a presence, a destiny: the finitude that clarifies and watches over meaning" (83). If we ask why no poem is fully adequate to experience we will get a response at odds with an influential contemporary view of language that draws from nineteenth-century philosophy and twentieth-century linguistics. On this understanding, the structures of language promote a fiction of presence. Thus for Nietzsche God is an effect of grammar, while for Saussure signification is formed in a linguistic system composed of negative differences.[37] Coming from the opposite direction, Bonnefoy teasingly suggests in a prose poem that one day in the eternal world of essences "words were invented, and through them absence."[38]

In this world, however, the situation is quite different. Here the concept obscures death, while language makes mortality a notional truth at best. How then can one hope by reading and writing poetry to discover the true place, the gleaming presence of the here and now, that depends on a full and unconditional acceptance of finitude? Bonnefoy sketches an answer, and he does so in harmony with Bataille's and Kojève's Hegel, the young thinker who declared that "Man is that night, that empty Nothingness, which contains everything in its undivided simplicity" and who went on to develop "a philosophy of death (or, which is the same thing, of atheism)."[39] For his part, Bonnefoy says that

> Nothing exists except through death. And nothing is true that does not prove itself through death.
>
> If there is no poetry without language [*discours*]—and Mallarmé himself said just that—how, therefore, can the truth and the grandeur of poetry be preserved, except by appealing to death? By the stubborn exigency that death be said—or, better, that it speak?[40]

An appeal to death may help to bring presence into view, but it cannot guarantee it can be grasped in language, even when language is charged with metaphor.

Another assurance is needed. Or perhaps I should say that the act of faith that presence is sacred calls forth another act of faith, that in mortal poetry the concept can be suspended or denied:

> this poetry which cannot grasp presence, dispossessed of all other good, will be in anguished proximity to the great accomplished act, as its *negative theology* . . . in authentic poetry nothing remains but those wanderers of the real, those categories of possibility, those elements without past or future, never entirely involved in the existing situation . . . They appear on the confines of the negativity of language, like angels telling of a still unknown god. A negative "theology."[41]

Let us pause before these remarks. We know that for Bonnefoy the word *theology* must be carefully guarded by quotation marks in case it should suddenly fly away to attend a transcendent God, but we need to consider what assumptions might be assigned night duty behind the words *death* and *negative*.

3

Blanchot responds to Bonnefoy in two phases: "Le Grand Refus" examines the assumptions of *L'Improbable* and opens them onto a more fundamental level of analysis where they uneasily resituate themselves, while "Comment découvrir l'obscur?" seeks to rework the themes by way of a discussion of possibility and impossibility. "I have always found concepts less important than obsessions": Bonnefoy quotes Jean-Pierre Richard's apothegm immediately after introducing Blanchot to English readers in 1958, and he may well have recalled the sentiment in September and October of the following year when reading Blanchot's critique of his book in the *Nouvelle Revue Française*.[42] For in that double review *L'Improbable* is absorbed into an intense meditation that began before the war and that would continue until Blanchot's final writings. One major aspect of that inquiry is a deepening reflection on Bataille's work, not least of all on the notion to which he lent the title of a late book, *L'Impossible* (1962), which he had once contemplated calling *Haine de la poésie*.

Hatred of poetry? The title declares Bataille's impatience with ornamentation and rhetoric, false unities, as well as his sympathy with literary terrorists. Bonnefoy will suggest that Bataille indicts the poets "because he is unwilling to follow their lesson and subordinate subjectivity to a higher reality, the one that in fact we can encounter in the slightest thing in the world, pebbles along a path or a gleam in the water."[43] Yet Bataille tells another story when explaining why he changed the title of his book. "It seemed to me that true poetry was reached only by hatred. Poetry had no powerful meaning except in the violence of revolt. But poetry attains this violence only by evoking the *impossible*."[44] We have already touched this notion in pondering inner experience. Bataille expands on it when distinguishing two kinds of communication. The first is familiar: it connects two beings, "laughter of a child to its mother, tickling, etc"; the second, however, is altogether strange:

> Communication, through death, with our beyond (essentially in sacrifice)—not with nothingness [*le néant*], still less with a supernatural being, but with an indefinite reality (which I sometimes call *the impossible*, that is: what can't be grasped (*begreift*) in any way, what we can't reach without dissolving ourselves, what's slavishly called God). If we need to we can define this reality (provisionally associating it with a finite element) at a higher (higher than the individual on the scale of composition of beings) social level as the sacred, God or created reality. Or else it can remain in an undefined state (in ordinary laughter, infinite laughter, or ecstasy in which the divine form melts like sugar in water).[45]

One ground against which this passage cuts its figure is Hegel, for whom the negativity of action is exhausted in realizing the world of the possible; and it is a difference over Hegel that marks Blanchot's divergence from Bonnefoy.

Hegel had been variously significant for both writers. At the threshold of *Du mouvement et de l'immobilité de Douve*, the poetry of his first maturity, Bonnefoy had placed an epigraph from the *Phänomenologie des Geistes*, a passage that speaks of how "the life of the mind is not one that shuns death and keeps clear of destruction; it endures death and in death maintains its being [*das ihn erträgt und in ihm sich erhält*]."[46] And in the late forties Blanchot had counterpointed Jean Hyppolite's and Kojève's readings of Hegel in a major speculative essay, "La Littérature et le droit à la mort," in which those same words ring out several times.[47] So while one can easily imagine the debate's involving other philosophers—and I will introduce another before very long—there are good reasons why it turns on Hegel. Certainly it is no surprise to open *L'Improbable* and find Bonnefoy, an ardent advocate of the here and now, alluding to Hegel's discussion of sense certainty at the beginning of the *Phänomenologie*. For there the philosopher shows that, far from presenting particulars, any uttering of a "here" or "now" will necessarily involve universals, that is, concepts. Now Bonnefoy is mistaken, Blanchot suggests, to imply that Hegel simply contributes to the great refusal of death.

The philosopher's account of the concept does not show that language is divine by dint of a purported ability to freeze a word and consequently form an eternal concept. Rather, the concept's force resides in an eerie ability to introduce the negativity of death into language, so that speech has, in Hegel's words, "the divine nature of directly turning the mere 'meaning' right round about, making it into something else."[48]

On Blanchot's understanding, Hegel alerts us to two rival tendencies in literature, a regard for the concept and a fascination with language. It is a claim whose broad features were sketched years before in *Comment la littérature est-elle possible?* (1942), Blanchot's first conversation with Jean Paulhan, and which was later explored with Hegel in mind in "La Littérature et le droit à la mort." Since that latter essay tracks the phased motifs of death and dying, let us turn to it for clarification. I interrupt the contemplation halfway through, just after Blanchot has quoted for the first time Hegel's evocation of the moment when life "endures death and in death maintains its being." In the first place, modern literature—roughly, that written since the French Revolution—is an affair of the concept; it "contemplates itself in revolution," conceives itself as a quest for what precedes its inevitable recourse to language, and assumes a tie between the concept and death. To name something is to annihilate its unique existence and make it into an idea as well. Literature, here, idealizes death by making it into a dialectical power: the negativity of death is given not in senseless dissolution of life but in its purported ability to shape "the life of the mind." In the second place, however, literature is linked to language; it is concerned not with the eternity of the idea but with retracing the passage from nothingness to speech. A word is not the representation of something that preexists it. Not at all: it is a sensible presentation, "a nonexistence made *word*," a matter of *Darstellung* more than of *Repräsentation* or *Vorstellung*.[49] Viewed in this way literature is no longer in the realm of possibility and power but rather attends to the materiality of words: "and thus it is meaning detached from its conditions, separated from its moments, wandering like an empty power, a power no one can do anything with, a power without power" (331; 320). Released from the concept's grip, literature shakes itself free of death as a shaping force and in that movement renders negativity unemployed. Literature will have no work to do—or, if you prefer, its work will *be* this nothing. At any rate, the very inability of literature to invest dying in meaningful action consigns it to speak endlessly of the "impossibility of dying," an anguished slipping away from both life and death.

At the beginning of this chapter, when I was introducing Blanchot's role in the discussion with Bonnefoy, I said that he was "speaking for the negative." Protocols of debating aside, it turns out that Blanchot is speaking both for and against the negativity, *Negativität*, of the dialectic. He does so by way of adjusting Mallarmé's distinction in "Crise de vers" between ordinary and poetic language.[50] "Common language" is animated by negativity, he says, while "literary language" reveals the weakness of the negative, its incapacity to impose the categories of being and nothingness. The one works with the realm of the possible, progressively determining that which is: it is the space of "meaningful prose," and Blanchot associates it with Mallarmé. The other unworks possibility—it is the "realm" of the impossible—and it is here the poets may be found, including Mallarmé, perhaps for Blanchot the only poet to follow both tendencies of literature in an exemplary fashion. Neither the one nor the other, literature is the doubling of common and literary language; it generates aporias of negativity and neutrality, death and dying, power and passivity. In no way then does this amount to a criticism that calls for "the death of the author," to use a phrase of Blanchot's that Roland Barthes made famous, for Blanchot would have us ponder the author's perpetual resuscitation into a state of interminable dying.[51] Nor is it an appeal to let death speak in poetry, such as Bonnefoy makes, since Blanchot insists that death cannot speak in poetry because it is forever interrupted by the murmur of an endless dying. The concept is not an enemy of poetry, that which prevents it from recognizing finitude; it is that which introduces mortality into poetry but, in doing so, compels poetry to speak of death as possibility and dying as impossibility.

4

The sacred is immediate presence, Bonnefoy tells us, while adding the rider that "The immediate does not give itself, one cannot reach presence through images."[52] Unable to attain immediacy, we cannot and should not divest ourselves of the desire for it.[53] Poetry comes from that desire and elaborates itself as a theology of earth. As such, it calls for a supplement of negative theology to ensure that it remains before the sacred radiance that only finitude can confer on the here and now. For there is always a danger that the poetic image can be regarded as absolute and so become an idol venerated by a cult. Or, adopting another perspective, the image can always seem indifferent to time and space and so become the value of a dangerous and false religion, a literary gnosticism.

Poetry not only campaigns against the concept but also conducts a struggle closer to home, in the home itself, a "war against the Image—against the claims of words, against the weight of what is written."[54] That was written in 1981. Years before, in "Le Dialogue d'angoisse et le désir," an important poem in *Pierre écrite* (1965), we had been told,

Nous n'avons plus besoin
D'images déchirantes pour aimer.
Cet arbre nous suffit là-bas, qui, par lumière,
Se délie de soi-même et ne sait plus
Que le nom presque dit d'un dieu presque incarné.[55]

The same disquiet with respect to the image can be heard years later in a letter that Bonnefoy wrote to his friend John E. Jackson: "Poetry that vanquishes the image in writing is love."[56] And in "Les Nuées" we are told that poetry would be a cleansing of the image: "Mais toujours et distinctement je vois aussi / La tache noire dans l'image, j'entends le cri / Qui perce la musique."[57] No poetry can grasp the immediate; the here and now can never fully present themselves to consciousness in a self-sufficient image, and therefore we must accept that the sacred reveals itself only in withdrawal. The most that we may legitimately hope for is a poetry that constitutes a negative theology of the unpresentable.

In clarifying this formulation it is tempting to begin by excluding the Kantian notion of the sublime in which the imagination sacrifices itself in an attempt to present what is strictly speaking unpresentable. After all, Bonnefoy is not concerned with a sensible presentation of the ideas of reason, and he has no wish to disclose a supersensible destination of humankind. It is equally tempting to say that, in terms of Kantian aesthetics, Bonnefoy is more attracted to the beautiful than to the sublime, as his favorite emblems suggest—a torn ivy leaf, the dark panes of an orangery, a window gleaming in the evening sun—and this is reinforced by recalling that for Kant aesthetic experience does not require the particular to be subsumed by a concept. Quoting Bonnefoy's conviction that "L'Imperfection est la cime" (Imperfection is the summit) scarcely counters this view.[58] There is no logical difficulty in loving natural beauty while rejecting the alexandrine, say. Accordingly, one could argue that for Bonnefoy the beautiful resists presentation. And yet he is in no way an apologist for the "merely beautiful," for beauty drained of the sublime. We must therefore distinguish two claims. First, immediate presence always abides in space and time, and poetry is an attempt to present it. Like the Jena romantics, Bonnefoy knows that no *Darstellung*, no sensible presentation, can wholly capture what is absent; unlike them, though, he eschews romantic irony in favor of honoring the referent. So much for the first claim. The second is that, following Jean-Luc Nancy's reading of the *Kritik der Urteilskraft* (1790), the sublime and the beautiful occur together. Sublimity is not raised above beauty but is a flaring of beauty at the limit, an effulgence that can be simple and serene rather than magnificent and violent, and beyond which there is nothing.[59] It is the sensing of the unconditioned beyond presentation, *das Unbedingte*, which constitutes the feeling of the sublime. While Bonnefoy offers no comment on it, Blanchot, as we shall see, almost never ceases to write of it, albeit in his own terms.

These various considerations, both "aesthetic" and "theological," can be brought into focus by turning to one of Bonnefoy's most haunting lyrics, "La lumière, changée":

> *Nous ne nous voyons plus dans la même lumière,*
> *Nous n'avons plus les mêmes yeux, les mêmes mains.*
> *L'arbre est plus proche et la voix des sources plus vive,*
> *Nos pas sont plus profonds, parmi les morts.*
>
> *Dieu qui n'es pas, pose ta main sur notre épaule,*
> *Ébauche notre corps du poids de ton retour,*
> *Achève de mêler à nos âmes ces astres,*
> *Ces bois, ces cris d'oiseaux, ces ombres et ces jours.*
>
> *Renonce-toi en nous comme un fruit se déchire,*
> *Efface-nous en toi. Découvre-nous*
> *Le sens mystérieux de ce qui n'est que simple*
> *Et fût tombé sans feu dans des mots sans amour.*[60]

Having achieved a mortal vision, like the older Wordsworth, the speaker has experienced a deepening of relations with nature and humans. Interpretation becomes more complex, however, at the beginning of the second stanza with the sublime prayer to the divinity "qui n'es pas." Is this the gnostic Godhead who transcends even the categories of being? Or is it a God who does not exist by dint of His transcendence? The latter is closer to the truth grasped by the lyric, despite its final line. The God whom Nietzsche's madman declared dead can return only as a fully incarnate divinity, a god of the earth. No longer separable from the world, our souls are to be mixed with nature; while the notion of a divine spark in humankind is to be renounced as firmly as the human longing to return to God. That achieved, we do not thereby eliminate mystery. On the contrary, we finally realize that transcendence is all about us, in simple things and ordinary acts.[61] It is a truth that has long been in us, hidden by our longings for excarnation which are at odds with human love and complicit with writing.

The sensible presentation that is poetic speech therefore acknowledges an inability to present the immediate. Let us listen to Bonnefoy again: "in authentic poetry nothing remains but those wanderers of the real, those categories of possibility . . . which are the wind, fire, earth, the waters."[62] And, as we know, he goes on to speculate that "they *are* words, being no other than a promise" and that they form, as we have seen, "A negative 'theology'" (114). We know why Bonnefoy would want to place scare quotes around "theology," but the word "negative" also needs to be interpreted. He does not do so until 1988, many years after Blanchot's review and perhaps with it in mind, when he explicates "negative" not by way of Hegel or the Pseudo-Denys but with Franz Kafka firmly in view. He broods on a fragment he first read in 1945 in the sequence of aphorisms or sayings that Max Brod entitled "Reflections on Sin, Pain, Hope and the True Way": "What is laid upon us is to accomplish the negative; the positive is already given."[63] Kafka's construal of the negative is profoundly dualistic rather than dialectical, and it carries a distinct flavor of gnosticism perhaps gleaned from Kabbalah, but Bonnefoy reworks Kafka's enigmatic utterance in his own way, and by the late eighties in a direction heading away at right angles from gnosticism.

"The positive?" Bonnefoy asks. "For me, it is this sufficiency, this peace flush with the spectacle of the world . . . that is no different than the simultaneity, contiguity, continuity—unity—of its parts (if this last word still makes sense)."[64] Language can only distance us from the positive, he thinks: "Who speaks can only hate what he desires, as long as he does not uncover—and is this possible?—the unknown feeling in the world of nature which will transcend this aporia" (10). Yet the very closeness we feel to the simplicity and immediacy of life as we live it encourages us, he believes, "to think that one can 'make the negative,' that is, fight in the same words what in them is a refusal of our origin" (11). The immediate must be approached by contesting language with the only thing that there is to use: language. And it follows from this that a poem must not aim for formal perfection. It is in the fault lines in the lyric that we can, he thinks, discern the radiance of presence, the beauty of transcendence, and the unity of things: there, only there, is the salvation that we can hope for. "In fact, *poetry* is what aims at an object," Bonnefoy says in another essay of the same period, "at this being right before us, in its absolute, or at being itself, at the presence of the world, in its unity."[65] And he adds, "Poetry is what attaches itself—and here is its specific responsibility—to what cannot be designated by a word of language; and this because what is beyond designation is an intensity, a plenitude we need to remember. The One, Presence—poetry can 'think' of them in writing, since the unusual relations that the forms of sonority in verse establish between words break up the codes, neutralize the conceptual significations, and thus open up something like a field for the unknown dwelling beyond" (198). Indeed, Bonnefoy in 1988 will even go so far as to say that "interruption is a starting point, the true origin of what is specifically poetry in a work" (199).

Almost a quarter of a century before Bonnefoy mused on Kafka, Blanchot was speaking of interruption. For him, however, it is precisely unity and presence that are to be shattered not regained.[66] In "Le Grand Refus" there is no such talk; there he remains close to the dialectic that he regards as conferring meaning and truth at the price of losing uniqueness. We think of that which falls outside the dialectic as the neutral, but that which precedes the dialectic would be neutral as well. "How can I find it again, how can I, in my speech, recapture this prior presence that I must exclude in order to speak, in order to speak it?" (36; 50) Language is "the lack of what it would say." In speech we have "*sacrificed* what we can find again only by rejecting it," Blanchot says; we have come upon "the most ancient tomb," and our contest "is no longer a Crusade or a Dispute over the empty Sepulcher, but the 'struggle over origins'" (36; 51). When Pope Urban II launched the First Crusade at the Council of Clermont in 1095, the *milites Christi* were required to vow that they would complete their pilgrimages by praying in the Church of the Holy Sepulcher in Jerusalem. The holy city must be won back from the Muslims, the Church decreed, and an indulgence was granted to all who devoutly helped to liberate Jerusalem. For Blanchot and Bonnefoy, though, there is no resurrected Jesus to be worshiped, no sacred site to be regained by force, even the gentle force of prayer: the sacred is to be found, if at all, Blanchot thinks, in the invisible tomb that is erected by speech. The very movement of speech, from the material world to its spiritual meaning, is sacrificial. This is not the sacrifice of the imagination that Kant evokes. Not at all. I turn to Bataille who speaks best on the theme: "on the level of Hegel's philosophy, Man has, in a sense, revealed and founded human truth by sacrificing; in sacrificing he destroyed the animal in himself, allowing himself and the animal to survive only as that noncorporeal truth which Hegel describes."[67]

"Can we . . . come upon . . . what is at stake in this contest . . . ?" Blanchot asks in "Le Grand Refus." We can, it seems, but only if we seek the help of Hegel's friend Friedrich Hölderlin, whose "speech and even his life" are marked by "this *sacrifice*" (36). Yet Hölderlin's sacrifice is of a wholly different order from that which marks the movement of Spirit and also needs to be distinguished from the Kantian sacrifice of the imagination. Before the difference can be made evident, though, we must examine the lines that Blanchot quotes from the German poet in order to clarify the concerns of the French poet:

Jezt aber tagts! Ich harrt und sah es kommen,
Und was ich sah, das Heilige sei mein Wort.

Or, in English,

But now day breaks! I waited and saw it come,
And what I saw, the holy be my word.[68]

5

When Blanchot seeks to illuminate the issues raised by Bonnefoy in *L'Improbable* by quoting two lines from Hölderlin's hymn "Wie wenn am Feiertage . . . " (1799?), he folds the poet into a disquisition on those lines that commenced in 1939 when Heidegger first attempted an explication of the hymn, and that Blanchot himself redirected in "La Parole 'sacrée' de Hölderlin" (1946), "La Folie par excellence" (1951), and the closing pages of *L'Espace littéraire* (1955). Indeed, Bonnefoy is brought into a discussion that stretches back to Pindar for an essential reference.

In "Wie wenn am Feiertage . . . " Hölderlin boldly seeks to recreate German meter in the image of Pindaric measure. As one commentator astutely remarks, the hymn "may be regarded as a declaration of allegiance to Pindar."[69] Heidegger says almost nothing of this aspect of the poem—he confines himself to observing that the bulk of the sixth stanza has a "Pindaric structure"[70]—although he uses Hölderlin's later translation of and commentary on a Pindaric fragment, "Das Höchste" (1803?), as a lens for bringing the hymn into focus. The title "The Most High" (Das Höchste) sits above both the translation and the rumination that follows it. First, the poem as Hölderlin translates it:

Das Gesez
Von allen der König, Sterblichen und
Unsterblichen; das führt eben
Darum gewaltig
Das gerechteste Recht mit allerhöchster Hand.

To which Hölderlin appends these observations:

The immediate, strictly speaking, is impossible [*unmöglich*] for mortals, as for the immortals; the god has to differentiate several worlds, according to his nature, because heavenly goodness, for its own sake, must be holy [*heilig*], unalloyed. Human beings, as cognizant ones, must also differentiate between several worlds, because cognition is possible only by contrast. That is why the immediate, strictly speaking, is impossible [*unmöglich*] for mortals, as for immortals.

But the strictly mediate is the law.

And that is why, compellingly, it guides the justest justice with a sovereign hand.[71]

Using this gnomic commentary to elucidate the hymn, Heidegger argues that chaos is the opening of nature, understood as primordial wholeness: both chaos and nature are "holy" (or "sacred": the two words are synonymous here) and "immediate," completely "unapproachable" by gods or mortals because the holy is "always former" (85).[72] Both gods and mortals derive from the holy, and, given this, we can regard it as the "mediatedness of the mediated" (84).[73] Far from being opposed to the law, the holy (or chaos, the immediate, nature) is *itself* the law. How then can the holy communicate itself to either the gods or mortals? The burden of responsibility is given to the poets. Not that they can intuit the holy, for they "must leave to the immediate its immediacy"; even so, they must "take upon themselves its mediation as their only task" (93). This is possible only because nature has lightly embraced the poets from the beginning: they have been initiated into the ways of the holy, although as mortals they remain attached to the earth. Not all their songs speak of the holy, only those that awaken "from the sun of day and warm earth" and that come as the result of good fortune, of the poet's being struck by "the holy ray" and thus turned decisively toward the holy which has always embraced him or her. "The poet's soul 'quakes,' to be sure, and so lets the quiet quaking awaken within itself; but it quakes with recollection, that is to say, with the expectation of that which happened before; this is the opening up of the holy . . . The holy word comes to be" (91).

Heidegger has no doubt that the holy *is* spoken by the poet, that it comes as event, even if it is not named directly: "the word will convey the holy" (90), we are told. Of course, there are difficulties when "the holy becomes word" (94), for the essence of the holy, its immediacy, is threatened; yet we are soon assured that "what sprang from the origin cannot do anything against the origin" (96), and the elucidation of the hymn can move calmly toward conclusion with the remark, "The holy bestows the word, and itself comes into this word" (98). If that is the case, when Hölderlin says in the hymn, "And what I saw, the holy be my word," his wish or his prayer is answered: the holy *becomes* his word, it is the very embodiment of the "now" that marks the dawn. Although Bonnefoy nowhere alludes to Heidegger's reading of "Wie wenn am Feiertage . . . ," one can easily imagine that he would respond sympathetically to it.[74] Thinking back to before Bonnefoy published his first collection of poems, however, it is precisely this claim that Blanchot disputes in "La parole 'sacrée' de Hölderlin" and that forms his preunderstanding of Bonnefoy's insistence on associating the here and the now with the holy. "How can the Sacred, which is 'unexpressed,' 'unknown,' which is what opens provided only that it is not discovered, which reveals because unrevealed—how can it fall into speech, let itself be alienated into becoming, itself pure interiority, the exteriority of song?"[75] The question is rhetorical, needless to say, and its tone of incredulity derives from Blanchot's adherence to the fundamentals of Heidegger's reading of the poem. He concludes: "In truth, that cannot really be, that is the impossible" (126; 128).[76] And if we need more caution about Heidegger's reading of Hölderlin, we have only to look at those scare quotes hovering on either side of "sacrée." They remind us that "sacred speech" is a theme chosen by Heidegger, not Blanchot, while also suggesting that the sense and function of "sacrée" for the Frenchman will not coincide with orthodox Christian understandings and uses of that word.[77] In no way would Blanchot accept the reading ventured by Erich Przywara that in his last works Hölderlin was consumed by the Holy Spirit.[78]

No one could ignore Blanchot's imputation of gnosticism to Heidegger—the "unknown" falls "into speech"—although he makes nothing of this insight into Heidegger's commentary on the hymn. The point he wishes to make is that the sacred cannot take place, and he does so while briefly considering "Das Höchste." Certainly the sacred cannot be experienced by the poet; he cannot become "the sacred necessity he obeys" (120; 123) because there can be no experience of chaos or the immediate.[79] The sacred is the day, as Hölderlin declares, but "not the day as it contrasts with the night, or the light as it shines from above" (121; 124). Not at all: it is an anterior sky. It is "a before-day, a clarity before clarity to which we are closest when we grasp the dawning, the distance infinitely remote from daybreak" (121; 124). The difference between Heidegger and Blanchot could hardly be more marked here: light from above, for the one, and the distance of a dark anterior sky for the other. When the speaker of the hymn declares, "But now day breaks! I waited and saw it come," it is the unearthly light that precedes the dawn that is witnessed in silence. It cannot be articulated, for "the ineffable remains always unexpressed" (129; 130), and yet the poet must declaim: "he speaks but does not speak, he leaves what he has to say unexpressed and leaves unmanifested what he shows" (129; 130). Before he sings, the poet does not exist; and when the poem is uttered, the sacred is still to come. Like the oracle at Delphi, the poet neither speaks nor remains silent but indicates. It is a painful experience for the poet: he speaks only in the moment when he loses the power to say "I," when he forfeits himself as an individual and becomes "no one," and when he is already turning to the neutral space of suffering.[80] "Impossible, the reconciliation of the Sacred with speech demanded that the poet's existence comes nearest to nonexistence" (131; 132). It is this demand that gives rise to the sacrifice to which Blanchot testifies; it is a kenosis more personal, more intimate, than the movement of Spirit that Hegel explored, and more wrenching than the sacrifice of the imagination that Kant conceived. For the poet is exposed to the endlessness of dying rather than transported to an immortal home.

If we move forward several years to "La Folie par excellence" (1951), we find Blanchot explaining that the good fortune experienced by Hölderlin, the sheer dazzle of the brightness with which he is struck, occurs only "against a background of extraordinary pain."[81] It is this experience, this exposure to the Other, that Heidegger occludes in his elucidation of "Wie wenn am Feiertage . . . " And if we move forward another two years to "La Bête de Lascaux" (1953) we hear Blanchot speaking of the same problem, but this time with René Char in mind. It is worth drawing attention to this: it is no distraction to our concern with Bonnefoy and Hölderlin, although this time the classical reference is not to Pindar but to Socrates and, beyond him, Heraclitus.[82] As is well known, in the *Phaedrus* Socrates objects to written language because it comes with no personal guarantee of veracity and can neither defend itself nor answer questions about the claims it urges. Less familiar is that Socrates also rejects "another form of impersonal language, the pure speech that gives expression to the sacred."[83] The objections against writing apply equally, though they are urged more respectfully, to the singing of hymns, for the performer "is simply the irresponsible vehicle of a language infinitely beyond his control" (10; 14). Only those men who are present, who can stand by their word, use language properly. Those people for whom language allows the origin to speak, whether as "poetry" or as "sacred hymn," are not to be entirely trusted. Blanchot comments:

> The language in which the origin speaks is essentially prophetic. This does not mean that it dictates future events, it means that it does not base itself on something which already is, either on a currently held truth, or solely on language which has already been spoken or verified. It announces, because it begins. It *points* towards the future, because it

does not yet speak, and is language of the future to the extent that it is like a future language which is always ahead of itself, having its meaning and legitimacy only before it, which is to say that it is fundamentally without justification. (12; 21)

Several threads need to be drawn from this. First, like inner experience, poetry and sacred hymn are without warrant; they carry their authority within themselves, their speech is profoundly impersonal, and the poet cannot ultimately defend or even explain what is said. Second, although this poetry is radically impersonal it is nonetheless intensely intimate: it speaks of what is closest to us, what does not offer itself as phenomenon yet still presses upon us. Third, the language of this original speech offers itself to the future not in words that are to come but in lines that have already been committed to memory or to paper. In "Le Grand Refus" Blanchot says, with a nod to Heidegger, "the Sacred must be speech" and then adds, "and even more, my very speech" (40; 56). It is the very singularity of the poet that lends itself to the demand and that, as Hölderlin found, requires nothing less than a sacrifice of that individuality (though not the poet's idiom). The "must" at issue in "the Sacred must be speech" does not take root in the present, however; it is a prayer or a wish. Blanchot acknowledges this and does not want to consign the sacred to subjective whim; it must be embodied in the very speech that brings forth the sacred. But how? By way of answer, Blanchot quotes a line from "Partage formel" in René Char's collection *Seuls demeurant* (1945), a sentence that appears to carry as much weight for him as Scripture for a believer, partly because for him it resonates with the couplet from Hölderlin that has been preoccupying us and partly because, for Blanchot, Char is—or might as well be—Hölderlin for us here and now. He is the one "whose destiny as a poet is bound to our own."[84] Char writes, "Le poème est l'amour réalisé du désir demeuré désir" (The poem is the realized love of desire that has remained desire).[85]

A poem is a poem and not mere talk because one day, somewhere, a poet has managed to put desire into words: a love for that desire has been realized, and yet the poem *is* a poem (and not mere talk) because the language in the air or on the page still bears within itself the ache, the longing, for what it intends. To the extent that a sequence of ordinary words is a poem, it is not only a response to the sacred and an address to the day in which we live but also an address to a time that is always to come. No poem lodges entirely or simply in the present: the struggle between the desire for form and the need to respond to the limitless Outside always exceeds the present. The struggle is irresolvable since it is not between two powers but between power and passivity, work and worklessness, and therefore the poem, which *is* the struggle, is always unresolved, dynamic, and can always speak in days to come. A formalism of ambiguity, irony, metaphor, and paradox can capture something of that desire, but still the poem slips through that grid. Any number of contexts—economic, historical, political, social—can be brought to bear upon the poem, but its longing can never be satisfied here and now. There is never a question of our being unable to grasp sensory presence because it is fleeting, and poetry therefore has to establish itself as a negative theology of the ephemeral. Were an immediate presence to impose itself, it could not be experienced—subject and object would have been fused—but the fact there is something like a poem tells us, indeed, it *insists*, that there is something other than the present to which it sends itself, something other than any and all future presents; and this indicates what Blanchot calls "the impossible."

Similar thoughts are evoked several years later in "René Char et la pensée du neutre" (1963), an essay collected in *L'Entretien infini*. Here what Blanchot values is the way in which poetry can maintain "the unknown as unknown" (300; 442) and thereby indicate the neutral or the impossible. Heraclitus's language alerts us to the neutral, but philosophy since then has moved in another direction entirely. "By a simplification that is clearly abusive," Blanchot says, "one can recognize in the entire history of philosophy an effort to acclimatize or to domesticate the neuter by substituting for it the law of the impersonal and the reign of the universal, or an effort to challenge it by affirming the ethical primacy of the Self-Subject, the mystical aspiration to the singular Unique" (299; 441).[86] The neuter of Heraclitus and Char has been covered by the philosophy of the neuter. Blanchot names no philosophers, implying that there would be too many. Only Heidegger has seen through this immense cover-up. His philosophy "can be understood as a response to this examination of the neuter and as an attempt to approach it in a non-conceptual manner" (299; 441).

Yet the philosopher's glimpse of the neuter "must be understood as a new retreat before that which thought seems only able to entertain by sublimating it" (299; 441). *Sein* invites us to think the neutral, and yet its relation with truth, its unfolding into clarity, and its association with light prevent Heidegger from thinking the neuter and the unknown in tandem. Metaphysics as the study of neutral being, neither divine nor created, has laid claim on the boldest attempt by a philosopher in centuries to think the neuter. Only Char, who values Heraclitus above all philosophers, can grasp the neuter and the unknown and thereby stand before the sacred.[87] Blanchot indicated what was at issue here years before in "René Char." In this poet, he tells us, "poetic imagination distances itself from reality in order to join this very movement of self-distancing to this reality, to make inside of what is, that which is not, and take that as its principle, as absence that makes presence desirable, irreality that allows the poet to possess the real, to have a 'productive knowledge' of it."[88] Perhaps more than in any other French poetry, Blanchot suggests, it is in Char's lyrics that we find the dark gaze.

Let us take a step back. Where Bonnefoy speaks of poetry and the sacred by way of "categories of possibility," Blanchot approaches the same concerns by evoking a relation of impossibility: "if the immediate is infinitely absent, exceeding and excluding any present, the only relation with the immediate would be a relation reserving in itself an infinite absence."[89] Blanchot does not deny that this relation can rightly be considered sacred, only that it can have any redemptive value: there is no question, here, of time having a forward direction, let alone a meaning. Indeed, in earlier pieces on Hölderlin he takes pains to preserve the word *sacred* while making it quite plain that he does not believe in the Christian God. For Hölderlin, the poet speaks in a space between two spheres: the withdrawal of the gods and the turning away from the gods by mortals. Like Heidegger, Blanchot agrees that the time evoked here is not merely the historical moment of Hölderlin—the double infidelity being a characteristic of the Enlightenment—but, more profoundly, the time of poetry.[90] So when Hölderlin calls the space of poetic speech "the sacred" he is, for Heidegger and Blanchot, saying something about *all* poetry, not only that which Hölderlin tried to keep alive by his own practice in a bad time for poets.

So Blanchot the atheist retains the space marked out by the double infidelity of gods and mortals as "this empty and pure place [*lieu*] . . . *the sacred.*"[91] Two things might be noticed. The first assimilates Blanchot to the world of *la religion sans religion*. The sacred, as conceived here, is a matter of revealability, not revelation: the poet is open to revelation, but no new credible one has yet been received, and we might well wonder if a revelation will come on terms that are determined by a human, even though he or she be a poet. The second is that, over the course of Blanchot's reflections on *L'Improbable*, Bonnefoy's passionate endorsement of the "here" and the "now" has been narrowed in Mallarméan fashion into a steady contemplation of the "now." I do not think this is an unintentional lapse on Blanchot's part, although his reasons for not focusing on place are given in a slightly earlier essay, "La Parole prophétique" (1957), which anticipates some of the themes of "Le Grand Refus" (1959) and "Comment découvrir l'obscur?" (1959). Prophetic speech, Blanchot says, has nothing essentially to do with predicting the future; rather, it interrupts the present and contests all its confidence in possibility. The secure foundations of the present are thoroughly shaken, and an "*other* time," that of the impossible or the Outside, is announced.[92] "Prophetic speech," we are told, "is a wandering [*errant*] speech" (113); it affirms nomadism as a positive value while opposing all fixity, rootedness, and rest, which, from its perspective, are pagan values.[93] The prophetic word responds to the "*other* time" that precedes the alternation of day and night, although it can never name that "ciel antérieur."

6

"Here and now, but everywhere beyond the here and now, under the canopy and in the forecourt of our place and our moment. Omnipresent and alive; one might say that they are the very speech of being that poetry draws forth. One might say that they *are* words, being no other than a promise."[94] Bonnefoy is speaking of "the wind, fire, earth, the waters," which he calls "categories of possibility" (114), and he adds that they appear "on the confines of the negativity of language, like angels telling of a still unknown god." As we have seen, these elements hint at a "negative 'theology'" (114): by negating all the concepts that they generate we can ascend until we gain an awareness of the presence and ultimate unity of wind, fire, earth, and water. This is not gnosticism, for the god who remains unknown is of the earth, and although one cannot hope for language, even when exquisitely deployed, to describe this divinity, one can and should direct language toward it. Poetry's task is to name the possible, Bonnefoy thinks, and it can do so properly only if it is committed to a mortal vision, one that testifies to the fleetingness of beauty and willingly embraces imperfection. Only in doing this can there "be some sense in saying 'I'" (161).

Blanchot does not simply reject this position either in his criticism or in his narratives. Take *Le Très-Haut* (1948), for instance, Blanchot's last novel and, as it happens, a work whose title translates Hölderlin's expression "Das Höchste." When Henri Sorge cries out in the moment of his death, "Now, now I'm speaking," he is truly then, and only then, the "most high" because only then is he no one: the final sentence of the novel bears out the truth of the opening sentence, "I wasn't alone, I was anybody," makes it possible (the entire narrative is spoken by a dead man), while also, in the same gesture, condemning Sorge to an endless dying.[95] In his criticism too Blanchot accepts that poetry must name the possible while adding that it must also respond to the impossible.[96] His reflection on Bonnefoy is not simply a doubling of the space that the poet chooses, as though the impossible were a realm that could be added to the possible, since Blanchot removes the sacred from the possible and identifies it with what he calls the impossible, the neutral, or the Outside. Decades later, in *L'Écriture du désastre* (1980), Blanchot will quote the first four lines of Bonnefoy's "Le Fleuve," the opening poem of *Dans le leurre du seuil* (1975), so that they make a fragment just by themselves:

Mais non, toujours
D'un déploiement de l'aile de l'impossible
Tu t'éveilles, avec un cri,
Du lieu, qui n'est qu'un rêve . . . [97]

No commentary is offered: the poet's word "l'impossible" is quietly folded into the thought that has absorbed Blanchot for most of his adult life. It is hard to imagine Bonnefoy being entirely happy with this use of his poem, and one can only recall some words from his inaugural lecture at the Collège de France the very year after Blanchot's collection of fragments appeared: "Poetry in Europe seems to have been the impossible: what eludes a man's lifelong search as immediacy does our words."[98] It is as though years after "Le Grand Refus" and "Comment découvrir l'obscur?" Blanchot were indicating that Bonnefoy, as a poet if not as a critic, were aware of the neutral dimension to which all poetry worthy of the name responds. And it seems that Bonnefoy has not changed his mind on his central conviction since he wrote *L'Improbable*.

For Blanchot, a poet can rightly say with Hölderlin, "das Heilige sei mein Wort" not because the sacred has been named in what has been written but because one may hope that the poem bears a trace of its response to the impossible. Once again, I turn to *L'Écriture du désastre* for assistance, this time to a fragment that comes shortly after the quotation from Bonnefoy's poem. "The poet is Narcissus to the extent that Narcissus is an anti-Narcissus," he says, and then adds, in a complex formulation, "he who, turned away from himself—causing the detour of which he is the effect [*portant et supportant le détour*], dying of not re-cognizing himself—leaves the trace of what has not occurred" (135; 205). One becomes a poet not by falling in love with oneself and giving way to unbridled subjectivity but by sacrificing the self and reconstituting it in the idiom of the poem that is written; the poem bears the trace of a response to the impossible—the inspiration of the poem—or, if you like, the sacred which has never been and can never be part of a lived experienced for the poet. The sacred is not transcendent, then, not even in the phenomenological sense of the word that Bonnefoy uses. Could it be regarded as transcendental? To the extent that the sacred is the very opening of nature, it is indeed the condition of possibility for life and all writing about life. Yet it would be just as telling, if not more so, to call the sacred a condition of impossibility: it interrupts any attempt to freeze the present and render it permanent.

"Why is art so intimately allied with the Sacred?" Answering his own question, Blanchot tells us that art looks to the sacred to supply "the profound *reserve* which it needs."[99] Art has always testified to the divine; it has been able to speak only as a response to the sacred, as a privileged way of conducting mystery without compromising it. The artist has been the one who lets the divine speak in the work, who makes the sacred manifest to the extent that it allows itself to become so. In turn, art has been sheltered by the divine: it withdraws in the presentation of the sacred, has nothing to say on its own account. "It is as if a secret law required of the work that it always be concealed in what it shows," Blanchot says, "and thus that it only show what must remain concealed, and that finally it only show what must stay hidden by concealing it" (232–33; 310). As soon as one no longer believes in the gods, the great odes of Pindar lose their intimate rapport with the origin; they begin to appear as poems. As soon as we no longer worship God, the Book of Job ceases to be a revelation of benign and malign powers and can be taught by a professor of English, as a prelude to reading Matthew Arnold's "Dover Beach" and Philip Larkin's "Church Going." In their very different ways, those two poems speak of the disappearance of the divine; and in art like that of Arnold and Larkin the divine is not so much a reserve as a trace. What happens when that trace is itself lost? Or, as Blanchot frames the question, "What will become now of art, now that the gods and even their absence are gone, and now that man's presence offers no support?" (233; 311).

We do not know. We know that without the sacred there can be no art and that for us there is no viable relation between art and the sacred. All that the poet can do, Blanchot thinks (with Hölderlin in mind), is maintain poetry in the space defined by the double infidelity of the human *and* the divine, which coincides with the space defined by the sense of the sacred that has vanished from the earth *and* the sense of the sacred that might come to us. "The poem's space is entirely represented by this *and*," he says. "But as for whether it is this *and* that unites and binds together, the pure word in which the void of the past and the void of the future become true presence, the 'now' of dawn—this question is reserved in the work" (247; 333). We have passed from the sacred as a reserve for art to art needing to reserve a question about the sacred. It is a grim scenario for art, as Blanchot understands it, though not a hopeless one. The possibility remains that one might be able to say, with Hölderlin,

Jezt aber tagts! Ich harrt und sah es kommen,
Und was ich sah, das Heilige sei mein Wort.

In its solitude the poem remains "prophetic," Blanchot tells us in the final line of the last chapter of *L'Espace littéraire*. This does means not that the poem speaks of a time to come but that it testifies to the *"other* time" of the impossible, Rilke's *Nirgends ohne Nicht.* Doubtless we are asked to recall an ontological attunement that constrains us to see something as both itself and as image, and to find ourselves transfixed by the dark gaze of being transmuting itself into nothingness. What frightens Bonnefoy about gnostic excarnation, its abandoning of sensuous particulars while questing for a higher order, is eerily reset by Blanchot. For the sheer presence of being is excarnated and turned into a hollow image of itself. A catastrophe occurred in the very moment of creation: not a fall from an original fullness in which the *pneuma* is nonetheless preserved but rather a fall from being to image. Viewed properly, Blanchot's theory of the imaginary is the fullest and strongest elaboration of the gnosticism that Bonnefoy most fears. It is also the most disturbing, not because the image can be manipulated by magic but because the place of the image, according to Blanchot, is a nonplace.[100] We do not desire it but are drawn to it despite ourselves and, finally, without ourselves.

Blanchot could never be accused of belonging to a cult of the image, yet if we stand far enough away from him, in both time and place, we can almost see him reviving a theology of the icon, albeit in a characteristically dark manner. "Icon," here, would need to be taken quite generally and would make no reference to the visual. I can best indicate what I have in mind by quoting a passage from Saint Theodore the Studite's *On the Holy Icons*, a remarkable ninth-century rebuttal of arguments against the use of icons in worship. In his third refutation of the iconoclasts, Saint Theodore makes the following pronouncement:

> The prototype and the image belong to the category of related things, like the double and the half. For the prototype always implies the image of which it is the prototype, and the double always implies the half in relation to which it is called double. For there would not be a prototype if there were no image; there would not even be any double, if some half were not understood. But since these things exist simultaneously, they are understood and subsist together. Therefore, since no time intervenes between them, the one does not have a different veneration from the other, but both have one and the same.[101]

No image without a prototype, Saint Theodore tells us, and also, more surprisingly, no prototype without an image.

In essence, Saint Theodore offers a version of the phenomenological argument used a thousand years later by Lévinas and Blanchot. We encountered it in the last chapter: when a thing or an event presents itself it also gives an image of itself in the very gesture of its appearing. In Saint Theodore's hands, the argument urges us to accept that Christ and His image are ontologically related. We cannot maintain a secure interval between an icon of Christ and Christ Himself: the distance between the two is, if I might adopt Blanchot's idiom, already within Christ, "the limitless depth behind the image . . . absolutely present although not given."[102] The experience of the person in prayer before an icon is one of fascination, being drawn endlessly toward the divinity. Before the icon, no one can trust in a clear disjunction of orders between the icon in the church or in the home and the divine world. Although the divinity of Christ cannot be circumscribed, it nonetheless abides in the icon. For Blanchot, literature is a part of that to which it exposes the author. The Outside cannot be circumscribed: it is infinite, impossible, otherwise. Yet the literary work cannot begin without moving toward the imaginary point that we call the Outside. From the perspective I have suggested, the stories and poems on which he broods—those by Beckett and Char, for example—are icons of the Outside. They embody it and indicate it.[103] And to the extent that Blanchot is prepared to call the Outside the sacred, we might say that he quietly suggests that the sacred has not disappeared so much as been refigured in literature. Bonnefoy would agree, though for different reasons: if poetry is iconic, it is because it uses the things of this world to illuminate the immediacy and unity that we desire.[104]

Perhaps too in Blanchot's talk of an "*other* time" we are invited to ponder a way of being in relation with one another that escapes both dialectics and fusion and that offers the hope of a communication of humanity at the limit of the possible. For Blanchot speaks now and then of a plural, mobile, dispersed way of being in relation, a society of the impossible, an "ultimate affirmation" of being human.[105] Hardly a refusal of death, this community is founded on the dying of the other person; and scarcely an endorsement of an "elsewhere," this vision is turned to the houses where we live, the streets and woods where we walk. I will return to this in the final chapter. Suffice it to say for now that our experience of socialism would bear no more than a faint resemblance to this unavowable community. That is partly because this community is always to come and partly because it is not a utopia, a "perfect society," but never lasts and turns on the "principle of a transparent humanity essentially produced by itself alone."[106]

If ever such a principle should be in evidence, the divine as Blanchot understands it would be dissolved entirely in society. With no project of salvation, the sacred would be joyfully consumed in what René Char called "commune présence," moments of explosive communication, instants of passion and acts of friendship in which life overbids itself. This is not quite what Bonnefoy understands by incarnation or transcendence, and yet there is some common ground. I think of Bonnefoy's remarks at the end of a lecture on Ronsard. Poetry, he says, is "passionately committed to clarity, and this is because it knows that the world, the revitalised relationship with the reality of the world, exists only insofar as the latter is, as I have said, a place: that is to say a social entity, constituting therefore as comprehensive and immediate an exchange with others as may be."[107] When things are put this way, one can almost imagine Bonnefoy drawing close to Blanchot, just as one does when about to have a long and serious conversation.

4

·

LOSING THE POWER TO SAY " I "

1

In a meditation on *L'Homme révolté* (1951)
Blanchot recalls Albert Camus's claim that "the movement of the absurd is the
equivalent of methodical doubt" and is then reminded of the further suggestion
that "the No of the man in revolt, this word that means 'I am in revolt, therefore we
are,' corresponds to the 'Cogito' of Descartes."[1] Before continuing his reflections on
the absurd, Blanchot turns for a moment to Descartes:

> The "Cogito" was that firm, unshakable, beginning [*commençante*] word,
> and apparently without anything to support it but its own evidency; truly
> a first [*première*] word, alone capable of stopping the moving march of
> the desert, in this case, doubt. That the "Cogito" should in turn be
> shaken by the unsatisfied exigency of a beginning still more beginning
> is a long story [*histoire*] that would be out of place here; it moreover
> leaves intact everything this word, by its suddenness and its imperious
> beginning force, gathers in the way of brilliance and decision. When, in
> a word, the beginning has spoken, we see it still illuminated by the light
> of the "Cogito." (176–77; 264)

The long story that cannot be related here, the narrative of a beginning older
than the "Cogito," is never directly told by Blanchot, and, as his récits suggest, it
cannot be told. And yet oblique approaches to it can be found in many of his narratives and essays. The very piece on Camus I have just cited, "Réflexions sur

l'enfer" (1954), is an example; for by the time you reach the passage just quoted you will have noticed a trace of the story. "Albert Camus said, 'I am in revolt, therefore we are,' placing all the decision of a solitary hope in a word. But those who have lost the power to say 'I' are excluded from this word and from this hope" (173; 259).

Commentary on Blanchot has tended to take its bearings from this story that shakes the "Cogito." Two examples will suffice. Early on in Blanchot's writing life, shortly after the publication of *Thomas l'obscur* (1941), Georges Bataille hinted at a quasi-mystical interpretation of the novel, a suggestion that for some readers would influence the reception of essays and narratives yet to be composed. Unlike Descartes, who submitted "the unknowable to the necessity of being known," Blanchot remains faithful to the unknowable.[2] Then Bataille says, in a passage I considered in the first chapter, that in *Thomas l'obscur* "the questions of the new theology (which has only the unknown as object) are pressing, though they remain hidden" (102; 120). In other words, the young novelist develops a negative atheology in a negative mode. Twenty-odd years later, in an equally bold act of appropriation, Michel Foucault cautions against associating Blanchot with negative theology while still valuing his writing for distancing itself from Cartesian thought. "The reason it is now so necessary to think through fiction—while in the past it was a matter of thinking the truth—is that 'I speak' runs counter to 'I think.' 'I think' led to the indubitable certainty of the 'I' and its existence; 'I speak,' on the other hand, distances, disperses, effaces that existence and lets only its empty emplacement appear."[3]

Must we choose between these two powerful interpretations, whether in reading Blanchot, in placing him with respect to Descartes, or in doing justice to the Cogito? I do not think so. When reading Bataille we must remember that "the unknown" in *Thomas l'obscur* attempts to present itself through an encounter with the Cogito and that the "I" is not dissolved but reconceived as the host of an absent Thomas. Moreover, "the unknown" functions differently for Blanchot and Bataille, and over the years that function changes for Blanchot: the everyday, as well as the mystical, comes to be figured as unknown. Bataille is not simply mistaken about Blanchot, however: the essays and narratives brood over gaps between "human being" and "possibility" and respond as best they can to the disconcerting approaches of what comes through those gaps. Nor is Foucault entirely on the wrong track: Blanchot is drawn to the negative power of speech, its eerie ability to destroy the particularity of things. But when reading Foucault we should be wary of aligning fiction and speaking here, and thinking and truth there. As the passage about Descartes I quoted at the outset hints, Blanchot does not prize writing for evading or disrupting the Cogito. He finds both an "I speak" and an "I think" in literary and philosophical texts alike.

Let us therefore approach Blanchot by a third path, one that keeps in view both the "beginning word" and the "beginning still more beginning." In this way perhaps we can come to understand what is involved in shaking the Cogito, and what it might mean to talk of losing "the power to say 'I.'"

2

The Cogito has been attacked and revised many times and from many quarters, and so, before setting out, let us be clear what Blanchot is *not* saying about it. Unlike Leibniz, Blanchot does not accuse Descartes of mistaking the Cogito for the sole primitive truth of reason.[4] There is no other foundation, whether a principle of noncontradiction or a principle of reason, that he urges us to accept. And unlike Kant, he does not condemn the Cogito for being a tautology: it has content, he thinks, though one that differs from what Descartes holds to be there.[5] Blanchot is not perturbed, as Schelling is, to find that Descartes uses *cogito* ambiguously, as both that which is doubting and that which reflects on the doubting, and that *sum* in the famous expression cannot mean "I am" in an absolute sense but only "I am *in one way or another.*"[6] Nor does Blanchot agree with Balzac that while Descartes says, "I think, therefore I am," he should really say, "I am, therefore I think."[7] And he is untouched by Gide's complaint that the real problem with the Cogito is the "therefore" and that the proposition could be defended only were it to read, "I think *and I am.*"[8] Blanchot is not pained, as Husserl is, to catch Descartes finding the ego as *substantia cogitans* once the *epochē* has taken place and so becoming "the father of transcendental realism, an absurd position."[9] Nor is he concerned to distinguish the true Cogito from psychological and intentional rivals, as Merleau-Ponty is.[10] And finally he does not seem bothered, as many analytic philosophers are, whether the Cogito is an inference or an intuition.[11]

Blanchot's suspicions about the Cogito begin to come into focus when seen by way of Heidegger's questioning in *Sein und Zeit* (1927), which Blanchot read shortly after it was published.[12] Now while Heidegger places great emphasis upon the phenomenological destruction of the Cogito, which he states without the *ergo* to avoid the appearance of a syllogism, he defers that demonstration to division 2 of part 2 of his treatise, pages that never saw the light of day. All the same, we can detect the outlines of the analysis in that work and see some developments and details in later publications. On Heidegger's reading, Descartes does not supply the ontological foundations of the *cogito sum* and believes himself excused from doing so because of the absolute certainty that the Cogito seems to offer. For

Descartes, the *res cogitans* is a *fundamentum inconcussum* that can be defined on-tologically as an *ens* which in turn is given only within the horizon of *ens creatum*. At the heart of the Cogito, then, long before we reach the ontological argument for the existence of God, there is a theological prejudice, and all the philosophy that answers to Descartes, the great "metaphysics of subjectivity," is marked by that orientation.[13]

Properly seen, Heidegger thinks, the philosophy of the subject begins not with Descartes but with Francisco Suárez whose massive and meticulous *Disputationes metaphysicae* (1597) has been "the strongest influence on modern philosophy."[14] It is Suárez on whom Descartes relies, "using his terminology almost everywhere" (80), and thereby keeps the Counter-Reformation reading of Thomas in play.[15] We can overcome this theological prejudice only when the ontology that determines *ens* as *ens creatum* is radically interpreted from the standpoint of temporality. When that happens, the *cogito sum* can be given a fresh ontologico-phenomenal confirmation. And then it becomes clear that *sum* is not consequent upon *cogito* but rather grounds *cogito*. "As such an entity, 'I am' in the possibility of Being towards various ways of comporting myself—namely, *cogitationes*—as ways of Being alongside entities within-the-world."[16] Yet it was Suárez who passed on to Descartes the view that the proper object of metaphysics is neither finite nor infinite being but rather a neutral concept of being. Aristotle's definition of meta-physics remained authoritative for Suárez, *ens in quantum ens reale*, yet lifted be-ing away from both God and creation. Heidegger remains closer to Suárez the metaphysician than to Descartes the epistemologist, and he also absorbs Suárez's emphasis on neutral being all the more readily by rejecting the notion of *ens* as *ens creatum*.[17] Being and God, as he will later say, have nothing to do with one another.[18] More broadly, the Heidegger who identifies metaphysics as onto-theology and seeks to overcome it has already inherited a concept of neutral being from Suárez, a concept that is itself constitutive of onto-theology or at least its modern phase.[19]

We know that reading *Sein und Zeit* was an "intellectual shock" for Blanchot in the late 1920s, and we can trace the effects of that encounter, especially the em-phasis on finitude and temporality, through to the meditations on literary space of the 1950s and, with diminishing emphasis, beyond them to his later fragmen-tary writings.[20] And we know too that, with the exception of a sharp jolt, he steadily maintained that Heidegger's work could stand as a valuable "new view-point" for contemplating art.[21] This affirmation of a fresh perspective was made in 1938 and in all likelihood was triggered by reading "Hölderlin und das Wesen der Dichtung," which appeared in *Das innere Reich* in late 1936 and was published in Munich by Albert Langen and George Müller in 1937. Blanchot would have been familiar with *Was ist Metaphysik?* (1929), the French translation of which was introduced by Alexandre Koyré in *Bifur* in 1931.[22] Heidegger's brooding on the "Nothing" (*Nichts*) that is prior to negation (*Verneinung*) and that is manifest in states of dread was doubtless important for an early essay like "De l'angoisse au langage" (1943). Yet negativity (*Negativität*) as much as Nothing imposes on Blanchot, and Hegel comes to join Heidegger as a vanishing point of his world.[23] Certainly the arch-philosopher's name was in the French air in the late thirties and early forties, but now standing for the dialectic and its passions rather than for a panlogism.[24] What grounds those passions is nothing other than negativity, that drive to determination wherein the Idea leaves its home in Logic and suffers alienation in Nature in order to find itself more truly in Spirit.

This is a vast theme. Let us narrow our focus, as Blanchot does in "La Littérature et le droit à la mort" (1947–48) and look at just one phase of the dialectic, when language engages with nature. Blanchot draws our attention directly to an early text of Hegel's, *Das System der speculativen Philosophie* (1803–4), and indirectly to a passage in the *Phänomenologie des Geistes* (1807) that treats of the same material. I shall have something to say about the later version in a minute, so let us look at Hegel's earlier formulation. "The first act, by which Adam established his lordship over the animals, is this, that he gave them a name, i.e., he nullified them as beings on their own account, and made them into ideal [entities]."[25] Which, when recast by as devoted a reader of Mallarmé as Blanchot, becomes the following: a word "gives me the being, but it gives it to me deprived of being. The word is the absence of that being, its nothingness."[26] Hegel regards the act of naming as a labor of the negative: the immediate being of an animal is annulled to reveal the dialectical necessity of mediation. Blanchot, though, declines to follow the speculation that passes from immediacy to mediation and instead focuses exclusively on the point that not all the negating power of language can be used by the dialectic.

Conceptual understanding occurs, the singular partly gives way to the universal: Blanchot readily concedes the dialectical move. Even so, language is left with a negative charge in excess of what is required of it. A word does not simply denote its concept; it also presents itself as a thing—a sound, a shape—that does not need an intending consciousness in order to signify. "Language speaks": in putting matters that way, it seems that Blanchot has gone by way of Hegel and Mallarmé to reach Heidegger—or, more exactly, to miss him by an inch or by a mile, depending on one's perspective. For while Blanchot maintains that language speaks, it is not being that is heard but death as the impossibility of dying. Language has the peculiar power to render things absent and to keep only the ghostly image of their presence. Close to the narrator's voice, he tells us, there is a narrative voice that speaks through the script; it is an impersonal murmur, a consciousness that does not answer to a living subject and that cannot be brought under its sway. It is scarcely a "voice" at all, since, strictly speaking, it is only the attenuated image of language, and it is unlike the narrator's voice in that no claims for self-identity are made on its behalf. Rather, this writing considered apart from speech is an anonymous and dispersed way of being in relation. It presents a world in its plurality while contesting any tendency, from within or without, to ascribe an overarching meaning to it.

The human "I," as Hegel portrays it, is the supremely active "power of the negative," achieving an identity by transforming nature or—it is the same thing— by the making of history.[27] Yet for Blanchot this negativity can no longer be invested in action, for Hegelian man has essentially completed the project of human being. Surfacing here is an anthropological reading of Hegel proposed by Kojève in the 1930s and relaunched from a new site by Bataille, a reading that Blanchot puts to his own ends. Having realized the idea of freedom, human beings wait without hope or reason at the end of history, replete not with satisfaction but with a sense of futility. All that offers itself under the sign of possibility has been achieved in essence if not in each and every detail, and all conflict between subject and object has been overcome. If human beings are metaphysical subjects—and not simply grammatical, legal, or psychological subjects—then "man is dead," and following the subject into oblivion are philosophy and war.[28] The human being who is not content with this state of affairs must, for Bataille and Blanchot, hazard the impossible: a communication with the unknown that approaches when immanence and totality begin to break up. Perhaps this communication will not be fully achieved and one will be like Marcel in À la recherche du temps perdu (1913–27) when he gazes at the three trees at Hudimesnil. Unable to place them in his past, he is unsettled by their strange allure and feels "behind them the same object, known to me and yet vague, which I could not bring nearer."[29] Or perhaps the communication will be more complete, and, like Bataille in Le Coupable, one will dissolve into the "indefinite reality" beyond life and death.[30] By 1941 Blanchot was calling the person who risks this experience "the last man," although the extraordinary récit bearing that title was not to appear until late in the next decade.[31]

A concern with lastness orients much of Blanchot's narrative writing. It forms the burden of Le Très-Haut (1948), his novel of the absolute state (which doubles as an adverse report on the state of absolute knowledge), whose narrator, Henri Sorge, is humiliated precisely because he is called to "read, write, and reflect"—activities that properly belong to history, not to the "perfect" society instituted after its end.[32] A few years after those words were written, in *Celui qui ne m'accompagnait pas* (1953), the thought of the end is loosened from Hegelian and Marxist theories of history. Now the "end of history" stands for our mortal state, death taking the place of world revolution as the *dénouement,* and writing bespeaks the dissolution of interiority as a privileged ground of experience. One could say that the emphasis is phenomenological rather than analytical, although "phenomenological" is stretched out of its usual shapes, for there can be no experience of death that gives itself to consciousness. What is experienced, if the word can be used here, is the perpetual deferment of this manifestation, a sense of the endlessness of the end. As the narrator of *Celui qui ne m'accompagnait pas* tells us, "I am almost no longer myself, but that's what it is, to write."[33] It is a significant statement. Kant spoke of the transcendental unity of apperception, the "I think" that accompanies all our representations and holds them together. It is perhaps not going too far to say that over the years Blanchot comes to propose a transcendental disunity of inscription, an "I write" that accompanies all our representations and sets them at variance with the unity of consciousness attributed to the Kantian subject.[34]

One consequence of reading Blanchot principally through the powerful lens of Bataille, as is usually done, is that his analysis of the "I" appears limited to a particular critique of Hegel. Find reasons for not regarding Hegel's sense of selfhood compelling, or promote a more attractive theory of the subject, and suddenly all talk of losing "the power to say 'I'" seems rather beside the point. It is important then to show that Blanchot casts his net somewhat more widely than that, though it needs to be kept in mind that he does not cast as broadly as he thinks he does. He takes as his quarry not only those philosophies organized by "the subject," as Heidegger thinks of it, but also notions of selfhood that eschew "the subject" while covertly relying on a determining trait of it. He takes the fundamental point of these theories to be a conception of the self by way of possibility. In using this word he is not evoking logical or epistemic possibility, and he does not interest himself in Kant's warning that we should distinguish logical and real possibility.[35] At first one might think he draws on Aristotle's notion of possibility as potentiality—or, as we would say now, ability—but his sense of possibility is more robust than that.[36] Besides, his concern is not with those moral problems that gather around a person's being able to do something but not doing it. What he has in mind, rather, is an ontological notion of possibility: "to be plus the power to be." "Possibility establishes and founds reality," he writes: "one is what one is only if one has the power to be it. Here we see immediately that man not only has possibilities, but is his possibility." And he adds: "Even death is a power . . . Retaining a relation to death, I appropriate it as a power."[37]

As I pointed out in the second chapter, Blanchot maintains that the modern sense of self is underwritten by three philosophers—Hegel, Nietzsche, and Heidegger—the last two of whom are usually valued precisely for their radical interrogation of the metaphysics of the subject. "The decision to be without being is possibility itself: the possibility of death," Blanchot writes, and it is possibility which determines how the self is conceived.[38] Of these three thinkers, it is Heidegger who goes the furthest in his questioning of the subject yet who develops the most persuasive account of death as possibility. Subjectivity, Heidegger argues, has been the main obstacle to a proper unfolding of the question of Being: the very emphasis on epistemology associated with Descartes, Kant, and Husserl has sidelined the more fundamental question of the being of *Dasein*. The consequence is that, ontologically, Dasein is furthest from itself, and we can only begin to grasp our being by attending to preontological clues. "Dasein is not something present-at-hand which possesses its competence for something by way of an extra; it is primarily Being-possible."[39] That is the general picture of Dasein. A replay of Dasein's last moments tells us more. For, properly understood, death for Dasein is *"the possibility of the impossibility of any existence at all."* And the thinker of Todtnauberg goes on: "Being towards this possibility discloses to Dasein its *ownmost* potentiality-for-Being, in which its very Being is the issue" (307). Which means that Dasein's final possibility grants it every other possibility: it is what enables the "I" to affirm itself. You could say that, with a backward glance to Descartes, Heidegger says, parodically, "I die therefore I am." It is against this background that Blanchot appears, arguing that death has two aspects. Death does not declare itself only as Dasein's final possibility but, through suffering or endless waiting, lets itself be understood as the erosion of all possibility.[40]

So one does not encounter the neuter as a possibility among other possibilities in the world. It is not to be found in negativity, not even in death as such, but in the incessant and interminable *approach* of death which is usually interpreted as a menace but which can be understood as a friend. Speaking the language of phenomenology, one would say that the neuter is transcendent; it does not belong to anyone's stream of experience.[41] To encounter it one would have to transgress the laws of phenomenology and indeed all laws. Having said that, one would be obliged to add that we are dealing not with transgression understood as a voluntary act, an extremist exercise of the mind or the will, but with what happens when power reaches its limit and plays itself out. No longer able to maintain itself by negation, and therefore without any resistance against which it can affirm itself, the "I" is cast adrift in a dead time that fascinates while it undermines any security the "I" may have had in itself as a constituted subject. And yet, this sovereign experience of the neutral—insofar as it is "an experience"—cannot offer a definite release from consciousness, now or ever. Although this way of seeing things differs from the Heideggerian theme of dread and nothingness, and in fact converges with the notion of "existence without existents" explored by Lévinas, it connects positively with the German thinker's suggestion that the position of an "I" or a subject occludes the phenomenal character of Dasein.[42] And this indicates Blanchot's heaviest debt to Heidegger. The distinction between subject and Dasein comes up early in *Sein und Zeit* when we read that "*Ontologically, every idea of a 'subject'*—unless refined by a previous ontological determination of its basic character—still posits the *subjectum* (ὑποκείμενον) along with it, no matter how vigorous one's ontical protestations against the 'soul substance' or the 'reification of consciousness.'"[43] Dasein's "essence" is given not in the contents of a constituting consciousness or in the positing of an "I think" around which everything else turns but in its being-in-the-world, its shared everyday existence.

Yet it would be misleading to regard Blanchot as a "Heideggerian" or as "anti-Cartesian," partly because he comes to reject the German thinker's emphasis that Dasein is "in each case mine [*jemeines*]" and partly because of the high value he places on a certain kind of doubt.[44] This is not the skepticism of an isolated *ego cogito* with respect to its representations but is akin to the primal σκέψις that Heidegger understands as a gaze past beings to being.[45] The young Blanchot entitled his *mémoire* for the *diplôme d'etudes supérieures* "La Conception du dogmatisme chez les sceptiques" (1930), while the mature Blanchot writes warmly of the "invincible skepticism" that characterizes Lévinas's later philosophy.[46] In his judgment, skepticism for Lévinas amounts to writing a work that "affirms nothing that is not overseen by an indefatigable adversary, one to whom he does not concede but who obliges him to go further, not beyond reason into the facility of the irrational or towards a mystical effusion, but rather towards another reason, towards the other as reason or demand."[47] This adversary is not a subject, however, since Lévinas's skepticism is not a philosophical position that can be attributed to consciousness. "*Language* is already skepticism."[48] And Blanchot suggests that the accent should fall on the adverb: not to indicate a movement of negativity or a transgression but to remind us that language unsettles both absolute knowledge and transparent verbal communication.[49] Within that horizon a question must surely take shape: if language is already skepticism, how can Descartes ever formulate the Cogito in speech or writing?

Blanchot's reading of Sextus Empiricus and other skeptics did not lead him to that question; it was not to be posed until he had pondered Lévinas's *Autrement qu'être* (1974), and we shall see it emerge a little later. There is no hint of it in his first article on the philosopher, "Une Vue de Descartes" (1941), a meditation on how Paul Valéry and Karl Jaspers have responded to the guiding spirit of the Cogito. What intrigues Blanchot there is more a problem of what is not written, a sense that, for all their proximity, Valéry and Descartes nonetheless miss one another; a sense that, even though the poet's lucid pages are to be admired, "the Descartes of Paul Valéry still remains to be written."[50]

In that early essay Blanchot makes nothing of the poet's claim that "I am" has no more content than "I am not." And as it happens, Blanchot could not have agreed with Valéry and could not have defended Descartes. He had already adopted a third position. The expression "I think therefore I am not" had in fact appeared in *Thomas l'obscur*, published the same year as Blanchot's review of Valéry, although the words function very differently in the novel than in the essay. Let us overhear part of Thomas's long meditation after the demise of his lover, Anne. Readers of the novel will recall that in an early scene Thomas throws himself into an open grave only to encounter the impossibility of dying. Phenomenologically at least, there is no exit from being. Because being is itself and the image of itself, it perpetuates itself as the absence of being: "it was not a misunderstanding. He was really dead and at the same time rejected from the reality of death. In death itself, he was deprived of death."[51] And now, several chapters later, it becomes increasingly evident to him that he is a divided being. There is one Thomas who has "existence and life" and another, obscure Thomas who possesses "reality and death" and who feeds parasitically on the living man. Brooding on this doubling leads Thomas to an ecstatic overturning of the Cogito: "It was then that, deep within a cave, the madness of the taciturn thinker appeared before me and unintelligible words rung in my ears while I wrote on the wall these sweet words: 'I think, therefore I am not' [*Je pense, donc je ne suis pas*]" (99; 217).

Immediately, Thomas is granted a vision of a flaming lens that becomes conscious of itself as a "monstrous I":

It began to speak and its voice seemed to come from the bottom of my heart. I think, it said, I bring together all that which is light without heat, rays without brilliance, unrefined products; I brew them together and conjugate them, and, in a primary absence of myself, I discover myself as a perfect unity at the point of greatest intensity. I think, it said, I am subject and object of an all-powerful radiation; a sun using all its energy to make itself night, as well as to make itself sun. (99; 218)

The narrative continues. In its first version, the novel of 1941, the lens goes on speaking, while in the "nouvelle version" of nine years later a slight change of punctuation renders it unclear whether it is the lens or Thomas who is speaking. "I think, it said, there at the point. . . ," we hear in 1941; while in the later version we read,

> I think: there at the point where thought joins with me I am able to sub-
> tract myself from being, without diminishing, without changing, by
> means of a metamorphosis which saves me for myself, beyond any point
> of reference from which I might be seized. It is the property of my
> thought, not to assure me of existence (as all things do, as a stone does),
> but to assure me of being in nothingness itself, and to invite me not to
> be, in order to make me feel my marvelous absence.[52] (99–100; 218)

In both versions of the story something fundamental to Descartes's enterprise is placed at risk, and while Blanchot presses into service an argument of Hegel's it is not one the philosopher himself uses against Descartes. What Hegel objects to in the Cogito is not that thought and being are identical but that Descartes does not think through the implications of the immediacy he presents. Thought does not contain a pure and simple immediacy, as Descartes believes it does, since it also harbors the determination to mediate itself with itself. Fichte was the first to realize that, Hegel tells us. Thus prompted we recall the *Wissenschaftslehre* (1794): "Thinking is by no means the essence, but merely a specific determination of existence; and our existence has many other determinations besides this. —*Reinhold* put forward the principle of representation, and in Cartesian form his basic proposition would run: *repraesento, ergo sum,* or more properly: *repraesentans sum, ego sum.* He makes a notable advance over Descartes."[53]

Rather than dwell on the unreflective nature of the Cogito, Blanchot attends to its status as a representation and, in doing so, makes use of the Hegelian reasoning that what is presented to consciousness is the absence and not the presence of being. I have already quoted a passage from the *Geistesphilosophie,* part 3 of *Das System der speculativen Philosophie.* I turn now to the second text that Blanchot cites, Kojève's gloss on a passage from section 7 of the *Phänomenologie des Geistes* where Hegel observes that "conceptual comprehension [*Begreifen*] . . . knows natural existence when cancelled and transcended."[54] Here then is Kojève lecturing on time and eternity in Hegel in the academic year 1938–39:

> the *conceptual* understanding of empirical reality is equivalent to a *murder*. To be sure, Hegel knows full well that it is not necessary to kill a dog in order to understand it through its Concept—that is, in order to give it a name or define it—nor is it necessary to wait for it actually to die in order to do so. However, Hegel says, if the dog were not *mortal*—that is essentially *finite* or limited with respect to its duration—one could not *detach* its Concept from it—that is, cause the Meaning (Essence) that is embodied in the *real* dog to pass into the *non*living word—into the *word* (endowed with a meaning)—that is, into the *abstract* Concept—into the Concept that exists not in the dog (which realizes it) but in the man (who thinks it)—that is, in something *other* than the sensible reality which the concept reveals by its Meaning . . . If the dog were eternal, if it existed outside of Time or without Time, the Concept "dog" would never be *detached* from the dog itself.[55]

And here is Blanchot's reverie, inspired by Hegel and Kojève, of course, but also haunted by Mallarmé:

> Of course my language does not kill anyone. And yet when I say, "This woman," real death has been announced and is already present in my language; my language means that this person, who is here right now, can be detached from herself, removed from her existence and her presence, and suddenly plunged into a nothingness in which there is no existence or presence; my language essentially signifies the possibility of this destruction; it is a constant, bold allusion to such an event. My language does not kill anyone. But if this woman were not really capable of dying, if she were not threatened by death at every moment of her life, bound and joined to death by an essential bond, I would not be able to carry out that ideal negation, that deferred assassination which is what my language is.[56]

Two claims are urged in this imposing paragraph—no "I" without death, no language without death—and it is important to recognize that they occur in a Hegelian or, better, Kojèvian context, though one that Blanchot maintains is not completely controlled by the dialectic. The particular moment of the dialectic is of course nature, where the Idea is alienated from itself; it is the realm of finitude, where everything is marked by contingency, externality, and singleness. Now in any act of representation these traits of natural being are negated in order to free what is universal. In another conception of nature it need not be so. Any reader of Milton's *Paradise Lost* (1667) can readily imagine Adam and Eve conversing before the Fall, two beings as yet untouched by mortality and their language making no existential threat whatsoever. And even in Hegel's less exalted vision of nature, the point at issue turns around finitude rather than death. I can say "This woman" while pointing to Daphne in Bernini's sculpture *Apollo and Daphne*, and, even if I concede that my death is bespoken in that act, the same cannot be said of Daphne, who is finite, not mortal. Naming, for Hegel, cancels what is immediate and natural while yielding what is mediated and spiritual. On Blanchot's account, as we have seen, there is a greater if more disturbing yield: a dialectical comprehension of language *and* a neutral fascination with language. Or, in terms of the anthropological twist that Blanchot keeps in his reading of Hegel, any representation will result in both death (negativity) and dying (unemployed negativity).

With these points in mind, I return to Blanchot on Descartes and, in particular, to *Thomas l'obscur*. The Cogito requires a reference to the present moment each time it is pronounced, for the argument or inference would not secure apodictic certainty if it relied on the vagaries of memory. Yet consciousness does not necessarily imply the presence of existence, it is claimed here, since the very ability to represent oneself as an "I" means that one has hollowed out the existence of that selfhood and now has only the absence of that self. To say "I," even to oneself, is to have lost the presence one claims to have secured. Thus the assertion "I think therefore I am not" is in no way a gratuitous or irrational reversal of the Cogito, subjectively verified by a moment of frenzied grief, as it might well seem on a quick reading of this passage. Rather, it is a dramatized statement of a lost moment in the dialectic, as interpreted by Kojève, that thinking not only grasps the existence of consciousness but also understands that this consciousness can abide without reference to a living presence.

Thomas takes upon himself the import of the lens's vision, not as a notional truth but as a limit experience:

> I think, also said Thomas, and this invisible, inexpressible, nonexistent Thomas I became meant that henceforth I was never there where I was [*je ne fus jamais là où j'étais*], and there was not even anything mysterious about it. My existence became entirely that of an absent person who, in every act I performed, produced the same act and did not perform it.[57]

At heart there is nothing mysterious about the parasitic Thomas. His obscurity arises from a clash of two necessities: consciousness is constrained to indicate him while being unable to present him. His gaze must remain dark.

3

Let us shift our angle of approach a little, just a hair's breadth some will say, and instead of viewing Blanchot listening to Hegel at Jena let us imagine him in conversation with the early German romantics. Here then is Blanchot quoting from Novalis's "Monologue," a short piece most likely dating from 1797–98. It is "a text of angelic penetration," Blanchot tells us, and, unlike Heidegger, he offers no warning about the poet writing within the horizon of absolute idealism.[58] Let us listen to this young poet. "It is amazing, the absurd error people make of imagining they are speaking for the sake of things; no one knows the essential thing about language, that it is concerned only with itself. That is why it is such a marvelous and fruitful mystery— for if someone merely speaks for the sake of speaking, he utters the most splendid, original truths. But if he wants to talk about something definite, the whims of language make him say the most ridiculous false stuff."[59] Unless one values irony over logic, one might be tempted to say that anyone who "speaks for the sake of speaking" is more likely than not to utter banalities and nonsense. But Blanchot prizes the risks of writing and minimizes its failures, even to the extent of entertaining the thought that perhaps there are no "bad narratives."[60] What he finds here and in other passages from Novalis is, first, "the non-romantic essence of romanticism," the movement's tendency to project itself into the past and future and thereby to lose all its specificity; and second, the realization, close to his heart, that "to write is to make (of) speech (a) work [œuvre], but that this work is an unworking [cette œuvre est désœuvrement]; that to speak poetically is to make possible a non-transitive speech whose task is not to say things (not to disappear in what it signifies), but to say (itself) in letting (itself) say, yet without taking itself as the new object of this language without object."[61]

"Speech is the subject [sujet]": this is what Blanchot chiefly values in Novalis's observations about language. It comes down to two motifs. Since poetic speech is all-important, a reference to the "I" is unavoidable; indeed, the lyric "I" must transcend the poem it makes and unmakes. The first motif, then, is a detached reflection on what is created: the unstable synthesis of the playful and the serious known as romantic irony. And in emphasizing that in the act of writing one passes from the first to the third person, Blanchot could be seen as detaching himself from the work even more thoroughly. "Detached from everything, even detachment," he will say in *L'Écriture du désastre*.[62] The second motif is one I have touched on and will return to, the election of presentation over representation; poetic language already *is* matter, like nature. Now in valuing the young poet for the idea that "speech is the subject," Blanchot could just as well have quoted from the—in all likelihood—still younger Novalis of the *Fichte-Studien* (1795–96). In this passage Novalis goes to the heart of Fichte's project, the derivation of the fundamental principle "I = I" from the law of identity, "A = A":

> In the proposition *a is a* lies nothing but a positing, differentiation, and joining. It is a philosophical parallelism. In order to make *a* more clear, *A* gets divided. *Is* becomes established as general content, *a* as determinate form. The essence of identity can only be erected in an illusory sentence [*Scheinsatz*]. We abandon the *identical* in order to present it— Either this only seems to occur—and the imagination would lead us to believe so—that *occurs*, which already *Is*—naturally or through imaginary division and unification—Or we present it through its nonbeing, through something not identical—sign.[63]

"I = I" may well be a *Grundsatz*, as Fichte thinks, but in order to be presented it must minimally assume a linguistic form and so become a *Scheinsatz*, an illusory sentence. The presentation of absolute identity must occur in language, a medium characterized by differentiation; and consequently only the "nonbeing" or absence of the *Grundsatz* can be presented.

The thematics of romantic irony and sensible presentation are bound together, if only because romantic irony unsettles any presentation by drawing attention to its status *as* presentation. Let us take them one at a time, beginning with the first.

1. Novalis's critique of the Fichtean principle "I = I" proceeds by way of romantic irony. Perhaps the possibility of that critique was already in Fichte, as Hegel hints, merely awaiting an extension of his epistemology into aesthetics.[64] Be that as it may, Blanchot closely follows in Novalis's footsteps when stalking the Cogito, both in an early novel like *Thomas l'obscur* and even more clearly in the late *L'Écriture du désastre*:

> What is strange in the Cartesian attitude "I think, therefore I am," is that it only presented itself by speaking, and that speech, precisely, caused it to disappear, suspending the ego of the cogito, consigning thought to anonymity without any subject—to the intimacy of exteriority—and sub-

stituting for living presence (for the existence of the I am) the intense absence of an undesirable and attractive dying . . . That is why one can say that Descartes never knew he was speaking, any more than that he was keeping still. It is on this condition that the lovely truth is preserved.[65]

What are we being told here? That an attempt to secure the "I" as an absolute ground will fail to the extent it ignores its mode of presentation.[66] And that once presentation is duly considered, the Cogito must yield to a beginning still more beginning, which remains obscure.

2. So much then for any attempt to secure transcendental subjectivity by way of the Cogito. But what of writing? It is involved in these arguments if only because Blanchot's argument shifts the discussion from "I am" to "I speak" (and, as he deepens his meditation over the years, to "I write"). For Blanchot as for Novalis, literature is produced under the sign not of *Repräsentation* or *Vorstellung*, both of which presume a mental content that exists prior to inscription, but rather of *Darstellung*, sensible presentation. The intention is to exclude mimesis, understood by way of imitation, as the essence of writing and, with it, all prizing of interiority. In the words that Blanchot gives to the allegorical figure of Literature in "La Littérature et le droit à la mort," "I no longer represent, I am; I do not signify, I present."[67] However, Literature knows something that Descartes does not: to say "I am" is also to say "I am not." What Literature presents is, in all rigor, the unpresentable *as* unpresentable. It is a romantic notion, to be sure, though unlike the Kantian sublime the Blanchotian sublime, if I can call it that, points us to the approach of the neuter rather than to the heavenly city.[68] Rather than a confirmation of the integrity of our souls, the Blanchotian sublime is a contestation of everything, including itself. In later years, once again in agreement with Lévinas, Blanchot will evoke a pure narrative Saying that never coincides with a Said: a standing invitation for skepticism to visit language, no matter how brutally it has been refuted by philosophers or even by itself. "Skepticism," for Blanchot, is another word for the infinite contestation of a consciousness without an ego; and rather than lead to a *Cogito ergo sum* it points to a far less reassuring statement, *Scribo ergo non sum*.

Let us pause for a moment and reflect on Blanchot's argument. It is this. As soon as Descartes pronounces or writes *cogito*, the "I" yields the absence of what it was intended to capture. Rather than correlating knowing and being, the Cogito links knowing and nothingness. The argument has force, then, for as long as one regards the "I" as a self-identical thing, what Heidegger calls "the soul substance."[69] It appears to be restricted to human beings and irreducible to the body. At no time does Blanchot suggest that animals can have selfhood or that bodies are part of selfhood; and from this perspective he seems remarkably Cartesian.

If we grant Blanchot's reasoning, he establishes that the subject of knowing is unpresentable. Note, though, that he does not actually conclude that there is no subject, let alone no self. The "lesson" of *Thomas l'obscur* is that when one says *cogito* one discloses an "invisible, inexpressible, nonexistent Thomas" who does not coincide with the living Thomas. And Blanchot deduces from this state of affairs that the "I" cannot be the source of one's desires and thoughts; whenever one is tempted to say "I think," the less delusive locution would be "it thinks." Now the neutral realm, from which the obscure Thomas approaches his living counterpart, is not the unconscious, or—in Freud's second map of the psyche— the "id" or "it," although the notions of the unconscious and id are placing shots for the more radical thought of the neuter. (A later placing shot, the Lacanian reading of Freud, in which the unconscious is structured as a language, would be far closer.) Relations with psychoanalysis aside, Blanchot's deduction that the "I" is not the source of thought is valid. Yet it follows equally that if there is an egological subject it cannot be presented. Of course it would have to be opaque rather than transparent. That said, one can imagine a reflexive philosopher, even a Kantian, not being worried by Blanchot's analysis.[70] After all, the "I think" that unifies my representations is not presentable to consciousness, and it is only in moral action that I can gain any sense of my self.

Since Kant has been mentioned, a rather unlikely pairing might be ventured. Kant talks of the "I" as an unknowable noumenon, while Blanchot evokes the unknowable that calls the "I" into question before it can be established. The differences between these positions are many and varied. Yet there is nothing in Blanchot's reasoning about the Cogito to disconcert a Kantian who holds that the unity of a self is presupposed rather than given. And one can imagine the Kantian talking (with as much justification as Bataille does, though not in the same tone or from the same site) about enigmatic moments of "communication" in which that self is apprehended. Needless to say, the Kantian would be open to all sorts of attacks, not least of all regarding the scope, status, and strength of the "I think," and so I take a second example, one that is closer to home. One can imagine a phenomenologist—Maurice Merleau-Ponty, for example—speaking of a subject that, while not able to be presented to consciousness, is nonetheless presupposed by each and every act of concrete constitution. In terms of the structure of consciousness, every active synthesis would be shown to open onto a prior passive synthesis; while in terms of genesis, the subject would be shown to develop from an anonymous sensibility.[71] Either way, the self would be always insufficient with respect to itself. And on reflection this is not so very far from what Blanchot entertains about the self when brooding on Freud.[72]

Let us shift perspective a little. Even if one proposes to dismantle the Cartesian knowing "I," one is not thereby obliged to abolish selfhood or subjectivity. A theory of selfhood need not be centered in egology and need not involve what a recent catch cry calls "a return to the subject," but some account of selfhood is needed in order to protect fundamental human rights. In their different ways this is precisely what Emmanuel Lévinas and Paul Ricoeur try to do. Ricoeur retains selfhood while insisting that "self" is to be understood not as a sameness, an *idem*, as with a post-Kantian idealist like Fichte, but as an *ipse*, a site where a singular but heavily layered hermeneutic project is being worked out in time.[73] Unconcerned with the thematics of a narrative project, Lévinas tries to determine a realm prior to theoretical consciousness; and it is this realm, he argues, that registers the claim of the Other on me before the Other can be set forth as the thematic content of my intentional consciousness. What this ethics offers, he suggests, is precisely "a new way of understanding the possibility of an I [*Je*]," in which selfhood is construed by way of responsibility rather than ontology: "In responsibility, which is, as such, irrecusable and non-transferable, I [*je*] am instituted as non-interchangeable: I [*je*] am chosen as unique and incomparable."[74] Selfhood is preserved, not in the nominative ("I") but in the accusative ("me"), although interestingly Lévinas does not seem particularly worried by writing "I."

That Blanchot wishes to defend human rights is clear from his left-wing dissident political activity since the Second World War. And when he does so he sounds more like a liberal than like someone who wishes wholly to erase the "I." Hear him talk to Madeleine Chapsal about the privilege of rights over duty in 1960 in his sole interview, the one he granted with respect to the *Manifeste de 121:* "Right is a free power for which each person, for his part and in relation to himself, is responsible, and which binds him completely and freely: nothing is stronger, nothing is more solemn. That is why one must say: the right to insubordination; it is a matter of each person's sovereign decision."[75] And it is also plain from his Bataillian reservations about projects that he would have more sympathy with Lévinas than with Ricoeur, though he is far less easy than Lévinas about using the first-person singular or even valuing the uniqueness of the "me":

The Other, if he calls upon me [*moi*], calls upon someone who is not I [*moi*]: the first come or the least of men; by no means the unique being I

[*je*] would like to be. It is thus that he assigns me to passivity, addressing himself in me [*moi*] to dying itself.

(The responsibility with which I [*je*] am charged is not mine and causes me not to be I [*et fait que je ne suis plus moi*].)[76]

In calling for a response, the other person does not address me as a unique person, an "I," but summons me in the accusative, as a "me." I am called not because of any particular abilities I may have or because of a responsibility that I personally bear toward the one who calls me. Not at all: the contract between me and the other person came into effect without our having to sign it. I am always and already responsible for him or her but not by dint of being "I." Rather, I am "the first come," the one on the spot, and the call is received by me only because it is addressed in principle to all human beings. Even so, someone (and not just someone or other) acts; and one can legitimately ask what distinguishes this person from the one who does nothing when given the same opportunity. One may be a "me without selfhood" ("un moi sans moi"), while also being a subject of action.[77] How else are we to understand Blanchot's emphasis on possibility as "to be plus the power to be"? But there are matters to which I must return before this one can be taken any further.

4

Scribo, an act of sensible presentation, does not assume a self-presence on the part of the writer, an authenticity that has been hidden by culture or society. And in recognizing that, we can distinguish Blanchot's conception of art from that proposed by most avant-garde groups, even revered ones like the surrealists, who take their cue from Descartes without knowing it and consequently without questioning it. Surrealism "needs to make a clean slate," Blanchot writes, "but above all it seeks its *Cogito* . . . it finds that it is an exact replica of Cartesian experience."[78] How can this association of Descartes and Breton be justified? One can point to an allusion by Breton in the first manifesto, "I believe more and more in the infallibility of my thinking about myself," but a general point provides the stronger link. "What Breton sought . . . is an immediate relationship with his true existence," Blanchot explains, and automatic writing provided exactly that (86; 91). "If I say, or better if I write, 'I suffer,' these words, provided they were written outside the control of my consciousness, not only express my awareness of suffering but are at heart this very awareness" (87; 92). For Blanchot, however, art does not offer an unmediated vision of a true existence, and one cannot elude consciousness while writing in order to assert what abides outside its domain. Neither dreaming nor writing uncovers one's true being, a depth or an immediacy disguised by civilization or reason. Consider Blanchot's meditation on Michel Leiris, who published a record of his dreams long after he left the surrealists:

> In the depths of the dream—admitting that it has a depth, a depth that is all surface—is an allusion to a possibility of being that is anonymous, such that to dream would be to accept this invitation to exist almost anonymously, outside of oneself, under the spell of this outside and with the enigmatic assurance of semblance: a self without self, incapable of recognizing itself as such because it cannot be the subject of itself. Who would dare transfer to the dreamer—be it at the invitation of the evil genius—the privilege of the *Cogito* and allow him to utter with full confidence: "I dream, therefore I am"? At most one might propose for him to say, "Where I dream, there it is awake [*Là où je rêve, cela veille*]."[79]

A self is not established then erased but abides in two dimensions at once, one of negativity and power (the "I") and one of neutrality and powerlessness (the selfless self of dreams).

While this formulation once more gives the lie to commentators who maintain that Blanchot simply disparages and disperses the "I," it stands in need of clarification. To begin with, the two dimensions that lay claim to what one of them would call the self cannot be harnessed into a dialectical relationship; the powerlessness of the neutral dimension exceeds any couple of "power" and "powerlessness" that might be sublated. Moreover, these dimensions are not symmetrical; in advance of whatever self may be erected by way of negativity, the neutral prevents it from becoming a subject in the Cartesian-Kantian sense of the word. "I think" must make room for "it thinks." The subject is immemorially dead, Blanchot will tell us; there never was a "self" to have been lost.[80] Yet if the self was never an *idem*, could it have been and still be an *ipse*? Yes, if by saying that one allows Blanchot to reset the word in his own terms. For he is committed to there being an "I" that is formed dialectically and that takes part in everyday life. This "I" does not neatly converge with the ethical self that is formed by virtue of the Other's call. Nor does this "I" precede the community to which it belongs.[81] It exists merely in terms of realizing possibilities, and in doing so generates effects of subjectivity. Although he makes nothing of it, this dialectical ego helps Blanchot to defend the rights of the individual against oppression without falling into self-contradiction, or to write in the first-person singular before remembering to place scare quotes around the "I."

To return to the question of literature and consciousness. Blanchot will tell us that literature is an experience—*une expérience* rather than *une vécue*—of perpetual assertion and contestation, a response to what he calls "the original experience" ("l'expérience originelle"), a relation to death as the impossibility of dying. Given this stress on experience, could one establish a literary criticism, as Kant erected a philosophical criticism, by adducing the conditions of possibility for literary experience? Yes and no. Yes, because literature inaugurates itself by seeking a condition of possibility. No, because literature elaborates itself by contesting that very condition of possibility, and because "experience" here is used more in a Hegelian than in a Kantian sense: to write requires putting the work (and the self as a work) at risk.[82] And yet, supposing the authority of experience to be thoroughly expiated in writing, there could be no writing, no movement of self-erasure, without an experience of the beginning. Is this beginning the "light of the 'Cogito'" that Blanchot speaks of when meditating on Descartes? No, for as Blanchot tells us, the Cogito is both shaken and left intact by "a beginning still more beginning." In order to approach this thought, I could turn to many places in Blanchot's criticism, but perhaps none is more lucid than the final chapter of *L'Espace littéraire* (1955):

What the work says is the word *beginning* [*commencement*]. But today the work is the work of art: art is its starting point. And it says "the beginning" when it says "art," which is its origin [*origine*] and whose essence has become its task. But where has art led us? To a time before the world, before the beginning. It has cast us out of our power to begin and to end; it has turned us toward the outside where there is no intimacy, no place to rest. It has led us into the infinite migration of error. For we seek art's essence, and it lies where the nontrue admits of nothing essential. We appeal to art's sovereignty: it ruins the kingdom. It ruins the origin by returning to it the errant immensity of directionless eternity . . . That the work is able to pronounce the word *beginning* precisely because the origin attracts it to the place where it risks utter ruin, and because, precisely, it must escape *with a leap* the implacable insistence of something having neither beginning nor end: this might well be said.[83]

To distinguish origin and beginning, as is done here, is to allow people to approach art under the sign of gnosticism. If the center of *L'Espace littéraire* is to be found in "Le Regard d'Orphée," as Blanchot indicates, we can understand that text only when we recognize that Orpheus is Orphic. Not that the dominant figure of that meditation is a movement from a primal fullness to an existential void but rather that creation for Blanchot is a fall, what he called a disaster long before composing *L'Écriture du désastre* (1980).[84] Literature is a quest for an obscure origin that comes into being only once the quest has commenced and that withdraws when approached. It leads to no vision but rather to a state of fascination before a magnetizing play of empty images. One is transfixed, unable to escape from this ghostly spectacle. So the writer encounters something—an approach—that, while it discloses itself only in the exhaustion of possibility, belongs to a time other than that of dialectic, meaning, and truth. "The Neuter does not come first, eternal follower that precedes": and with this gesture Blanchot acknowledges the strange logic of an experience *après coup*, what he elsewhere calls the "original experience."[85] To put this in the terms we have been using, the neuter is the "beginning still more beginning," and one can start to write only by freeing oneself from the fascination it exerts, by pronouncing a decisive *"Cogito."* Consequently the work will consist of two inseparable and irreducible movements that must be forced to engage one another and thereby produce a communication between the impossible and the possible.

From this description it might seem that the artist, especially the romantic artist, is the one who is compromised by the "beginning still more beginning" that shakes all certainty, including the Cogito, and who must live within the tension of bringing the possible and the impossible together. This squares with Blanchot's reading of Rilke: "it is correct to say that the artist's experience is an ecstatic experience and that it is . . . an experience of death."[86] Years later, though, when the influence of Bataille has been modified in certain respects, Blanchot makes it plain that this would be a special case. Impossibility "would not be the privilege of some exceptional experience, but behind each one and as though its other dimension."[87] This needs some clarification, as Blanchot realizes, although his explanatory remarks are themselves offered at a high level of abstraction. An example: "it is perhaps given to us to 'live' each of the events that is ours by way of a double relation. We live it one time as something we comprehend, grasp, bear, and master . . . we live it another time as something that escapes all employ and all end, and more, as that which escapes our very capacity to undergo it, but whose trial we cannot escape . . . The experience of non-experience."[88]

This kind of formulation is familiar in religious writings, and the resemblance is liable to introduce confusion. For example, in his major work on the philosophy of religion S. L. Frank maintains that *"Everything that is known, habitual, familiar, does not stop being an unknowable mystery for us."*[89] And Bataille, on whom Blanchot is commenting in the passage I quoted in the previous paragraph, tells us that "Within the experience of un-knowing of which I speak, there remains a religious experience."[90] But Blanchot is not affirming a religious transcendence in what we know, even though the unknown is transcendent in the phenomenological sense of the word. "Non-experience," for him, answers to something far more common than religious transcendence, for "it is offered in the most common suffering, and first of all in physical suffering" where we subsist in an endless present we cannot master; "we are delivered over to another time—to time as other, as absence and neutrality."[91] Again, though, this appears to be a special kind of experience. There are times when we suffer, other times when we enjoy life. To which Blanchot responds that the suffering he has in mind is "not that of a paroxysmic state where the self cries out and is torn apart, but rather of a suffering that is almost indifferent" (44; 63). This suffering must be common to everyone, approaching us at all times, while not something we can actually undergo. It is akin to what Heidegger would call an "ontological attunement." Let us try to characterize it more narrowly.

5

Nowhere does Blanchot find a "suffering that is almost indifferent" more memorably than in Robert Antelme's relation of his internment in an SS labor camp, *L'Espèce humaine* (1947). Early on in that remarkable narrative, we witness a disassociation of the self when the narrator hears a roll call: "Laughter when my name is called, and I reply 'Present.' It sounded outlandish in my ear; but I'd recognized it. And so for one brief instant I had been directly designated here, I and no other had been addressed [*on s'est adressé à moi seul*], I had been specially solicited—I, myself, irreplaceable [*moi, irremplaçable*]! And there I was. Someone turned up to say yes to this sound, which was at least as much my name as I was myself, in this place."[92] And later we learn how, although extreme hardship reduces differences between the prisoners, each clings to a sense of singularity. "And, since it's impossible here to fulfill anything of that singularity, you are able to believe sometimes that you are outside life, on some sort of horrible vacation from it. But this is a life we are leading, it is our real life; we don't have any other to live . . . So you also have to struggle not to allow yourself to sink beneath anonymity, not to cease demanding of yourself what one doesn't demand of another. You discover that you can let go of yourself to an extent you never imagined possible before" (87). And later still, as the narrator touches the boundaries of nature, he realizes with "absolute clarity" that "there are not several human races, there is only one human race" (219). At the limit of affliction, when one is almost dispossessed of selfhood, one can still affirm a "we" that cannot be destroyed by those wielding force. To say "I" requires a power, a possibility of negating nature, and the same would be true of saying "we" in the sense of a collective subject. The "we" that those in the labor camp can affirm, however, has neither a positive nor a negative relation to power. As Antelme writes, the executioner "can kill a man, but he can't change him into something else" (220).

In fact, however, it is precisely the change that occurs in a human being that most interests Blanchot in *L'Espèce humaine*. Over the course of a dialogue about the book, two unidentified voices explore the thought that in extreme suffering, such as in the camps, it is indeed possible to lose the power to say "I" and to become the Other. "Each time the question: Who is '*Autrui*'? emerges in our words I think of the book by Robert Antelme," begins the first voice.[93] It is a jolting remark because *Autrui* is a word intimately associated with Lévinas and one that Blanchot has considered earlier in *L'Entretien infini*.[94] For Lévinas, *Autrui* is the other person who calls me to responsibility, who makes me a self though only in the accusative ("me") and never in the nominative ("I"). Not only does Blanchot seek to rethink *Autrui* from the perspective offered by Antelme but also he focuses on something that Lévinas would never countenance: a movement whereby the self becomes *Autrui*. The first speaker notes that "human power is capable of anything"; the SS, or any group like them, can master the subject, the *ego cogito*, and erase the horizon that surrounds him or her. No longer a subject, the deported one is unable to maintain selfhood: work gives him or her no meaning, no value, but only brings dying all the more close through pointless exhaustion. The SS control all possibility, the second speaker concedes: they can treat the other person as *autre*, but they cannot master the relation of impossibility in which the other is disclosed as *Autrui*, the stranger, the dispossessed, the suffering one in whom the irreducibly human is revealed. At the extreme limit, the man or woman of the camps responds to the pressure of *Autrui* by surviving, not on one's own account but by maintaining an attachment to life that is almost impersonal. As the second speaker puts it, in suffering one affirms "*an egoism without ego*" (133; 196). The first speaker responds, "It is as though in nourishing myself at the level of subsistence it is not I whom I nourished; it is as though I received the Other [*l'Autre*], host not to myself but to the unknown and the foreign" (133; 196). Elsewhere, Blanchot notes that in the "absolute absence of hope," as in the camps, the final human needs are rendered "sacred."[95]

In the extremity of suffering there is formed then a new self; it is no longer a subject but is a representative of what is irreducibly human in humankind. It receives the human "in the justice of a true *speech*" (134; 197), as the second speaker has it, while the first speaker notes that inevitably this new self, precisely because it is a *self*, is placed back in "a situation of dialectical struggle so he may once again consider himself as a force" (134; 197). And he adds, "We always come back, then, to the exigency of this double relation" (134; 198), an engagement with the possible as well as a response to the impossible. In the camps, however, there can be no speech for *Autrui*: that must wait for the liberation, if it comes in time. Speech is held in reserve. "It is this truly infinite speech," the second speaker tells us, "that each of those who had been handed over to the impossible experience of being for himself or herself the 'other' [*autrui*] felt called upon, now back in the world, to represent to us in speaking endlessly, without stopping, for the first time" (135; 199). *L'Espèce humaine* is narrated from an impossible site, where the Self became Other and is now returning to itself in and through the act of writing; and it is in listening to this voice, authoritative and strange, that we can begin to hear the authentic tones of humankind. Indeed, it is this murmur that indicates, Blanchot thinks, a communism "beyond communism" (xii; viii). Where *Autrui* is first and foremost an ethical figure for Lévinas, for Blanchot it takes hold first of all at the level of community.

The "I" that returns to the social world, if it is able to do so, loses its character as *Autrui* and finds itself faced once more with others outside the self. This is not to say that the "I" simply reforms; it remains a "canonic abbreviation" because it cannot ground itself, not because it is the sum of its diverse experiences.[96] Blanchot cannot concur with Marcel's musings about self-identity in *À la recherche du temps perdu*. "I was not one man only, but as it were the march-past of a composite army in which there were passionate men, indifferent men, jealous men . . . "[97] Not at all: for Blanchot, the "I" may be a plurality of selves but they are always in question as selves. To give due weight to this point let us overhear the narrator in *Le Dernier Homme* (1957): "slowly—abruptly—the thought occurred to me that this story had no witness: I was there—the 'I' was already no more than a Who?, a whole crowd of Who?s . . . "[98] The point is phenomenological. Already in lectures composing *Die Grundprobleme der Phänomenologie* (1927), Heidegger was telling his students that Dasein "cannot at all be interrogated as such by the question *What* is this? We can access to this being only if we ask: *Who* is it? The Dasein is not constituted by whatness but—if we may coin the expression—by *whoness*."[99] Being human is to be grasped not by appeals to the *animal rationale* or to the "I" as *subjectum* but by attending to something more fundamental, something that does not coincide with an "I." As we hear in *Sein und Zeit*, "It could be that the 'who' of everyday Dasein just is *not* the 'I myself.'"[100] Or, as one of the voices puts it in a dialogue signed by Blanchot, "'Who,' without claiming to once again put *the ego* into question, does not find its proper site, does not let itself be assumed by Me: the 'it' that is perhaps no longer the it of it is raining, not even the it of it is, but without ceasing to be personal, does not let itself be measured by the impersonal, either, and keeps us at the edge of the unknown."[101]

The argument Blanchot uses to support the view that an "I" does not coincide with a "me" is that the "I" is open to both the possibility of death and the impossibility of dying. In his world, a subject would not be the transcendental ground of experience, as Kant maintains. Rather, an "I" would be both affirmed and contested in experiencing an aporia of death and dying. This is a long way from the constituted subject sketched by Descartes and filled in by Kant; but there seems to be no reason to take Blanchot at his word in prizing suffering in the dissolution of the subject. Since the "I" is vulnerable to the endless approach of dying, there is a suffering that, strictly speaking, concerns no one because in its passivity the self is already other than itself. And one need not be on one's deathbed to experience this approach. Searching for an example, I interrupt the narrative of *Celui qui ne m'accompagnait pas*:

> When did I give myself up to this risk? Perhaps while sleeping, perhaps in the course of a night when, by an unreflecting movement, by a single word into which I had put all of myself, the decision of time, having been shaken, caused me to pass into the indecision of the absence of time, there where the end is always still the unending. But if that is an imprudence, why mightn't I have committed it? could I live without committing it? did I regret it? Free not to surrender myself to this risk, don't I surrender myself to it from one moment to the next? and at present, is this beginning again? but nevertheless it is not beginning again, it is an absolutely different moment, without any parallel, without any tie to the past, without any concern for the future, and yet it is also beginning again, is the same, is the emptiness of repetition, the infinite pain that always passes through the same point again, and always, at whatever moment it may be, this is said, and eternally I express it.[102]

The suffering depicted in living an event as an image is entirely credible, and I have no wish to diminish it. Nevertheless, Blanchot indicates alternate ways in which the "I" yields to a "Someone"—a "he," a "we," or a "Who?"—that are less anguished. True, he maintains that community is founded on the dying of another, and so for him the possibility of sociality is associated from the very beginning with a foretaste of mourning.

We can be more precise about this by entertaining a counterexample. One might object that while it is true that we are exposed collectively to death, there is a case to be made that an experience of birth also invokes community. A pregnant woman in her third term is approached by people she does not know; her belly is patted and she is wished well. The father, pushing a stroller down the road, is hailed wherever he goes by people whose names he does not know. And both incidents are neither personal nor impersonal; they are moments of communication. The force of the counterexample must be acknowledged. Yet what underwrites this eruption of community is not simply a recognition of new life but a relaxation of one's fear of death: humankind will survive, even though I will not. If community turns on the dying of the other person, it also involves an adumbration of my death. That said, not all of Blanchot's meditations on community are directly touched by a tone of mourning. The sense of belonging to a community that is unavowable in the first-person singular can be an occasion of joy for Blanchot, as his warm evocation of May 1968 attests.[103] And indeed he appeals time and again to the feeling of calm that comes with losing the power to say "I," whether in writing or in ordinary acts of human exchange. In the words of L'Attente l'oubli (1962): "With what melancholy and yet with what calm certainty he felt that he would never again be able to say 'I.'"[104]

Yet Blanchot continues to say "I," despite his disbelief that the Cogito reveals a stable origin. And he talks in this way without contradicting himself or relying on a convenient formula, because a self—a subject of action, not a metaphysical subject—is created by any dialectic of possibility. While dying approaches us endlessly, it does so amid a tangle of acts that have civic, fraternal, and sororial significance. The possibility that is "to be plus the power to be" is not to be dismissed or slighted, even though the locus of our desires and thoughts does not simply trace out a human face. In a late text Blanchot acknowledges this more clearly than in his more hyperbolic statements about selfhood: "Write in order that the negative and the neutral, in their always concealed difference—in the most dangerous of proximities—might recall to each other their respective specificity, the one working, the other un-working [l'un travaillant l'autre désoeuvrant]."[105] No one, not even Nietzsche, avoids this doubleness. He too speaks now "of the whole" and now "of the fragment, of plurality, of separation": the self is affirmed to be strong and at the same time is disarticulated.[106] None of this allows the self to be figured as a subject, needless to say, although there are times when Blanchot is prepared to envisage the possibility of something's taking the place of the subject. There is a danger, he says, that we will die inattentively, and another danger that, being distracted from death, we do not realize that the distraction is itself deathly. The danger is to be welcomed, for it keeps watch, and "this vigilance is the 'subject' of the experience, that which undergoes it, leads it, precipitates it, and holds it back in order to delay it at its moment of immanence."[107]

Blanchot may tell us that there is no self-present, unified subject, but in fact he shows us something else. First, if there is a transcendental subject of knowing, it cannot be presented to consciousness. Second, the presence and presentability of a *cogito* are not necessary conditions for subjectivity: a subject of action is created by being summoned by another person, not by virtue of possessing intentional consciousness. And third, although the suffering Self becomes the Other and is attached to life in an almost impersonal way, as soon as this Other represents a "collective structure" it is returned to play a dialectical role in society: even at extreme limits the "I" is never simply abandoned or lost. If we see Blanchot's critique as breaking with a style of thinking inaugurated by Descartes and variously explored by the romantics and postromantics, we would be only partly correct. The Cogito may be shaken by Blanchot's meditations on the neuter but every beginning word that he writes is, as he says, "illuminated by the light of the 'Cogito.'"

5

•

BLANCHOT'S "TRIAL OF EXPERIENCE"

1

On May 5, 1943, Blanchot headed his regular review for the *Journal des Débats* with the title of Bataille's new book, *L'Expérience intérieure*. It was the first time he had elevated the word *expérience* to the rank of title, although it was neither the first nor the last time that he would ponder the concept. How life and work interact, how rhetoric sits with lived events, how mystics touch the divine, how the other person always escapes one's consciousness: all these topics presume a reference to experience, and since Blanchot broods on them week after week it is hardly unexpected that he uses both the word and the concept. From the beginning of his career as a critic, though, Blanchot shows himself to be far less interested in the standard epistemological topics in the philosophy of experience—sensation and perception, the "given," the foundations of knowledge—than in how experience and writing are related.[1] Romanticism hails literature as experience, we are told, and the example of Jean-Paul (1763–1825) reveals that the writing of literature permits us to find "a more authentic life," a notion Blanchot will question and develop.[2] He does not deduce the experience of writing from a rigorously determined notion of experience but rather proceeds in exactly the opposite direction: we will learn something important about experience if we approach literature in the right way. So we come across titles such as "L'Expérience de Proust," "L'Expérience magique d'Henri Michaux," "Gide et la littérature d'expérience," and "L'Expérience de Lautréamont."[3]

Read in the broad context of French criticism before and after the Second World War, none of these titles is at all unusual. Indeed, as Jean Pfeiffer remarked in 1950, "For the past thirty years, the term 'experience' has enjoyed a singular favor in literature."[4] Certainly the word had been essential to modernism, in both its artistic and theological manifestations, and certainly the prestige of phenomenology had conferred a luster on the word. With the fifth of the *Logical Investigations* (1900), Husserl had led the way back to experience while all the time stressing that he was not advocating a thoroughgoing subjectivism. What interests Husserl is not the flow of actual experience registered by an "I" but the intentional relationship maintained by consciousness with respect to the world. The ego does not contain external events that have been mentally lived through but rather has "the relevant acts of perceiving, judging etc., with their variable sense-material, their interpretative content, their assertive characters, etc." It follows, as Husserl says, that "there is no difference between the experience [*erlebten*] or conscious content and the experience itself [*Erlebnis selbst*]."[5] If classical phenomenology had lost some of its appeal by mid-century, the theme of experience had not: in 1950 Heidegger published a beautiful and important work, "Hegel's Concept of Experience [*Erfahrung*]," in *Holzwege*.

Thirty years before, in his War Emergency lectures of 1919, Heidegger had made his audience aware that things had changed in the passage from the nineteenth to the twentieth century. Our contemporary existence is all too often shaped by a theoretical attitude to life, he warns us, an attitude that reduces the possibility of authentic experience. In order to evoke this situation he coined the word *Entleben*, "de-experience," and in order to affirm the inherent meaning of life he sought to identify phenomenological and hermeneutical intuition. When we allow life to express itself by way of hermeneutical intuition we have "experience of experience" ("Erleben des Erlebens") in which no theoretical and objectifying positings can find a place to stand.[6] It takes only a step or two from here for Heidegger to be in a position to make his fundamental criticisms of Husserl: to focus on *Erlebnisse*, individual private perceptions, is to ignore, first, that experience is temporal and, second, that it cannot be evoked in abstraction from one's concrete involvement in the shared, public world about one. In sum, we might say that if twentieth-century literature values experience it is partly because it aligns itself with life rather than with theory.

Life to come or life that has been lived? Aristotle tells us in *Posterior Analytics* 100a that experience (ἐμπειρία) means having many memories of the same thing. "Experience" for Pfeiffer, however, is not directed from the present to the past but an opening of the present to the future. In contemporary terms, this understanding takes its cue not from psychoanalysis, which teaches that infantile memories are buried deep within the self, but from surrealism which urges that the voices that speak to us are always ahead of us. For the writer, the experience to be valued is that which takes shape as one writes. One reason the word *expérience* has received special treatment over the period from 1920 to 1950 is that it denotes both experiment and experience; and, as Pfeiffer reminds us, the influence of surrealism did much to promote artistic experiment. He could have cited Michel Leiris writing about "expérience" in *Biffures*, which appeared in 1949, not least of all because Leiris straddles the border between a literature of experiment and of experience.[7] But he does not. Instead, he suggests that, with the exception of surrealism, all the other contemporary senses of *expérience* are at heart gathered in Bataille's notion of "expérience intérieure."

For an essay written after the glory days of *Lebensphilosophie*, phenomenology, and vitalism, all of which touched French literature in one way or another, this is a very odd proposal. There is nothing in "inner experience" that would have pleased Dilthey. No Bergsonian would find "primal experience" there, and no Husserlian would find "intuition" there either. Besides, Bataille explicitly draws a line between his understanding of experience ("a voyage to the end of the possible of man") which pursues the path of unknowing and that of a phenomenologist like Husserl who speaks of *Anschauung, Erfahrung*, and *Intuition* with a view to establishing and grounding our knowledge of the world.[8] One might object that Bataille drew this distinction too boldly or too quickly; after all, Husserl prized the principle that intuition exceeds concepts. There is always more experience to be had of an object once one has performed the *epochē* and pursued the reduction, no matter how much one has observed it. This is not Pfeiffer's concern, however. He is less interested in detail than in the broad sweep of events: the frequency with which "expérience" appears in criticism testifies, he thinks, to an uneasiness or malaise with respect to literature. It is as though literature is no longer sufficient unto itself.[9] "It wants to be something else, or something more than what it is. It wants to be an experience, it wants to know itself, it wants to be lived" (55).

Having said that, Pfeiffer immediately turns to Blanchot. It is appropriate, given the importance he attributes to "inner experience," since, as we know, Bataille does not get very far into his book before acknowledging the influence of his new friend. One day Blanchot "stated simply this principle, that experience itself is authority (but that authority expiates itself)."[10] Yet while Pfeiffer takes Blanchot to have defined "experience" for writers, it is not this remark he has in mind but a passage of *Lautréamont et Sade* (1949). I will consider it in a moment. Beforehand, let us see how Pfeiffer answers the central question he poses, "What is 'experience' for Blanchot?" He begins by focusing on *Thomas l'obscur*, *Aminadab*, and *Le Très-Haut*. These novels record the "lived experience" of their characters, we are told, but because "the language of experience is not different from the experience of language," each work is not so much an image of a completed event as that of "its incompletion, its obsession and its drama" (56). Thomas in *Aminadab* and Sorge in *Le Très-Haut* descend into hell; it is not only "a subjective experience" but also "an experience of subjectivity itself" (57). Each descent resembles an initiation or, better, a "*counter-initiation*" (58), for Thomas and Sorge live whatever happens to them without assigning meanings to occurrences or deducing projects from them.

When Pfeiffer reaches *L'Arrêt de mort*, he recognizes the strange power of this récit to suspend the categories of plausibility and implausibility. The narrative allows us to glimpse how "the experience of being slides on the plane of literature and language" (60). Seeking a passage to cite in support of his judgment, he finds he need go no further than the first paragraph: "If I have written books, it has been in the hope that they would put an end to it all. If I have written novels, they have come into being just as the words began to shrink back from the truth."[11] After pausing to take in that second sentence, Pfeiffer suggests leaving "the plane of particular exploits" in order to approach "the problem of the writer." *The* problem? Is there just *one*? Doubtless Blanchot believes there to be a central issue around which the writer circles endlessly, and in the second sentence that Pfeiffer quotes he announces it. When read attentively, this sentence unfolds much of what Blanchot has to tell us about literature, and it does so while intimating his distance from Heidegger's view of art. "The nature of art, on which both the art work and the artist depend, is the setting-itself-into-work of truth," says the philosopher in the mid 1930s.[12] Art involves words shrinking back from the truth, replies the writer in 1948. His point is Hegelian. In the *Phänomenologie des Geistes* we are told of "the divine nature" of speech, its ability to turn "the mere 'meaning' right round about, making it into something else, and so not letting it come the length of words at all."[13] Of course Blanchot and Heidegger are not as starkly opposed as this somewhat artificially staged exchange suggests. "Truth" for Heidegger is a re-veiling as well as a revealing, and when Blanchot separates truth and words he is scarcely endorsing the untrue. Yet their emphases are more than rhetorical. The philosopher is concerned with art lighting up the world, the writer with art's strange relation—a relation so strange it is "without relation"—with a neutral realm in which there is neither light nor meaning, neither truth nor falsity.

To return to Pfeiffer. It is in passing from the novels and récits to "La Littérature et le droit à la mort," he believes, that he will be able to answer his question about the meaning of "expérience" for Blanchot; and as though to stress the importance of generality, he fastens onto a philosophical reference in that essay, a line that Blanchot adapts from Hegel's *Phänomenologie*. For Hegel, "the life of the mind . . . endures death and in death maintains its being" (93). Blanchot gives a dialectical twist to this proposition by figuring language as the life of the mind. In doing so, he can explain precisely why the life of mind works through death. As Hegel himself saw, the very act of calling a particular cat "cat" annihilates its absolute singularity.[14] Two things quickly follow from this. First, to speak is to bespeak one's demise. Pfeiffer quotes Blanchot: "Therefore it is accurate to say that when I speak, death speaks in me."[15] Second, to pronounce any common noun is to possess not the singular being that it names but only its being as a concept. Again, Blanchot is quoted, and this time one can hear Mallarmé as well as Hegel murmuring in the background: "The word gives me the being, but it gives it to me deprived of being."[16]

Faced with Blanchot's recasting of Hegel, Pfeiffer approaches the French writer as though he were a wayward French Hegelian, influenced no doubt by Kojève, and proceeds to interpret him in those terms. Although all circumstances in life are marked by death, "there is no experience of death or the void; there is only experience of negation or, rather, negation is the very motor of experience" (64). Negation affirms, we are reminded, and self-negation affirms all the more strongly. Pfeiffer is right: there is a Hegelianism in Blanchot. And we have also seen that there is a Blanchot who discerns something in art that resists the dialectic, such as when he tells us that "art and the work of art . . . assert, behind the hope of surviving, the despair of existing endlessly."[17] In creating a work the writer also detaches consciousness from self. Outside the dialectic of being and nothingness, and therefore unable to die, this consciousness is condemned to an interminable dying. All this eerie talk is bypassed in the remark that language never loses the ability to deny and destroy. To which Pfeiffer adds, "That's why negation is not death, but life, and there is something in life that cannot be destroyed because life is also the negation of itself. It is why life depends on death, but also why it destroys death, because it cannot know it" (64). This sounds like a Hegelian account of *Erfahrung* as speculative adventure: the exile and return, as mediated, of what was once supposed to be immediate to consciousness.[18] Yet while experience, on Pfeiffer's understanding of Blanchot, is dialectical, it is not teleological. Nor is it religious. If it has a rapport with mysticism, he suggests, it is only because the mystics challenge the authority of theology (64). The judgment is entirely defensible. Even so, we should not be too quick to agree with it: maybe Blanchot can tell us more than that about the relations of literature and religion, among other things.

2

Pfeiffer orientates himself with respect to Blanchot's essay on Lautréamont, specifically the passage that addresses the relationships between lucidity and obscurity in "Maldoror's experience."[19] *Les Chants*, Blanchot tells us, is a "work of lucidity, *par excellence*" (90), although this clarity first loses and then denounces itself. Lucidity, he reminds us, can function while absent as well as while present. That, indeed, is essential to the dialectic of composition. For the writer "institutes between his work [*ouvrage*] and his lucidity [*lucidité*] a movement of composition and of reciprocal development" (90). It is not only a movement but also a labor, one that is "important and complex, a task that we call *experience* [*expérience*]" (90). At the completion of this process, the work will have made use of the spirit while serving it, and it will be "absolutely lucid, if *it is the work of lucidity* and if *lucidity is its work*" (91). Never perhaps has Blanchot sounded so Hegelian, and never perhaps has *lucidité* sounded so German.

And yet no sooner has Blanchot made this general statement than he qualifies it. *Les Chants* is not one work among others; it is exemplary, a model for work that has no model. It is more arresting than either Rimbaud's *Les Illuminations* (1886), which overwhelms the spirit, or *Une Saison en enfer* (1873), "which instead of an experience is the narration of an experience" (91). The distinction is intriguing, for it seems that *Les Illuminations* is too condensed and too powerful to be coaxed into a dialectic while *Une Saison en enfer* is too faint as experience to possess much negativity. Before one can weigh up the merits of those two works, we are drawn to a footnote that acknowledges that "in Rimbaud, by other paths, poetry is experience itself" (91). Exactly what that judgment might mean is suggested by Blanchot when he places himself beside the young poet about to begin writing *Les Chants:*

> What did Lautréamont have in mind, the night he wrote the first words, "May it please heaven that . . . "? It is insufficient to say that, in this first moment, Lautréamont did not have, completely formed, the recollection of six songs that he was going to write. One must say more: not only were the six songs not in his mind, but this mind did not yet exist, and the sole end that he could have had was this distant mind, this hope of a mind which, at the moment when *Maldoror* would be written, would bring to him all the desired force to write it. (91)

Again, one thinks of Hegel telling us in the *Phänomenologie des Geistes* that the content of *Erfahrung*—namely *Geist*, mind or spirit—is inherently substance; and this spirit "is the development of itself explicitly to what it is inherently and implicitly." In experience a transformation occurs, "of Substance into Subject."[20]

Blanchot developed the same thought with regard to Michel Leiris in 1947. "Writing is nothing," he wrote, "if it does not involve the writer in a movement full of risks that will change him in one way or another."[21] These risks are detailed more fully when he writes about André Gide. There we are told that literature "is an experience that is essentially deceiving, and that is what creates all its value . . ." Why construe literature's value by way of deceit? Because literature prizes itself while also calling itself into question. Needless to say, a poem or a novel might condemn the poetry or the fiction of an earlier generation, but in doing so it does not denounce art itself as "mystification or deception," even though there are very good grounds for doing so.[22] Now let us hear how Blanchot finishes the sentence about the author in general and Gide in particular: "but this illusion, deceiving him, carries him away and, carrying him away by the most ambiguous movement, gives him, as he chooses, a chance either to lose what he had already thought he found, or to discover what he can no longer lose."[23] The ambiguity is between the possible and the impossible, death and dying, that which confers meaning and that which cannot be ascribed a meaning. To write is to risk losing one's relation to meaning and the world or, equally, to risk finding oneself in relation with what has no meaning and no world (which means it will be a relation without relation). With such things in mind we are less likely to think of experience in Hegel's sense, of substance transformed into subject, than of Bataille observing that experience is "a voyage to the end of the possible of man." We are less likely to think with Pfeiffer that Blanchot's characters undergo both "a subjective experience" and "an experience of subjectivity itself" than to recall one reason why Blanchot approved of the surrealists. They show that "Language no longer has anything to do with the subject, it is an object that leads us and can lose us; it has a value beyond our value."[24]

When Blanchot renders literature as experience or experiment and finds its value in leading the writer "to attain the inaccessible," as he does when writing about Leiris, he is not regarding literature as simply a means to an end. Unlike Sartrean engagement, contestation respects the literary functioning of a text, and, if anything, it grants a slight privilege to poetry over prose. Yet unlike Hegel, for whom writing contributes to the development of the subject, Blanchotian contestation calls the subject into question. Michel Foucault was alert to this, seeing Blanchot as an exemplary witness to a historical mutation, a new *episteme* characterized by the erasure of the subject, that would definitely remove us from the age that stretches from Descartes to Hegel and from Hegel to Husserl.[25] Regarding literature as experience is valuable, Foucault thinks, not so much for what it tells us about literature but for what it reveals about experience. In Mallarmé and Kafka, in Bataille and Blanchot, literature offers a way of wresting ourselves from the power of the "I think" so that, through the multiplications of "I speak," we may encounter what Blanchot calls "the Outside."[26] The Pseudo-Dionysius might have caught sight of this Outside, we are told, although we are also assured that for Blanchot the neutral state has nothing to do with mysticism. There is no "shelter in which experience can rest" (53), no "Word" that can "wrap and gather oneself in the dazzling interiority of a thought that is rightfully Being and Speech . . . even if it is the silence beyond all language, and the nothingness beyond all being" (16).

If we can hear Foucault's firm rejection of Christianity in these lines, we can also wonder a little about his reasons. He is right to call an association of the Pseudo-Dionysius and Blanchot "rash" (17). It is true to say that the Pseudo-Dionysius contemplated something exceeding the limits of western thought, a vision of the deity as above or beyond what is unified, although he did not do so without the support of Plotinus and Proclus. In the *Divine Names* and the *Mystical Theology* God is imagined to abide beyond the reach of the distinction between unity and multiplicity, to subsist beyond all conceivable ways of being. So the Pseudo-Dionysius does, in a sense, evoke an "outside." Yet while the divinity exceeds all being, it is not to be regarded by way of absence or emptiness. On the contrary, it is overfull; it perpetually spills over into beings. (The Areopagite speaks of the deity's "exceeding fullness.")[27] Compare that understanding of what is beyond being with Blanchot's conception of the Outside. As we have already seen, what intrigues Blanchot is that a being or an event presents itself as both itself and its image. The imaginary, he tells us in an essay on Proust, is a "moving absence, without events to hide it, without presence to obstruct it, in this emptiness always in the process of becoming." It is a place where one can no longer apply psychology, for "there is no more interiority, for everything that is interior is deployed outwardly, takes the form of an image." To which he adds, "the essence of the image is to be entirely outside [*au-dehors*], without intimacy, and yet more inaccessible and more mysterious than the innermost thought, without signification, but summoning the profundity of every possible meaning unrevealed and yet manifest."[28] This Outside is transcendent in the phenomenological sense of the word but not in the religious sense that fits the Pseudo-Dionysius's superabundant deity, and it is entirely consequent upon the ontological attunement that makes us stall in fascination before the image.

There is no common thread joining the Areopagite and Blanchot, but this is not because the Pseudo-Dionysius advocates "going 'outside of oneself' . . . in order to find oneself," as Foucault would have it. Not at all: *The Mystical Theology* teaches its addressee, Timothy, that the soul attains union with the deity only by detaching itself from beings and seeking the dark path of unknowing. As Timothy is assured, "you will unknowingly be elevated, as far as possible, to the unity of that beyond being and knowledge" (998b) where no self may be found. All the same, we can discern in the notion of selfhood a motivation for Foucault's rejection of Christianity. "Do not go abroad. Return within yourself. In the inward man dwells truth": such was Saint Augustine's advice in *Of True Religion*.[29] Blanchot is valuable for Foucault precisely because he resists the attractions of interiority, both in Christianity and in phenomenology. This conjunction should not be completely surprising: those very sentences by Saint Augustine were quoted by Husserl in the conclusion of his *Cartesian Meditations* (1929), which was the last great attempt to secure the privilege of the "I am" and to forestall the dangers of "I speak."[30] Foucault is undoubtedly trying to be faithful to Blanchot in associating interiority and phenomenology and then rejecting both. Even so, from Blanchot's perspective he moves a little too quickly with respect to both theology and phenomenology.

Meditating on *Les Mots et les choses* (1966), the very work in which he and others are held to herald a new *episteme*, Blanchot doubts whether atheism is even possible.[31] "I can very well tell myself, and believe with a strong conviction in so doing, that every form of affirmation in which the name or the idea of God would arise is foreign to me; yet 'I' am never atheist." Why not? Because "it is always God as *light* and as *unity* that one continues to recognize" (252; 377); strictly speaking, we should not talk of the "One God" but say that "Unity . . . is God, transcendence itself" (433; 635). The self functions as "a center who says 'I am,' says its relation to an 'I am' of height who always is" (252; 377). No "I" without God, or at least an idea of God, for Blanchot, and also no God without an "I." What are we to make of this position? In the first place, Blanchot's phrasing leads us to assume that he distinguishes the idea of "One God" as inherited from the Jews from the "Unity" of the Platonists, and that he wishes to distance us from the latter. Whether he objects to Plato's One that unifies the one and the many or to Plotinus's One that is beyond *noesis* and *ousia* is not addressed. He would be critical of both.[32] The heavy accent on transcendent unity is first heard in Christianity with the Pseudo-Dionysius who regards unity as the last, most difficult, and most exalted of the divine names: it bespeaks the complete and utter transcendence of the deity, and as such has neither name nor logos. His doctrine surely derives from Plotinus's insistence on the preeminence of the One and from Proclus's primary principle that transcends being, cause, time, and unity.[33]

Certainly Christian theologians have steadily maintained that God is one; it is the only way to avoid infinite regress, Irenaeus informed the gnostics.[34] Equally certainly, however, not all theology has relied on the Neoplatonic notion of a transcendent unity. It has proven hard in practice to maintain this hyperaffirmative unity while also confessing the triune nature of God. The temptation of modalism, the heresy that God is triune only in His dealings with creation *ad extra*, has never been the sole preserve of Sabellius. Both the Areopagite and Eckhart show conceptual strain in this regard. There is no sign of that particular tension in Saint Thomas Aquinas, who absorbed Neoplatonism by way of the Pseudo-Dionysius and Boethius, although one can find difficulties there of another sort. Thomas clearly affirms the divine unity; indeed, he argues that God's existence and unity properly belong to the *preambula fidei*, not to revealed faith, and can therefore be known rationally by men and women.[35] The claim is not without difficulties, for the profession of faith begins, "We believe in one God," requiring any Thomist to argue that the expression "We believe" encompasses the whole creed, not just its first proposition, or to engage in special pleading for those without a philosophical cast of mind.[36] Thomas does not overvalue unity with respect to the divine names, however. Before he considers that God is one, he affirms Him to be the highest good, and moreover uses this as the ground of his main argument for God's unity. "For it is not possible that there be two highest goods, since that which is said by superabundance is found in only one being. But God, as we have shown, is the highest good. God is, therefore, one."[37]

It is the homology between the "I" and the idea of God, Blanchot thinks, that makes any affirmation of atheism impossible in the first-person singular. To make such an affirmation would be to court self-contradiction. But the claim is far from self-evident, since the unity ascribed to the deity is not the same as that usually urged in arguments about personal self-identity. Only God enjoys a *unitas singularitatis*, a unity of singularity, and a *unitas simplicitatis*, a unity of simplicity. For anyone sympathetic to Christian Platonism, God's unity transcends any and all distinctions between unity and multiplicity, whereas the unity of self-identity is at most transcendental, as with Kant, and at least a unity of stages, as with Hume.[38] Neither Kant's nor Hume's notion of unity supports a repetition of the divine in the subject. Of course, if you look hard enough, the thought of such a unity can be found: Proclus held there to be a unitary faculty in the soul that allows us to attain ecstatic fusion with the primary principle. This faculty is "the most sublime of our activities," he says in *Alcibiades I*; "by this we become divinely inspired, fleeing from all multiplicity, converging upon our actual unification, becoming one, and operating after the manner of the One."[39] But his account of this "unitary portion" was not taken up by the Church.

Doubts and queries aside, however, let Blanchot's claim stand. It is an original interpretation of atheism, and one that calls for discussion. To begin with, it tells us that atheism cannot be rigorously established by rejecting the ontological argument for the existence of God or by finding contradictions in the very idea of God. And it tells us that atheism would not be possible on the basis of particular experiences that run counter to God's existence or his love, because these could be appropriated by the "I." Protest atheism would be covertly in league with theism, in Blanchot's mind, and the only authentic rejection of God would draw from an experience that radically unsettles the "I."[40] That said, and it is rather a lot, let us focus on the question in hand. Can there be an experience that shatters the "I"? If we follow Aristotle, there is no reason at all to think that experience grants unity: it gives only the constituents out of which a unity is conferred by cognition. Is there an experience that cognition cannot unify? Of all the questions that are raised by Blanchot's linking of the "I" and God, this is the only one he addresses. It comes to him in a modern form: Can there be an experience that destroys the "I"? Modern as it is, the question strikes us at first as peculiar, since without a subject—or at least some sort of a self—it is difficult to conceive that there can be experience. And yet modern narrative, when it follows Flaubert in using the *style indirect libre*, gives us many hundreds of pages of "experience without a subject."[41]

In the same essay, "L'Athéisme et l'écriture: L'humanisme et le cri" (1967), Blanchot defends Husserl against charges that Foucault will make explicit only later, in the foreword to the English edition of his book. Readers of *The Order of Things* (1970) learn something that readers of *Les Mots et les choses* (1966) do not. For the English, "a more serious public," are informed by Foucault that he rejects "the phenomenological approach" because it "gives absolute priority to the observing subject, which attributes a constituent role to an act, which places its point of view at the origin of all historicity."[42] This is a somewhat blurry representation of what is presented in *Logical Investigations, Ideas I*, the *Cartesian Meditations*, and the *Crisis*, and Blanchot rightly notes that phenomenology "contributed to the task of removing man, the psychical, from the status of natural causality; then to removing consciousness from its naive characterization as a site of conscious states."[43] Quite so: the doctrine that all consciousness is intentional in structure means that consciousness is neither internal nor external, neither subjective nor objective. In a sense, then, it is neutral.

Be that as it may, Blanchot readily concedes that phenomenology maintains the primacy of the subject with regard to speech. "Language, the expression of a meaning that precedes it, that it serves and safeguards: meaning, the ideality of light; a primary light that originates in the Subject with which a beginning occurs;

finally, experience (an experience that is rather difficult to determine; at times empirical, at times transcendent, and yet neither the one nor the other): source of signification" (251–52; 376). Without accepting or rejecting phenomenology, Blanchot quietly changes its central metaphor: light is to be removed and replaced with speech. That this has consequences for the delineation of experience Blanchot develops is evident. No longer can it be a dialectic of *ouvrage* and *lucidité*. It also has consequences for his understanding of religion. All talk based on the metaphor *lumen fidei* (light of faith) is put to one side while attention is given to the dialogue between God and human beings.

3

Why is Foucault so taken with Blanchot's thought of the Outside? In *L'Espace littéraire* we are told that the Outside is "the realm of the most dangerous indecision, toward the confusion from which nothing emerges"; it is "bereft of intimacy and of repose"; it "prevents, precedes, and dissolves the possibility of any personal relation"; it is "menacing," "vague and vacant," "nil and limitless," "a sordid absence, a suffocating condensation where being ceaselessly perpetuates itself as nothingness."[44] Could anything be less attractive? Of course, as Foucault fully realizes, the pull of the Outside does not rest on any charm, but his evocation of it suggests what draws him to it of his own accord. It lays bare "what precedes all speech, what underlies all silence: the continuous streaming of language."[45] It must be said that this description of the Outside seems far more benign than the dark gaze that comes from the heart of being to which Blanchot repeatedly testifies. And when one hears Gilles Deleuze saying that for Foucault not only does thinking come from the Outside but also so does "a certain idea of Life, a certain vitalism," one begins to suspect that Foucault's Outside must be rather different from that detailed in *L'Espace littéraire*.[46] For Blanchot, the Outside is intimately bound up with experience, so let us approach it from that perspective. I take my bearings not from *L'Espace littéraire* but from a less well-known piece, "À toute extrémité," which was also published in 1955 and which serves as a better introduction to "expérience" as Blanchot has come to use the word.

Immediately after considering a passage from Gide's journal, Blanchot reflects that the word *expérience* can be misleading in the context of literature or poetry because it tends to make us think it is associated with a "particular psychological phenomenon."[47] Just as the popular understanding of Heidegger's "Was ist Metaphysik?" suggests that anxiety supplies the key to metaphysics, so too people might think that a special mental condition is required for writing literature. "But literary experience . . . flies over experience and tests [*épreuve*] what does not test itself [*s'éprouve*]." It is not a matter of entering a "strange state" whether "distressing or delightful" (290). Not at all: it is as though literature opens "another space" above or below existence. Blanchot says nothing here of the characteristic Heideggerian move from an ontic to an ontological state, of rejecting anxiety at the level of psychology and affirming it as an attunement to being. Yet he makes exactly the same move in his own way, as we shall see. Now, though, in "À toute extrémité," he approaches experience by way of Proust. He does not have in mind the novelist's well-known view that "experience of oneself" is "the only true experience."[48] On the contrary, Proust brings us close to grasping a pass or plight, which is "very different from all others, even mystical experience," he says. It is experience "of what is not given in experience" (291).[49] In other words, this is an event that is not lived; it escapes the present moment. How experience can occur outside the present is very far from clear, and since Blanchot directs us to Proust it is to him that we must go for help.

"L'Expérience de Proust," Blanchot's first reflection on the novelist, revolves around the possibility of the author's enjoying "an actual mystical experience."[50] Hardly religious, in any of the usual senses of the word, this event would be a matter of feeling time as a vast loss, akin to death, or of powerful chance events of memory. In the end, what weighs on Proust is "a revelation of time" in which "one does not die but exists in generally unknown but not unknowable perspectives" (46; 57). This chimes with the theme we have encountered. Yet when Blanchot was writing "À toute extrémité" he was more than likely thinking of his more recent discussions of Proust. In the first, "mystical experience" is elucidated as "total experience." Here literature is "the very passion of its own question," and Proust is not someone who writes but "the very demand to write, a demand which employs the name of Proust, but does not express Proust, which only expresses him by disappropriating him, by making him Other [*Autre*]."[51] This understanding of an event implies a metaphysics sharply at odds with Hegel's, and from an angle that Hegel would never have imagined. Creative writing, Blanchot tells us, implies a turn from the everyday and its governing categories of being and nothingness. When he is writing, as Blanchot says in a second piece on the novelist, Proust becomes a "he," or even an "it," and in this state time itself changes "into an imaginary space (the space unique to images)"; it is a place "where there is no more interiority, for everything that is interior is deployed outwardly, takes the form of an image."[52] It is as though time has allowed itself to become a *khôra* even stranger than the one that Plato conceived. *Timaeus* 52 b–c describes a placeless place where the Forms are inscribed. Blanchot conjures a timeless time where images gather only to dissimulate themselves.

When one writes fiction or poetry, Blanchot thinks, the act of composition brackets the natural attitude. Husserl would have been inclined to agree. Yet neither "À toute extrémité" nor *L'Espace littéraire* details the reduction that the philosopher had in mind. For on picking up a pen, a writer takes a detour from the everyday world one might record in a journal to this strange space where time has stagnated and turned sour. Far from encountering being as it is, in all the hidden or undisclosed horizons of intentionality, I am faced with language as radically prior to me as subject. I realize that I touch being not as concretely determined but only as attenuated, as ghostly images, moving according to merely formal laws of grammar and rhetoric, words "deprived of being" that in no way lead me closer to being or to the Word. There is no origin here, for everything has always and already commenced and everything returns eternally from a past that never was. To be sure, this encounter threatens the work by holding the writer in the grip of fascination, and the work can occur only as a leap from this abyss, from that which cannot be lived to that which can be lived. Unless one brushes against this imaginary space, the work will become at best a cultural monument; it will not be literature in the modern sense because it will not have incorporated literature as a question, as questionable, as the "original experience." Maybe the final stanza of Paul Verlaine's "Ars poetica" comes to mind:

Que ton vers soit la bonne aventure
Éparse au vent crispé du matin
Qui va fleurant la menthe et le thym . . .
Et tout le reste est littérature. [53]

The poet's adventure for Blanchot has no morning freshness about it, people will say, recalling that for him writing exposes us to an endless dying. Yet we should also remember that writing for him is also an excess of life that life cannot contain, an event that disturbs the *conatus essendi* and that exposes us to "a blossoming, a smile of the whole of the space," a "tranquil smile of no one, intended for no one, and near which one could dwell near oneself." [54]

The writer who best testifies to this "original experience," Blanchot thinks, is not the supreme novelist of time lost and regained but the exquisite poet of the void, Stéphane Mallarmé. His letter of April 1866 to Henri Cazalis is quoted: "by digging this thoroughly into verse, I have encountered two abysses which make me despair. One is Nothingness." Immediately Blanchot supplies a gloss, "the absence of God," which is more or less what Mallarmé had in mind when writing that we have "invented God and our soul." [55] Then Blanchot adds, "the poet enters that time of distress which is caused by the gods' absence."[56] Notice how the paraphrase quietly translates a Christian into a pagan reference: Blanchot wishes to think of Mallarmé's loss of faith under the sign of Hölderlin rather than of Nietzsche. He does so because "this absence of the gods is not a purely negative form of relation," as in Nietzsche, but "a relation which threatens ceaselessly to tear and disorient us, with that which is higher than the gods, with the sacred itself or with its perverted essence."[57] Notice also how Blanchot generalizes what he takes to be Mallarmé's other point, his sense of personal ill health: "Whoever delves into verse dies; he encounters his death as an abyss."[58] The whole of L'Espace littéraire revolves around this conjunction of writing and dying, and this understanding of both occurs by way of what Hölderlin called "the categorical reversal." As mortals turn away from the gods, so too the gods withdraw from mortals, leaving the poet to protect the interval between the two which is the new abode of the sacred.

"L'Expérience de Mallarmé" begins by evoking not a "categorical reversal" but a "radical reversal" that occurs in the act of writing. Only toward the end of L'Espace littéraire, though, is this reversal explained. It is introduced by way of a question I quoted and considered in chapter 2. Is it not the case that when man has art, "he entertains with death a relation which is not that of possibility, which does not lead to mastery or to understanding or to the progressive achievements of time, but exposes him to a radical reversal"? Now it is time to listen to Blanchot answer that question. He does so with another question:

> *This reversal:* would it not seem to be the *original experience* [*l'expérience originelle*] which the work must touch, upon which it closes and which constantly threatens to close in upon art and withhold it? The end, in this perspective, would no longer be that which gives man the power to end—to limit, separate, and thus to grasp—but the infinite: the dreadful infinitude on account of which the end can never be overcome. (241; 323)

On one level, Blanchot's argument is an attempt to find an atheistic interpretation of artistic creation, but in order to see that clearly we will have to take several steps back. And in doing so we will be better able to find an answer to the question raised a little while back: how can experience occur outside the present?

The first move is taken in recalling Blanchot's association of the "I" and "God." Because the divine "I AM" of Exodus 3:14 is repeated in each and every affirmation of the first-person singular, the sentence "I am atheist" involves a covert self-contradiction. If we unpack the "I AM" a little, we will quickly find that it presumes a link between the "I" and the possible. God says not merely

"I AM" but "I AM THAT I AM." He is not merely being but wholly self-determining being. In Blanchot's terms (and here he is surely remembering Nicholas of Cusa), God is possibility itself. He is not thinking of logical possibility, "what is not at variance with the real, or what is not yet real, or, for that matter, necessary."[59] Nor is he recalling Kant's definition of the word in the first *Critique*—"That which agrees with the formal conditions of experience, that is, with the conditions of intuition and of concepts, is *possible*"—even though, as we shall see, that notion is not irrelevant to his thought.[60] Rather, he wishes to consider possibility in an ontological sense of the word, "to be plus the power to be" ("être, plus le pouvoir de l'être").[61] In a theological age, such as he takes ours to be, it is the same for human beings as for God: "man not only has possibilities, but is his possibility" (42; 59). Even death is seized as possibility, as Hegel, Nietzsche, and Heidegger saw in their different ways. Now if it can be shown, Blanchot thinks, that human being maintains a relation with the impossible, men and women would be freed from the religious anthropology in which we still find ourselves. It is art that reveals a relation to the impossible; and, as we saw in chapter 2, it does so in terms of the image. So let us return to that argument and follow it a little further. It is found a few pages after the lines I have quoted from *L'Espace littéraire*, in an appendix that ventures an answer to a question posed at the beginning of the book, "what is the image?" (34 n. 3; 32n).

There are two versions of the imaginary, Blanchot suggests. Classically understood, the image is "life-giving negation, the ideal operation by which man, capable of negating nature, raises it to a higher meaning."[62] Here the image is experienced. Yet the image gives us not being but the absence of being, and "having become image" an event or a thing "has become that which no one can grasp, the unreal, the impossible" (255; 343). And here the image cannot be experienced. Since modern philosophy has grasped death by way of possibility, it is not as strange as it might seem that Blanchot approaches the impossible by way of the corpse, a body that is now only externality. What intrigues him is that after death "the mourned deceased begins to *resemble himself*" (257; 346). Consider Blanchot in the essay:

> The cadaver is its own image. It no longer entertains any relation with this
> world, where it still appears, except that of an image, an obscure possibil-
> ity, a shadow ever present behind the living form which now, far from
> separating itself from this form, transforms it entirely into shadow . . .
> And if the cadaver is so similar [*ressemblant*], it is because it is, at a cer-
> tain moment, similarity [*la ressemblance*] par excellence: altogether sim-

ilarity [*ressemblance*], and also nothing more. It is the likeness, like to an absolute degree, overwhelming and marvelous. (258; 347)

And consider Blanchot in *Thomas l'obscur*, when Thomas contemplates Anne's corpse:

> She was not sleeping. She was not changed, either. She had stopped at the point where she resembled only herself [*au point où elle ne ressemblait qu'à elle-même*], and where her face, having only Anne's expression, was disturbing to look at. I took her hand. I placed my lips on her forehead. I treated her as if she were alive and, because she was unique among the dead in still having a face and a hand, my gestures did not seem insane. Did she appear alive, then? Alas, all that prevented her from being distinguished from a real person was that which verified her annihilation. She was entirely within herself: in death, abounding in life. She seemed more weighty, more in control of herself. No Anne was lacking in the corpse of Anne. (89–90; 100)

The corpse is a limit case: we experience it par excellence as an image. Yet, strictly speaking, we cannot say that we *experience* an image, since the image is precisely the disappearance of the object that we encounter and the appearance of its ghostly double. And here we find an answer to the question raised a little while ago. If Proust encounters the realm of the imaginary while writing, he is brought into a passive relation with that which cannot appear as a phenomenon; and this event, the very index of literary experience, does not strictly take place in the present.

There is more to say about the matter at hand. Blanchot recalls Heidegger's analysis of the broken tool in *Sein und Zeit* § 16: a damaged hammer is no longer part of my seamless world of sense and use, for it has become conspicuous; it interrupts the world in which I have been absorbed. For Heidegger, the piece of useless equipment reveals itself no longer as *zuhanden* (ready to hand), but merely as *vorhanden* (present to hand). Losing the unity of my life and my world, I become a subject faced with an object until I can regain the rhythm of work and restore the nonthematic absorption that I had in my world. Notice that even as he explicates *Sein und Zeit* § 16 Blanchot changes the vocabulary, introducing a word that Heidegger does not use except when discussing Kant (and even then in a different form). A damaged hammer "becomes its *image*," he says, and "no longer disappearing into its use, *appears*."[63] Granted, Blanchot wants us to conceive the appearance of the image as disrupting our world; yet the image, as he figures it, is neither a real nor an intentional object. This becomes all the more apparent when he considers the limit case of the corpse. There we are not dealing with the conspicuousness of a broken thing or even with the obstinacy of an event, as when I no longer know my way around a situation and must address it in an explicit and deliberate manner. Instead, the dead body obtrudes upon us. The corpse is close to being a "thing" (257; 345), Blanchot says. Well, yes and no, we might reply. Heidegger grants that it is "the Being-just-present-at-hand-and-no-more of a corporeal Thing which we encounter" and that "The *end* of the entity *qua* Dasein is the *beginning* of the same entity *qua* something present-at-hand."[64] Yet almost immediately he concedes that although the corpse is also "'more' than a *lifeless* material Thing" because "we encounter something *unalive*, which has lost its life" (282; 238), and he notes that although the dead one has left our world, "*in terms of that world* those who remain can still *be with him*" (282; 238).

Blanchot is more brusque: with death, he says, "the feeling of a relation between humans is destroyed" (257; 346), and while he confides that "he who dies 'in your arms' is in a sense your brother forever," he adds, without missing a beat, "But now, he is dead" (257; 345). We sense that for him the Dasein of the dead person has become *vorhanden* without an interval of solicitude. It is a chilling moment until we recall Thomas's tenderness with the dead Anne and remember that, for Blanchot, the death of the other person abolishes the infinite distance between the two of us, leaving no relation of ethical substance. With death, "*everything sinks back to indifference,*" a matter of "*profound grief,*" not callousness.[65] Although Blanchot implies that he introduces Heidegger's analysis of *Zuhandenheit* and *Vorhandenheit* merely as a passing analogy, the comparison lingers in his treatment of the corpse. In the terms of the analogy, the corpse would be completely obtrusive. We would be helpful, simply in "the mode of just tarrying alongside" the dead one, and we would encounter dead bodies "purely in the *way they look.*"[66] Yet in *his* analysis of the corpse, Heidegger withholds the moment of the gaze. He underlines that "In tarrying alongside him in their mourning and commemoration, those who have remained behind *are with him,* in a mode of respectful solicitude" (282; 238). For Blanchot, the situation is reversed; it is the dead one who remains *with us.* "What haunts us is something inaccessible from which we cannot extricate ourselves," he says. "It is that which cannot be found and therefore cannot be avoided. What no one can grasp is the inescapable" (259; 348). We do not experience the image, constitute it as meaningful, so much as suffer it to pass through us and deconstitute us. We are transfixed before it, and we risk standing where our "here" will crumble into "nowhere."

It is when things obtrude upon us, Heidegger argues, that we begin to adopt a theoretical attitude. For his part, no sooner has Blanchot completed his phenomenological description of the corpse than he begins to philosophize—or, rather, theologize. "Man is made in his image: this is what the strangeness of the cadaver's resemblance teaches us" (260; 350). The doctrine that man is formed in God's image is not reversed as in the old joke that first God created man in his image and then man immediately returned the compliment. Rather, the deity is left out of the picture altogether. Man is not *imago dei*, for we are the image of ourselves, and never more truly than when lying in state: "He is more beautiful, more imposing; he is already monumental and so absolutely himself," says Blanchot of the corpse (258; 346). He does not stop at what could be reconciled to a humanism, however, and offers a bold reading of his doctrine: *"man is unmade* [défait] *according to his image"* (260; 350). There is no way in which a person can prevent an image from being formed of him or her: it is a condition of our mortality. Yet to have a relation to the imaginary, even one that is entirely passive, is to be associated with the impossible as well as the possible, and in responding to this neutral realm one falls outside the space defined by the "I."

Although he wishes to distance himself from all theology, Blanchot's account of experience and the Outside remains very close to a venerable problem in that discipline. It is best approached by way of a question: can one have experience of God? It would seem not, some people say, for the deity is hardly the kind of being—if that phrase even be appropriate—that can be perceived; and even if we credit the raptures of the mystics, they do not involve the senses and therefore cannot be called experiences.[67] If one begins from this general conviction, then one's theology will turn on the ability of reason to establish that there is a God and that he is in relation with us. Or one will say that believing in the Gospel establishes an allegiance to Christ and does not open the way to distinctive experiences. Or one will say that "the presence of the Word of God is not an experience, precisely because and as it is the divine decision concerning us."[68] Yet this broad position is far from invulnerable. For other people will say that the life of faith is not a matter of accepting exterior doctrines; it requires the believer to relive what has been witnessed and taught in the past. And if one is to live the faith then one must have an intentional relationship, if not an actual encounter, with the object of faith. To deny the possibility of that relationship would be to deny that revelation has occurred.

Now if one develops this line of thought then one's theology will revolve around finding a sense of "experience" that can cohere with talk of God. One might speak with Origen of "spiritual senses," as some of the mystics have done, even to the point of praising the "Odor divinio" as Jacopone da Todi does in one of his poems.[69] Or one might, like Friedrich Schleiermacher, evoke a moment "which you always experience yet never experience" ("den Ihr jedesmal erlebt, aber auch nicht erlebt").[70] Or one might reflect with Karl Rahner on a transcendental experience that is, when properly understood, an experience of transcendence.[71] Or one might come to talk with Eberhard Jüngel of an "experience with experience" ("eine Erfahrung mit der Erfahrung").[72] Disregarding all these individual responses, it is this second main approach to which Blanchot is close, not because he affirms the One who transcends the distinction between unity and multiplicity but because the Outside, as he imagines it, cannot be set forth in terms of being and nonbeing regarded as mutually exclusive categories. And we can best see how he elaborates his position by distinguishing it from those developed by Kant and Hegel. For ease of exposition, it is better to begin with the latter.

In his lectures on the philosophy of religion, both in 1821 and 1824, Hegel considers the very question I raised a moment ago: how can the finite mind comprehend the infinite? One must begin from where one is, Hegel declares, and that is in nature, the realm of finitude. Yet there can be no passage from the finite to the infinite, there is no *scala paradisi* or *scala perfectionis* for the philosopher, and in fact none need be constructed. For nature is the realm of contradiction: in its self-negation, the finite sublates itself and reveals itself to be a moment in the infinite. In 1821 Hegel puts it as follows: "To philosophical cognition, the progression is a stream *flowing in opposite directions*, leading forward to the other, but at the same time working backward, so that what appears to be the *last*, founded on what precedes, appears rather to be the *first*—the foundation."[73] One can pass from the finite to the infinite only because the infinite has dialectically preceded the finite; and so it makes decent philosophical sense to speak of experiencing the deity. Assuredly, God may not be found in "external experience" (the senses) or in "inner experience" (illumination), but is to be known in the final reaches of *Erfahrung*, understood speculatively as the return of absolute spirit to itself (1:258).[74]

I do not know if Blanchot has ever come across this argument. Perhaps he hit upon a version of it himself when seeking a phenomenological description of what happens when one writes a poem or a story and in doing so evoked what abides just beyond the limit of phenomenology. At any rate, in literature it is time that "changes direction" ("change de sens"), that "has radically changed its meaning and its flow [*changé de sens*]."[75] The writer has been distracted from the finite task of producing a literary work and has become fascinated by the infinite movement of writing; it has already transformed the "I" into a "one." The finite work has been enveloped by the infinite movement of writing, and the finite life has been interrupted by death understood as infinite dying. The present moment in which the author writes has been dispersed, and as we have seen this "original experience" does not occur in the present moment. The event does not allow one to represent it in the first person, for "by the fact that we experience it, it escapes our power to undergo it" (45; 63). Accordingly, Blanchot calls this event "the impossible"; and with this word it is timely to turn from Hegel to Kant.

In the first *Critique* Kant defines the possible as "that which agrees with the formal conditions of experience, that is, with the conditions of intuition and of concepts" (A218/B265). He says nothing there about that which would not agree with these conditions, although one could readily imagine Blanchot not ignoring that state of affairs, calling it the impossible, and noting that it cannot be constituted by a subject but rather calls the sovereignty of the self into question. One person who dwells explicitly on Kant's definition of possibility is Jean-Luc Marion, and it is instructive to enter his world, all too briefly, and see how his report on "the possibility of the impossible" differs from Blanchot's figure of the impossible.[76] Marion notes that for Kant possibility is linked to phenomenality, and, further, that a phenomenon can give itself only in terms established by the categorical structure of the subject. Marion proposes and tests the hypothesis that there is a "saturated phenomenon," one in which givenness exceeds intention. The saturated phenomenon would contradict the conditions of possibility set for experience, and consequently Marion speaks of "counter-experience" (215–16). Far from being able to constitute this phenomenon, the "I" is constituted by it; and it should be noted that we cannot ascribe a simple unity to this phenomenon: it calls forth many and varied horizons and sets in motion what is in principle an endless process of interpretation. Notice though that Marion is concerned with a phenomenon, one that is so rich in intuition it cannot be aimed at or borne; it is absolute and irregardable. By contrast, Blanchot is not preoccupied with a phenomenon at all and denies that we can have any intuition of the impossible. Of course, the impossible cannot be aimed at, borne, or regarded, although it is not so much absolute as holding us in a "relation without relation." No experience is offered to us; the "I" is deconstituted, and there can be no talk of unity. This then is not a counterexperience but a "trial" of experience, and its passivity is of another order from that envisaged by Marion.[77] One has no power over it, not even the power of constituting its meaning, for it has no meaning. No longer is experience a relation of *ouvrage* and *lucidité* for Blanchot, and no longer is it even a work. On the contrary, it is worklessness.

4

L'Espace littéraire firmly rejects Heidegger's characterization of a virile Dasein grasping death as the last possibility. Even so, one might be forgiven for finding in the same text a heroic image of the artist who runs up against the menacing Outside, encounters dying in losing the power to say "I," yet is unable to draw upon religious consolation as the mystic is supposed to do. It is doubtful that Blanchot would credit this image of the hero since he sees undertaking the detour as utterly passive and therefore unheroic. Equally doubtful is that any of the mystics would endorse Blanchot's caricature of mysticism, or that Foucault had the artist as hero in mind when he hailed "the thought from Outside." Indeed, on Deleuze's understanding, Foucault wished to situate himself in the Outside because it was a "murmur without beginning or end."[78] To be sure, Foucault said that he "preferred to be enveloped by speech, and carried away well beyond all possible beginnings," and he affirmed, "the murmur of indifference: 'What matter who's speaking?'"[79] This question has an interest and a pertinence of its own, but we may well wonder if Foucault is talking about the menacing Outside to which Blanchot testifies in *L'Espace littéraire*.

I do not think that Foucault was mistaken about the Outside. Instead, I think that Blanchot had come to adjust how he thought of it some years before "La Pensée du dehors" appeared in 1966. As we have seen, Blanchot had earlier distinguished the journal, which details the everyday, from the artwork, which traces a detour from the everyday. There are writers who confirm this way of putting things. Polish poet Adam Zagajewski, for one, tells us that "A writer who keeps a personal diary uses it to record what he knows. In his poems or stories he sets down what he doesn't know."[80] I suspect, though, that Blanchot found his own distinction too divided and equivocal to bear the burden of speculation about the Outside. Not all writers use diaries to anchor themselves to the quotidian, not even Franz Kafka, one of Blanchot's exemplary writers. Nor do all writers distinguish the creative and the quotidian in quite the way that Blanchot does. And we can only wonder whether, for the Blanchot of *L'Espace littéraire*, literary critics and editors need to keep diaries. At all events, by the mid- to late 1960s he had come to rethink the Outside by way of *la parole plurielle* or *écriture* instead of *littérature*. As already seen, for Blanchot the metaphor of light had led phenomenology toward the One, despite the built-in resistance provided by intentionality. Now this metaphor is definitively replaced by speech or writing, both understood by way of "plural speech" or "writing" in Derrida's sense of the word.

Although Blanchot passes from literature to writing for his new model of the

Outside, he does not stop talking about "the artistic experience." Not at all: rather than figuring the Outside on a distinction between the everyday and art he develops accounts of it based on both art and the everyday. Let us begin with the first. Thinking of Thomas Mann and the *ars nova*, he maintains that "the artistic experience can be realized *only* in works given over to the fragment." More surprising is the political work that this artistic experience is held to do, for the presence of the fragment "suffices to unsettle [*à ébranler*] the *entire* future of culture and *every* utopia of happy reconciliation."[81] It is a bold claim, and I shall return in chapter 7 to consider an assumption buried deep inside it: that the movement of endless contestation has a social endpoint, "communism, recognized as ultimate affirmation," as he puts it in *L'Entretien infini*.[82] Now, however, I wish to consider very briefly Blanchot's understanding of the fragmentary from two directions: whether it necessarily unsettles the religious, and whether it forms a de facto totality of another kind.

Not to be confused with the aphorism, the essay, or the maxim, the fragmentary can be of any length. Its distinguishing trait, as it were, would be that it resists incorporation into a totality, a unity, or even a program that would itself thematize fragmentation. It is coordinate with the "end of history" or a "change of epoch" and answers to a negativity that cannot be employed. So it is a writing that cannot be related to a unifying beginning or end. Yet if, as Blanchot insists, "There is no experience" of the fragmentary, one can only wonder how it can ever unsettle a culture.[83] Of course, what Blanchot has in mind is that the fragmentary cannot be encountered in the first-person singular, only in the third-person singular. The experience of writing involves a turn from the "I" to the "one," and in that movement I lose the power to say "I": I become a "who?"—the subject of a question. So Louis-René des Forêts's *Ostinato* (1997) would be fragmentary because its fragments ceaselessly call the "I" into question, while Henri de Lubac's *Sur les chemins de Dieu* (1956) would not be, for even though it is (in its first edition) a collection of fragments it does not question a belief in the unity of man or God.[84] Here Blanchot seems to converge with Adorno's claim that twentieth-century life is characterized by the "impossibility of experience [*Erfahrung*]," an insight the critical theorist shared with the young Heidegger, at least to the extent that *Entleben* points in the same direction.[85] Yet Blanchot thinks the issue differently. For him, the putting into question of the subject is the first stage of a movement of contestation that is the very opening of experience and that I have raised before and will discuss again.

Returning to Adorno for a moment, it is characteristic that Blanchot does not engage with the dialectical version of his claim that life here and now is drained of experience, namely, the view that experience today is given to us only in and through the fragmentary. That idea is most closely associated with Walter Benjamin, and it can be found in his intriguing claim that a translation, "instead of imitating the sense of the original, must lovingly and in detail incorporate the original's way of meaning, thus making both the original and the translation recognizable as fragments of a greater language, just as fragments are part of a vessel."[86] Here Benjamin's sense of a fragment that indicates a larger whole than even the language in which it is written and that cannot be properly expressed recalls his debt to the Jena romantics' reflections on the fragment.[87] No one would be surprised to hear that when Blanchot considers Benjamin's sense of a pure language he does so by way of his favorite romantic poet, Friedrich Hölderlin, whose *Antigone* and *Oedipus* sought to unify German and Greek. These were among the poet's last works before madness descended upon him; and this event is no accident, Blanchot thinks, for those translations exposed him to "the unifying power that is at work in every practical relation, as in any language" as well as "the pure scission that is always prior."[88] To hold together both the movement toward unity and the pure difference that precedes the movement is impossible, and to do so with a passion as fierce as Hölderlin's is to go to the limit of sanity.

Elsewhere, Benjamin offers insights that cannot be traced to Friedrich Schlegel or redirected to Hölderlin. "The value of fragments of thought is all the greater the less direct their relationship to the underlying idea," he says, "and the brilliance of the representation depends as much on this value as the brilliance of the mosaic does on the quality of the glass paste."[89] A fragment can redeem something greater than itself, Benjamin suggests, and it does so precisely by being dialectical. When a fragment is recognized in the here and now, its lost moment—cultural, historical, and social—once more begins to sparkle. The *Urgeschichte*, that is, all the ordinary hope, love, and suffering that has been discarded or overlooked by the decades or centuries in their rush to establish themselves as "History" is suddenly redeemed in the observer's eye. That Benjamin's notion of historical redemption draws deeply from Jewish theology is well known, and rather than rehearse that theme I simply note that religion is the focus for his contemporaries Franz Rosenzweig and Simone Weil, for whom the fragment opens toward eternity rather than recaptures what has been lost in history. "He who denies the totality of being, as we do, thus denies the unity of reasoning": it is not Blanchot who is speaking but Rosenzweig, and he does so in sketching for us the "star" of redemption rather than in talking about the disaster.[90] "We have to accomplish the possible in order to be able to seize upon the impossible": again, it is not Blanchot who is speaking. This time it is Weil; I have quoted a fragment from one of her notebooks.[91]

One can imagine a religious sensibility that rejects the totality of a theological system in favor of an openness to the eternal, that finds faith not in the fullness or even the evacuation of experience but rather in our frustrations and brokenness, that prizes the singularity of the other person, and that conceives God in terms of excess rather than the original being, the highest being, or the being of beings. For this sensibility, discerned by some in our own time, religion is a matter of living in the fragmentary and having no desire to reconstitute a lost unity or to devise a new one.[92] Jean-Louis Chrétien could be cited as a partial witness to this, since his work has been to explore and affirm the wound caused by the inadequacy of our response to the overwhelming call of the divine.[93] A more spirited avowal of fragmentary existence, as compatible with Christianity, is given by David Tracy, whose writings I have already cited. The fragmentary, here, would be neither a part nor the whole; it would be neutral. And this raises a problem, since understanding occurs only with reference to a whole. Does this mean that someone committed to the spiritual life by way of the fragmentary would be condemned to live without understanding? I do not think so: the required reference is to *a* whole, not *the* whole. Logical difficulties obtrude only when one denies the possibility of a provisional whole, and then they affect not only believers but also nonbelievers.

Blanchot is not unaware of the risks of affirming the fragmentary, and in *L'Écriture du désastre* he quotes Jacques Derrida's warning to him: "There is reason to fear that, like ellipsis, the fragment—the 'I say practically nothing and take it back right away'—makes mastery over all that goes unsaid possible, arranging in advance for all the continuities and supplements to come." To which Blanchot adds, "Let us heed this warning" (134; 203). The response is hardly reassuring, but he has already taken note of the problem to the extent that he sees it as structural rather than stylistic. As noted in the previous chapter, he insists that we must learn to live in two slightly phased registers, one dialectical and the other neutral, the one a mode of activity, the other a passivity beyond all dialectical passivity. "In the same way," he adds, "each of us ought both to be a free and speaking subject, and to disappear as passive, patient."[94] This doubling in Blanchot, which is bound to disturb any movement toward unity, is not always noticed, not even by some of his warmest admirers. When Deleuze and Félix Guattari, for example, applaud his concept of the fragmentary, they do so because it bolsters their sense of the desiring machine as "pure multiplicity, that is to say, an affirmation that is irreducible to any sort of unity."[95] What is ultimately wanted here is the "one" without the "I," an assemblage without a subject; but this is not quite what Blanchot is telling us about the turn from the first to the third person.[96] Or not always, for he is not quite consistent. When meditating on Foucault, for example, he takes care to defend him from the charge of doing precisely what Deleuze and Guattari do. "The subject does not disappear," he says; "rather *its excessively determined unity* is put in question"; and then we are reminded that the subject is not erased but dispersed, becoming "no more than a plurality of positions and a discontinuity of functions."[97] Within a sentence we have passed from the pressure of too much unity to no unity whatsoever, and there is reason to be doubtful about the rhetoric. For one can reject the substantial unity of the subject, as Foucault does, yet one cannot simply wipe away unity as a horizon of intelligibility. To do that is to make insuperable difficulties for recognizing a unity of parts or phases. At best, one can show that the horizon is disrupted here and there and try to work out the effects of such breaks.

5

Foucault prizes Blanchot because he marks an exit from phenomenology, and yet an engagement with Husserl and a reworking of his thought are a part of his intellectual life. Like Lévinas, what chiefly interests Blanchot in Husserl is not the reduction but intentionality. It is a valuable notion because it "maintains the empirical and the transcendental within a powerfully structured relation."[98] This has consequences for both: experience cannot be wholly converted into knowledge, while the transcendental cannot be localized in consciousness or "natural reality." The transcendental will abide, rather, "in the emergence of a network of relations that neither unite nor identify but maintain what is in relation at a distance, and make of this distance, recaptured as form of alterity, a new power of determination" (251; 375). If we link the empirical and the transcendental, as conceived here, we can make out another image of the Outside. It may not derive from the journal, but it answers to what Blanchot believed the journal was designed to record: the everyday.

For the Blanchot of the late 1950s and early 1960s, the "original experience" is no longer the sole preserve of the artist. It is now to be rendered by way of writing, not literature, and so Blanchot must find an experience open to all. "This is an experience we do not have to go very far to find," he says, "if it is offered in the most common suffering, and first of all in physical suffering."[99] In reading this, one is reminded of what Blanchot said in "À toute extrémité," namely, that the experience that interests him does not depend on a special psychological state. As we have seen, he alludes there to a popular understanding of Heidegger's "Was ist Metaphysik?"—namely, that anxiety, considered as one affective state among others, projects me into nothingness. For Heidegger, however, in anxiety I am not simply concerned about my finitude but also concerned for it. Anxiety is therefore not an ordinary emotional state; it is a fundamental attunement that must be awakened if Dasein is to be granted its subsistence and possibility.[100] Suffering fulfills the same role for Blanchot: we must regard it not as exceptional, a special state of consciousness, but as a structural feature of human life. It is "a suffering that is almost indifferent, not suffered, but neutral (a phantom of suffering) insofar as the one who is exposed to it, precisely through this suffering, is deprived of the 'I' that would make him suffer it" (44–45; 63). To turn from "I" to "one" is part of being human, but this attunement does not reveal possibility, as in Heidegger, only impossibility. To suffer, to be exposed to dying, is not a matter of aging, or of always being old enough to die, for these considerations cohere with death as a possibility, a power—whereas dying is the complete lack of power. Outside the dialectic, this passivity is therefore outside time, and it follows that dying is logically anterior to each and every one of us as individuals.

In his first formulation of the Outside, Blanchot portrays the journal as linking the writer to the everyday, the realm of negativity and possibility, because literature would carry him or her into the timeless time of fascination, the *Nirgends ohne Nicht* of which Rilke spoke. When rethinking the Outside, however, Blanchot aligns it with the everyday. Now the everyday cannot be approached by way of fusion: I am not taken into the Other, even if it is regarded as the sovereign state. Similarly, the everyday stands outside the dialectic; it is approached as that which escapes the distinction between being and nothingness, and several things immediately follow from this. The everyday cannot be comprehended; it does not allow the distinction between true and false to take hold; and it allows no origins or ends. Seen only from this perspective, the everyday would seem to share traits with the mystical. "In this consists its strangeness—the familiar showing itself (but already dispersing) in the guise of the astonishing."[101] Indeed, in the everyday there is no present moment, "we slide in the leveling out of a steady slack time" (242; 361), and consequently we have no opportunity for experience. Everyday human beings exist as "he" or "she," not as "I," and consequently, "The hero, while still a man of courage, is he who fears the everyday; fears it not because he is afraid of living in it with too much ease, but because he dreads meeting in it what is most fearful: a power of dissolution" (244; 365). We live in the Outside but cannot experience it, or if we do then only by way of the peculiarly modern attunement that Heidegger called boredom.[102] Foucault may not have been attracted by either boredom or suffering, but what he retained from Blanchot was the endless murmur of the Outside, of human beings on the streets escaping "all authority, be it political, moral, or religious" (245; 366).

Once Blanchot has affirmed the everyday as neither fusion nor dialectic, he has little trouble in declaring it to be a place where no God reigns. It is here that human beings can be atheists, for only in everyday life is "I" unable to be pronounced. To pass from "I" to "one" is at heart to undergo a counterconversion. The assumption of unity that bound human beings to their Creator has been discharged, it seems, simply by people walking the streets. Heidegger and Adorno thought that the cost of modernity is the impossibility of experience, but their position is not the same as Blanchot's. For him, the cost of atheism is nonexperience, and there can be no doubt that he does not think it too high a price to pay. In its own way, this neutral world is, as he says, "sacred," but the sacred no sooner appears than it expiates itself.[103] It is as though Blanchot were adapting for his own purposes Durkheim's contention that "the god and the society are one and the same."[104] What could "nonexperience" mean here? In an Aristotelian vocabulary, it would be the absence of ἐμπειρία, different memories of the one event. In Hegelian terms it would be no return, as mediated, of what was initially seized immediately by consciousness. In Husserl's world, it would be having no intentional acts. And so on. For Blanchot, however, nonexperience means undergoing a "trial of experience," glimpsing the ordinary in such a way as to recognize, albeit fleetingly, that it is not completely undergirded by the possible but opens onto the impossible. The ordinary and the familiar thus appear as "an anonymous, distracted, deferred, and dispersed way of being in relation," and not, as we expect, comforting, known, and readily mastered.[105] This trial gives rise to what Blanchot calls an experience "that one will represent to oneself as being strange and even as the experience of strangeness,"[106] and we think inevitably of his own "(Une scène primitive?)." The mystics know this sense of strangeness well, though Blanchot will try to tell them that mystery abides in how one sees, not in a transcendent being, in the dark gaze rather than in the *lumen fidei*. The poets know it too, that silent moment when the world suddenly seems eerie and fragile. As one of them, the Argentinian Roberto Juarroz, tells us, "Lo impossible no levanta nunca la voz" (The impossible never raises its voice).[107] But the poets, because they are human, are as likely to be drawn to the divine as to the Outside.

No one lives wholly in the everyday, and insights into the strangeness of the world will be transient at best. Blanchot recognizes this and, with it, that atheism cannot be affirmed as a position in quite the way that theism can. His main point is that "possibility is not the sole dimension of our existence" and that there is quite another claim made upon us:

it is perhaps given to us to "live" ["*vivre*"] each of the events that is ours by way of a double relation. We live it one time as something we comprehend, grasp, bear, and master (even if we do so painfully and with difficulty) by relating it to some good or to some value, that is to say, finally, by relating it to Unity; we live it another time as something that escapes all employ and all end, and more, as that which escapes our very capacity to undergo it, but whose trial we cannot escape.[108]

We cannot escape this trial because experience itself *is* contestation. The challenge we face is not merely to increase our understanding of the world about us or even of ourselves, but rather to elaborate ourselves as a question. To be human, for Blanchot, is a matter not only of being able to say "I am" but also of asking "Who?" The question is posed time and again when making or responding to art, when living out an everyday existence, when following "a secret way of seeing," whenever one recognizes that existence opens onto the impossible as well as the possible.[109]

How is one's self called into question? Blanchot speaks of an ontological attunement that he associates with mystery, understood in his own sense: the neutral. He also insists, especially in his later writings, that appearances to the contrary this sliding away from the self requires the proximity of the Other which, for him, is always the other person. One must be open to the Other, he says, and in affirming that gesture of vulnerability, above and beyond any act or word, one also affirms the shifting distance that separates and maintains us in a relation in which each transcends the other. If this is so, transcendence is an irreducible aspect of contestation or experience. Plainly, this is neither the Unity of the Platonists nor the One of the Jews. Yet Blanchot is more intrigued with the latter than with the former, and his struggle with the One God of Israel is an encounter that needs to be closely examined.

6

·

"THE NEARNESS OF THE ETERNAL"

1

"How for example to think the nearness [*voisinage*] of the Eternal in the Bible?"[1] It is Blanchot who is speaking, and the conjunction of the questioner and the question should be allowed a little time to echo. I am quoting from his essay "Paix, paix au lointain et au proche" (1985), the title of which is a quotation from the Bible: "Peace, peace to him that is far off, and to him that is near, saith the Lord; and I will heal him" (Isa. 57:19). We do not readily associate Blanchot with the Bible, and it is strange to find him opening the Scriptures and inquiring about the Eternal. We would not be at all surprised to hear him meditating on the eternal return, Friedrich Nietzsche's "revelation of Surledj," as he calls it, but that does not seem to be what is at issue in the sentence I have quoted.[2] One might think that, following Moses Mendelssohn's bold translation of Genesis, Blanchot is using "the Eternal" as one of the names of God.[3] Again, though, that thought completely misses the point of the question. Before trying to establish what the word *Eternal* might mean here, it is worth considering the sort of question that is being posed. There is nothing here to make us think of semiotic, structural, or narratological readings of the Bible; it is not the kind of question that comes up in rhetorical or psychoanalytic approaches to Scripture; nor does it have the air of a probe that will uncover a deep politics of exodus or redemption or, for that, of any biblical theme. Of course, this is not to say that Blanchot is unconcerned with biblical events and figures. Even casual readers will recognize motifs of call and response, creation and apocalypse, law and exile, mystery and suffering, death and resurrection, in both his criticism and his narratives; and they will also see that each of these is reset in such a way that it cannot readily be folded back into the Bible.

The phrasing of the question does not make us think of someone about to engage in historical criticism, and nothing there makes us think of biblical scholarship, even when broadly understood. In fact, when removed from its context the question is more than likely to strike us as premodern, to recall a world in which Scripture and faith directly nourished one another. We might almost be tempted to think that Blanchot is approaching the Bible with a view to eliciting a new sort of spiritual understanding. And—why not?—we might even take up the thought that he is attempting an allegorical reading of Scripture. "When after the Fall Jahweh asks Adam 'Where are you?' this question signifies that henceforth man can no longer be found or situated except in the place of the question."[4] On reading this passage out of context one might imagine that one has stumbled across a forgotten paragraph of Origen's homilies on Genesis rather than a page near the beginning of *L'Entretien infini*.[5] If so, the very next sentence would snap one back to the appropriate century: "Man is from now on a question for God himself, who does not question" (14; 17). But the confusion with Origen is not entirely misleading. If we understand "allegory" to indicate a search for a meaning or a significance other than at the level of the letter, and seek neither to pass from letter to spirit nor to forget that Blanchot insists on there being a dimension of literature that can never be brought to light, then we have good reason to keep the word in play.[6] The question's insistence on *thinking* (and not believing in) the nearness of the Eternal and on taking the Bible as an *example* (and not as spiritually exemplary) should make it sufficiently clear that Blanchot is distancing himself from all biblical theology.

And yet it remains a question about the Bible. We should therefore respond with care, not because Scripture must always call forth piety in its readers but because a question about it is likely to involve hermeneutics and poetics and to work on cultural and political as well as confessional levels. Given that, we would do well to step back a little and ask ourselves about the sense and function of the word *Bible* in Blanchot's writings. The first thing is to determine which set of documents is intended when he speaks about Scripture. There is the Christian Bible in its different versions and translations, and any reader of *L'Espace littéraire* (1955) will recall how Blanchot uses lines from the Vulgate. "Noli me legere," he writes, adapting Jesus's command to Mary Magdalene after the resurrection: "noli me tangere, nondum enim ascendi ad Patrem" (Touch me not; for I am not yet ascended to my Father) (John 20:17).[7] Which means for him that a text forbids its author to read it: an interdiction that is in place as soon as the author begins to write and that, unlike Jesus's words, is disobeyed time and again. "Lazare, veni foras" (Lazarus, come forth) (John 11:43), he later quotes, recalling the story of Jesus's raising of his dead friend at Bethany.[8] This time he is seeking to suggest how a reader calls to the work to enter the light of understanding, and this time he repeats the Vulgate word by word.

More often, however, Blanchot's reference is to the Hebrew Bible or Tanakh, which Christians have reordered and called the Old Testament.[9] That description would irritate Blanchot, since for him Jewish Scripture is not a long preface to the revelation that Jesus is the Christ. Indeed, the New Testament would be the prime instance of what he calls "messianic *impatience.*"[10] His approach to Jewish messianism favors those commentaries that suggest "the relation between the event and its nonoccurrence": the Messiah being here among us, perhaps even "at the gates of Rome among the beggars and lepers" yet still not coming.[11] All the same, the notion of Scripture as testament has abiding value for him. Neviim and Ketuvim, the Prophets and the Writings, are part of Israel's witness to the nations until the Messiah comes. Yet Blanchot is always drawn to Torah, the foundation of Israel's testimony of divine revelation. Abraham leaving his home in quest of a land that will be shown to him, Moses receiving the Tablets from God at Mount Sinai, the wandering of the Jews on their way to the promised land: these are motifs to which he returns time and again.

Less important from Blanchot's perspective but highly significant for his readers is what I will call the "Bible effect" in his work. First of all, I am thinking of verses that function as holy writ for him. We have already encountered them in earlier chapters. René Char: "Le poème est l'amour réalisé du désir demeuré désir." And Friedrich Hölderlin: "Jezt aber tagts! Ich harrt und sah es kommen, / Und was ich sah, das Heilige sei mein Wort."[12] Blanchot invests these lines among others with an authority akin to revealed truth. More generally, when reading Blanchot discussing those who loom from on high in his canon—Kafka and Mallarmé, in particular—one could sometimes be forgiven for believing he is explicating another testament with its own "'sacred' speech."[13] The influence of Heidegger's elucidations of Hölderlin, or at least a deep sympathy with them, is apparent. In the second place, there is a Bible effect when readers respond to Blanchot's writings as though to Scripture. When talking of the récits Christopher Fynsk testifies to "the strangeness of their language: a force, at times, that one associates with sacred texts";[14] and when reading *Thomas l'obscur* (1941) George Quasha and Charles Stein declare that it seems "to echo in some impossible way *The Gospel of Thomas*" and ask, "Is there a secret affinity held in reserve?"[15] Since the Coptic translation of the Gospel of Thomas, the only complete version of the text, was discovered at Nag Hammadi in December 1945, thirteen years after Blanchot started writing the novel and four years after it was published, the echo is decidedly "impossible."[16] Yet empirical falsification hardly affects the quality of the impact that Quasha and Stein feel when reading Blanchot's fiction. That eerie sense of "spiritual" or counterspiritual authority needs to be analyzed, although I will not be doing that here.

I will be thinking instead about how Blanchot uses the Bible, both as a text and as an idea. It is a large topic, one that resists neat formulations, and all I will be able to do in this chapter is follow one or two paths that beckon to me. Doubtless, I should start with what Blanchot says about Scripture. If we assemble all the relevant bits and pieces, spoken in his own voice and by his narrators and characters, we will come up with a mixture of allusions to biblical figures, reworking of narratives, twisting of themes, texts that invite allegorical readings almost as though they were Scripture, and polemic pronouncements. Sometimes there is nothing much to be done with the information. Sometimes it is hard to tell if it even *is* information. Take for example *Le Très-Haut* (1948), the very title of which gives an image of divine authority and transcendence. Critics readily invoke Hegel and Kojève when writing about this novel, and with good reason, for it describes what happens when history has been brought to an end. The state is absolute, and so at long last "inside and outside correspond."[17] "The end of history" is itself a major biblical theme, of course, while the title of the novel is a biblical epithet for God (Heb. *elyon*). The divine name is used by Melchizedek, king of Salem, in Genesis 14:18, and Abram adopts the Canaanite epithet just four verses later.[18] Thereafter it is used very frequently in the Hebrew Bible. One has only to recall that psalmists promise to "sing praise to the name of the LORD most high" (Ps. 7:17) and evoke "the tabernacles of the most High" (Ps. 46:4), while the narrator of Daniel testifies "that the most High ruleth in the kingdom of men" (Dan. 4:17) and Hosea laments that none of his people would exalt "the most High" (Hosea 11:7). In the Bible there is no one verse that unlocks the novel's allegory, if there is one, while in the novel the only direct reference to Scripture occurs when Henri Sorge casually reports of a fellow employee that "he opened an enormous dossier, bulkier than a Bible" (33; 38). No particular allusion to holy writ is needed, though, for readers to be aware of the irony that Blanchot's "Most High" is an ordinary citizen who does not give the Law but, right up until the dénouement, incarnates the law completely. And no one who is familiar with the importance that Hölderlin has for Blanchot would be taken aback to learn that there are Greek as well as Hebrew motifs to be respected in the novel. Alongside the biblical themes of law and theophany one must take account of the figures of Antigone and Orestes.[19]

At other times readers face the difficulty of knowing what to do with biblical information when it has been found. For example, one picks up Blanchot's second novel, *Aminadab* (1942), and being puzzled by the title checks a concordance and finds that the word is a proper name: the son of Ram and the father of Nahshon. We learn in Ruth 4:19–22 that Aminadab is a link in the Davidic line, a piece of genealogy that is repeated by Matthew and Luke, who extend the line backward to Adam and forward to Jesus by way of Joseph (Matt. 1:4, Luke 3:33). Or we find an Amminadib in Canticles 6:12, as we did in chapter 2, which some commentators regard as a figure of Satan while others discern there a figure of Christ.[20] Or we learn of an Aminadab who is a chthonic servant in one of Nathaniel Hawthorne's stories.[21] Or we discover that Emmanuel Lévinas had a younger brother of that name who was killed by the Nazis.[22] Yet Aminadab himself is mentioned just once in the novel, almost at the end, and then only in passing. A young man tells Thomas that he would have been wise to have descended under the earth rather than attempt to climb to the top floor of the house he has entered. Down there, in the cool caves, he would have come upon a barrier of wood and a little latticework that the local tenants imagine to be a great door guarded by a man called Aminadab. "In reality, access to it is very easy," the young man adds; and we hear no more of the guard.[23] So there is perhaps more reason to look for significance in the name itself—"my people are generous (or noble)"—than for a thematic relation with a biblical character. Even then, text and title do not suddenly fall into alignment. Our research will have told us more about the name Aminadab than we knew before, but it has hardly put us in a better position to read Blanchot's novel.

Another sort of difficulty may be found in a récit published several years later, *Au moment voulu* (1951). It concerns a first-person narrator and two women, Judith and Claudia, although the narrative perplexes anything that might seem to be a clear sense of the relations between these three, including whether they even answer to these names. Toward the end of his story the narrator tries to make sense of the relation or nonrelation he has had with Judith. He says, "she was not bound to me by a relation of friendship or enmity, happiness or distress; she was not a disembodied instant, she was alive." Then he reflects:

> And yet, as far as I can understand, something happened to her that resembled the story of Abraham. When Abraham came back from the country of Moria, he was not accompanied by his child but by the image of a ram, and it was with a ram that he had to live from then on. Others saw the son in Isaac, because they didn't know what had happened on the

mountain, but he saw the ram in his son because he had made a ram for himself out of his child. A devastating story.[24]

Judith is compared with Abraham—"I think Judith had gone to the mountain"—and, beyond the recounting of the Akedah or binding of Isaac, this identification makes us wonder about the biblical counterparts of the other characters in the story. There has been debate whether Claudia or the narrator stands for Isaac.[25] Here, though, I am less interested in pondering that question than in pointing out how Blanchot allows one biblical narrative to haunt another. The very name Judith, meaning "Jewess," recalls the deuterocanonical book of that title, and it is difficult to exclude the biblical character from a reading of the récit.[26] In *Au moment voulu* the narratives of Abraham and Judith quietly engage one another and produce an irregular pattern of interference that cannot be stopped or calculated in advance.

2

Blanchot's readings of Greek myths—Orpheus and Eurydice, Odysseus and the Sirens—are given a central position when critics try to come to terms with his understanding of literature. Less familiar, almost unremarked by Blanchot himself, and yet very important, is his use or abuse of biblical material. I have already noted his citation of "Lazare, veni foras," and I would like to return to it for a while. In *L'Espace littéraire* Blanchot takes one of Christ's miracles and recasts it as a perfectly ordinary literary event. Reading is a "'miracle,'" he says, one that allows us to discern "the sense of all thaumaturgies": the tomb is not only the space of absence but also the means by which presence appears. "To roll back the stone, to obliterate it, is certainly something marvelous, but it is something we achieve at every moment in everyday language."[27] He has in mind the act of reading, and he develops the conceit: "At every moment we converse with Lazarus, dead for three days—or dead, perhaps, since always. In his well-woven winding sheet, sustained by the most elegant conventions, he answers us and speaks to us within ourselves" (195). We learned at the start of *L'Espace littéraire* that "the writer [is] dead as soon as the work exists" (23; 16). Yet reading is figured here not as a resuscitation of the author but as the bringing forth of "the work" ("l'œuvre"). The book is not a stone to be rolled away, for the work is hidden in the book. Reading or resuscitation involves a "violent rupture" (196; 258), and it can never be guaranteed that we have brought literature to light. Some part of it must remain buried in the tomb, the Lazarus "who already smells bad, who is Evil, Lazarus lost and not Lazarus saved and brought back to life."[28]

Several years before speculating on the death of the author in *L'Espace littéraire*, Blanchot had quoted the same three words from the Vulgate—"Lazare, veni foras"—in "La Littérature et le droit à la mort" (1947–48) when making a slightly different point by way of Hegel. To name something, the German philosopher wrote in the *Jenaer Systementwürf* (1803–4), is to annihilate it. Which becomes for his French admirer: "The 'existent' was called out of its existence by the word, and it became being."[29] Blanchot continues to paraphrase Hegel, yet now he goes by way of the Gospel. "This *Lazare, veni foras* summoned the dark, cadaverous reality from its primordial depths and in exchange gave it only the life of the mind" (326; 316). The name both destroys the absolute singularity of the creature named and preserves what truth it has at the level of the concept. Having evoked the Gospel, Blanchot reaches further back in the Bible to Exodus 33:20. The story is familiar. Moses has petitioned God, "shew me thy glory," but the Lord says, "Thou canst not see my face: for there shall no man see me, and live." Blanchot comments, "Whoever sees God dies. In speech what dies is what gives life to speech: speech is the life of that death, it is 'the life that endures death and maintains itself in it'" (327; 316). It is a curious conjunction, for in speaking one does not see God, and as likely as not we will recall that Hegel, whose *Phänomenologie* is quoted here, testifies in the same work to "the divine nature" of speech, its ability to turn "the mere 'meaning' right round about, making it into something else."[30] For Blanchot, who is writing on behalf of literature, "God" stands for any immediate singularity, since that which transcends all concepts and that which falls beneath them are both ineffable.[31] Literature wants precisely what it cannot have, the absolutely singular, and it cannot have it because this singularity is destroyed by the very conceptuality that makes literature possible. It seems that, despite complaints and ruses, literature must content itself with a false resurrection of a "this" into a concept. Far from being a triumph over death, however, the concept, as Hegel shows, is complicit with death. Only because of this allegiance can there be a dialectic at work.

Before saying any more about this situation, I would like to pause in order to note that resurrection is not only a defining motif of the Christian Bible for Blanchot but also a principal site of his contestation of that complex document and the spaces it opens. One can find evidence for this in his narratives as well as in his criticism. In *Thomas l'obscur* the fifth chant ends with an evocation of Thomas as an antibiblical character, "the only true Lazarus, whose very death was resurrected" (38; 42). Later, when Thomas reflects on Anne's death, he says, "A body without consolation, she did not hear the voice which asked, 'Is it possible?' and no one dreamed of saying of her what is said of the dead who lack courage, what

Christ said of the girl who was not worthy of burial, to humiliate her [*pour l'hu-milier*]: she is sleeping."[32] The allusion is to a story told in all the Synoptic Gospels, Jesus reviving Jairus's daughter, usually taken to be a tale of faith rather than humiliation.[33] Let us focus on the version given in Mark 5:21–43. Since the biblical narrative is important to *L'Arrêt de mort* (1948), Blanchot's strongest récit, I will stay with it for a while. Jairus petitions Jesus to save his child from death: "come [*veni* (Vulgate)] and lay your hands on her" (Mark 5:23). He agrees and is on his way to the sick house when he is distracted by "a certain woman." After he has dealt with her, word comes from the house that the girl has died, yet Jesus goes there anyway. Seeing the little girl, he asks those standing about, "Why make ye this ado, and weep? the damsel is not dead, but sleepeth" (Mark 5:39). The people standing by mock him, but "when he had put them all out," he goes to her, "And he took the damsel by the hand, and saith unto her, Talitha cumi; which is, being interpreted, Damsel, I say unto thee, arise. And straight-way the damsel arose, and walked" (Mark 5:40–42).

In *L'Arrêt de mort* the narrator himself partly assumes the role of Jesus when his friend J. dies of a sickness that "had made a child" of her (8; 18). To be sure, it is not his only role, and he does not play it fully or in a straightforward manner. Even so, we are hardly prepared for it. J.'s doctor tells the narrator, "'I am fortunate enough to have faith, I am a believer'" (9; 19). He asks the narrator, "'What about you?'" No answer is forthcoming, and we know he thinks the doctor is a vulgar fellow. Instead, we are told the following:

> On the wall of his office there was an excellent photograph of the Turin Sudario, a photograph in which he saw two images superimposed on one another: one of Christ and one of Veronica; and as a matter of fact I distinctly saw, behind the figure of Christ, the features of a woman's face—extremely beautiful, even magnificent in its strangely proud expression. One last thing about this doctor: he was not without his good qualities; he was, it seems to me, a great deal more reliable in his diagnoses than most. (9; 19–20)

One detail here calls for some explication, for at first the narrator seems to have made a simple error of fact. What people venerate as the Shroud of Turin is known in Greek as the *sindon*, meaning "linen cloth," which is supposed to contain an image, front and back, of the entire body, including the face, of Jesus after his crucifixion. Where Mark, Matthew, and Luke agree to speak only of a *sindon*, the Fourth Gospel also mentions a *sudarium* or napkin that was placed over Jesus's face (John 20:6–7). Those who argue for the authenticity of the Shroud have always been troubled by the addition: either the Gospel is mistaken or the image of Jesus's face must have passed through the *sudarium* to the *sindon*. At any rate, there may well be a "Turin Sindon" but there is no "Turin Sudario."

Popular traditions have risen about images of Jesus's face. One of the oldest stems from the fourth century when word spread of an "Image of Edessa": a supernatural portrait of Jesus's face that the Messiah created to help a king who had become a leper. Deriving from this tradition in the fourteenth century is another with even less historical support. Here we are told that a woman called Veronica gave Jesus a cloth with which to wipe his face while he was struggling with his cross along the Via Dolorosa. An image of his face was said to have been imprinted there. Now no one has ever claimed to see a woman's face on the *sindon* or on the *sudario*, presumably now lost if it ever existed. Yet the narrator is not reporting a confusion on the doctor's part or confirming an odd interpretation of the Turin Shroud. Once we recognize that Blanchot is resetting the story of the revival of Jairus's daughter, we are likely to remember that this story, as told by Mark, intercalates another pericope, quite likely from a pre-Markan source. This is the narrative of the woman who distracts Jesus on the way to Jairus's house in the hope that, by touching his garment, she will be cured of "an issue of blood" she has had for twelve years (Mark 5:25). According to pious legend, this woman's name is Beronice or Veronica, and she is the same person who will later help Jesus on the Via Dolorosa.[34] We know that she had "suffered many things of many physicians . . . but rather grew worse" (Mark 5:26). Perhaps it is this suppositious Veronica who truly stands behind the image of Jesus in the photograph on the doctor's wall and whose "extremely beautiful" face and "strangely proud expression" are both admired by the narrator. That she has had such trouble with doctors for so long makes us think of J., sick for ten years, whom the narrator also introduces by way of an image, a photograph.[35]

Eventually J. dies, and the narrator is summoned by J.'s sister, Louise, to the apartment. When he arrives, Louise retreats, sensing that "something was about to happen that she knew she did not have the right to see, nor anyone else in the world" (19; 35), and so she takes the other mourners away. The narrator is left alone with J. "I leaned over her, I called to her by her first name; and immediately—I can say there wasn't a second's interval—a sort of breath came out of her compressed mouth, a sigh which little by little became a light, weak cry" (20; 36). In the Gospel the little girl arises "straightway" and walks, then Jesus sensibly tells those standing around and gawking to get her something to eat. In Blanchot's narrative, however, another detail is added:

At that moment, her eyelids were still completely shut. But a second afterwards, perhaps two, they opened abruptly and they opened to reveal something terrible which I will not talk about, the most terrible look [*le regard le plus terrible*] which a living being can receive, and I think that if I had shuddered at that instant, and if I had been afraid, everything would have been lost, but my tenderness was so great that I didn't even think about the strangeness of what was happening, which certainly seemed to me altogether natural because of that infinite movement which drew me towards her, and I took her in my arms, while her arms clasped me, and not only was she completely alive from that moment on, but perfectly natural, gay and almost completely recovered. (20; 36)

What is this "terrible look"? Earlier, when the narrator was not in her apartment, J. asked her nurse, "'Have you ever seen death [*la mort*]?'" The nurse replied, "'I have seen dead people, Miss,'" only to hear the ominous rejoinder, "'No, death! . . . Well, soon you will see it'" (16; 30). It is tempting to read J.'s dark gaze as death itself looking at the narrator, rather than the nurse; and, as we will see, this is in fact what occurs. Yet when J. suffers a fatal relapse, the narrative forbids us to yield to that temptation in order to explain J.'s remark. Let us return to that episode. It begins with J. declining a shot of morphine, and ends with J. fulfilling her promise to her nurse. "Then she turned slightly towards the nurse and said in a tranquil tone, 'Now then, take a good look at death [*la mort*],' and pointed her finger at me" (28; 48). If the narrator, half accepting a silent prompt from Louise that perhaps originates in him, comes to be a latter-day Jesus, the role of death is explicitly assigned to him by J. He is *la mort*. Does it matter that the noun is female and he is male? In one sense, not at all; and yet, once raised, the question opens another dimension of the récit.

Far from enjoying good health, the narrator has earlier revealed that J.'s doctor has told him that by rights he should be dead. But J. indicates *death* with her finger, not a man who should be dead. Perhaps she remembers that he agreed with her proposal to kill herself—"I can see how bitter she had felt when she heard me agree to her suicide" (5; 13)—and perhaps this is sufficient for him to represent death. It needs to be recalled that the narrator does eventually help J. to die: "'Quick, a shot,'" J. instructs him, without exactly imploring him to help her die. "I look a large syringe, in it I mixed two doses of morphine and two of a sedative, four doses altogether of narcotics" (30; 52), we are told, and several minutes later J. dies again. Keeping all that in mind, we must admit that the récit tells a more complex story than has been suggested thus far, for the narrator is called to the apartment when J. is dying. "Come, please come [*Venez, je vous en prie*], J. is dying"

(17; 31), pleads Louise (and maybe we recall "I pray thee, come [*veni* (Vulgate)] and lay your hands on her" [Mark 5:23]). Yet the narrator does not at first arrive as healer. We learn a little later that "the receiver had hardly been hung up when her pulse, the nurse said, scattered like sand" (19; 34). Before J. identifies the narrator as death, the narrative leaves open the possibility that he is suited to that very role. Yet when J. points her finger at him and indicates to the nurse that *he* is death, she has already been saved from death by the narrator. We know that J. was not aware of having died, but perhaps there is more at work here than her inability to experience her own demise. In yet another meditation on "Lazare, veni foras," this time in *L'Entretien infini*, Blanchot makes an observation that helps to explain this strange state of affairs. He suggests that the force that brought Lazarus back to life "is no doubt admirable" but that it is "precisely a force" and that it "comes in this decision from death itself."[36] In reviving J., the narrator is colluding with death considered as a force, the very death that Hegel assimilated to the negativity of the dialectic.

Is there a death other than the one that reveals itself in negativity? There is, Blanchot assures us, although it cannot show itself in the order of phenomena, and therefore Hegel bypasses it in the *Phänomenologie*. It is not death in its dialectical guise, because this darker side of death "manifests existence without being, existence which remains below existence, like an inexorable affirmation, without beginning or end."[37] This is not death as a force, which would mark a clean break with life by way of either nothingness or an afterlife, but death as radical passivity: an endless dying that cannot be experienced but that no experience ever quite eludes. Blanchot regards this aspect of death, *le mourir*, as the neuter or the "he" (*il*). And this, I take it, is what is revealed to the narrator when J. raises her eyelids: the reluctant withdrawal of "the *He* of Sovereign Death" ("le *Il* de la Mort souveraine").[38] This is not the death that, for Hegel, conspires with negativity in order to constitute the "I" (*Je*) but the death that cannot be suborned by negativity and that undoes the "I." It is "a death that no individual death satisfies."[39] The narrator glimpses the *il* before J. is once again *elle*; it is "something terrible which I will not talk about, the most terrible look [*le regard le plus terrible*] which a living being can receive" (20; 36).

After Jesus raises the little girl to whose deathbed he has been summoned, we hear no more of her. The Gospel narrative moves along briskly, "And he went out from thence, and came into his own country; and his disciples follow him" (Mark 6:1). We know without having to be told that Jairus's daughter must eventually die again. In Mark's narrative, her resuscitation foreshadows Jesus's resurrection. Blanchot rewrites and redirects the biblical story by adding the completion that

Mark omits. As he tersely puts it in another work, "The dead came back to life dying."[40] The first part of *L'Arrêt de mort* is not simply a resetting of Mark 5:35–43; it twists the narrative beyond belief, and not only because it involves the myth of Orpheus and Eurydice.[41] The story of J. ends with the narrator reflecting on what has happened:

> I myself see nothing important in the fact that this young woman was dead, and returned to life at my bidding, but I see an astounding miracle in her fortitude, in her energy, which was great enough to make death powerless as long as she wanted. One thing must be understood: I have said nothing extraordinary or even surprising. What is extraordinary begins at the moment I stop. But I am no longer able to speak of it. (30; 52–53)

The passage progresses by coding the extraordinary as the ordinary and vice versa. One event, the narrator's judgment that J.'s fortitude is "an astounding miracle," can be explained naturalistically: it comes as a change in perspective and is a characteristic modern response to the world of the Bible. Also we need to remember that, for the narrator, J. had already lived another life before dying the first time: "for her those few minutes had been a lifetime, more than that eternity of life they talk about" (19; 34). Yet when the narrator regards J.'s return to life as unimportant, his judgment is itself extraordinary precisely because our response to it is shaped by the Bible. Think of Mark 5:42, for example. When those who mocked Jesus for saying "the damsel is not dead, but sleepeth" saw her brought back to life, "they were astonished with a great astonishment." In denying the importance of J.'s resuscitation, and in saying "I have said nothing extraordinary or even surprising" when he himself has described it as "the miracle that I had brought about" (27; 47), the narrator moves away from the Gospel, but in which direction it would be hard to say.

Resurrection, for Blanchot, is both beholden to death and utterly ignorant of what death truly is. It draws its force from death considered as negativity, while disregarding its obscure dimension: a dying that never begins and never ends but eternally repeats itself and therefore dissimulates "itself." To affirm resurrection from the dead would be not to acknowledge the eternal return of dying. This anterior or impossible death never offers itself to comprehension, although one can become vaguely aware of it when suffering or pointlessly waiting. We cannot experience dying, for we come upon it only when there is no ground, no traction, for consciousness to take hold. Yet its sheer alterity dangles before us the thought of having an experience par excellence. The thought is delusory; at most, dying interrupts us, puts us to the test, but it can never be lived in the present. Indeed, it disperses the present and undoes any assurance we might have in the unity of the "I." Frightful as this dying might seem, it is to be affirmed, Blanchot tells us in a récit, for it announces "the renunciation of mystery, the ultimate insignificance of lightness."[42] If death enters into the life of the concept, dying declines any invitation to take part in either comprehension or history; it does not abolish the particular but, as it were, hails its singularity while not being able to speak of it.

There can be no gainsaying the fact that for Blanchot the Christian Bible is an invitation to enter mystery, an affirmation of significance, and a commitment to weight. This is one reason why critics have tended to read his work wholly by way of Greek mythology, especially the story of Orpheus and Eurydice which is, in its own way, an account of a failed resuscitation. That this story is central to Blanchot is not to be disputed: the author himself has underlined its importance, and rightly so.[43] Yet the Greek reference need not exclude a biblical equivalent. Before J. dies she murmurs, "Quick, a perfect rose [une rose par excellence]" (25; 44), later echoed in a macabre way by "Quick, a shot" (30; 51–52); and anyone who reminds us that the rose is an Orphic symbol is of course entirely right.[44] However, one should not thereby forget that the rose, along with the lily, is the preeminent biblical flower in European translations of the Scriptures. Nor should one automatically exclude the pertinence of Christian tradition for a writer brought up as a French Catholic. Chances are that Blanchot would have known the medieval tradition of giving a perfect rose in order to honor royalty, and a reader with such cultural knowledge might well find in J.'s final words an allusion to "sovereign death."

As a coda to this brief discussion of L'Arrêt de mort, I would like to say that, for all the passion that the primal poet has for his wife, the myth of Orpheus, as Blanchot reads it, speaks of the relative powers of art and death. And to this I add that Blanchot has also pondered the biblical conceit "for love is strong as death" (Cant. 8:6). Some Christian exegetes have seen this as an adumbration of the resurrection, although, to be sure, Blanchot takes it quite differently.[45] Nonetheless, it would be a weak reader who does not find Blanchot's novels and récits to be as profoundly about love and death as they are about art and death.

3

Let us return to our guiding question, "How for example to think the nearness [voisinage] of the Eternal in the Bible?" In thinking about it, admittedly at a distance, it has come to seem a strange question for Blanchot of all people to ask. After all, he is the one who insists that the eternal is a "temptation," the suspect thought of refusing to accept death.[46] It might seem even more strange if we recollect that he is intensely suspicious of the figure of the Book. Christ is the sole divinity represented in ancient art with a book scroll, and the Tanakh abounds with positive images of the book.[47] Why then should Blanchot take a positive interest in the Bible, the Book of books? *L'Entretien infini* begins by placing the Book in counterpoint with writing, understood in a fresh way as "an anonymous, distracted, deferred, and dispersed way of being in relation" (xii; vii). This relation disallows the Other to be subsumed dialectically by the Same and, equally, rejects the idea of the Self dissolving in the Other. It forms the basis of Blanchot's aesthetics (a poetics of the fragmentary), his ethics (a double dissymmetry of Self and Other), and his politics (a communism beyond communism). Once this new sense of writing begins to take hold, it brings everything into question, "first of all the idea of God, of the Self, of the Subject, then of Truth and the One, then finally the idea of the Book and the Work" (xii; vii). Moreover, this writing "far from having the Book as its goal rather signals its end" (xii; vii). It comes as no surprise to read in the last few pages of *L'Entretien infini* that "The book begins with the Bible" (427; 627). What remains unaccountable is that Blanchot wishes to think "the nearness [*voisinage*] of the Eternal in the Bible."

Extended remarks directly about the Bible are very rare in Blanchot, so it is worthwhile to see how he characterizes Scripture when he devotes more than a few sentences to it. In the meditation from which I have already quoted, he has already distinguished the book as an empirical artifact from "book" as the condition of possibility for reading and writing, and he has recalled the Jena romantics' project of the "absolute book." He alludes to Novalis, although we are just as likely to remember Friedrich Schlegel telling us in a fragment that "Bible" *means* "the book per se, the absolute book."[48] Recalling the Jena romantics' talk about the book as such cues him to mention Hegel, although the absolute book for the philosopher would be his *Enzyklopädie der philosophischen Wissenschaften* (1830) and not the Bible, which needs to be interpreted as religion before it can present the truth as such.[49] And he will of course evoke the quite different rigor of Lautréamont's *Les Chants de Maldoror* and Stéphane Mallarmé's project of *Le Livre*.[50] Having documented all that, Blanchot offers a fragment of his own about the Bible. Here are its first sentences:

> The book begins with the Bible in which the logos is inscribed as law. Here the book attains its unsurpassable meaning, including what exceeds its bounds on all sides and cannot be gotten past. The Bible refers language to its origin: whether it be written or spoken, this language forms the basis for the theological era that opens and endures for as long

as biblical space and time endure. The Bible not only offers us the pre-eminent model of the book, a forever unparalleled example, it also encompasses all books, no matter how alien they are to biblical revelation, knowledge, poetry, prophesy, and proverbs, because it holds in it the spirit of the book. The books that follow the Bible are always contemporaneous with it: the Bible doubtless grows, increases on its own through an infinite growth that leaves it identical, it being forever sanctioned by the relation of Unity, just as the ten Laws set forth and contain the monologos, the One Law, the law of Unity that cannot be transgressed, and that negation alone cannot deny. (42; 627)

Those last remarks on unity cannot be assailed by recalling that the word "Bible" derives from the Greek τὰ βιβλία, the books, for Blanchot has in mind the idea of the Bible, not its empirical form; and that idea, though formulated differently for the Tanakh and the Christian Scriptures, is certainly of a unified revelation.[51] In their different ways, Tertullian, Saint Irenaeus, and Origen all insisted on the unity of the Scriptures.[52] And until we rid ourselves of that revelation of unity, Blanchot thinks, we cannot enter "a nontheological future."[53]

Students of the Bible are likely to be puzzled by the expression "the logos is inscribed as law." Blanchot is not suggesting any relation between the Logos of John 1:1 and Torah. As becomes clear in the fourteenth fragment of his essay, he is exploring Talmudic and Kabbalistic distinctions between written and oral Torah. Now rabbinic Judaism teaches that written Torah, as preserved on the scrolls, is supplemented by oral Torah, which God gave to Moses along with written Torah, and which yields not only the Mishnah, the first written summary of the oral law, but also the principles and processes of reasoning about the law.[54] Blanchot relates a teaching from the Jerusalem Talmud concerning how Torah existed before creation: "It was written with letters of black fire upon a background of white fire" (Shekalim, 13b). He then adds the remarkable suggestion of Rabbi Isaac the Blind, father of Kabbalah, that the true written Torah is to be found in the white fire, the black fire being oral Torah.[55] On this interpretation, the Bible preserves oral Torah as legible and written or mystical Torah as illegible. Only Moses could steadily contemplate this ur-text. The greatest prophets can merely glimpse a little of its splendor, and as a whole it will remain invisible until the Messiah comes.

"The 'oral Torah' is therefore no less written than the written Torah," Blanchot says, "but is called oral in the sense that, as discourse, it alone allows there to be communication."[56] Kabbalah holds a fascination for Blanchot. He applauds its "striking search for anonymity" and notes its authors' general distaste for talk of divine union.[57] But his concern in citing it here is not so much to commend Hebraic mysticism as to introduce a more general distinction between "first" and "second" writing. The first is without origin, it is "the greatest violence, for it transgresses the law, every law, and also its own" (xii; viii), while the second is precisely the writing of the law that attempts to contain this anarchic writing but is forever interrupted by it. It is this second writing in which logos—language, reason, speech—appears as the law and the law as articulate, reasonable speech. By inscribing logos as law and law as logos, the Bible opens us to knowledge, even in its anti- and nonbiblical forms. If we object, as some people are likely to do, and make a competing claim for Plato over Moses, the Dialogues over the Bible, as the decisive opening of western thought, Blanchot will answer that writing for Plato remains alien and external to speech whereas, for Moses, it is what guarantees memorialization.[58]

God is the one who inaugurates "second writing," Blanchot thinks, not only because He writes the Ten Commandments on tablets of stone but also because He is committed in advance to unity. "God," we are told,[59] "is God only in order to uphold Unity and in this way designate its sovereign finality"; and he adds, "It is therefore of consequence to say: not the One God but Unity, strictly speaking, is God, transcendence itself" (433; 635). It is striking how readily Blanchot suborns Jewish faith in the one Lord to a philosophical concept of unity that comes from Greece.[60] This bypasses the possibility of reading *Elohim* as plural, which can be forgiven if Blanchot is aware of a theological tradition that imports Trinitarian assumptions into the passage; and it trusts exclusively to reading *Elohim* as proclaiming God's preeminence. Even more to the point, it elides the important distinction between Jewish monolatrism (in which only YHWH was worshiped, but the existence of other gods was conceded) and the absolute monotheism declared by Isaiah and Jeremiah in the postexilic period. There was no philosophical interest in God's unity in biblical times or even over the centuries when the Talmud was composed. For that, one has to wait until Moses Maimonides (1135–1204), and even then his concern was with demonstrating that God is one.[61] The proposition that God answers to Unity would have shocked him. Even the God of Lurianic Kabbalism, while remaining one, nonetheless manifests Himself in ten *sefirot*, from *Keter* to *Shekinah*. When Blanchot includes monolatrism and monotheism in what he rejects as "the One," he reaches a limit in what he can affirm of "being Jewish." Not all Jews pray the Shema—"Hear, O Israel: The LORD our God is one LORD" (Deut. 6:4)—and certainly not all Jews confess belief in the Lord or study Torah. Yet "being Jewish" minimally bespeaks a historical reference to Abraham and to monolatrism.[62]

At first one might be tempted to say that "being Jewish," for Blanchot, is to be grasped by way of exile and wandering in preference to affirming the one God. This would be too hasty, for he prizes the Tanakh as testimony. Consider how he continues his fragment on the Bible:

> The Bible: the testamentary book where the alliance, the covenant is declared, that is to say, the destiny of speech [*la parole*] bound to the one who bestows language [*le langage*] and where he consents to dwell through this gift that is the gift of his name; that is to say, also, the destiny of this relation of speech to language [*la parole au langage*] that is dialectics. It is not because the Bible is a sacred book that the books deriving from it—the entire literary process—are marked with the theological sign and cause us to belong to the theological realm. It is just the opposite: it is because the testament—the alliance or covenant of speech [*l'alliance de la parole*]—was enfolded in a book and took the form and structure of a book that the "sacred" (what is separate from writing) found its place in theology. The book is essentially theological. This is why the first manifestation of the theological (and also the only one that continues to unfold) could only have been in the form of a book. In some sense God only remains God (only becomes divine) inasmuch as He speaks through the book. (427–28; 627)

Blanchot rejects the common view that the book is a secularization of the Bible and is therefore haunted by theological assumptions. On the contrary, Israel's testament to the nations is held to be primary, and the presentation of this covenant in a book, the Tanakh, is regarded as generating the "sacred." Those scare quotes are Blanchot's and serve to indicate his distance from any confession in the theophany at Mount Sinai. Such distance is warranted, he thinks, because the sacred as traditionally understood can establish itself only with respect to "second writing," which, as we have seen, can always be interrupted by "first writing."

If this fragment seems to distinguish speech from writing, we have only to recall that *L'Entretien infini* begins with a long meditation on "Plural speech" which is coded as "the speech of writing" ("parole d'écriture") and which he describes in terms of the neutral. This "neutral" or "Outside" has been repressed in the western philosophical tradition, he thinks, yet it is always able to interrupt us in our most assured moments. We are told of "the glistening flow of the eternal outside."[63] On hearing this, biblical scholars are likely to murmur of eschatology, thinking of one or more of its senses; and for his part Blanchot will tell us that Israel's most significant bequest to us has been an anticipation of plural speech, or "first writing." It is, he admits, an unusual way of characterizing Israel's legacy:

> Here we should bring in the great gift of Israel, its teaching of the one
> God. But I would rather say, brutally, that what we owe to Jewish mono-
> theism is not the revelation of the one God, but the revelation of speech
> [parole] as the place where men hold themselves in relation with what
> excludes all relation: the infinitely Distant, the absolutely Foreign. God
> speaks, and man speaks to him. This is the great feat of Israel.[64]

What "we owe to Jewish monotheism" will depend a good deal on who "we" are, and the obligation is never going to be simple or straightforward: God's unity is one inheritance, without a doubt, but so too is purity of soul. That said, we need to notice that for Blanchot the preeminent divine predicate would be infinity, not being, goodness, love, or unity, and God's exemplary act would be speech. This is important, for he will come to argue that, strictly speaking, "the infinite" is announced in the speech of the other person, *Autrui*, who is to me as the Most High. It is the other person, not God, who creates "the fruit of the lips" (Isa. 57:19), whose each word is, simply by being a spoken word, a promise of peace to those who mourn, who must live without the face of God. This is a remarkable argument, central to the discourse of "religion without religion," and one that we should approach with care, and so I return to the passage I have just quoted.

The passage in question was published in 1962. Several years before, in 1959, Blanchot had broached the same thoughts in another essay. Here the recognition that Israel's "great feat" is dialogism, not monotheism, is not given with an air of muscular independence ("I would rather say, brutally . . .") but is credited to Martin Buber. As Blanchot phrases it, dialogue with God is to be prized over His Unity. In point of fact, Buber says something different, that Israel "pointed out that this God [i.e., "the one real God"] can be addressed by man in reality, that man can say Thou to Him."[65] Buber does not contend that monotheism is secondary to dialogism. Not at all: what is decisive in monotheism, he thinks, is the Jewish people's trusting relation to God, not the metaphysical claim that He is a unity.[66] Blanchot goes on to rephrase Buber:

> Speech alone can cross the abyss; the voice of God alone, God as voice, as
> power that addresses without letting itself be addressed in turn, makes
> this separation the locus of understanding. In every religion, no doubt,

there have been relations between Creator and creature through sacrifice, prayer, inner rapture. But in Israel, a unique relation of familiarity and strangeness, of proximity and distance, of freedom and submission, of simplicity and ritual complication comes to light, a relation whose speech—the mystery and friendship of speech, its justice and reciprocity, the call it conveys and the response it awaits—constitutes the principle of the substance.[67]

"Being Jewish," for Blanchot, turns on the uniqueness of a "relation of familiarity and strangeness." This "relation without relation," as he also calls it, can be found in the Bible, although only if we wrest the work from the book and suffer the consequences of the rupture. It would be a violent wrenching, for it would require us to read Torah without reference to the one God and would therefore transform Scripture from a confession of trust in God to a sketch of a possible ethics, an ethics of the impossible.

There has been a "change of epoch," a speaker suggests in one of the dialogues in *L'Entretien infini*, because we have finally started to experience what writing is. It is also ventured in the same piece that we are for the first time also in the position of being able to destroy ourselves, of ending history. "But are you sure it's the first time?" the other speaker asks. "Perhaps you've forgotten your Bible. Biblical man constantly lives from the perspective you describe as new" (269; 402). Be that as it may, this "change of epoch" requires us to recognize that the ethics that are attested in Torah can be seen more generally in "first writing" which is, as we have seen, "an anonymous, distracted, deferred, and dispersed way of being in relation" (xii; vii). Now one might object that Blanchot can get this far only by stretching Buber whose views, even when faithfully stated, are a bold reinterpretation of Judaism. Also, one might accuse Blanchot, like Philo Judaeus long before him, of allegorizing Judaism out of history, of figuring "speech" as "the promised land" (128; 187). "Being Jewish," it might be said, has become nothing more than an ethics of relationality: "the emergence of a network of relations that neither unite nor identify but maintain what is in relation at a distance, and make of this distance, recaptured as a form of alterity, a new power of determination" (251; 375). Moreover, this ethics is announced under the title "Atheism and Writing."

In self-defense Blanchot could fairly say that in calling speech "the promised land," he is indicating that conversation is the alternative to murder and gives us our best chance for peace. Even Christian theologians will sometimes say that the Kingdom of God comes to speech *as* parable.[68] Also, far from trying to allegorize the Jews out of history, he is seeking to indicate their uniqueness. Because of the revelation at Mount Sinai, the Jews are "set apart" from all other peoples—a judgment that causes problems of its own.[69] ("This is the justification for all ghettos," Blanchot says elsewhere, "and they in turn anticipate the sinister concentration camps, where there was nothing save waiting for death.")[70] Also, he would surely insist that he is not trying to shrink Jerusalem so that it fits inside Athens but rather showing us that Jerusalem cannot rightly stand for "singular" while Athens stands for "universal." On his understanding, when God declares, "all the earth is mine" (Exod. 19:5), he renews "the exigence of universality from which Jewish singularity cannot turn away."[71] Jewish singularity must, in responding to its vision of God, open itself toward that universality; and this is, he admits, an "Infinite task" (52). Without a doubt, the Jews have negotiated this double call of singularity and universality in a historically unique manner. All the same, for Blanchot the Jewish turn toward universality is a retreat from monotheism. Transcendence is to be conceived no longer in the time-honored terms of positive religion, a God abiding above or beyond the phenomenal world, but rather by way of the elevation of *Autrui*, the other person. God's refusal to be seen by Moses on Mount Sinai is exemplary here. For as the Jews come of age they eschew "religious experience" and stand as witnesses to the trace of the Infinite, opening themselves to an ethics based on responsibility. Lévinas would not be in complete agreement with all these claims as phrased here, although the view that religious transcendence derives from a primary ethical transcendence is one of his signature theses.[72] It is worth remarking the extent to which Blanchot subscribes to his friend's views. He was doubtful about what he took to be the veiled theological project of *Totalité et infini* (1961), yet was drawn to the revision of this that culminated so magnificently in *Autrement qu'être ou au-delà de l'essence* (1974). Let us therefore spend a little time with Lévinas in the years around and between these two books.

4

In "Judaïsme et temps présent" (1960) Lévinas asks with respect to Israel, "is one trying to preserve oneself within the modern world, or to drown one's eternity in it?"[73] Reason refutes "biblical cosmology," to be sure, yet no sooner has that scientific demonstration taken place than an inner life arises to stare down modern reason: "Eternity was rediscovered within the fortress-like inner life which Israel built on an unshakable rock" (211; 296). Almost immediately, though, "modern thought denounces the eternity of Israel by questioning whether the inner life itself is a site of truth" (211; 296). For

Lévinas, this social disengagement is a "false eternity" (213; 298), and Judaism, he thinks, "has always wished to be a simultaneous engagement and disengagement" (213; 298). What he has in mind is made more clear in "La Signification et le sens" (1964), one of the most important essays in carving out the passage that would lead from *Totalité et infini* to *Autrement qu'être*: "To be *for* a time that would be without me, *for* a time after my time, over and beyond the celebrated 'being for death,' is not an ordinary thought which is extrapolated from my own duration; it is the passage to the time of the other. Should what makes such a passage possible be called *eternity*?"[74] The explicit allusion is to Heidegger's discussion of Dasein as being-toward-death in *Sein und Zeit* §§ 46–53, which Lévinas regards as allowing ontology to hide the prior claim of ethics. It is the death of the other, he argues, and not my death that is truly significant for human being. I put this claim aside, since it will interest us in the following chapter, and consider instead how the passage I have just quoted is framed. Lévinas evokes "an eschatology without hope for oneself" (92; 45) and recalls the story told in Deuteronomy 3:23–28 of Moses praying to see the Promised Land and being rebuked by God and told that Joshua is to lead the people of Israel into the land of Canaan. We are later told in Deuteronomy 32:48–52 that Moses must climb Mount Nebo and see the Promised Land but die on the peak without entering the land himself. The land flowing with milk and honey, for Lévinas, is not for the Self to grasp but rather is to be freely given to the Other. Introduced with a Hebraic reference, the passage is concluded with admiring attention to a detail of Greek culture. The ethical "work" of which Lévinas approves is the passage from my persistence in being, the *conatus essendi*, to my being for the other. And this work has its concept fixed "with a Greek term 'liturgy,' which in its primary meaning designates the exercise of a function which is not only totally gratuitous, but requires on the part of him who exercises it a putting out of funds at a loss" (92–93; 45). Lévinas cannot be understood unless it is recognized that ethics, in his sense of the word, is prior to the cultural and theological division between Athens and Jerusalem.

"Eternity," then, is to be figured eschatologically, but in favor of the Other's future rather than the Self's. I am obliged to yield my *conatus* to the other person, yet I must not ask the Other to do the same for me. Several pages after putting things this way, however, Lévinas once again evokes eternity, and this time construes it by way of a past impossible to possess rather than of a future that I will never possess. I interrupt a long, difficult, and important meditation on the trace:

> The allegedly immediate and indirect relationship between a sign and
> the signified belongs to the order of *correlation*, and is thus still a recti-

tude, and a disclosure which neutralizes transcendence. The signifying-ness [*signifiance*] of a trace places us in a "lateral" relationship, uncon-vertible into rectitude (something inconceivable in the order of disclo-sure and being), answering to an irreversible past. No memory could follow the traces of this past. It is an immemorial past—and this also is perhaps eternity, whose signifyingness [*signifiance*] obstinately throws one back to the past. Eternity is the very irreversibility of time, the source and refuge of the past. (103; 64–65)

Eternity is the time of the Other; it is an "immemorial past," Lévinas says, by which he means that my responsibility for the other person is formed not in a present encounter or in a contract formed in a past present but in a time that is wholly the other person's and that has never been present to my consciousness. I am summoned by the Other not because of anything I might have done or not done, and not because of any rational or prudent agreement I might have made with either church or state. Eternity has no relation with the Cogito that would seek to conquer time; it has nothing to do with the perpetuation of one's being, or even with a present that does not pass. To prize the time of the other, to loosen the strings that join us and make me regard him or her as a modification of my con-sciousness, is for Lévinas to think the nearness of the eternal. "A trace qua trace does not simply lead to the past, but is the very passing toward a past more remote than any past and any future which still are set in my time—the past of the other, in which eternity takes form, an absolute past which unites [*réunit*] all times" (106; 68–69). Eternity does not offer itself for contemplation, it does not offer it-self at all: but it passes in acts of responsibility.

So when Blanchot asks, "How to think the nearness of the Eternal in the Bible?" he is at heart asking how we are to approach the Bible in terms of the ethics that Lévinas has elaborated and that he extends in the direction of "beyond good and evil," how we are to discern the time of the Other, alterity, in the Book of books, the very model of Totality, that speaks of God, the archetype of Unity. No-tice, though, that while Blanchot distances himself from all talk of Unity, Lévinas explicitly affirms that the immemorial past "unites all times." It will be worth-while to see if in fact the two friends disagree on this point, and the best way of do-ing so is to take a steady look at "La Signification et le sens." In its broadest sweep, the essay affirms the primacy of ethics in a time of cultural crisis brought about by the disclosure of an apparently irreducible plurality of linguistic and symbolic meanings. Nietzsche's proclamation of the death of God is coordinate with this "loss of unity," Lévinas suggests. He is far from simply lamenting the contemporary lack of belief in a transcendent deity or, indeed, in any meaning that subsists only in internal relations. After all, his favored philosophical method, phenomenology, maintains that the access to meaning always contributes to that meaning. Nonetheless, modern atheism has roots in this multiplication of sense. Lévinas himself is not prepared to abandon belief in God, even though he has little or no sympathy with Christian attempts to render the divinity intelligible by bringing it into correlation with the "I."

In his philosophical writings on God, essays such as "Enigme et phénomène" (1965) and "Dieu et la philosophie" (1975), Lévinas makes no appeal whatsoever to the authority of theology. Quite rightly, he sees that theology can be done only within the dimension of faith and that philosophical arguments cannot rely on theological insights. He does not offer a noncorrelational theology such as Karl Barth does, for example, but he does sketch a philosophy of religion that turns on a failure of correlation between the human being and the deity. One cannot have an intentional rapport with God, for the deity is not a phenomenon that can be situated in any horizons of consciousness whether known or unknown. Nor can the deity be reduced to a theme. Yet He can and does pass in the face of the other person: one discovers God not in commending oneself to a transcendent "Thou," let alone in mystical fusion, but in taking care of the material needs of the widow, the orphan, the stranger. Like Kant, Lévinas seeks to save religion from relying overly on the positivity of revelation; unlike Kant, he finds no moral law that is binding on all men and women but only a trace that disturbs the security of the subject in the present moment. Certainly he does not wish to devalue the importance of the positive religions, but he readily concedes that they are faced with a pressing difficulty. "The crisis of sense [sens] is thus experienced by our contemporaries as a crisis of monotheism."[75] In speaking of contemporaries he may well be thinking of his old friend Maurice Blanchot, among others. Against this general view, and perhaps even his friend's particular statement of it, he asserts that meaning, "the unity of sense" ("l'unité de sens") (87; 36), is to be found only in ethics; and because its provenance is the immemorial past it is therefore prior to history and the proliferation of meanings that characterizes our historical moment.

Where is this unity of meaning to be found? In the vulnerability of Saying, the exposure of the Self to the Other, regarded as the Most High, before a word is uttered. Of course, Saying inevitably declines into the Said, all the sentences that have been spoken and preserved, and so what begins as openness toward the Other can eventually be gathered into a totality. The works of the saints give way to the lives of the saints and to the metaphysics of the saints. Only the writing of poetry (understood broadly) in which the Said unsays itself can frustrate this gradual hardening into totality. Yet a meaning that is irreducible to the order of intelligibility can be found in any genuine movement from Self to Other; and since this responsibility is the sole "meaning" ("sens") that is not circumscribed by culture, Lévinas feels justified in speaking of "unity of meaning." Without this pretheoretical notion of unity, he argues, no one would be able to judge cultures: the utopic hope of a better world for those who are to come would give way to a dystopic world here and now in which cultures would lord it over the Good. Only the trace, venturing from a past that has never been present, disturbing and exceeding all immanence, prevents such dystopias from forming and remaining in place permanently; and it is this trace, arising from the absolute past of the other person, that Lévinas thinks gives us our approach to eternity. The implication is that the transcendence spoken of by the positive religions derives from a fundamental ethical insight.

Although Lévinas rejects totality, he is committed on ethical grounds to unity. To be sure, this unity does not belong to the realms of ideality or even intelligibility; and so it remains obscure. If we inquire more closely what he means by it, we find an answer in "Langage et proximité" (1967). In the sixth part of that essay Lévinas reminds us that Descartes in the *Discourse on Method* weighs the ancient view that animals can communicate in their own languages although we cannot understand them. This is false, we are assured. "For if this were true, since they have many organs which are allied to our own, they could communicate their thoughts to us just as easily as to those of their own race."[76] Rather than object to the disparagement of animals, Lévinas approves Descartes's insight that there could be "a language that would be imprisoned in the particularisms of a species."[77] "Language," he insists (thinking only of humans), "is the possibility of entering into relationship independently of every system of signs common to the interlocutors" (122; 232). In other words, there is a Saying without a Said, an exposure to the Other that precedes any and all conventional signs. "Like a battering-ram, it is the power to break through the limits of culture, body, and race," he says, then adds, "Our analyses have brought us to see fraternity with the neighbor as the essence of the original language; it finds universality, or, more precisely, universalization, starting with absolute singularities" (122; 232). Unity, then, is to be grasped as a capacity for ethical action, one that is complete in itself and is held by all human beings, regardless of their differences.

Blanchot firmly agrees with Robert Antelme that "there are not several human races, there is only one human race [*il y a une espèce humaine*]" and that because the SS "have sought to call the unity [*l'unité*] of this human race into question that they'll finally be crushed."[78] And so he is not likely to disagree with Lévinas's claim about the unity of ethical action. Nor perhaps would he wish wholly to dissociate himself from Lévinas's phrasing when his friend says, "Peace is a mode of unity superior to the unity of the One."[79] Yet when Blanchot tells us, as we have already heard, "The Bible refers language to its origin," he is not evoking an Adamic ethical meaning but is rather drawing attention to "the law of Unity that cannot be transgressed" because even the thought of God, which is always excessive, is subservient to Unity.[80] The unity at issue in ethics—nonideal, nonintelligible—can be affirmed, it seems, while the unity spoken of in metaphysics is to be rejected or at least seen to be part of a double relation. The question remains whether God must be thought according to metaphysical unity. Blanchot skirts the question when acknowledging that Judaism has been a witness to the temptation of presence, and he observes that the disciples on the road to Emmaus confessed belief in the divine presence only after Jesus had left them.[81] But the question whether divinity is necessarily linked to presence is never rigorously posed by him, let alone answered.

5

It is entirely reasonable for Blanchot to announce that his inquiry into "being Jewish" does not proceed from any "religious exigency."[82] However, it is regrettable that this inquiry finds it necessary to strip religiosity from "being Jewish." Lévinas is sometimes vulnerable to the charge of overweening ethicity. Not content with recasting ethics as "first philosophy," he allows it to dominate the whole of philosophy. So runs one objection. In showing how ethics brings God to thought he indicates a path from the world to God, an endless à-dieu in which our spiritual hungers are satisfied in meeting the material needs of others. It is impressive, though part of its force comes precisely from minimizing God's fundamental interruption to earthly existence, namely, revelation. So runs another objection.[83] And, as with all talk of religion without religion, there is a reduction of God to just one of the transcendentals: He is approached by way of Justice, while Being and Beauty, Truth and Unity, are bypassed. So runs a third objection. Even Lévinas, who distrusts the sacred because of its associations with fusion and magic and instead favors the holy, which he takes to be "ethical meaning as the ultimate intelligibility of the human," does not see desacralization as removing mystery or religious ritual from the world.[84] It is Blanchot more than Lévinas who seems the more poorly defended against the charge of a reductive ethicity, at least with respect to religion.

"Ethicity" is not to be confused with ethics in any of its usual senses, if only because Blanchot affirms an "ethics" that is beyond good and evil, something already noted in passing and that will concern us in the following chapter.[85] For Blanchot it is as though monotheism were merely the seed from which, at one time or another, this "ethics"—in order to drop the scare quotes, let us call it an ethics of relationality—could grow. In a letter written to Salomon Malka in 1988 he recalls the 1940s: "It was obviously the Nazi persecutions . . . that made us feel that the Jews were our brothers, and that Judaism was more than just a culture, more than just a religion even, because it was the foundation of our relationship to others [autrui]."[86] And earlier, in 1962, he asked rhetorically, "Is there not in Judaism a truth that is not only present in a rich cultural heritage, but also living and important for the thought of today—even if this thought challenges every religious principle?"[87] Judaism exists, he suggests, "so [pour que] the idea of exodus and the idea of exile can exist as a legitimate movement [mouvement juste]; it exists, through exile and through the initiative that is exodus, so that [pour que] the experience of strangeness may affirm itself close at hand as an irreducible relation" (125). In order to understand this bold claim we need to recognize that Blanchot has not one but at least two targets in his sights.

In the first place, and obviously so, Blanchot is attempting to detach Judaism from its religious contexts. The move is ultimately Hegelian. Judaism belongs to a dialectical movement: things happen so that other things might be generated in turn. Yet Hegel would pay a little more attention to the specifics of religious practice. No mention is made by Blanchot, for instance, of the *Shekinah*, the abiding presence of God in the Tabernacle. With the destruction of Jerusalem in 587 BCE and the beginning of the Babylonian exile, the divine presence was believed to dwell with the Jews in the Tabernacle throughout their sojourn outside Israel. Unity with the divine was reconfigured: along with His people, God suffered the *galuth* or exile. The sense of unconditional unity between God and Israel was not called into question by the exile. "God himself separates himself from himself," Franz Rosenzweig says, "he gives himself away to his people, he shares in their sufferings, sets forth with them into the agony of exile, joins their wanderings."[88] To which André Neher, a scholar whose views on prophecy influenced Blanchot, adds, "The *Shekinah* resides with every exiled fragment of the Jewish people. In every particle of land trodden by a Jew in exile the presence of God is revealed. Far from being an outward road leading the Chosen People farther and farther away from the center of their election, the Exile is for Israel a mission, each stage of which strengthens the bonds between the Jew and the God who accompanies him."[89]

"The Jew can only be understood theologically, because—and in this he is unique among mankind—he exists theologically."[90] I have quoted the Catholic theologian Heinrich Schlier, although one could cite any number of Jewish and Christian writers who make the same point though not always in the service of the same end. A word or two of clarification is needed. There are orthodox Jews who insist that the Jew exists theologically and that this existence is absolutely primary with respect to other dimensions of life. From them, as for liberal and reformed Jews, no Gentile who holds the Jewish faith and follows the prescribed rituals is therefore already a Jew: a formal process of conversion is required. By the same token, an atheist Jew is still a Jew, even for the most orthodox rabbi, even though, from that perspective, he or she might be regarded as partly blind to what it means to be Jewish. Now I take it that Schlier does not wish to suggest that the Jew does not live in several dimensions at once. His point is that the Jew is historically unique in that a theological dimension cannot be eliminated from his or her existence, regardless of personal belief or lack of belief. We might well ask if Blanchot is rejecting an orthodox view (a Jew is anyone whose mother is Jewish or who has been properly converted) or a reformed view (a Jew is anyone, raised as a Jew, who has at least one Jewish parent). The answer, I think, is both. In saying that, however, I am not suggesting that Blanchot is endorsing the redefinition of "being Jewish" proposed at the very end of the nineteenth century by Asher Ginzberg (Ahad Haam). He is no more a "spiritual Zionist" than he is a rationalist. Unlike the spiritual Zionists, he vigorously declares that Israel should exist as a political state, and he does not affirm cultural over theological categories.[91] Nor is Blanchot a "political Zionist," inheriting ideas from Theodor Herzl. Rather, he preserves theological categories in order to interpret them in a manner that is incompatible with monotheism as he understands it. Blanchot does not exclude revelation so much as construe it in terms of positivity and then drain it of that positivity.

I do not think that Blanchot entirely allegorizes the Jews out of history. He maintains that Judaism is a rupture within time, one that allows Jews to participate "in history in an entirely other manner" and that allows all human beings to hear "the original rupture, which is anterior to history," that is, the eternal murmur of the Outside.[92] What is specific to the Jews, not by their nature but by their being regarded as *Autrui*, allows all men and women to recognize the human relation. "Judaism is an essential modality of all that is human": so Lévinas said to Salomon Malka in an interview.[93] In firm agreement with his friend, Blanchot perhaps goes further than Lévinas would in identifying a second target. Not only is the sacred to be liberated from religion (and recoded in terms of the experience of strangeness), but also the faith of the Jews in God is to be rethought in terms of faith in the other person. The Jew teaches us, not to believe in the Lord God, but rather to acknowledge that when the other person speaks he or she speaks as God. This deity is not the original rupture in history. The otherness that fascinates Blanchot is that of the Outside, and it enters history through the Jews. They have grasped the truth of revelation in the Talmud. It is that the other person is strictly unknown and therefore approaches me in a movement of the neutral. Frightening as this alterity is, I must have faith in that other person, sufficient faith to talk with him or her. In scholastic terms, this is the substitution of credence for faith.[94]

The relation of particularity and modality in Judaism will concern us in the next chapter. In concluding this chapter, however, I would like to note that Blanchot's emphasis on the historical evolution of Judaism from a religion to an ethical relation beyond good and evil has difficulties of its own. To begin with, seizing only on exodus and exile as distinguishing traits of Judaism is to give an excessively stripped-down interpretation of being Jewish.[95] And one might object that the concentration of just these traits ignores the beginnings of the two stories: Abram's exile from his homeland begins as an act of obedience to God, and the exodus from Egypt takes place in the promise that God gave first to Abram and then to Moses. If "being Jewish" has passed from a response to the transcendence of God to a response to the transcendence of *Autrui*, the Jew who follows the God of Abraham, Isaac, and Jacob is informed that this belief is superfluous to his or her being a Jew. How can this not be taken as an affront? Blanchot asserts that an ethics of relationality "challenges every religious principle." He is led to this position by relying overly on a dubious etymology of "religious": "that which binds, that which holds together."[96] What offends Blanchot in religion is its presumptive claim to unity; and yet, as Lévinas has shown us, ethics *itself* relies on a unity.

More positively, there is another way of interpreting the Jewish struggle between singularity and universality, one that Blanchot does not consider precisely because of his conviction as an atheist. A turn to universality can be grasped in terms of the Jews' developing consciousness of monotheism. Judaism began, as we have seen, in the monolatrism of the early tribes and continued down to the monarchy. "If the LORD have stirred thee up against me, let him accept an offering: but if they be the children of men, cursed be they before the LORD; for they have driven me out this day from abiding in the inheritance of the LORD, saying, Go, serve other gods" (1 Sam. 26:19). Yet monotheism began to be forcefully felt in Deutero-Isaiah. "I am the Lord, and there is none else, there is no God beside me: I girded thee, though thou hast not known me" (Isa. 45:5). There is no reason to think that this blossoming of monotheism in Judaism is not capable of further theological development. If God created everything, then all that lives is related to everything else, and all men and women are called upon to respect that life. When God declares, "all the earth is mine," He plainly calls for a universality that is tied to monotheism; and it should be noted that the call is not only for responsibility for other human beings, to which Blanchot, like Lévinas, restricts it, but also for life as such. From this vantage point, one could envisage a historical evolution of monotheism, one in which respect for life expands from an ethnic group to include all men and women and that finally will come to encompass animals and insects, forests and oceans.

"How for example to think the nearness [*voisinage*] of the Eternal in the Bible?" By reinterpreting the Eternal as the time of the Other, the Most High, who calls me "to a relation that is 'incommensurable with a *power* exercised, a conquest, a joyful possession or a knowledge.'"[97] Blanchot quotes Lévinas, and then paraphrases him, "All true discourse . . . is discourse with God, not a conversation held between equals" (56; 80). Not to recognize the elevation of the other person, Blanchot says elsewhere, would be to repeat the terrible story of Cain and Abel.[98] It might be said that Blanchot could equally have invoked Buber, who has surely influenced Lévinas on just this point: "Every particular *Thou* is a glimpse through to the eternal *Thou*; by means of every particular *Thou* the primary word addresses the eternal *Thou*."[99] Yet to cite Buber would be to miss what Blanchot is urging us to accept: that *Autrui*, the other person, *is* the Most High. For Buber, the Bible records the Jews' colloquies with God, although these events continue outside the Book and even outside its laws. Blanchot the atheist would not put things in quite this way, and he conceives the work that we must wrest from the Bible to be an ethics: an endless conversation between self and other, to be sure, but also a conversation that turns on the irruption of the infinite in the space between self and other and that reveals both speakers to be irreducibly strange because they are human. Nowhere does he do this more fully than in *L'Entretien infini* itself, a text that, for all its concern with Greek mythology and philosophy, contests, reworks, displaces, and yet perpetuates the Bible.

7

•

THE HUMAN RELATION

1

Since our last conversation [*entretien*], I've been thinking that if what you [*vous*] say points in the right direction [*une direction juste*], the human relation, as it affirms itself in its primacy, is terrible.

—Most terrible [*terrible*], but without terror [*terreur*].

—It is most terrible because it is tempered by no intermediary. For in this view there is between man and man neither god, nor value, nor nature. It is naked relation, without myth, devoid of religion, free of sentiment, bereft of justification, and giving rise neither to pleasure [*jouissance*] nor to knowledge [*connaissance*]: a neutral relation, or the very neutrality of relation. Can this really be asserted?[1]

I would like to replay this brief exchange as slowly as I can, listening for what is said, for what is not formulated as clearly or as fully here as elsewhere, for what the form of the text might tell us, and for what is perhaps claimed too firmly. "We must try not to hurry" (60; 85), one of the speakers says a little later in the dialogue, "Tenir parole" (1962). It is very good advice for himself and his interlocutor since, after all, they are attempting to sketch a new mode of being in the world: a way of living and dying that would take place without reference to God, value, or human nature. To move too quickly would be to risk remaining in thrall to unity and all the old ways by which being human has been regulated. "We do not seek to rid ourselves all at once of unity," one of the speakers concedes in a later exchange; "what a joke that would be" (67; 95–96). Not to hurry is sound advice for the reader as well, although Blanchot would be the first to point out that reading and talking, like reading and writing, are not the same.

To read is "to allow the book to *be*," to erase the author from the sentences, paragraphs, and chapters that claim your attention.[2] Now, as you hold it in your hands and begin to read it, the story, novel, poem, or dialogue "has become a book minus the sometimes terrible [*terrible*], the always formidable experience which the reader effaces" (193; 254); it is "the experience of creation . . . the torments of the infinite" (196; 259), "the movement which exposes the creator to the threat of the essential solitude and delivers him to the interminable" (197; 259). Unlike writing, reading seems to be a "weightless yes" (197; 260), a welcome to the work, a space in which the work can be simply itself, unencumbered by its author.[3] Because of this lightness, the reader experiences "the joy of plenitude, the sure evidence of complete success, the revelation of the unique work" (197; 260). In a sharp twist of romantic doctrine, Blanchot sees reading, not writing, as better evoking "the divine aspect of creation" (197; 260). If reading puts us in mind of creation, it also makes us think of resurrection: the "Lazare, veni foras" that I touched on in the previous chapter is the call of the reader to the work buried in the book. Yet can the lightness and innocence of reading ever be a problem when reading certain works? Could it be that to follow Blanchot's speakers in "Tenir parole" as they explore what is most terrifying is, by the very act of reading, to reduce the gravity of their concern?

Not at all: the welcome extended by reading need not perpetually defer all analysis. Reading for Blanchot is not the same as comprehension or interpretation, let alone judgment. It is part of the work, he says, and this insight modifies how we understand the innocence of reading. Every work, regardless of its genre, is at heart a "dialogue," he assures us.[4] The claim boldly reverses a sense of a text that has been firmly in place for several centuries. It was Peter Ramus (1515–72) who ushered dialogue out of both dialectic and rhetoric, giving pride of place to monologue; and his strict framing of method in terms of logic—mono-logos—has been extraordinarily successful.[5] His influence on Descartes's understanding of method is well known; the philosopher learned logic from a post-Ramist textbook at La Flèche. To think of a text as dialogue is to acknowledge a distant world oriented more to auditory than to visual perception. It is also, as we saw in the previous chapter, to align oneself with the Jewish notion of a God with whom one can talk across the infinite distance between the human and the divine.

Notice that Blanchot places scare quotes around "dialogue." He has good reasons for using them, for he has something more like a fight than a discussion in mind. In each and every work, he thinks, there is a "more original combat of more indistinct demands, the torn intimacy of irreconcilable and inseparable moments which we call measure and measurelessness, form and infinitude, resolution and indecision" (199; 264). Reading does not pass like an angel above the work; it is within it, a part of its primal agon, a response to a call that quietly comes from beyond that struggle, from "before" it even commenced, if the expression be allowed. There are therefore two calls in the act of reading: the reader's imperious summons for the work to enter the light of understanding, "Lazare, veni foras," which can never be obeyed fully, and a more gentle if unnerving solicitation that comes to the reader from far within the work itself. To read is to respond to that second call and, in doing so, to make the work communicate. That last verb must be taken in a robust sense. For Blanchot, the reader as well as the writer is a *makar*.

So when we are taught that reading allows a book to *be*, we are told only a part of what is at issue, since reading also puts us in relation with the book. Intimate as reading can be, the relationship is never personal. The book is unconcerned with me as an individual: *I* am never uniquely addressed, even though I might like to think I am. While the singularity of our encounter is to be respected, a distance between book and reader is also to be preserved, and it is in this interval that communication takes place. If we ask what is communicated we will get an unusual answer, since Blanchot is interested in something more fundamental than semantic content. It is the ceaseless struggle that we have just heard about that is communicated, a combat between a text's origin and its beginning, between the writer's fascination with the Outside and the leap into writing that breaks the grip of that implacable gaze on the writer. The exact form of this conflict will differ from work to work and from writer to writer, and no struggle is ever communicated in a simple, undifferentiated manner. In reading, Blanchot thinks, we respond to a call that increasingly reveals itself to come from the obscure origin of the work: the narrative voice rather than the narrator's voice, the eternal murmur of the Outside and not the more or less articulate speech of characters, narrators, and author.[6] Dialogue and narration provide the opportunity for the murmur to be heard, if one is sufficiently attuned to it and attentive to its call. And so the reader as well as the writer can be exposed to "a neutral relation, or the very neutrality of relation."

It would seem then that there is a rapport between reading and the "human relation," as Blanchot sketches it. Or, if you like, there is an affiliation that allows us to slip from "communication" to "community," one that brings to mind Hölderlin's well-known lines in "Friedensfeier":

> *Viel hat von Morgen an,*
> *Seit ein Gespräch wir sind und hören voneinander,*
> *Erfahren der Mensch; bald sind wir aber Gesang.*[7]

Less certain is whether this alliance can be discerned, rendered intelligible, and finally hailed as knowledge. In *La Communauté inavouable* (1983), Blanchot quotes a sentence by Edgar Morin and finds himself very much at home in his words: "Communism is the major question and the principal experience of my life. I have never stopped recognizing myself in the aspirations it expresses and I still believe in the possibility of another society and another humanity."[8] These are dignified words, and in reading them over Blanchot's shoulder we must remember that communism is anything but homogeneous, either in "itself" or as deployed in political acts. Elsewhere, Blanchot distinguishes Marx's "three voices" and notes the danger of construing communism in terms of an "immanence of man to man."[9] And more generally he doubts that communism can be thought properly by way of possibility in the first place. Even so, at first blush and even long after, we might well think that his understanding of community is more heavily marked by mysticism than by communism. It is developed in terms of transcendence; it passes by way of the sacred instead of the state; and there is far more talk of ecstasy than economics. Similarly, Blanchot's sense of communication appears to have less to do with a shared world of symbols that precedes and exceeds the individual than with a limit-experience that, while never presuming an isolated subject, can occur in episodes that are in principle private.

I would like to look back to the "last conversation" mentioned by the first speaker to see how the two characters have reached their current position. This earlier dialogue is entitled "Connaissance de l'inconnu," and it is the first of three pieces in *L'Entretien infini* (1969) that respond to Emmanuel Lévinas's *Totalité et infini* (1961). The third is "L'Espèce humaine," which is intriguingly devoted to Robert Antelme rather than Lévinas, and which Blanchot separated from the first two when he came to arrange the texts that constitute *L'Entretien infini*.[10] I would also like to glance ahead to the conversation that follows the first two in the book, "Le Rapport du troisième genre (*homme sans horizon*)," to find out how the "human relation" is specified in more detail. Since the exchange I quoted at the very start is a part of a wider discussion that Blanchot has been holding for many years with writers and philosophers, political thinkers and mystics, I will take the opportunity to look backward and forward, now thinking about terror and the terrible, now reflecting on community and friendship. The human relation, Blanchot says, posits no "god" and is "devoid of religion"; and yet the effort of breaking new ground, of moving into a "nontheological future" (262; 392), is offered under the sign of "prophetic eschatology" (58; 83) and turns on a "revelation" (55; 79). At the very least, this phrasing is curious; and a little close reading is called for if Blanchot's work is itself to be properly communicated.

2

The first of the conversations held by our nameless speakers converges on the question of how we can become aware of the unknown. It begins with Bataille's suggestion that contemporary philosophy arises out of fear rather than wonder, his allusion being to Socrates' remark to Theaetetus when the latter confesses to getting dizzy when pondering the puzzles of being and becoming. "This sense of wonder is the mark of the philosopher. Philosophy indeed has no other origin" (*Theaetetus*, 155d). Plato would hardly have agreed with Bataille, since he held fear to be a "foolish counselor" (*Timaeus*, 69d). Doubtless it is; but the fear that exercises Bataille differs from what the great philosopher despised, as we shall see. Fear is to be distinguished from anguish and terror, two other important words in Blanchot's vocabulary, the one associated with Heidegger's analysis of *Angst* and the other with violence, whether political or literary.[11]

What falls outside us and is other than us is the truly frightening. The two conversation partners agree about that without any worries about what it means and whether it even makes sense. If there is something that is radically other than us, then it is doubtful that we could be aware of it. The argument goes back to Plato, specifically to Parmenides demonstrating to Socrates that because the forms exist independently of us they are strictly unknowable (*Parmenides*, 133b–135d). Of course, one might say, as the young Karl Barth does, that God is the Wholly Other, that He exceeds the category of Same and Other, and do so in order to recall people to a sobering sense of the divine aseity. Yet Barth's hyperbole makes sense only when one sees it as a stark refusal of the liberal constructions of the deity he encountered as a student and young pastor. It is an extension, and a very striking one, of a series of negative divine attributes with which we are familiar. God is *eternitas, infinitas, immensitas, immutabilitas,* and so on; we speak with Luther of the *deus absconditus* at the heart of the *deus revelatus,* and we proclaim with Saint Augustine that *deus semper maior.*[12] Were a broad context like this to be missing, one would need assurance that the attribute "Wholly Other" fits the deity, since there could well be another "wholly other" that threatens divinity. "God," Lévinas reminds us, "is not simply the 'first other,' the 'other par excellence,' or the 'absolutely other,' but other than the other [*autre qu'autrui*], other otherwise, other with an alterity prior to the alterity of the other, prior to the ethical bond with another and different from every neighbor, transcendent to the point of absence, to the point of a possible confusion with the stirring of the *there is* [*il y a*]."[13] A God who transcends the world so completely that He could be confused with the *il y a* or (in Blanchot's vocabulary) the Outside is frightening indeed. "It is a fearful thing to fall into the hands of the living God" (Heb. 10:31), but it is even more frightening if one cannot tell this God from the fissure in being from which images come.

At any rate, no objection is raised by either partner in the conversation when this sheer alterity is given a name that Blanchot has already deeply considered, "the Outside." "Philosophical fear" would be a reaction to what resists being known, what cannot properly be brought into the realm of phenomena. The Outside would not be a belated version of Kantian noumena, however. It does not have the solid reality that Kant ascribes to God, freedom, and immortality. Besides, neither speaker has the slightest inclination to introduce the hope of salvation, whether it be justified in theoretical or practical terms. And yet even as the speakers reject theological categories they tacitly agree to use them in a new way. The fear in dispute is not an anguish that can be more or less accommodated by a sovereign self. Rather, it pushes a person beyond his or her limits. What happens at the crumbling edge of the self takes place "in fear and trembling" (50; 71), Blanchot says, quoting Paul's injunction ("work out your own salvation with fear and trembling" [Phil. 2:12]). The allusion is ironic, needless to say, and it would remain so even if directed to Kierkegaard's quotation of Paul in the title of his pseudonymous book *Fear and Trembling* (1843). The fear examined by Johannes de Silentio with regard to the Akedah, Abraham's binding of Isaac, arises when the ethical is suspended in favor of the religious, while the fear of the Outside is, as we shall see, at the base of both the sacred and ethics for Blanchot.

Yet Blanchot's talk of fear and trembling also passes by way of the religious, even if it has no confessional role to play. The fear that pushes one beyond his or her limits "constitutes an ecstatic, properly speaking, a mystical movement" ("un mouvement extatique, mystique à proprement parler") (50; 71). The Outside cannot be known, nor can it be experienced in any clear or familiar sense of the word. At the same time, it can be rightly said that the encounter of an "I" with what is truly Other is the defining mark of experience as such. As we have seen over the course of this study, much of Blanchot's writing, in all its styles—narrative, discursive, and fragmentary—engages and displaces the tension between these two statements. While keeping this in mind, let us stay close to the matter in hand. Were the Outside able to be mediated, it could offer itself to experience and knowledge, but we are told that no dialectic can find traction there. Were it to be immediate it could communicate itself by way of "ecstatic confusion" or "mystical participation" (51; 73). In that case, there could be no relation between the self and what falls outside the self: all talk of relation would fade in favor of simple identity. Since neither mediation nor immediacy is appropriate, the speakers agree to settle on a third term to designate the relation between Self and Other: the "non-mediate" (51; 73).[14]

Let us assume for the moment that the category of the nonmediate makes sense, that it genuinely indicates a position between immediacy and mediation. It would bespeak a mode of experience distinct from both intellectual intuition and positive knowledge. Or if "experience" cannot be held apart from "knowledge," we should talk as Blanchot sometimes does of a test, trial, or ordeal, *une épreuve*, that occurs at a limit that passes through all human existence, not just at the extremities visited by the spiritual élite. What is outside us and other than us is met as an ordeal, one that we must undergo and to which we can only respond. And it is in this sense that we can hail the Outside as other and grasp that it is other: it is apprehended though never understood, if I might adapt a distinction drawn by John Henry Newman.[15] As we have seen in chapters 1 and 2, Blanchot believes that mystics and their exegetes have tended to mistake the nonmediate for the immediate. We have also seen that he believes theology and philosophy to be dominated in overt and covert ways by the possible. I pointed out in chapter 5 that Blanchot shows no concerted interest in distinguishing logical and epistemic possibility or logical and real possibility, but that he holds to an ontological sense of the word, "to be, plus the power to be" ("être, plus le pouvoir de l'être").[16] Possibility is not something one *has*, as Aristotle suggests in his notion of δύναμις or potentiality; and it is more than mere susceptibility to change, as it usually is for the Philosopher. Rather, possibility is what enables one to be what one is and to continue in that state or, if desired, to change it. (Blanchot is therefore far closer to Plotinus's sense of δύναμις than Aristotle's.)[17] It is with this ontological sense of the word in mind, then, that Blanchot believes he can affirm that "Possibility establishes and founds reality" (42; 59). Aristotle's prizing of necessity over possibility is plainly not a part of this world, nor is the scholastic insistence that the very existence of an *ens possibile* presumes the existence of an *ens necessarium*.

And yet Blanchot keeps a conception of the deity as a constant target, and it is easy to see what he has in mind. Plotinus taught that all possible beings abide in the divine and that the necessary overflowing of the One means that they are sure to be realized. Because the One is perfectly good, "to be possible" converges in principle and eventually in fact with "to be." It is not a view that could be acceptable to an orthodox Christian, for it severely compromises God's freedom. Hence the distinction between *potentia absoluta*, God's absolute power, and *potentia ordinata*, His ordained power. Although the deity comprehends the entire realm of what is possible, only those things are actualized and sustained that do not contradict the order of nature.[18] Equally heterodox is Nicholas of Cusa's arresting doctrine of God as *possest*, that which is and can be. It fits neatly into Blanchot's general sense of the western tradition's prizing of possibility, although it must be said that its influence has been limited. One does not have to reach back to *De apice theoriae* (1464), let alone look to the mystics, to find an instance of possibility being pressed into the service of the Church. Following the scholastics, Leibniz argued in the *Monadology* (1714) that "God alone . . . has this prerogative that if he be possible he must necessarily exist."[19] We get closer to the position that intrigues and disconcerts Blanchot, though, when we come upon Heidegger arguing in *Sein und Zeit* (1927) that "possibility as an *existentiale* is the most primordial and ultimately positive way in which Dasein is characterized ontologically."[20] As Heidegger goes on to say, Dasein has always and already projected itself into the future, regardless of a plan of action, and is already pressing into possibilities. "Being-a-whole" is a possibility for Dasein that especially interests Heidegger, and he explores the notion by way of Dasein as "being-toward-death" (§§ 46–53).[21]

In thinking of these themes, have we left theology? Not at all, Adorno insists in his 1965 lectures on metaphysics. Heidegger seeks "to rescue structures of the experience of death as structures of *Dasein*, of human existence itself," we are told in the fourteenth session.[22] But there is a difficulty, Adorno warns, since "these structures, as he describes them, only existed within the world of positive theology, by virtue of the positive hope of resurrection; and Heidegger fails to see that through the secularization of this structure, which he at least tacitly assumes in his work, not only have these theological contents disintegrated, but without them this experience itself is no longer possible" (107). The steady emphasis on the naked self confronting an inexorable death is inherited from many Christian writers, and Karl Jaspers had reason to joke about the theological tone of *Sein und Zeit*. Yet Heidegger does not rework an ontic doctrine of resurrection at the level of the ontological. *Sorge*, the sense that Being is an issue for us, no more relies on a notion of the world as a vale of tears than it does on a psychological understanding of being weighed down by the troubles of life. It is the other way round; for Heidegger, these religious and psychological notions derive from the general ontological structure he is analyzing. People were bothered by Being, by what it is *to be*, long before the resurrection of Jesus. Witness the *Theaetetus* and the *Parmenides*; recall the Psalms, the Book of Job, and the Epic of Gilgamesh. The possibilities into which Dasein presses have nothing essentially to do with the resurrection of the flesh.

One could elaborate a vision of modernity and even postmodernity by way of the possible, but it would not be Blanchot's way of going about things.[23] His interest, as we have seen, is in naming the possible and responding to the impossible. To be sure, it is not an evenhanded policy: we are embroiled in the realm of the possible, even if we are not fully aware of being so, and we are not yet sufficiently attuned to the impossible. To become attuned to it, he implies, would be to risk opening ourselves to other ways of relating with people at the levels of fraternity, friendship, and love, ways that are truly *other*.[24] What Robert Musil calls "the other state" ("der andere Zustand"), when thinking of the relations between Ulrich and Agathe, is just one instance.[25] Admirers of Musil will recall the scene where Agathe cries out, "there's really no such thing as good and evil, but only faith—or doubt!" To which comes this response from Ulrich, "'Yes, the moment one slips away from a life of inessentials, everything enters into a new relationship with everything else. I would almost go so far as to say into a nonrelationship. For it's an entirely unknown one, of which we have no experience, and all other relationships are blotted out.'"[26] Putting such adventures aside, this attunement to the impossible would also allow some awareness of communism, so long as we acknowledge, as Blanchot wrote in a tract that followed in the wake of May 1968, that communism is "that which excludes (and is itself excluded from) any already constituted community."[27] It is also cut off from any continuing future; it must not last.[28] Those conditions make it sufficiently plain that no sustained political theory turns on the impossible, and no continuous political practice does so either. Blanchot's primary concern is not with the regulative, in a Kantian sense, but with contestation. The new political thinking, he says, does not result in programs of reform; and yet he does not deny that such programs have their value. The task is to affirm a politics of rupture that keeps all programs, even revolutionary ones, open and that remains critical of its own temptation to become a vitalism.[29]

3

In a meditation on Kafka, Blanchot wonders how a writer, "a man without mandate," can ever enter "the closed—the sacred—world of the written?"[30] How can a literary person venture "to add a strictly individual word to that Other, old, terrifyingly old Word [*l'Autre Parole, l'ancienne, l'effroyablement ancienne*] that covers, comprehends, and encompasses all things, all the while remaining hidden in the depths of the tabernacle from which it has perhaps disappeared?" (392–93; 575). The terrifyingly old Word here is Torah which, as a well-known midrash in *Bereishit Rabbah* has it, preceded the creation of the world. "In human practice," we are told, "when a mortal king builds a palace, he builds it not with his own skill but with the skill of an architect. The architect moreover does not build it out of his head, but employs plans and diagrams to know how to arrange the chambers and the wicket doors. Thus God consulted the Torah and created the world."[31] Since it is eternally underwritten by God, Torah proclaims the fullness of divine meaning, which the Talmud explains by saying that the Mosaic books offer themselves to all the nations of the world, that is, to seventy interpretations. "Every single word that went forth from the Omnipotent was split up into seventy languages" (*Shabbath* 88b).[32] Intimidating as it might be, especially for a Jew like Kafka, Torah and the wealth of Talmudic commentaries do not form the sole image that Blanchot gives us for causing the writer's fear. There is another image he presents, although he phrases it in the same words that he uses when evoking Torah as that "terrifyingly old Word."[33] It is appropriate since he has in mind the mystical or written Torah that I discussed in the previous chapter, the neutral "first writing" that interrupts all other writing.

Consider this passage from *Celui qui ne m'accompagnait pas* (1953). An unnamed male character cries out brusquely to the narrator, "'You're speaking!'" and he in turn tells us that the sound "seemed to me to come from a different mouth—oh, from an infinite past" (23; 46). Then he reflects,

Yes, I recalled his reply, the violence of his repudiation, by which he had apparently tried to break me, but I could not "take it badly," I could only acknowledge that he was right, I who alone was still right, and exactly what had happened? Surely, this went farther back, surely, when this had been said, something quite different had come to light [*s'était fait jour*] through this remark, had sought a way out, something older, dreadfully old [*quelque chose de plus ancien, d'effroyablement ancien*], which had perhaps even taken place at all times, and at all times I was tied to the spot.[34]

The passage evokes a limit-experience or, better, the eternal return as a limit-experience: not a vision granted to mystics but a fleeting awareness of that which abides behind each and every experience. In a limit-experience one becomes aware of that which exceeds the whole, whether that "whole" be an epoch that has been comprehended, a self that believes itself to be firmly grounded in the Cogito, or an artwork that reposes in a declaration of its aesthetic value. Here the narrator is carried away by "the anonymous, the nameless" (47; 90), and the récit is an obsessive reflection on that which obsesses. Notice that this "sordid, sterile neutrality" (47; 90) discloses itself in speech, specifically in the male character's harsh cry, "You're speaking!" (23; 46). German allows us to capture this disclosure better than either French or English: there is a slip from *Stimme* to *Stim-mung*, from speech to mood or attunement.

What is communicated through this ordeal? First of all, a contestation of selfhood. The narrator says he must remain "always on my feet . . . without being relieved of myself, but always confronting a demand that gave me the feeling I myself had also disappeared" (34; 67). Is this a revelation of some dark truth? Not quite: the narrator is "sworn to sustain" what is given in the test, to "make it more real, more true and, at the same time, push it farther, always farther, to a point truth can no longer reach, where possibility ceases" (34; 67). Rigorously neutral, the Outside turns aside the venerable distinction between truth and falsity. Later in the narrative we return to the event and to the fear "that drove that instant back toward another sort of time, older fearfully old [*un temps autre, plus ancien, effroy-ablement ancien*]" (30; 47). It is a "frightening ordeal," we are told. "It has no lim-its, it knows neither day nor night, it concerns itself with neither events nor de-sires" (64; 121). The syntax is that of negative theology, although if we recall Lévinas's line about alterity that I quoted a moment or two ago, we should think of the *il y a* rather than the deity beyond being. Nevertheless, the narrator does not hesitate to draw on a familiar religious metaphor: "It may be that at one time I thoughtlessly obeyed its call, but then who doesn't obey? He who is not called? But obeying proves nothing about the call, the call always takes place, it doesn't need anyone to answer, it never really takes place, that is why it isn't possible to answer it" (64; 121–22). Unlike the gentle call of the Spirit, the Outside is unconcerned about those it calls, and its reality, though anterior, is not absolute but consequent upon the doubling that occurs in the presentation of a phenomenon.

Consider also this passage from *L'Espace littéraire* (1955) in which the same phrase is used:

> the work is always original and at all moments a beginning. It is thus that it appears ever new, the mirage of the future's inaccessible truth. And it is new "now," it renews this "now" which it seems to initiate, to render more immediate. And finally it is very old, frightfully ancient [*très anci-enne, effroyablement ancienne*], lost in the night of time. It is the origin which always precedes us and is always given before us, for it is the ap-proach of what allows us to depart—a thing of the past, in a different sense from what Hegel said.[35]

In the introduction to his lectures on aesthetics, Hegel observes that "art, con-sidered in its highest vocation, is and remains for us a thing of the past."[36] Taken out of context, the remark seems eccentric, if not downright philistine, for it was pronounced in the 1820s when Goethe and Wordsworth were writing, when Beethoven was composing, and when Constable, Delacroix, and Turner were painting. Yet no amount of hindsight diminishes the force of Hegel's point: he was arguing that *Geist* no longer manifests itself in art, as it did for the Greeks, and consequently that art can no longer meet our spiritual needs. The past that interests Blanchot is not historical; it is the origin of the work that he identifies with the Outside. As we have seen in chapter 5, an author cannot avoid the "original experience," a limit-experience, in the very act of composing a literary work. It is this approach of the Outside that allows the author to pass from being a self-assured subject, an "I," to existing in the third person.

Finally, consider, this fragment from *Le Pas au-delà* (1973), a text in which Blanchot meditates at length about fear, especially what he calls "the ancient fear." The expression "terrifyingly ancient" occurs there four times, twice in quotation marks. In the first passage Blanchot has been brooding on irrevocability, and then he turns to make the following comment:

What has just taken place, would slip and would fall right away (nothing more rapid) through irrevocability, into "the terrifyingly ancient [*l'effroyablement ancien*]," there were nothing was ever present. Irrevocability would be, in this view, the slip or the fragile fall that abolishes time in time, effaces the difference between the near and the far, the marks of reference, the so-called temporal measures (all that makes contemporary) and shrouds everything in non-time, from which nothing could come back, less because there is no return than because nothing falls there, except the illusion of falling there.[37]

And in the second passage he adds a gloss on the first:

If, in the "terrifyingly ancient [*l'effroyablement ancien*]," nothing was ever present . . . it is because (whence our cold presentiment) the event that we thought we had lived was itself never in a relation of presence to us nor to anything whatsoever. (15; 25)

Irrevocability, here, does not simply name that which cannot be recalled or recovered because it now abides in the past. What is important is not so much the irreversibility of the past as its emptiness. The point differs from Saint Augustine's worry in *Confessions* 11 about the physical (but not psychic) nonexistence of the past, as well as from modern concerns about whether "being past" can be properly ascribed to a continuant. As we have seen in previous chapters, for Blanchot as for Lévinas there can be no thing or event that does not resemble itself. An event is never wholly and exclusively real, present to itself; it is partly unreal, marking an absence from itself by dint of its sensible qualities that offer themselves to the imagination to be reconstituted or recombined. The fall occurs with each and every event: not a Fall from grace to sin, but a slip from the real to the unreal, from the possible to the impossible. It is this unreality that is seized and immobilized in an image. Not only does art respond to the unreal but also it insists on substituting the unreal for the real: such is the ground of Lévinas's distrust of art. Blanchot, however, approaches the situation from the exact opposite side. He sees in art a veiling and unveiling of the Outside from which human beings have tried to shield themselves by religion and philosophy.[38] Neither subjective nor objective, the Outside precedes this distinction, though Blanchot does not specify its mode of priority.

Nothing could ever have been present in this anterior space, this realm of the imaginary, and it can never be made present to consciousness. It is not "ancient" in terms of historical time, but we must recognize that it is strictly prior to our thoughts and acts. By dint of its otherness, it is irreducible to the realm of phenomena, to the distinction between phenomena and noumena and to all related polarities, including that of time and eternity; and this is what makes it frightening. It follows from Blanchot's understanding of the fall into the "terrifyingly ancient" that we never truly live an event in the present. The disaster has always and already occurred, and our longed-for experience of being has vanished into the imaginary. *Erlebnis* is never possible in the strict sense, and *Erfahrung* is to be understood as combining the traits of nonexperience and experience.[39] What presents itself as other, thereby opening the space of experience in its most radical sense, eludes our grasp; and yet the fear that marks this encounter is sufficient evidence that there has been experience. It has happened but not occurred, as Blanchot would have us say. Because the slip from the real to the unreal occurs in time, it is always possible for the Outside to return in an involuntary manner, such as we have seen in *Celui qui ne m'accompagnait pas*. Unlike Proust's instantaneous recoveries of lost time, those apprehensions of "a fragment of time in the pure state," Blanchot's limit-experiences testify to the emptiness of the past, the excess of nonexperience over experience.[40]

4

Writing would attract us to the Outside, Blanchot hints, were we "to write within the secret of the ancient fear."[41] So it is a secret, this brushing against the unknown. Has Blanchot revealed it to us? The matter is not so simple. Recall the last sentences of "(Une scène primitive?)," a text that evokes the "terrifyingly ancient" without naming it: "He says nothing. He will *live* henceforth in the secret. He will weep no more."[42] In a conversation that reflects on these sentences, one of the speakers in the "Tenir parole" dialogue implies that the secret presumes a moment when the whole has been made manifest. To which the other responds, *"The un-knowledge* [non-savoir] *after absolute knowledge which does not, precisely, allow us to conceive of any 'after.'"*[43] Then the other voice replies, *"Except as introduced by the imperative of the return, which 'designifies' every before, as well as every afterward, by untying them from the present, rendering them foreign to every tense"* (137; 208).

Overhearing this conversation, one is likely to recall Bataille and Laure telling us that the sacred *is* communication: a sudden fracturing of the sphere of the "I" in which selfhood is lost and one is joined with an indefinite reality, "the impossible."[44] Blanchot does not disagree. Like the divine, the neuter slips between distinctions, he says, while also implying the point he wishes to defend, that people have mistaken the neuter for the sacred.[45] For him, the neutral *is* the sacred, the "terrifyingly ancient," which can be grasped as the mystical or written Torah that we discussed in the previous chapter. Although, with Hölderlin, he speaks of the mystery of the gods' departure, he certainly does not associate the sacred with mystery, which, for him, is ultimately no more than "a secret way of seeing."[46] It is closer to the mark to think of the neuter or the unknown, as he says in *Celui qui ne m'accompagnait pas,* as "the renunciation of mystery, the ultimate insignificance of lightness."[47] The sacred, for him, is a secret; but in putting things this way we should not mislead ourselves and think that this is a secret that, if discovered, would offer itself directly to experience and knowledge. It cannot be kept hidden within the interiority of an "I." It is precisely that interiority that has been contested in the ordeal, and the secret abides, to return to the dialogue, *"in the inequality of difference, in the absence of community, by virtue of the un-common of communication"* (137; 208).

The secret is that there is no secret, Blanchot thinks; there is only what he calls an "empty depth."[48] It has not always been so. When the Greeks believed in the gods, they lived in the light of their presence. But with the gods' departure, we are left only with the realm of the imaginary pressing upon us. If we talk now of the sacred, it is of the terrifying without any benevolence. Blanchot's 1985 reply to the question "Why do you write?" is relevant here. "I will borrow from Dr. Martin Luther," he says, "when, at Worms, he declared his unshakability: *Here I stand, I cannot do otherwise. May God help me.* Which I translate modestly: *In the space of writing—writing, not writing—here I sit bent over, I cannot do otherwise and I await no help from the beneficent powers.* "[49] The space of writing puts us in contact with the ancient fear, the sacred; and it does so, as our guiding passage indicates, in good Lutheran fashion, without the tempering of any "intermediary." Luther would be less pleased with the thought that writing points us to the absence of the gods or, if you like, the default of God. Nor would he be at all sympathetic to Henri Sorge's revelation that we have already noted in *Le Très-Haut* (1948): "Until very recently people were only fragments and they projected their dreams onto the sky . . . But now man exists."[50] For us, as the narrator of a later fictional work, *Celui qui ne m'accompagnait pas* (1953), puts it, there is an "'outside' of all speech [*ce dehors de toute parole*], apparently more secret and more interior than the speech of the innermost heart, but, here the outside is empty, the secret is without depth, what is repeated is the emptiness of repetition, it doesn't speak and yet it has always been said already."[51] To which it must be added that this secret cannot be told, only communicated. One lives in it and never has it hidden within the self.

Especially in *La Communauté inavouable* (1983), where he remains close to Bataille, Blanchot gives the distinct impression that community and communism can be glimpsed only by way of an ecstatic limit-experience. If we go back thirty years and read his review of Dionys Mascolo's *Le Communisme* (1953), which he reprinted in *L'Amitié* (1971), we find a more complicated account of the relation. "We have two lives that we must try to live together, although they are irreconcilable," he says.[52] "One life is tied to the future of 'communication,' when the relations between men will no longer, stealthily or violently, make things out of them" (96; 112–13). This is the daily life of politics, of reasonable discourse, of protesting against injustice and working for a better world. But there is another life to be lived, and in this existence the quotation marks around "communication" are removed, as though Hubert and Mauss's sense of the word—communication as the sacred—is primary rather than derived. In the other life, one "greets communication outside the world, immediately, but on condition that this communication be a disruption of the 'immediate,' an opening, a wrenching violence, a fire that burns without pause, for communist generosity is also this, is first this, this inclemency, this impatience, the refusal of any detour, of any ruse, and of all delay: an infinitely hazardous freedom" (96; 113). In this second life, "*Man can become the impossible friend of man, his relation to the latter being precisely with the impossible*" (95–96; 112). Can we separate these two lives so readily? That is the question Blanchot considered when he included the review in *L'Amitié*, and he was surely led to do so by recalling the conversation with which I started this chapter. Here is Blanchot's addition to the review:

Is it so easy to distinguish between private and collective relations? In both cases, is it not a question of relations that could not be those of a subject, nor even of a subject to a subject, but relations in which the re-lationship of the one to the other affirms itself as infinite or discontin-uous? This is why the exigency and the urgency of a relation through de-sire and through speech, a relation that is always being displaced, where the *other* [autre]—the impossible—would be greeted, constitute, in the strongest sense, an essential mode of decision and political affirmation. (296; 112)

The human relation is prior to private and collective relations, Blanchot comes to think. More importantly, he suggests that it is not an external relation linking two previously constituted subjects.[53] On the contrary, self and other are related by an infinite distance between them, one that prevents any solidification of self into an "I" and that never resolves itself into a unity.

This relation is "devoid of religion," one of Blanchot's speakers tells us right at the start of "Tenir parole," and the statement can only strike one as surprising. First of all, if one knows Blanchot's writings at all well, a passage from "L'Itinéraire de Hölderlin" is likely to come to mind. "Hölderlin," he tells us there, "conceives pro-foundly that this absence of the gods is not a purely negative form of relation. That is why it is terrible [*terrible*]."[54] The explanation stands in need of explanation, which is immediately given. "It is terrible not only because it deprives us of the gods' benevolent presence . . . but because it substitutes for the measured favor of divine forms as represented by the Greeks (gods of light, gods of the initial naïveté) a rela-tion which threatens ceaselessly to tear and disorient us, with that which is higher than the gods, with the sacred itself or with its perverted essence" (275; 372). Doubt-less Blanchot, like Heidegger, believes that those of us who come after Hölderlin have lost touch with even the withdrawal of the gods, and one might well infer that we have accordingly lost all rapport with the sacred. There are times when he im-plies that this is so, "(Une scène primitive?)" being one of them. Yet if we follow him closely we can hear him saying that here and now we are threatened by being in a re-lation with the sacred or the Outside. One might argue whether Blanchot's notion of the Outside is a perverted version of the *sacred,* let alone a perverted *essence,* but it is plain that Blanchot wishes to preserve the sacred without religion. Less obvious is that the human relation is a recoding of the faith that people have with God. As he says in "Le Rapport du troisième genre," contrary to Lévinas on God ("other than the other" ["autre qu'autrui"]), the other person is "more Other than all that is other" ("plus Autre que tout ce qu'il y a autre") (72; 102). Nonetheless, rather than being "devoid of religion," the human relation has folded religion tightly into itself and, in doing so, changed its senses and functions.

It is also surprising to find that the very account of the relations between self and other is based on Descartes's argument for the existence of God. Completely unsurprising is that it is introduced by way of an appreciation of *Totalité et infini*. In "Connaissance de l'inconnu" we are told that one of "the strongest aspects of Lévinas's book is to have led us . . . to consider *autrui* from the basis of separation" (53; 75). Of the four paths that Lévinas takes, the first goes by way of Descartes's argument for the existence of God in the third of his *Meditations on First Philosophy* (1641). The kernel of Descartes's argument is breathtakingly simple: the infinite is not the negation of the finite, since the notion of the infinite is by far the richer of the two. And so the philosopher is led to conclude that "in some way I have in me the notion of the infinite earlier than the finite—to wit, the notion of God before that of myself."[55] Whether the argument works, whether this infinite is *God*, and whether this God is the Creator of heaven and earth are questions that Descartes debated with his critics.[56] None of them need detain us here, however.

For when reflecting on Descartes's argument, Lévinas begins by suspending the questions both of its validity and of whether the conclusion reached by philosophical means can be translated into an ecclesial dogma. The transcendence at issue is phenomenological, not theological. And so he emphasizes "that the transcendence of the Infinite with respect to the I which is separated from it and which thinks it, measures (so to speak) its very infinitude."[57] The point is reinforced by elegant restatement: "Infinity is characteristic of a transcendent being as transcendent; the infinite is the absolutely other [*autre*]" (49; 41). Then it is put to ethical rather than theological ends: "To think the infinite, the transcendent," Lévinas begins, then quietly adds "the Stranger" before concluding the sentence, "is hence not to think an object" (49; 41). Indeed not, and in making that remark Lévinas sweeps away all appeals to the pagan gods as transcendent.[58] The infinite, rather, is "a being [*un être*] that maintains its total exteriority [*son extériorité totale*] with respect to him who thinks it" (50; 42). Very quickly, the sort of exteriority in question is changed. As I pointed out earlier, in the *Parmenides* Plato entertains the thought that the Absolute abides without the possibility of external relations. Lévinas declares this position to be "purely abstract and formal" and tells us, "The absolute exteriority [*L'extériorité absolue*] of the exterior being is not purely and simply lost as a result of its manifestation; it 'absolves' itself from the relation in which it presents itself" (50; 42). We have moved, it seems, from Descartes's assertion that the idea of the infinite precedes the idea of the finite (and hence that God exists) to the claim that the other person, *Autrui*, is absolutely exterior to me, and that this exteriority cannot be thought by way of a representation. There can be no analogy that spans the distance between me and another person, for responsibility cannot be thought in terms of proportion.

Thus Lévinas paraphrasing and displacing Descartes. When Blanchot in turn summarizes Lévinas, there is another slide. It begins in the passage from thinking of *Autrui* as "absolutely exterior" to pondering "a relation with what is absolutely outside myself: the other [*absolument hors de moi-même: l'autre*]."[59] (53; 76). We pass from *Autrui* to *autre*. What for Descartes was God, and for Lévinas was infinity, has become for Blanchot the unknown or the Outside, an "absolute relation" ("rapport absolu") (51; 73) that does not fall under any concept and that must therefore be considered "strange." Turning away from unity, the absolute relation finds no shelter under multiplicity, which is just as much a concept as unity; the relation's strangeness consists in being neither the one nor the other. Not that this commits Blanchot to believe, if it is possible to do so, in a conceptual scheme that is irreducible to the one to which we usually appeal. Like Lévinas, he holds that responsibility cannot be subsumed by any category and thereby rendered finite and determinate. The distance between me and the other person is infinite in the sense that no bound can be placed on it: my responsibility for the Other is unlimited. Transcendent, the other person always speaks to me from a height: it is why the appropriate response to the other is always the formal *vous*, not the informal *tu*.[60] Also, though, the presence of the other person weighs on me, calling forth a sense of unlimited responsibility. "Presence," here, signifies neither a temporal present nor the self-presence of a self-conscious subject but rather the sense I have, and cannot put away, that my persistence in being, my *conatus essendi*, has been interrupted by the call of the other person. The desire at work in the human relation does not incorporate his or her being into mine or dissolve me into his or her being. Neither dialectical unity nor mystical fusion is at issue here. Instead, I stand before the other person, unmediated by anything in the realm of the possible, and must acknowledge that the situation is terrifying.

Why is it terrifying? Because it is sacred, giving rise to the fascination of a *mysterium tremendum*, would be an answer, one that is entertained in *L'Entretien infini*, although overall Blanchot is less comfortable there with the proposal than he was in *L'Espace littéraire*.[61] Because "all the mystery of the neutral passes, perhaps, by way of the other [*autrui*]" is the answer preferred in that later text (72; 102). And because I am faced with the alternative "speak or kill" (62; 88) is the legitimate extension of that answer. It is not a vacuous disjunction: the other person might be "Other than man, close to what cannot be close to me: close to death, close to the night, and certainly as repulsive as anything that comes to me from these regions without horizon" (72; 102). Blanchot could have tested this alternative with respect to the marquis de Sade whose works, as he knows well, are replete with murders. Sade's world is without nature. It is without God, except in the sense that he and his characters hate God into being, and it is without religion, although it promotes a perverted "gospel of evil."[62] The fury of destruction in Sade's fiction arises from an infinite negativity of the sovereign individual, and yet the libertines speak endlessly to one another and, by a dialectical twist, need one another: "the notion of God and the notion of neighbor"—Blanchot paraphrases Klossowski—"are indispensable to the conscience of the libertine."[63] Yet no amount of speech prevents even one grisly outcome, since while "everything is said, also everything is disguised" (36). For Sade, the infinite is a means of rendering everything visible and therefore accessible to desire. Such is the clear message of *Philosophie dans le boudoir.*[64] For Blanchot, however, the infinite is the contestation of the visible and the primacy of the human relation.

Instead of considering the dire alternative "speak or kill" in Sade's fiction, Blanchot turns in *L'Entretien infini* to the Bible. In the somewhat Alexandrian style of biblical interpretation to which he is partial, he has one of his speakers interpret Genesis 4:8 as follows: "Cain says to Abel: your dimension as infinite and absolutely exterior, that which you claim to surpass me, that which puts you beyond my reach—I will show you that I am its master; for as a man of power, I am master also of the absolute and I have made death into my possibility" (61; 87). A little later the same speaker adds, in the same allegorical style, "I notice that Cain says to Abel, when he wants to have it out with him: 'Let's go outside [*Allons au dehors*],' as though he knew that the outside [*le dehors*] were Abel's place, but also as though he wanted to lead him back to the destitution, to the weakness of the outside [*du dehors*] where every defense falls away" (61; 87). The Outside is the space of impossibility, not possibility, the space of dying and not death, and also, as is clear from this interpretation of the biblical story, the space required if there is to be an ethics. There can be no ethics, Blanchot suggests, without an infinite distance between the "I" and the other, without the unlimited responsibility for the other person falling on the "I" (and thereby dividing it immemorially).

Close as they are in many respects, Lévinas and Blanchot appear to differ on just this point. The one regards being-for-the-other, ethics, as marking an exit from the *il y a*, while the other maintains that ethics can begin only if there is an Outside.[65] Reflecting on *L'Espace littéraire*, Lévinas recognizes that Blanchot's understanding of art differs profoundly from Heidegger's, that his friend's affirmation of exile and nomadism is at variance with his teacher's stress on rootedness and the fourfold. The prizing of being over beings cancels in advance any possibility of a Heideggerian ethics, he insists. But what of the thought of the Outside?

Lévinas remarks only that Blanchot "also abstains from ethical preoccupations, at least in explicit form."[66] Does the Outside implicitly lead one to ethics? Perhaps. Certainly the author of *L'Espace littéraire* thought it led us to experience the sacred, "a relation which threatens ceaselessly to tear and disorient us" (275; 372). As we have seen in chapter 5, Blanchot's understanding of the Outside changes over the years, and by the time of *L'Entretien infini* (1969) the word's meaning seems to have expanded quite considerably. It can still indicate, as it did in *L'Espace littéraire* (1955), an imaginary realm where being perpetuates itself as nothingness, the final attenuation of the sacred first experienced by the Greeks. And it can also denote a way of being in relation that does not appeal to unity as a horizon.

At no stage does Blanchot imply that these various understandings of the Outside fundamentally differ. On the contrary, as late as *L'Amitié* (1971) he stresses that at least two of them coincide. Nothing is said of the sacred as a metaphor of the Outside. Only literature and politics attract his attention. "It is undoubtedly the task of our age to move toward an affirmation that is entirely *other*," he writes. "It is to this task that communism recalls us with a rigor that it itself often shirks, and it is also to this task that 'artistic experience' recalls us in the realm that is proper to it. A remarkable coincidence."[67] No word, then, of mystical experience or experience of the sacred. What Blanchot calls "artistic experience" is, as we saw at the beginning of this chapter, "terrible" because it exposes us to essential solitude and the interminable murmur. The essential solitude is the work's, not the author's: on finishing the work, the author is pronounced dead. Yet the work can always be communicated. The human relation, which Blanchot sees as the *Abgrund* or perhaps the *Ungrund* of communism, is also "terrible" precisely because it leads us on an interminable detour, one characterized by an infinite responsibility. It too can be communicated, and it too turns on a death: not that of the author but, as we shall see, that of another person.

Understood in this way, the difference between Blanchot and Lévinas consists of a less sharp disagreement than it first seems. Blanchot stretches the meaning of the word *Outside* so that it encompasses responsibility as well as the imaginary and the sacred while, at the same time, he wishes to rethink ethics under the horizon of communism (or, if you like, communism within the horizon of ethics). Both can be settled under the sign of the "entirely *other*," he implies, though we are likely still to wonder if there are not different sorts of alterity involved. Is the alterity of the sacred the same as that of ethics? Unlike Kierkegaard, Blanchot declines to answer the question. There is another point at which they differ, however, and it is appropriate to consider it before we turn to the significance of the other's suffering and death. Blanchot insists that the human relation cannot be elucidated in terms of external or internal relations, by way of empiricism or idealism. It is "a neutral relation, or the very neutrality of relation," and consequently beyond the main alternatives of western philosophy. Blanchot infers that because this "relation without relation" refuses both dialectical mediation and mystical immediacy it is therefore without religion. It opens instead onto a nontheological future in which God has no place. "Let us leave aside God" ("Laissons Dieu de côté"), says one of the speakers in "Connaissance de l'inconnu" (50; 71). Could this decision be a little hasty? Reading *Totalité et infini* (1961) might lead us to believe so, since there we find a quite different scansion of the expression "relation without relation," one that is both close to and very distant from Blanchot's. "For the relation between the being here below and the transcendent being that results in no community of concept or totality—a relation without relation—we reserve the term religion."[68] How can it be that the very notion that removes the human relation from religion for Blanchot is what defines it for Lévinas?

The answer can be found in "Enigme et phénomène" (1965), where Lévinas offers a brief sketch of a noncorrelational philosophy of religion. Someone can always bring a phenomenon into an intentional rapport with himself or herself, but not so with another human being who remains an enigma for phenomenology and whose meaning makes sense only in ethics:

A face can now appear as a face, as a proximity interrupting the series, only if it enigmatically comes from the infinite and its immemorial past. And the infinite, to solicit desire, a thought thinking more than it thinks, cannot be incarnated in a desirable, cannot, qua infinite, be shut up in an end. It solicits across a face, the term of my generosity and my sacrifice. A you [*Tu*] is inserted between the I and the absolute He. Correlation is broken.[69]

I am summoned immemorially to be for the other person, Lévinas argues, by nothing or no one that I can point to or name. This is the "absolute He" that, since "La Trace de l'autre" (1963), Lévinas has dubbed "illeity," and that cannot be accommodated by either presence or absence, being or nonbeing, because we encounter it only as a trace of what has long passed. To speak of an "absolute He," then, is not to hail a hyperessential divinity but to indicate that this "He" approaches us from an absolute past. It is more appropriate to say *à-Dieu* than *Dieu*, it is suggested; we move toward God in helping the other person, although we never reach Him. Our religion, in being worked out by way of ethics rather than immortal longings, finally becomes one that is appropriate to adults: we say *adieu* to our selves, to our desire to be eternally ourselves, and also *adieu* to the God with whom we can speak directly and with whom we can become intimate.[70]

When we speak the word *God* outside confessional creeds it is this "absolute He," this illeity, that comes to mind, Lévinas thinks. By the same token, we can risk calling this illeity "God" if we are careful not to import doctrinal assumptions into it, especially a dogmatic sense of transcendence, for this illeity is a philo-sophical rather than a theological construction. "The revealed God of our Judeo-Christian spirituality . . . shows himself only by his trace, as is said in Exodus 33. To go toward Him is not to follow this trace, which is not a sign; it is to go toward the others who stand in the trace of illeity."[71] *Only* by His trace? We might wonder about biblical theophanies, and above all Ezekiel's vision: "Now it came to pass in the thirtieth year, in the fourth month, in the fifth day of the month, as I was among the captives by the river of Chebar, that the heavens were opened, and I saw visions of God" (Ezek. 1:1). To ignore such theophanies and insist that gen-uine belief must presuppose ethics is likely to bring not God but Kant to mind, es-pecially the severe reducer of *Die Religion innerhalb der Grenzen der blossen Vernunft* (1793). Yet Lévinas proposes not a universal moral law but an endless obligation to the singular neighbor, and rather than arguing that morality "leads ineluctably to religion," as Kant does, he redefines "religion" so that it is centered in ethics.[72]

Illeity cannot be experienced or revealed in the present but calls men and women to lives of holiness, being-for-the-other. Perhaps it is nothing other than this call, perhaps it is the philosophical name of the revealed God. At any rate, Lévinas insists, this illeity is primary with respect to the doctrine of God that is supplied by theologians when they reflect on Scripture. Revealability precedes revelation, he steadily maintains. The God of a positive religion, if He be the true God, must coincide exactly with the "absolute He" beyond being and nonbeing who calls us endlessly to assume responsibility for the other person. Keeping this in mind, if I confess to belief in the Almighty, I can say that I fulfill my obligations to Him by welcoming and responding to those who have placed a demand on me. I relate to the deity by turning to the stranger, the widow, the orphan, and not di-rectly to Him; and so my piety is a "relation without relation." In a noncorrela-tional theology this would be completely inadmissible because it would give no place to what is primary: the adoration of God. No theology could allow ethics to subsume doxology. That, however, is not a problem for a noncorrelational philos-ophy of religion, the business of which is not to interpret revelation but to reflect on its conditions of possibility, its meaning, and its claim to truth. A philosophy of religion can propose and test an alternate ground for religion, and in their different ways Kant and Lévinas do just that, but philosophy moves beyond its proper limits when it tries to build an edifice on that ground.

"We propose to call 'religion' the bond that is established between the same and the other without constituting a totality."[73] I have quoted Lévinas again, and it must be noted that, unlike the definition I discussed earlier, this one makes no mention of God. From the perspective of this definition, then, what Blanchot calls the human relation is religious. One could hardly expect Blanchot to agree, although in *L'Espace littéraire* he did not hesitate to speak of a relation with the sacred. Interestingly, as late as *L'Écriture du désastre* (1980), he has Lévinas say something quite different from the sentence I have quoted from *Totalité et infini*. "Lévinas affirms," he tells us, that "religion is etymologically that which binds, that which holds together," and then he breaks off without adding "without constituting a totality."[74] This enables him, rhetorically at least, to mark his distance from his friend on the question of religion. He asks, "what of the non-bond which disjoins beyond unity—which escapes the synchrony of 'holding together,' yet does so without breaking all relations or without ceasing, in this break or in this absence of relation, to open yet another relation? Must one be nonreligious for that?" (64; 106–7). No, Lévinas would answer, one must have another reason, and besides one should distinguish the unity at issue in affirming there is one human race, without which ethics cannot gain a purchase on pluralism, and the unity between Same and Other that is contested in the name of ethics. That said, Blanchot is able to call on additional support. In "Connaissance de l'inconnu" one speaker approvingly quotes Lévinas's dictum, established by way of the *Phaedrus*, that "Discourse is discourse with God and not with equals."[75] It is to be interpreted, we are told, "in the strongest sense," to mean that the Other speaks from above, in an intersubjective space that curves upward in favor of him or her. "This 'curvature of space' is, perhaps, the very presence of God," as Lévinas phrases it.[76] Blanchot would add that the curvature has a negative sign that prevents unity.

Later, in "Le Rapport du troisième genre *(homme sans horizon)*," Blanchot allows doubt to be cast on the asymmetry of the ethical relation. One of his speakers suggests that "if it is true that *autrui* is never for me a self, for *him* the same is true of me," a commonsensical point, though one that threatens to flatten the space of ethics and return it to the world of dialectics.[77] His interlocutor resists the threat and argues instead that "it signifies a double dissymmetry, a double discontinuity" (70–71; 100). There is no question of ethical space being straightened out to allow the reassertion of universal laws and contractual obligations.

Rather, ethics is imagined to take place in something akin to a non-Euclidian geometric space. It is "as though the empty space between the one and the other were not homogeneous but polarized: as though this space constituted a non-isomorphic field bearing a double distortion, at once infinitely negative and infinitely positive, and such that one should call it neutral if it is well understood that the neutral does not annul" (71; 100–101). Here we glimpse Blanchot beginning to rethink ethics by way of community: a community of disaster, not oriented by any star, whose members are bound together solely by each other's death. Doubtless he does so partly to imagine a communism beyond communism. In his words, "the question: 'Who is *autrui*?' has no direct meaning" and "must be replaced by another: 'What of the human "community"?'" (71; 101). And partly he does so in order to erase the relation of *Autrui* and God.

Under pressure from Derrida, Blanchot withdraws the criticism that Lévinas's ethics presents itself in a "theological context," but he nonetheless wishes to eliminate the deity from the human relation.[78] In *L'Espace littéraire* he maintained with Hölderlin that revealability (the sacred) is prior to revelation (God or the gods), and that the poet has a privileged role with respect to revealability. So he has already indicated that the human relation can be thought without reference to the deity. In *L'Entretien infini* he can keep God out of the conversation only by sheering away illeity, in much the same way as Fichte stripped the noumenon from the critical philosophy by declaring it unknowable and therefore useless. Yet even in a world where double dissymmetry holds sway one could still be bothered by questions that cannot be brushed aside. If the other person is infinitely other and thereby cannot be assimilated to me, by what right can I reduce the alterity in question to the scale of the human? The immemorial past of the other person can always call God to mind. And one can also ask, if the other person ruptures the order of being, by what right can one limit this to the realm of the human, the being who clings to being?

5

The human relation is terrifying because it confronts us with a dire alternative, "speak or kill," options that need to be examined in more detail. The disjunction is not directly thematized in *Totalité et infini*, although Lévinas presents ethics by way of conversation. Ethics has nothing to do with the gaze that, as we have seen in Husserl, "transforms relations into correlatives."[79] For the Other to be always visible, forever brought into an intentional rapport with me, would be the end of ethics in its Lévinasian sense. "The relation with the Other, or Conversation [*Discours*], is a non-allergic reaction, an ethical relation" (51; 43), Lévinas announces; it is "to have the idea of infinity" (51; 43). Lévinas's *discours* which gives *l'idée de l'infini* becomes for Blanchot *l'entretien infini*.

If Blanchot's *entretien* is in any way a translation of Lévinas's *discours*, it certainly goes by way of what Blanchot takes to be Antelme's emphasis on *parler*, so much so that Blanchot finds that he can have one of his speakers say in the third of the three dialogues in *L'Entretien infini* in response to *Totalité et infini*, "Each time the question: Who is '*Autrui*'? emerges in our words I think of the book by Robert Antelme, for it not only testifies [*est . . . un témoignage*] to the society of the German camps of World War II, it also leads us to an essential reflection."[80] As we hear a little later, "it is a question not of telling one's story, of testifying, but essentially of *speaking*" ("témoigner, ce n'est pas de cela qu'il s'est agi, mais essentiellement *parler*") (134; 198).[81] Where testimony turns upon the individual self, speech, as figured here, is what proceeds from the Other—or, more exactly, from the Others, for *Autrui*, here, is thought by way of a community that is the extreme absence of community.

There were times in the camps when camaraderie became possible in snatches, and at those times the prisoners were once again in a dialectic. These moments, however, were accidental to the strangeness of the camps, for "what in this situation remains essential, its truth, is the following: the camp confined no more than a bondless entanglement of Others [*hommes Autres*], a magma of the other [*Autrui*] face to face with the force of a Self that kills, and that represents nothing but the untiring power to kill" (134; 199). The speech that has come from the camps, and from *L'Espèce humaine* in an exemplary way, is the speech of the Other. It is a reserved speech, one that could not be uttered in the camps but that overflowed when the war ended. "We wanted at last to speak [*parler*], to be heard."[82] Yet this essential speech could not be spoken fluently: "it was impossible. No sooner would we begin to tell [*à raconter*] our story than we would be choking over it. And then, even to us, what we had to tell [*à dire*] would start to seem *unimaginable*" (3).

An executioner "can kill a man," Antelme says, "but he can't change him into something else" (220). Nor can the executioner converse with a human being. As Blanchot puts it, when threatened, the prisoner tries "to preserve the true speech that he very well knows is at this instant merged with his silent presence—which is the very presence of *autrui* in himself" (132; 195). There may be no external limit to terror—given the proper resources, the SS could have killed all day and all night—but Antelme discloses an internal limit, which I quoted in the previous chapter: "the variety of the relationships between men, their color, their customs, the classes they formed into mask a truth that here, at the boundary of nature, at the point where we approach our limits, appears with absolute clarity: namely, that there are not several human races, there is only one human race" (219). The literary terrorism that intrigued the young Blanchot in his first critical writing is based on a deep distrust of language. Political terrorism, which more directly interested the same young Blanchot for a short while, is a refusal to speak or no longer to speak. The older author realizes now that political terrorism calls forth a similar refusal, one that keeps authentic speech in reserve. True speech can hardly be heard because, as Antelme says, it chokes the speaker and begins to evoke something that seems completely impossible. When we hear it, if we ever do, we recognize that it is, as Blanchot says, "silently affirming that were all relation is lacking there yet subsists, there already begins, the human relation in its primacy" (135; 199). It is a "truly infinite speech" ("parole vraiment infinie").

We can better understand the infinity of this speech by turning away from Antelme, whose work should not be encumbered by commentary, and listening instead to Blanchot thinking of another friend, Bataille:

> What is present in this presence of speech, as soon as it affirms itself, is precisely what never lets itself be seen or attained: something is there that is beyond reach (of the one who says it as much as of the one who hears it). It is between us, it holds itself between [*cela se tient entre*], and conversation [*l'entretien*] is approach on the basis of this between-two [*entre-deux*]: an irreducible distance that must be preserved if one wishes to maintain a relation with the unknown [*l'inconnu*] that is speech's unique gift.[83]

No surprise, then, that Blanchot's conversations are not forensic cross-examinations, as one finds in the Platonic dialogues. They are more meditative than maieutic. Lévinas insists with reason that conversation includes an element of teaching, yet Blanchot's conversations are not elegant pedagogical devices that allow for conflicting views to be presented and criticized, as Cicero does in his philosophical writings. They are more interrogative than didactic. Indeed, Blanchot does not stage an exchange of views by more or less stable, identifiable characters, as one finds in the philosophical dialogues of Augustine or Berkeley, Hume or Malebranche, Herder or Gide.

Heidegger's "Aus einem Gespräch von der Sprache" is closer to Blanchot's way of proceeding. Composed in 1953–54, it appeared in *Unterwegs zur Sprache* (1959), a year before Blanchot's first dialogues, "Entretien sur un changement d'époque" (1960) and "La Marche de l'écrevisse" (1960), the title of which conjures the crawling and nocturnal burrowing of a crayfish.[84] Let us listen to a short stretch of Heidegger's conversation between a Japanese and an Inquirer. "We Japanese do not think it strange if a dialogue leaves undefined what is really intended, or even restores it back to the keeping of the undefinable," says the unnamed man from Japan.[85] A little later, he reflects on how their conversation has been going, "Then our dialogue drifted away into the undefined," to which the Inquirer ("Heidegger") adds, "Fortunately" (28). Such wandering is the very style of Blanchot's infinite conversations. More telling is this exchange:

J: How would you present the hermeneutic circle today?
I: I would avoid a presentation as resolutely as I would avoid speaking *about* language.
J: Then everything would hinge on reaching a corresponding saying of language.
I: Only a dialogue could be such a saying correspondence.
J: But, patently, a dialogue altogether *sui generis*.
I: A dialogue that would remain altogether appropriated to Saying [*der Sage*].
J: But then, not every talk between people [*Miteinanderreden*] could be called a dialogue [*Gespräch*] any longer. (51–52)

Because it is an authentic dialogue, an attending to the unsaid, and not a mere idle conversation, the two men are borne along by it and language comes to meet them. This is what Heidegger calls a "relation."

To get a better idea of this relation, we need to overhear an earlier passage in the dialogue:

I: Man is used for hearing the message.
J: This you called a while ago: man stands in a relation [*Der Mensch steht in einem Bezug*].
I: And the relation is called hermeneutical because it brings the tidings of that message.
J: This message makes the claim on man that he respond to it . . .
I: . . . to listen and belong to it as man.
J: And this is what you call being human, if you here still admit the word "being."
I: Man is the message-bearer of the message which the two-fold's unconcealment speaks to him. (40)

Human beings stand in a relation with the unconcealing of being in beings, and, because of this, we stand in relation with one another. *Logos* is not something we manipulate; it is communication, a sharing, a dia-logos, the opening of community: a thought that Heidegger does not pursue but one that Blanchot does, though at an angle to the German thinker's preoccupations, by way of Lévinasian *Dire* rather than Heideggerian *Sage*.

Dire or Saying is not essentially a modality of speech; it is vulnerability before the other person, a willingness to address his or her needs even before words are spoken and begin their inevitable slide toward a hardening of meaning: archive, contract, dialectic, law. To be before the other person is not necessarily to see him or her; it is to be addressed from above, and it is in this speech, not in anything visible, that the revelation of *Autrui* occurs.[86] At its deepest level, *Dire* is an exposure to the certainty of the other person's death, an acknowledgment that he or she is finite, threatened by hunger, loneliness, and disease. The other person is always and already marked by a death to come; it is what enables a relation to be formed between us and, beyond that, exposes us to community.[87] More than a tacit acceptance of mortality is called for, however; the death of the other person calls me into question, contests any claim I might have to be a sovereign self. It is as though the smiles or frowns of the other person could always be interrupted now and then by a dark gaze, "the most terrible look which a living being can receive [*quelque chose de terrible*]," that of an endless dying, and it is this thought that solicits our unbounded solicitude.[88] Standing before the other person, *I* am called upon to respond not because of any special qualities I might have but only because I am here, now, before him or her. Blanchot and Lévinas do not call upon us to be passive with respect to the other person—on the contrary, they invite us to *act*. As Blanchot said with regard to South Africa in 1986, "the European community's inertia does discredit to the ideals and civilization that community claims to represent. Let us realize, therefore, that we too are responsible and guilty when we do not voice an appeal, a denunciation, and a cry."[89] That said, Lévinas and Blanchot ask us to recognize that ethics *as such* begins in a passivity that is prior to the alternative of passivity and action. Blanchot would add to this that community also begins in this absolute passivity, and not in any social work that one might do.

So we return to contestation. For Blanchot, it is always a questioning of the primacy of the self, a rejection of attempts to transform human relations into intentional correlations. Conversation is essential to this movement, as Raymond Carpentier makes plain in language that is reminiscent of Blanchot:

Dialogue, when it is really open to the other, when it is goodwill that is not some vague expectation but an active desire to receive, to listen, to seek to go out of oneself, and to admit the universe of another, could not proceed to its ultimate conclusions without the sacrifice [*l'immolation*] of one of the partners: that is to say, without repudiating itself as a dialogue. Truly to engage in a dialogue would be to question one's own being [*mettre en cause son être proper*] through the information that comes from another. It would be to accept the risk that the other might remold us in his image and destroy all that makes us what we are.[90]

Several years later, in *L'Écriture du désastre*, Blanchot phrases the matter as follows:

> To converse [*S'entretenir*], it seems, is not only to turn away from saying what, thanks to language, *is*—the present of a presence. To converse is also to turn language away from itself, maintaining it outside of all unity, outside even the unity of that which is. To converse is to divert language from itself by letting it differ and defer [*différer*], answering with an always already to a never yet.[91]

By contesting what is present and possible, conversation opens us to the impossible. It does not endorse a political project, this sort of socialism or that brand of communism, which, no matter how appealing, can always be contested further in its particular actions and in its party platform. Rather, it indicates an impossible politics, one that is always still to come but that, if forgotten or bypassed, will leave us with a more cramped or less generous way of living than could have been ours otherwise.[92] "The kingdom of heaven is ethical," writes Lévinas at the end of *Autrement qu'être*, putting his own spin on Jewish and Christian calls for what the New Testament names the βασιλεία.[93] No longer a monarchist or a Christian, not for several decades, Blanchot would distance himself from such a formulation, even one where the predicate is allowed to reflect negatively upon the subject; and yet he would affirm that the "negative community," the one we can discern only now and then in moments of communication, is ethical. That community tends to be experienced as the absence of community is no argument against ethics or a concession of the failure of community.

When the other person dies, the relation that has held us together and apart no longer obtains. Now there can be no further interruption of my being by this person, there can be no commerce between us. Hard as it is, I must admit that he or she has gone forever. "It is with that absence—its uncanny presence, always under the prior threat of a disappearance—that friendship is brought into play and lost at each moment, a relation without relation or without relation other than the incommensurable."[94] Just before saying this Blanchot had been talking about community. Notice that he has silently passed from the human relation to friendship. It is not the only time that this happens, partly because the very high level of generality at which he is thinking does not allow him to distinguish social and friendly relations, and partly because he construes friendship more broadly than is usual. Distinguishing his understanding of l'amitié from the Greek notion of φιλία, he tells us that friendship is "openness to the *Other*, the discovery of the Other as responsible for the Other, the recognition of the Other's pre-eminence, the awakening and sobering by the Other who never leaves me alone, the enjoyment (without concupiscence as Pascal puts it) of the Other's Highness, which makes the Other always nearer the Good than 'me.'"[95] Yet this is precisely the human relation phrased in a later version of Lévinas's idiom than was available when writing the dialogues now contained in *L'Entretien infini*, and it will surely be objected that we are not—can not be, and should not be—friends with any or all individuals. It is one thing to help the widow, the orphan, and the stranger; quite another to be friends with any of them.

Blanchot would seem to agree. "Faithfulness, constancy, endurance, perhaps permanence: these are the key traits of friendship" (35; 34), he says in *Pour l'amitié* (1996), while knowing very well how rare these qualities are. Elsewhere, he ponders whether ethics and love share the same dissymmetric structure. "Love [*L'amour*] may be a stumbling block for ethics," he admits (perhaps thinking of Lévinas's objections to love as *egoisme à deux*), "unless love simply puts ethics into question by imitating it."[96] The same can be said of friendship: it calls ethics into question—that is, expands its usual range of meaning—by adopting the same structure of double dissymmetry that characterizes ethics. The community that we glimpse beyond all communities, even those of good friends or faithful lovers, is one that bears the traits of friendship or love. That this community is impossible does not mean it is a utopia: the impossible and the possible are not contradictory terms in Blanchot's logic. His claim is that it leads us to contest all the more fiercely aspects of the communities in which we live. The position is fundamentally Kantian, although, as with Lévinas, the emphasis is on the singular other and not on a universal law.

"A tous mes amis, connus et inconnus, proches et lointains": so runs the dedication to *Pour l'amitié*, "To all my friends, known and unknown, near and far." Listening carefully, one can almost hear Blanchot alluding to the verse from

Trito-Isaiah that I discussed in the last chapter, "Peace, peace to him that is far off, and to him that is near, saith the Lord; and I will heal him" (Isa. 57:19). The merismus is set in reverse order: "far and near" becomes "near and far," and the hint of catastrophe contained in the verse is passed over in the dedication.[97] It is appropriate since, for Blanchot, the disaster has always and already occurred, and it is our relation (without relation) with it that is important. In a letter to Bataille Blanchot leaves us in no doubt what that relation is: "friendship is the truth of the disaster."[98]

More curious than the second pair of adjectives is the first, for the question inevitably arises whether can one have unknown friends. Surely not; but since Blanchot imagines death as a friend and conceives the community beyond community to be characterized by friendship, one can at least see how the question could be answered affirmatively. Blanchot's point, however, is that even one's friends are both known and unknown. In the words of one of his most beautiful meditations, "L'Amitié," which he wrote after the death of Bataille:

> We must give up trying to know [connaître] those to whom we are linked by something essential; by this I mean we must greet them in the relation with the unknown [l'inconnu] in which they greet us as well, in our estrangement [éloignement]. Friendship, this relation without dependence, without episode, yet into which all of the simplicity of life enters, passes by way of the recognition of the common strangeness that does not allow us to speak of our friends but only to speak to them, not to make of them a topic of conversations (or essays), but the movement of understanding in which, speaking to us, they reserve, even on the most familiar terms, an infinite distance, the fundamental separation on the basis of which what separates becomes relation.[99]

It is not the human that is wonderfully strange, as Sophocles declared, but the human relation; and what makes it irreducibly strange is that our relations with others, even friends, involve a reference to the unknown or, if you like, the impossible or the sacred.

We do not speak *of* the friend, only *to* the friend, Blanchot tells us, and adds that such talk occurs in an interruption of being (291; 328).[100] Once again we see how religion is inscribed in the human relation, not evacuated from it: in the liturgy we talk only to God and not of Him.[101] Friendship is not a different sort of relation that we have with others, a special kind of affinity. It is a species of the human relation; it lets us glimpse what being with others could be: a contestation of being, a rejection of the security of the *conatus essendi*. For Bataille, inner experience is friendship, and Blanchot does not fail to add that friendship is "the most tender of names."[102] We would read Blanchot badly were we not to recognize that this tenderness occurs in a world without God, and we would read him equally poorly if we did not also find coiled there—displaced and strange—tightly folded references to the sacred and faith.

CONCLUSION:
THE COUNTERSPIRITUAL LIFE

1

I began this study by evoking an image, unremarked by most readers of Blanchot, in which the young novelist, in conversation with Bataille, tries to make sense of what a "'spiritual' life" would be. Reporting their discussion, Bataille recorded his friend saying that such a life would be predicated on renouncing all hope of salvation and would be grounded in "inner experience," an authority that would "expiate itself."[1] Since inner experience involves a ravaging of the self and no contact with the deity, there is good reason for the scare quotes in "'spiritual' life." No one could fail to notice, however, that the notion of expiation restores the category of the sacred in the very gesture in which the possibility of faith in God is rejected. Blanchot adds a third clause to his understanding of the new spirituality: it would be "contestation of itself and nonknowledge [non-savoir]" (102; 120). About the time of that conversation, Blanchot found support for his views in the writings of Meister Eckhart who, along with Saint John of the Cross, is the only Christian mystic whose writings he affirms almost without reservation. Nonknowledge for Eckhart is a rupture with discourse, a break with all that is possible, and an affirmation of the impossible. "That mystical demands dominate his entire way of thinking and that this way of thinking bears witness to a spiritual experience [une expérience spirituelle] of great amplitude and richness—this is what seems certain as we read his principal writings."[2]

This is a rare moment in Blanchot when he allows the feasibility of a "spiritual life" without adding or implying scare quotes around the word "spiritual."

Eckhart is a representative of "faith's supreme experience" in which "notions of salvation, hope, and bliss no longer count" (27; 36); and so we see, if only for an instant, Blanchot conceding that Christian faith can have a role in the spiritual life he affirms. What appeals to Blanchot is Eckhart's relentless contestation of dogmatic notions of God until he comes to the Godhead, absolute no-thing-ness, to which one can be joined through unknowing and which would allow one truly to say, "I am already dead." On my reading of Blanchot, the "spiritual" life has two poles, the sacred and faith, both of which contest the integrity of the "I" and both of which are to be detached from their usual confessional settings. The sacred, for him, is not the *mysterium tremendum* to be found in biblical theophanies. As becomes clear in his readings of Heidegger and Char, it is the revelation, consequent upon an ontological attunement, that the distance between being and image is always and already within being itself. This event occurs, it does not happen; and, following Nietzsche, Blanchot holds that it eternally returns without ever becoming present. It cannot be lived, in the sense of *Erlebnis*, although Blanchot insists that it can be experienced as other. When it occurs, one is fascinated by it, as though it were the *mysterium tremendum*. I have called it a dark gaze partly in order to distinguish it from the sacred as usually understood and partly to identify a powerful sequence of motifs in Blanchot's criticism and narratives.

The dark gaze comes from *une réalité antérieure*, and, when it transfixes us, we witness the frightening transformation of presence into absence, being into image.[3] Yet some of us can assume this gaze ourselves. The artist, in particular, appropriates it in the very exercise of art; and so we find Blanchot venturing a new link between the artist and the sacred. He does so with both the Greeks and the German romantics in mind (itself a romantic gesture). On the one hand, the sacred is the neutral that Heraclitus discerned and that so much literature, philosophy, and theology have noisily talked down. If, with Lévinas, we can point to Parmenides as the instigator of the philosophy of the neuter, we can also indicate how a neutral conception of being was taken up by Duns Scotus, developed by Francesco Suárez, and perpetuated as much as castigated by Heidegger. Hölderlin and Char have exposed this philosophy of the neuter and have recovered the mobile, plural neutral, of which Blanchot's main figure has been the Outside. On the other hand, it is the poet who, in an instant of explosive communication, recognizes the fissure within being. He or she sacrifices words and selfhood in order to receive the gift of the poem, those ordinary words now charged as *other* and offered as a response to the "anterior reality." That poem will be sacred speech, regardless of its theme or the piety of its author. It does not dictate a divine word (all external authority is expiated in the act of writing), nor does the poet offer a personal warrant for what it says. The poem is prophetic, Blanchot insists, because it is always ahead of itself, never frozen into an acceptable meaning. It is the fire's part; it burns and does not illuminate. Sacred, sacrifice, prophecy, revelation: Blanchot does not hesitate to draw freely from a traditional religious lexicon, even while disassociating the sacred, in his sense of the word, from religion which he regards as fatally bound up with unity and therefore with the philosophy of the neuter.

The "'spiritual' life" turns on faith as well as the sacred, and I retain the quotation marks in order to emphasize what I have just said about Blanchot's rejection of religion. Faith, here, is worked out by way of the human relation, a notion that Blanchot explores by adapting the Jewish experience of prayer. Monotheism is not the greatest heritage that the Jews have bequeathed to us, Blanchot asserts. It is prayer, understood as dialogue between God and humans, that is our richest inheritance: "And the LORD spake unto Moses face to face, as a man speaketh unto his friend" (Exod. 33:11). Unlike Lévinas, who distinguishes God from *Autrui*, Blanchot insists that man is "more Other than all that is other" ("plus Autre que tout ce qu'il y a d'autre").[4] The word *autrui* must be withdrawn, presumably in favor of *communauté*, understood by way of double dissymmetry between human beings. The alterity of the other person does not bring God to mind, Blanchot tells us; rather, it is what conducts the mystery of the Outside. If the sacred contests the "I" by exposing it to an anterior reality, faith—understood as the human relation—similarly calls the "I" into question by exposing us to the mortality of the other person. The faith of the Jews, *he'emin*, opens onto the human relation partly because it rejects human autonomy and partly because it evokes a history of both trust and fear. Blanchot invites us to pass from a theocentric to an anthropological understanding of faith, to pass from the Jews in prayer, to the bareness of the human relation. Trust and fear are to be rethought in terms of "Speak or kill"; hope is to be retained in the form of a communism beyond communism; while obedience is reconceived in terms of double dissymmetry, an infinity that passes from the other to me and, without being returned, from me to the other.

Blanchot's deep empathy for the Jews can be seen to develop after the Second World War, although its beginnings were nourished by his early friendship with Lévinas. The young Blanchot was certainly not an anti-Semite as Robert Brasillach and Lucien Rebatet were, and he may not have been so in any other sense, either.[5] Yet he came to recognize that in the late 1930s and early 1940s he had been insufficiently vigilant with respect to the Jews in his association with the far right of French politics, and that this lack of sustained attention made him, like so many, culpable for what happened in Auschwitz and the other death camps.

Unlike many others, Blanchot acknowledges his guilt and newfound sense of responsibility, albeit in oblique ways. Thus he devotes a long if interrupted meditation on the Hebrew Bible as containing the best image of the human relation, an image that must be properly interpreted and endlessly opened to the rest of the world. In the 1960s Karl Rahner coined the expression "anonymous Christians," by which he meant those people of good faith, religious or not, whom Christians must believe are redeemed by Christ—a Christ in whom those people do not explicitly believe.[6] It is a deeply problematic expression, and this is not the place to debate it in any detail.[7] I raise it only because I think one could regard Blanchot as turning all the peoples of the world, including the Jews, into anonymous Jews.

A just ethics exists in ovo in the Hebrew Bible, Blanchot maintains, and it can and should be hatched and allowed to leave the nest. Since this ethics turns on a sliding from the "I" to the "one," Blanchot would presumably wish to defend the adjective "anonymous" with more zest than Rahner was able to do. The Catholic theologian upset Christians who thought their faith was anything but anonymous, and he faced the irritation or ire of Jews and Buddhists, Hindus and Muslims, who did not want to be known as anonymous Christians. Perhaps some of their distress would have been allayed had it been put more plainly to them that Rahner affirmed a double dissymmetry of his own. He, and others like him, should be regarded as an anonymous Jew, an anonymous Buddhist, and so on. Even so, one can readily imagine a Hindu, for example, insisting that there is nothing anonymous about being Hindu: it involves a complex set of beliefs and practices that should be respected, and the very idea of someone's being an "anonymous Hindu" shows a lack of respect for the religion that is practiced at some pains to himself or herself. My sense is that Blanchot's embracing of the Hebrew Bible leads in some interesting directions, not the least rewarding of which is the importance of dialogue rather than visual perception. However, the Judaism he affirms is an impoverished version of the religion, one that redefines the Jew's relation to Scripture and Israel's calling, while erasing both monotheism and monolatrism. Although he does not quite allegorize the Jews out of history, he comes very close to doing so when observing that the Jews exist so that we may have the ideas of exodus and exile, so that "the experience of strangeness may affirm itself close at hand as an irreducible relation," and so that we might speak with our neighbors rather than kill them.[8] I think of Adorno, hardly a friend of religion, who astutely observed, "If religion is accepted for the sake of something other than its own truth content, then it undermines itself."[9]

2

For a long time Blanchot regarded the artist as living the "'spiritual' life" in an exemplary way. It is in art that we find ourselves having to admit that human being is not entirely determined by way of possibility but is turned toward the impossible. In classical Greece the artist worked under the protection of the gods, and, with inevitable accommodations, the situation remained more or less intact for almost the first two millennia of Christianity. Doubtless this is partly why Blanchot can speak so admiringly of Eckhart. For the Meister it was still possible to believe in God, and his radicalism had to occur within the horizon of Christianity. Hölderlin was the first to diagnose that mortals have turned away from the deity and the deity has turned away from mortals. He was the first to realize that without the sacred the work of art cannot find "the profound *reserve* which it needs," the obscurity and distance "which constitute its space and to which it gives rise as though thus to come into the light."[10] Hölderlin saw that the artist must occupy the space created by the double infidelity. Now that divinity has left us, and now that we do not expect it to return, what becomes of art? It is a serious question for Blanchot, as it was for the Heidegger to whom he is close here. Nothing is left of the sacred but the eternal murmuring of the Outside, a stale and empty depth in which nothing truly begins but only begins again. It is more infernal than heavenly, as Blanchot indicates in "Le Regard d'Orphée." Without divinity, art points us to a state that is entirely other than the world of possibilities, a space of pure wandering that Rilke called *Nirgends ohne Nicht*, "nowhere without no." It is, as Blanchot reminds us, a state in which there is neither truth nor falsity. Without divinity, art can only point us in the direction of nihilism.

One might think that a thoroughgoing nihilism would be the ruin of all community. Not so, Blanchot says, for the thought of the human relation points us in exactly the same direction. In their different ways, art and communism both indicate a community to come that is characterized by friendship or love or, if you like, the "'spiritual' life." The word *communism* slipped quietly into that last sentence, as though it were no more than a gloss on "community," but it needs to be asterisked for attention. From the time he abandoned his youthful enthusiasm for French monarchism, Blanchot seems never to have swerved from his commitment to a future for which communism supplies the horizon. "Communism," he insists is "always beyond communism": not because it is regulative rather than constitutive but because it is touched only in instants of intense communication.[11] Unsympathetic readers will accuse Blanchot of special pleading in his politics, and not without reason.[12] "The Inquisition destroyed the Catholic religion, at the same time that it killed Giordano Bruno," he solemnly informs us.[13] There is not the slightest doubt that the Church has done dreadful things in the name of Christ. Yet one could equally point to Stalin summarily arranging for the deportation and death of Osip Mandelstam and say that he destroyed communism in that act. Neither judgment is just.

Blanchot is no Marxist in any simple sense, and the community to come that he evokes cannot be figured in terms of a dialectic: it falls outside the thought of *Geist*. This existence would not be so much a spiritual life, whether oriented to God or culture, as a counterspiritual life. In one sense of the word *counter*, this existence must be seen to oppose the hope of a Christian, Muslim, or Jew, because Blanchot readily identifies himself as an atheist, albeit one who recognizes the philosophical difficulties of affirming that position. Yet "counter" can also denote making an angle with, as happens when Joë Bousquet talks of "counter-writing," when Pierre Klossowski evokes "counter-mystery," and when Jacques Derrida rethinks "counter-signature."[14] In English the notion of counterspirit comes to us from William Wordsworth, specifically from his "Essays on Epitaphs," a part of his corpus one can easily imagine being of great interest to Blanchot:

> Words are too awful an instrument for good and evil to be trifled with: they hold above all other external powers a dominion over thoughts. If words be not (recurring to a metaphor before used) an incarnation of the thought but only a clothing for it, then surely will they prove an ill gift: such a one as those poisoned vestments, read of in the stories of superstitious times, which had power to consume and to alienate from his right mind the victim who put them on. Language, if it do not uphold, and feed, and leave in quiet, like the power of gravitation or the air we breathe, is a counter-spirit, unremittingly and noiselessly at work to derange, to subvert, to lay waste, to vitiate, and to dissolve.[15]

If counterspirit is demonic for Wordsworth, for Blanchot it marks the possibility of any encounter we might have with the Messiah. The two writers would agree that counterspirit is a disaster, but the word would mean quite different things for each of them. To derange, subvert, lay waste, vitiate, and dissolve, for Blanchot, would be precisely what the language of the Messiah offers us. More generally, to remove the quotation marks around "spiritual" would be quietly to change the word to "counterspiritual."

3

"For it would be wrong to speak of the Messiah in Hegelian language," Blanchot declares.[16] The Messiah is not to be assimilated to any talk of Absolute Spirit or Christian supersession, national spirit or spiritual revolution, nor are these to be annexed to any proclamation of the Messiah. The messianic does not happen as spirit, it occurs as counterspirit. Adorno's notion of "negative dialectics" gives us a rough indication of what this might mean, although something more is at issue than the *Nicht-identität* (nonidentity) of the particular and the universal, culture and society, in the final instance.[17] First of all, messianic time would be "a time more future . . . than any prophesy could ever foretell" (142; 215). The future announced in messianic time is impossible in that it is discontinuous with ordinary time: no project can pass from historical to messianic time. Now no attempt is made by Blanchot to evoke a temporality that is theologically appropriate to either the Hebrew or the Christian Bible.[18] Instead, he folds messianic time into his understanding of the Outside: the prophets expose us to the strange realm of the imaginary (or the sacred) where nothing can be accomplished and one can only wander.[19] This is not an aestheticizing of religion. To acknowledge a reference to the Outside, Blanchot insists, is to remove writing from the aesthetic, which is one reason why he will never associate the Outside and the sublime. The consequence is ethical, not aesthetic. People who have glimpsed the messianic transformation of time into space are "stripped of their power and separated from the possible (the widow and the orphan), exist with each other in the bare relationship in which they had been in the desert and which is the desert itself" (81; 112). Messianic time, like the time of writing, reveals the human relation, then, and is finally to be understood by way of community, not redemption.

It would not be quite right to say that counterspirit, as Blanchot conceives it, *resists* spirit either in history or in writing. Its passivity falls outside the dialectic of active and passive and does not wrest language back from the transcendence of spirit to the immanence of the letter.[20] Geoffrey Hartman, for whom Wordsworth is a constant passion, is characteristically insightful when he adapts the poet's expression in reading Blanchot. Counterspirit, he observes, "scandalizes because it suggests a passivity that cannot be spiritualized (interpreted as martyrdom for example) yet honors sheer endurance," and elsewhere adds that Blanchot's later writing "*is* this counter-spirit."[21] As Blanchot says, the language of prophecy is "Language that is not spiritual and that nonetheless is spirit."[22] (83; 115). And to this I would add only that we have to keep in play two languages, that of the dialectic and that of the neuter, the possible and the impossible, spirit and counter-spirit. Messianic time interrupts history; its language is "of transport and of being carried away" (83; 115). We might say that it is an inaugurated eschatology, already here yet still to come, but (unlike biblical eschatology) never to come in fullness and always to be completely without power.

Throughout this study I have tried to show that Blanchot rethinks the sacred and faith rather than dismissing them altogether, as most of his critics have assumed or desired. We cannot begin to understand this man's writing unless we can make sense of his spirituality, and we cannot come to terms with his epoch unless we recognize the ways in which its religious concerns are treated by him: in an exemplary way, I would insist, meaning by that with far more rigor than one usually finds. At the same time, I have underlined that we must respect Blanchot's convictions as an atheist and as a nihilist. Neither word satisfies him: atheism is not something that one can affirm as an individual, while nihilism is coordinate with the impossible, not the possible. To read Blanchot in the hope of finding a negative theology, an oblique rapprochement with the Christian or the Jewish God, would be dishonest in the extreme. As a Christian, I take it to be a very serious task to listen to atheists, partly in order to understand their convictions and their protests and partly because one or more forms of atheism cross and recross the most devout faith. People of faith can learn something from Blanchot and those from whom he draws.

What I have called Blanchot's counterspirituality is itself partly derived from Judeo-Christian spiritualities that are not as well known today as they could be, and it can be used to check the excessively philosophical, triumphalist, or political forms that Judaism and Christianity have taken in recent decades. I do not follow the strain of "religion without religion" that passes from Kant through Blanchot and finds a distinguished contemporary expositor in Jacques Derrida, but I do find the philosophy of the neuter troubling and think that Lévinas was entirely correct to name his friend as one of the people who identified it in western thought. The neutral will not serve, for me or for any believer, as an antidote to that philosophy; and I have discreetly indicated other ways of approaching the issue in these chapters. To flesh them out has not been my interest here; it could be done more economically by way of Hans Urs von Balthasar and Karl Rahner, Karl Barth and Eberhard Jüngel, to give only the barest indices. To think Jesus as the Messiah outside Hegelian language, and all that it swept up in its difficult and brilliant movement, to think Him outside supersession, national spirit, and spiritual revolution remains a pressing task to be undertaken at many levels and for many years. To rethink spirituality by way of the fragmentary would be a part of this, and to develop monotheism beyond the homology of the human "I" and "God" would be another part.

4

One argument against regarding Blanchot as a major figure is that he is not original: all his important thoughts are drawn from Nietzsche or Heidegger, Mallarmé or Kafka, Bataille or Lévinas. He adapts rather than creates. Another argument is that he is overly original: no other writer in the entire history of the West has ever testified to encountering the Outside, and so one would hardly be inclined to trust his account of literature. My response to this dispute is twofold. I have no doubt that Blanchot is a formidably strong writer of prose narrative: *Thomas l'obscur, L'Arrêt de mort*, and *Celui qui ne m'accompagnait pas*, in particular, strike me as being the most powerful fiction in French literature since Proust. Also, I have no doubt that Blanchot gathers in his critical writings, as well as in his narratives, a profound if often unacknowledged sense of our times. I hesitate to call this a religious sense because he would recoil from the very word, but I am content to talk of his counterspirituality because it contains both his rejection of received religion and the angles he makes with it.

Few people have thought longer or deeper about the relations between literature and the sacred than Maurice Blanchot. His understanding of those relations is unsettling for readers of literature as well as for the faithful, not because he is an atheist but because he takes the sacred seriously. He believes that we have lost the sacred and that this loss is a disaster. Literature now exposes us to the eternal murmuring of the Outside; it points us to a nihilism that is not the destruction of all community but a sociality that is grasped by way of the human relation. We are not full members of this "negative community" and never shall be, yet we remain faced, Blanchot thinks, with a stark alternative, "speak or kill." To speak is to take part in an infinite conversation, one that has been going on since biblical times, and one that begins because the infinite precedes the finite. Blanchot would never subscribe to a correlation between the human and the divine, and he distances himself from a religion that is elaborated in the breakdown of correlation. He realizes that such a religion requires an act of faith, both *interiori fidei actu* and *exteriori fidei actu*, and he chooses to live without it. It is a life that was never less than fully human. In the absence of such faith, however, he still repeats in his own way what was first written a long time ago, "Peace, peace to him that is far off, and to him that is near, saith the Lord; and I will heal him" (Isa. 57:19). Let us respect those words, regardless of who speaks them or cites them. Let us learn to hear them in all contexts and in all tones. And let us learn to live them in all their difficulty and in all their simplicity.

NOTES

INTRODUCTION

1. Maurice Blanchot, "Ars Nova," *The Infinite Conversation*, trans. and foreword by Susan Hanson (Minneapolis: University of Minnesota Press, 1993), 350; *L'Entretien infini* (Paris: Gallimard, 1969), 513–14.

2. Georges Poulet, *The Metamorphoses of the Circle*, trans. Carley Dawson and Elliott Coleman (Baltimore: Johns Hopkins University Press, 1966), xi.

3. Pascal formulates the claim as follows: "C'est une sphere infini dont le centre est partout, la circonférence nulle part." Blaise Pascal, *Pensées* (Paris: Éditions Garnier Frères, 1960), 2:72. The lines from the *Commedia* run as follows in English: "In the profound and clear ground of the lofty light appeared to me three circles of three colours and of the same extent, and the one seemed reflected by the other as rainbow by rainbow, and the third seemed fire breathed forth equally from the one and the other." *The Divine Comedy of Dante Alighieri*, trans. and commentary by John D. Sinclair, vol. 3: *Paradiso* (London: John Lane, Bodley Head, 1946), 485.

4. Blanchot says in a late text that "The Inquisition destroyed the Catholic religion, at the same time that it killed Giordano Bruno." See his "L'Inquisition a détruit la religion catholique . . . ," *La Règle du jeu*, no. 10 (May 1993): 206. Blanchot earlier discussed Bruno, in conjunction with Nicholas of Cusa, in "La Religion de Rabelais," *Journal des Débats*, August 4, 1943, 3.

5. Poulet, "Phenomenology of Reading," *New Literary History* 1 (1969): 59. See Sarah N. Lawall, *Critics of Consciousness* (Cambridge: Harvard University Press, 1968).

6. See Blanchot's comments on the circle in "Broch," *The Book to Come*, trans. Charlotte Mandell (Stanford: Stanford University Press, 2003), 125; *Le Livre à venir* (Paris: Gallimard, 1959), 172. Also see his use of the circle in *The One Who Was Standing Apart from Me*, trans. Lydia Davis (Barrytown, N.Y.: Station Hill Press, 1993), 76–77; *Celui qui ne m'accompagnait pas* (Paris: Gallimard, 1953), 144–45.

7. Poulet, *Metamorphoses of the Circle*, 223. Poulet also contributed an essay to the special issue of *Critique* devoted to Blanchot. See his "Maurice Blanchot, critique et romancier," *Critique* 229 (1966): 485–97. The essay was an expansion of a piece published in *Yale French Studies* 7 (1951): 77–81.

8. Marcel Raymond–Georges Poulet, *Correspondance 1950–1977*, ed. Pierre Grotzer, foreword by Henri Gouhier (Paris: José Corti, 1981), 86.

9. Pierre Klossowski, "The Marquis de Sade and the Revolution," *The College of Sociology, 1937–39*, ed. Denis Hollier, trans. Betsy Wing (Minneapolis: University of Minnesota Press, 1988), 226.

10. Saint Augustine, *Confessions*, 3.6.11. In his translation, Henry Chadwick renders the expression as "more inward than my most inward part and higher than the highest element within me." *Confessions* (Oxford: Oxford University Press, 1991).

11. See Paul Veyne, *René Char en ses poèmes* (Paris: Gallimard, 1990), 35, and Emmanuel Lé-

vinas, *De Dieu qui vient à l'idée* (Paris: J. Vrin, 1992). Also see Roger Laporte's remark that Blanchot is "mystique quoique athée," in his "Une Passion," included with Bernard Noël's "D'une main obscure," in *Deux Lectures de Maurice Blanchot* (Montpellier: Fata Morgana, 1973), 57. Laporte repudiated the essay and recast it as "Une Passion (Nouvelle version)" in *À l'extrême pointe: Bataille et Blanchot* (Montpellier: Fata Morgana, 1994). Thinking of earlier generations of thinkers, Ernst Robert Curtius observes that "It is only in France that we find the phenomenon of 'Catholic Atheism.'" *The Civilization of France*, trans. Olive Wyon (New York: Macmillan, 1932), 153.

12. See Ernst H. Kantorowicz, *The King's Two Bodies: A Study in Medieval Political Theory* (Princeton: Princeton University Press, 1957). It is worth drawing attention in this context to two early pieces in which Blanchot discusses the figure of the king. The first addresses the theme of death, "Sur la pièce de M. de Montherlant," *Journal des Débats*, March 31, 1943, 3. The second concerns the theme of speech, "De la louange à la souveraineté," *Journal des Débats*, June 2, 1943, 3.

13. Jules Michelet, *Introduction à l'histoire universelle. Tableau de la France. Préface à l'Histoire de France* (Paris: Armand Colin, 1962), 67.

14. See Michelet, *Origines du droit français cherchées dans les symboles et formules du droit universal* (Paris: Hachette, 1837), xxx.

15. Michelet, *Histoire de la Révolution française*, 2 vols. (Paris: Gallimard, 1952), 2:190. A lucid discussion of Michelet's responses to the regicide is developed by Susan Dunn in her *The Deaths of Louis XVI: Regicide and the French Political Imagination* (Princeton: Princeton University Press, 1994), especially chaps. 1 and 2.

16. Émile Durkheim, *The Elementary Forms of Religious Life*, trans. Karen E. Fields (New York: Free Press, 1995), 351. See Michèle Richman, "The Sacred Group: A Durkheimian Perspective on the Collège de sociologie," *Bataille: Writing the Sacred*, ed. Carolyn Bailey Gill (London: Routledge, 1995), 58–76.

17. Georges Bataille, *Death and Sensuality: A Study of Eroticism and the Taboo*, no trans. (1977; rpt. Salem, N.H.: Ayer, 1984), 22; *Oeuvres complètes*, 12 vols. (Paris: Gallimard, 1970–88), 10:27.

18. Georges Bataille and Michel Leiris, "Notes," in Laure, *The Collected Writings*, trans. Jeanine Herman (San Francisco: City Lights Books, 1995), 87.

19. Blanchot refers to *le Dehors* and *le dehors*, the Outside and the outside. It seems that he chose the capital letter, especially in *L'Espace littéraire*, to suggest its difference from a physical outside, and then later preferred the lower case in order not to mislead readers into believing that it was a metaphysical realm. In the interest of clarity I have decided to use the capital letter. The choice does not imply that I take Blanchot to be indicating a distinct metaphysical realm, such as the world of the Forms.

20. See my discussion of Bataille's conversation with Blanchot in chapter 1. Also see Roger Caillois, *Man and the Sacred*, trans. Meyer Barash (1959; rpt. Urbana: University of Illinois Press, 2001), 35.

21. See Martin Heidegger, epilogue to "The Thing," *Poetry, Language, Thought*, trans. Albert Hofstadter (New York: Harper and Row, 1975), 184; *Contributions to Philosophy (From Enowning)*, trans. Pavis Emad and Kenneth Maly (Bloomington: Indiana University Press, 1999), 20.

22. Marlène Zarader goes as far as to grant Blanchot epochal status. Evoking his work, she says that "The epoch does not cease to contemplate itself there." See her *L'Être et le neutre: À partir de Maurice Blanchot* (Lagrasse, Fr.: Éditions Verdier, 2001), 20. Hélène Merlin-Kajman makes the bold claim, "In the seventeenth century people 'spoke Balzac' or 'Vaugelas.' It seems clear to me that in the twentieth century we will have spoken Blanchot." "Réflections d'une dix-septiémiste à propos de l'amitié selon Blanchot," *Maurice Blanchot: Récits, critiques*, ed. Christophe Bident and Pierre Vilar (Tours: Éditions Farrago/Éditions Léo Scheer, 2003), 323. For Blanchot's concession that transcendence always wins, even in a negative form, see *The Writing of the Disaster*, trans. Ann Smock (Lincoln: University of Nebraska Press, 1986), 91; *L'Écriture du désastre* (Paris: Gallimard, 1980), 143.

23. Pierre Verstraeten goes so far as to suggest, "En réalité, Blanchot ne fait que transposer à l'expérience profane de l'écriture la fonction remplie traditionnellement par la figure du Christ." "Pour une confrontation entre le statut de l'écrivain chez Sartre et chez Blanchot," *Violence et éthique: Esquisse d'une critique de la morale dialectique à partir du théâtre politique de Sartre* (Paris: Gallimard, 1972), 425.

24. See Blanchot, "Atheism and Writing, Humanism and the Cry," *Infinite Conversation*, 252; *EI*, 377. In this regard also see Blanchot's discussion of the atheist's closeness to God in "Affirmation (desire, affliction)," *Infinite Conversation*, 111; *EI*, 160. I think that Jean-Luc Nancy misses the point closely when he argues that Blanchot affirms "un simple évanouissement" of God. See his "Le Nom de Dieu chez Blanchot," *Magazine Littéraire* 424 (2003): 67.

25. On the need to resist this temptation with respect to Nietzsche, see Tyler T. Roberts, *Contesting Spirit: Nietzsche, Affirmation, Religion* (Princeton: Princeton University Press, 1998), especially the introduction.

26. See Blanchot's essay "Interruption (as on a Riemann surface)," *Infinite Conversation*; *EI*, 106–12.

27. Blanchot does not consider the possibility, considered as likely by some cosmologists, that the curvature is neither positive nor negative.

28. Cited by Lincoln Barnett, *The Universe and Dr. Einstein* (New York: New American Library, 1950), 109.

29. See for example Roger Hazelton, *God's Way with Man* (Nashville: Abingdon Press, 1956); Émil Cailliet, *The Recovery of Purpose* (New York: Harper and Bros., 1959); and Georgia Harkness, *The Providence of God* (Nashville: Abingdon Press, 1960).

30. Whitehead's account of relativity differs considerably from Einstein's. See A. N. Whitehead, *The Principle of Relativity with Applications to Physical Science* (Cambridge: Cambridge University Press, 1922). Process theology was developed by Charles Hartshorne, principally in *The Divine Relativity: A Social Conception of God* (New Haven: Yale University Press, 1948) and *The Logic of Perfection and Other Essays in Neoclassical Metaphysics* (La Salle, Ill.: Open Court, 1962).

31. A. N. Whitehead, *Process and Reality: An Essay on Cosmology* (1929; New York: Free Press, 1969), 521.

32. Thomas F. Torrance, *Reality and Scientific Theology* (Edinburgh: Scottish Academic Press,

1985), 93. More generally, his third and fifth chapters are indebted to Einstein's understanding of science.

33. The dialogue, originally entitled "La Marche de l'écrevisse," appeared in *La Nouvelle Revue Française* 91 (July 1960): 90–99. With a change of title, it was later included in *L'Entretien infini*, 28; *EI*, 39. Also see Blanchot's comments on light and the sun in "Reflections on Nihilism," *Infinite Conversation*, 160, 162; *EI*, 239–40, 243.

34. See Michel de Certeau, *The Mystic Fable*, vol. 1: *The Sixteenth and Seventeenth Centuries*, trans. Michael B. Smith (Chicago: University of Chicago Press, 1992), 77.

35. See Lucie Christine, *Journal spirituel* (Paris: Beauchesne, 1910), and Félix Klein, *Madeleine Sémer: Convertie et mystique (1874–1921)* (Paris: Bloud et Gray, 1923). Also see Edouard Récéjac, *Essai sur les fondements de la connaissance mystique* (Paris: Félix Alcan, 1897). In Britain, indices of the new interest would include Friedrich von Hügel, *The Mystical Element of Religion*, vol. 1 (London: James Clarke, 1908); Evelyn Underhill, *Mysticism: A Study of the Nature and Development of Man's Spiritual Consciousness* (1911; rpt. New York: E. P. Dutton, 1961); and Dom Cuthbert Butler, *Western Mysticism: The Teaching of Augustine, Gregory and Bernard on Contemplation and the Contemplative Life* (London: Constable, 1922).

36. On these themes see Henri de Lubac, *Medieval Exegesis*, 4 vols., vol. 1: *The Four Senses of Scripture*, trans. Mark Sebanc (Grand Rapids: William B. Eerdmans, 1998), xvi, and Kevin Hart, *The Trespass of the Sign: Deconstruction, Theology and Philosophy*, expanded ed. (New York: Fordham University Press, 2000), especially the introduction and chapter 7.

37. On the return of Valentinian gnosticism, see Cyril O'Regan, *Gnostic Return in Modernity* (Albany: State University of New York Press, 2001).

38. Emmanuel Lévinas, *Totality and Infinity: An Essay on Exteriority*, trans. Alphonso Lingis (The Hague: Martinus Nijhoff, 1979), 298. Also see his "The Poet's Vision," *On Maurice Blanchot*, in *Proper Names*, trans. Michael B. Smith (Stanford: Stanford University Press, 1996), 137; *Sur Maurice Blanchot* (Montpellier: Fata Morgana, 1975), 23. For Blanchot's comments on the neuter, see "L'Étrange et l'étranger," *La Nouvelle NRF* 70 (1958): 681, and "René Char and the Thought of the Neutral," *Infinite Conversation*, 458 n. 2; *EI*, 441 n. 2. The expression "le mode neutre" appears as early as "Les Treize Formes d'un roman," *Journal des Débats*, May 26, 1943, 3. I leave aside Roland Barthes's account of the neuter as developed in his course "Le Neutre" (Collège de France, 1977–78). See Bernard Comment, *Roland Barthes, vers le Neutre* (Paris: Christian Bourgois, 1991).

39. Hans Urs von Balthasar, *The Glory of the Lord: A Theological Aesthetics*, 7 vols., vol. 5: *The Realm of Metaphysics in the Modern Age*, ed. Brian McNeil and John Riches, trans. Oliver Davies et al. (Edinburgh: T. and T. Clark, 1991), chap. 1. Also see Étienne Gilson, *Being and Some Philosophers*, 2nd ed. (Toronto: Pontifical Institute for Medieval Studies, 1952), 106.

40. See Duns Scotus's remark that Avicenna, rather than Averroes, is correct that God is not the proper subject of metaphysics in his "Questions on the Metaphysics," in *Duns Scotus, Metaphysician*, ed. William A. Frank and Allan B. Wolter (West Lafayette, Ind.: Purdue University Press, 1995), 27. Also see Jean-Luc Marion, *Sur l'ontologie grise de Descartes*, 2nd ed. (Paris: Vrin, 1981). The contemporary "radical orthodox" theologians, clustered

around John Milbank, rely on a stripped-down version of Balthasar's account of the philosophy of the neuter, which they see as constituting modernity. The best work in this area is done out of school by Michael Allen Gillespie, *Nihilism before Nietzsche* (Chicago: University of Chicago Press, 1995).

41. See Blanchot, "The Relation of the Third Kind (*man without horizon*)," *Infinite Conversation*, 72; *EI*, 102.

42. Thus one finds Whitehead, for example, observing that "the purpose of philosophy is to rationalize mysticism: not by explaining it away, but by the introduction of novel verbal characterizations, rationally coordinated." *Modes of Thought* (Cambridge: Cambridge University Press, 1938), 237.

43. Wallace Stevens, "Flyer's Fall," *Collected Poems* (New York: Alfred A. Knopf, 1954), 336. It is worth noting that Stevens testified to his love of Blanchot in one of his last letters. See his letter to Peter H. Lee of April 1, 1955, in *Letters of Wallace Stevens*, ed. Holly Stevens (New York: Alfred A. Knopf, 1972), 879.

44. For Blanchot's reservation about the word *ethics*, see "Keeping to Words," *Infinite Conversation*, 63; *EI*, 89.

45. Jacques Derrida, *The Gift of Death*, trans. David Wills (Chicago: University of Chicago Press, 1995), 49. Interestingly, there is no such neat phrase in the original French. Also see John D. Caputo, *The Prayers and Tears of Jacques Derrida: Religion without Religion* (Bloomington: Indiana University Press, 1997).

46. Maurice Blanchot, *Thomas the Obscure*, trans. Robert Lamberton (New York: David Lewis, 1973), 15; *Thomas l'obscur* (Paris: Gallimard, 1941), 15.

47. Blanchot, *Aminadab*, trans. and introd. Jeff Fort (Lincoln: University of Nebraska Press, 2002), 154; *Aminadab* (Paris: Gallimard, 1942), 176.

48. Maurice Blanchot, *Faux Pas*, trans. Charlotte Mandell (Stanford: Stanford University Press, 2001), 8; *Faux Pas* (Paris: Gallimard, 1943), 15.

49. Blanchot also considers Jouhandeau in "Le 'Je' littéraire," *Journal des Débats*, June 1, 1944, 2–3. His influence on Blanchot's thought remains to be studied.

50. Blanchot, "Literature and the Right to Death," trans. Lydia Davis, *The Work of Fire*, trans. Charlotte Mandell (Stanford: Stanford University Press, 1995), 331; *La Part du feu* (Paris: Gallimard, 1949), 319.

51. Blanchot goes on in this essay to relate this implacable and neutral gaze, this look without light, to an idea formulated by his close friend Lévinas. He says that the philosopher speaks of the *il y a*, an "anonymous and impersonal flow of being that precedes all being" (332n; 320n), and elsewhere cites the passage about night that I have already noted as an admirable description of this state. See Lévinas, *Existence and Existents*, trans. A. Lingis (1978; rev. ed. Boston: Kluwer, 1988), 63n; *De l'existence à l'existant*, pocket ed. (1963; rpt. Paris: J. Vrin, 1990), 103n. Also see Lévinas's comments on the *il y a* and Blanchot in his "Préface à la deuxième édition," 10. Bataille contrasts Blanchot and Lévinas with respect to the *il y a* in "De l'existentialisme au primat de l'économie," *OC*, 11:292.

52. Blanchot, "The Essential Solitude," *The Space of Literature*, trans. Ann Smock (Lincoln: University of Nebraska Press, 1982), 32; *L'Espace littéraire* (Paris: Gallimard, 1955), 29;

"Rilke and Death's Demand," *Space of Literature*, 151; *EL*, 196; *Death Sentence*, trans. Lydia Davis (Barrytown, N.Y.: Station Hill Press, 1978), 20; *L'Arrêt de mort* (Paris: Gallimard, 1948), 36. Also see *Death Sentence*, 60; *AM*, 98. I will argue that this is the gaze of death as the impossibility of dying.

53. Blanchot, "Essential Solitude," *Space of Literature*, 32; *EL*, 29. Trans. slightly modified.

54. See ibid. and "The Narrative Voice (the 'he,' the neutral)," *Infinite Conversation*, 384; *EI*, 563.

55. When thinking of Simone Weil, Blanchot also evokes a gaze of love that is far from dark. See "Affirmation (desire, affliction)," *Infinite Conversation*, 122; *EI*, 178.

56. See Blanchot's comments on the influence of the story of Orpheus and Eurydice as quoted by Evelyn Londyn, "L'Orphique chez Blanchot: voir et dire," *French Forum* 5, no. 3 (1980): 261. Also see Chantal Michel, *Maurice Blanchot et le déplacement d'Orphée* (Saint-Genouph, Fr.: Librairie Nizet, 1997). Larysa Mykyta explores the male gaze with respect to Blanchot in "Thomas l'obscur: The Tangled Web of Sexuality and Textuality," *Enclitic* 6, no. 2 (1982): 14–20.

57. See the exergue to *The Space of Literature*.

58. Blanchot, "Keeping to Words," *Infinite Conversation*, 60; *EI*, 86.

59. Blanchot, *The Unavowable Community*, trans. Pierre Joris (Barrytown, N.Y.: Station Hill Press, 1988), 52; *La Communauté inavouable* (Paris: Éditions de Minuit, 1983), 87.

60. On the Greek emphasis on the visual, see Hans Jonas, "The Nobility of Sight: A Study in the Phenomenology of the Senses," *The Phenomenon of Life: Toward a Philosophical Biology* (Chicago: University of Chicago Press, 1982).

61. Blanchot, "Des diverses façons de mourir," *Journal des Débats*, June 29, 1944, 2–3. Cf. "Rilke and Death's Demand," *Space of Literature*, 151; *EL*, 196.

62. Jean-Paul Sartre, *Being and Nothingness: An Essay on Phenomenological Ontology*, trans. and introd. Hazel E. Barnes (New York: Philosophical Library, 1956), 540–41.

63. Martin Heidegger, *Parmenides*, trans. André Schuwer and Richard Rojcewicz (Bloomington: Indiana University Press, 1992), 103. Also see David Michael Levin's discussion of the distinction between the assertoric and the alethic gaze in his *The Opening of Vision: Nihilism and the Postmodern Situation* (New York: Routledge, 1988), 440.

64. Blanchot, *Writing of the Disaster*, 43; *ED*, 73.

65. Edmund Husserl, *Ideas: General Introduction to Pure Phenomenology*, trans. W. R. Boyce Gibson (London: Collier Macmillan, 1931), § 79. See Lévinas, *Totality and Infinity*, 95; *Totalité et infini: Essai sur l'extériorité*, 2nd ed. (1971; Paris: Kluwer Academic, 1990), 96. Also see in this regard Jacques Lacan's distinction between seeing and the gaze in *The Four Fundamental Concepts of Psychoanalysis*, ed., Jacques-Alain Miller, trans. Alan Sheridan (Harmondsworth: Penguin, 1979), 182–84.

66. Blanchot, "Le Roman pur," *Journal des Débats*, December 4–5, 1943, 2; "Reflections on Hell," *Infinite Conversation*, 177; *EI*, 264. Clearly, Blanchot rejects the prizing of sight as one of the two "theoretical senses" as elaborated by Hegel. See *Hegel's Aesthetics*, trans. T. M. Knox, 2 vols. (Oxford: Clarendon Press, 1975), 1:38. Indeed, in *La Folie du jour*, it is light that blinds the narrator rather than enables him to see.

67. Blanchot, "The Essential Solitude," *Space of Literature*, 26; *EL*, 21. Also see "The Narrative Voice (the 'he,' the neutral)," *Infinite Conversation*, 386; *EI*, 566–67. On this general theme

see Martin Jay's survey, *Downcast Eyes: The Denigration of Vision in Twentieth-Century French Thought* (Los Angeles: University of California Press, 1993).

68. Saint Augustine, "Soliloquies I," *Soliloquies and Immortality of the Soul*, ed. and trans. Gerard Watson (Warminster, Eng.: Aris and Phillips, 1990), 25; *Confessions* 7.10.16. Also see his *Exposition on the Book of Psalms*, ed. Philip Schaff, Nicene and Post-Nicene Fathers, 8 (1888; rpt. Peabody, Mass.: Hendrickson, 1999), Ps. 42:2.

69. Saint Augustine, *Confessions*, 10.34.52. Also see his *The Trinity*, 12.15.24.

70. Saint Thomas Aquinas, *Commentary on the Book of Causes*, trans. Vincent A. Guagliardo et al. (Washington, D.C.: Catholic University of America Press, 1966), prop. 6.45; also see *Summa theologiae*, I q. 104 art. 1, and III q. 5 art. 2 ad 2. Saint Bonaventure, *On the Reduction of the Arts to Theology*, *Works of Saint Bonaventure*, vol. 1, ed. and trans. Zachary Hayes (St. Bonaventure: Franciscan Institute, 1996).

71. See Saint Thomas Aquinas, *Faith, Reason and Theology: Questions I–IV of his Commentary on the "De Trinitate" of Boethius*, trans. and introd. Armand Maurer, Medieval Sources in Translation (Toronto: Pontifical Institute of Medieval Studies, 1987), q. 3, art. 1. Aquinas points out that religion is a moral, not a theological, virtue, in *Summa theologiae*, 2a2æ, q. 81 art. 5, ad 3. Also see Blanchot, "The Clarity of the Novel," *Book to Come*, 159; *LV*, 219. "Vast as the Night," *Infinite Conversation*, 318; *EI*, 465. *Writing of the Disaster*, 7; *ED*, 17. Paul de Man observed of Blanchot's critical writings that "the light they cast on texts" differs from that of other critics and that "Nothing, in fact, could be more obscure than the nature of this light." "Impersonality in Blanchot," *Blindness and Insight: Essays in the Rhetoric of Contemporary Criticism*, 2nd ed. rev., introd. Wlad Godzich (Minneapolis: University of Minnesota Press, 1983), 62–63.

72. Blanchot, "Prophetic Speech," *Book to Come*, 84; *LV*, 117; "Idle Speech," *Friendship*, trans. Elizabeth Rottenberg (Stanford: Stanford University Press, 1997), 119; *L'Amitié* (Paris: Gallimard, 1971), 139. The contrast between clarity and fire goes back to Blanchot's critical response to Ernst Robert Curtius's *Die Französische Kultur* (1930), "La Culture française vue par un Allemand," *Revue Française* 10 (March 27, 1932), 363–65.

73. See Rudolf Otto, *The Idea of the Holy: An Inquiry into the Non-Rational Factor in the Idea of the Divine and Its Relation to the Rational* (New York: Oxford University Press, 1958). Blanchot does not speak directly of "faith," and yet his account of the human relation resonates with the Hebrew sense of faith as *he'emin*, a relationship with truth. The other person calls on me in an attitude of faith that I will take responsibility for him or her, and I call on the other person in the same way.

74. See Durkheim, *Elementary Forms of Religious Life*, 351.

75. See Lactantius, *Divine Institutes*, 4.28, and Blanchot, *Writing of the Disaster*, 64; *ED*, 106–7.

76. See Cicero, *De natura deorum*, 2.72; Augustine, *City of God*, 10.3. Aquinas remains uncommitted to any of the etymologies. "Whether religion is derived from frequent re-reading (*relectio*), from a repeated seeking of something lost through negligence (*reeligere*), or from the fact that it is a bond (*religare*), religion implies a relationship to God." *Summa theologiae*, 39, trans. Kevin D. O'Rourke (London: Eyre and Spottiswoode, 1964), 2a2æ q. 81, art. 1.

77. Blanchot, "Orpheus's Gaze," *Space of Literature*, 171; *EL*, 226–27.

78. On this issue, see John Milbank, "Stories of Sacrifice: From Wellhausen to Girard," *The-*

ory, Culture and Society 12 (1995): 15–46. Of course, it does not follow from Bataille's reliance on nineteenth-century assumptions about religion that Bataille's work can be unified simply in terms of "sacrifice."

79. See Laure, "The Sacred," *Collected Writings*, 37–94.

80. Blanchot, "Orpheus's Gaze," 173; *EL*, 231.

81. Sophocles, *Tragedies and Fragments*, trans. E. H. Plumptre, 2 vols. (New York: D. C. Heath, 1865), vol. 1, *Antigone*, 1.335.

82. As is well known, Husserl ends the *Cartesian Meditations* by quoting Augustine: "in te redi, in interiore homine habitat veritas" ("Go back into yourself. Truth dwells in the inner man"), *Cartesian Meditations: An Introduction to Phenomenology*, trans. Dorian Cairns (The Hague: Martinus Nijhoff, 1977), 157.

83. See Blanchot, "Literature One More Time," *Infinite Conversation*, 402–3; *EI*, 590–92, and "Reflections on Nihilism," *Infinite Conversation*, 149; *EI*, 224.

84. See the entry for "cosmos" in *Theological Dictionary of the New Testament*, ed. Gerhard Kittel, trans. Geoffrey W. Bromiley, 10 vols. (Grand Rapids: Wm. B. Eerdmans, 1965), 3:873.

85. On this issue, I would cite Mark C. Taylor's testimony to the importance of Kierkegaard for Blanchot. Blanchot wrote just one short piece on Kierkegaard in *Faux pas*, but indicated to Taylor in a series of letters that the Danish philosopher had figured more largely in his intellectual life than that short item would suggest. See Taylor, "Withdrawal," in *Nowhere Without No: In Memory of Maurice Blanchot*, ed. Kevin Hart (Sydney: Vagabond Press, 2003), 22–23.

86. See Georges Bataille, *Inner Experience*, trans. and introd. Leslie Anne Boldt (Albany: State University of New York Press, 1988), 102; *OC*, 5:20.

87. Blanchot, "Literature and the Original Experience," *Space of Literature*, 233; *EL*, 311.

88. See Blanchot, "Rilke and Death's Demand" in *The Space of Literature*, 137, 159; *EL*, 175, 208. In the first passage the French text contains an error: "c'est le monde et jamais un Nulle part sans nom"; it should be "sans non."

89. Stephen Mitchell translates the passage as follows:

> *Never, not for a single day, do we have*
> *before us that pure space into which flowers*
> *endlessly open. Always there is World*
> *and never Nowhere without the No: that pure*
> *unseparated element which one breathes*
> *without desire and endlessly knows. A child*
> *may wander there for hours, through the timeless*
> *stillness, may get lost in it and be*
> *shaken back. Or someone dies and is it.*
> *For, nearing death, one doesn't see death; but stares*
> *beyond, perhaps with an animal's vast gaze.*

The Selected Poetry of Rainer Maria Rilke, ed. and trans. Stephen Mitchell, introd. Robert Hass (New York: Vintage Books, 1984), 193.

90. On the approach of the literary space, see Joseph Libertson, *Proximity: Levinas, Blanchot, Bataille and Communication* (The Hague: Martinus Nijhoff, 1982), 148–56.

91. I take the expression from "The Limit-Experience," *Infinite Conversation*, 210; *EI*, 311.

CHAPTER ONE

1. Stéphane Mallarmé, *Poésies*, preface by Jean-Paul Sartre (Paris: Gallimard, 1978). "Les Fenêtres" was composed in 1863 although then Mallarmé wrote "je songe" rather than "je meurs." "Mysticité" is to be translated as "mysticalness" or "the mystical." Littré defines it as "Qualité de ce qui est mystique." It can denote intense faith. The word is to be distinguished from *mysticisme*, which in English is "mysticism" and which denotes the corpus of events and discourses associated with the path to union with God. On the formation of the substantive *la mystique*, as late as the sixteenth century, see Certeau, *Mystic Fable*, 1:75–78.

2. For the importance of windows in modern French literature, see Sima Godfrey, "Baudelaire's Windows," *L'Esprit Créateur* 22, no. 4 (1982): 83–100, and Susan Harris Smith, "The Surrealists' Windows," *Dada/Surrealism* 13 (1984): 48–69.

3. Mallarmé to Théodore Aubanel, July 16, 1866, and to Henri Cazalis, May 14, 1867, *Correspondance*, ed. Henri Mondor with Jean-Pierre Richard, 2 vols. (Paris: Gallimard, 1959), 1:222, 240.

4. See Blanchot, *Space of Literature*, 23, 158; *EL*, 16, 207–8. The synthesis of Mallarmé and Heidegger here will become one of Blanchot's signature moves as a critic.

5. Bataille observes, "mystical experience seems to me to stem from the universal experience of religious sacrifice." *Death and Sensuality*, 23; *OC*, 10:28

6. See Bataille and Leiris, "Note" in Laure, *Collected Writings*, 87. Blanchot partly defends Bataille against the charge of fusion (and the politics that follow from it) in *The Unavowable Community*, 7–8; *CI*, 17–20.

7. See Angela of Foligno, *Le Livre de l'expérience des vrais fidèles* (Paris: E. Droz, 1927). The mystic's book in English may be found in her *Complete Works*, trans. and introd. Paul Lachance, preface by Romana Guarnieri (New York: Paulist Press, 1993). Amy Hollywood relates Bataille's *L'Expérience intérieure*, by virtue of its form, to several female mystics, including Mechthild of Magdeburg and Marguerite Porete, while conceding that Bataille is unlikely to have read them. See her "Bataille and Mysticism: A 'Dazzling Dissolution,'" *Diacritics* 26, no. 2 (1996): 74–85. Peter Tracey Connor criticizes Hollywood's argument in his *Georges Bataille and the Mysticism of Sin* (Baltimore: Johns Hopkins University Press, 2000), 10–11, and Hollywood responds in her *Sensible Ecstasy: Mysticism, Sexual Difference, and the Demands of History* (Chicago: University of Chicago Press, 2002), 308 n. 36.

8. Jean-Paul Sartre, "Un Nouveau Mystique," in *Situations I* (Paris: Gallimard, 1947). André Breton heckled Bataille by calling him "mystic" and "priest" in *Nom de Dieu* (1943). See José Pierre, ed., *Tracts surréalistes et déclarations collectives, 1922–1939*, 2 vols. (Paris: Le Terrain Vague, 1980), 2:9. Nicolas Calas speaks of "atheistic mysticism" with regard to Bataille, "Acephalic Mysticism," *Hémisphères* 2, no. 6 (1945): 7. Bataille evoked the figure

of the "atheistic mystic" in his "Hegel, Death, and Sacrifice," trans. Jonathan Strauss, *Yale French Studies* 78 (1990): 17 n. 6; *OC*, 12:333n, and Walter Stace observes, "Atheism is not as such, I believe, inconsistent with introvertive mystical experience" (*Mysticism and Philosophy*, rpt. [London: Macmillan, 1960], 124–27). Also see Jean-Claude Renard, *L' "Expérience intérieure" de Georges Bataille ou la négation du Mystère* (Paris: Seuil, 1987). Bataille's final riposte to his critics on this score can be found in *OC*, 5:491. On Sartre's review of *L'Expérience intérieure* see Jean-Michel Heimonet, "Bataille and Sartre: The Modernity of Mysticism," *Diacritics* 26, no. 2 (1996): 59–73.

9.   Jacques Derrida, for instance, asserts, "Bataille above all is not a new mystic." "From Restricted to General Economy: A Hegelianism without Reserve," *Writing and Difference*, trans. Alan Bass (London: Routledge, 1978), 272. Bataille himself says, "when I was treated as a 'new *mystic*,' I was able to sense myself the victim of a truly mad error." "Aphorisms for the 'System,'" *The Unfinished System of Nonknowledge*, ed. and introd. Stuart Kendall, trans. Michelle Kendall and Stuart Kendall (Minneapolis: University of Minnesota Press, 2001), 174; *OC*, 8:582–83.

10.   Georges Bataille, *The Accursed Share*, trans. Robert Hurley (New York: Zone Books, 1988–91), 3 vols., 1:197 n. 22; *OC*, 7:179n. The French word *expérience* can mean both "experience" and "experiment."

11.   Bataille, *Inner Experience*, 102; *OC*, 5:120. In his review of *L'Expérience intérieure*, Gabriel Marcel took exception to Bataille's attitude toward salvation. See his "The Refusal of Salvation and the Exaltation of the Man of Absurdity," *Homo Viator: Introduction to a Metaphysic of Hope*, trans. Emma Craufurd (Gloucester, Mass.: Peter Smith, 1978), especially 185–200.

12.   See Bataille, *Death and Sensuality*, 23; *OC*, 10:28.

13.   Consider Saint Augustine: "No studious man, no inquisitive man, therefore, loves the unknown, even when he presses forward with the utmost eagerness to know the unknown. For he either already knows it by the genus which he loves, and is now eager to know it in some particular thing or things which he does not know, but whose praises he has perhaps heard, and, therefore, represents it in his mind by an imaginary picture by which he will be aroused to love . . ." *The Trinity*, trans. Stephen McKenna (Washington, D.C.: Catholic University of America Press, 1963), 10.2.4.

14.   In *Inner Experience* Bataille dissociates poetry and inner experience on pp. 5, 147, and 175 (*OC*, 5:17, 170, 427–28), yet associates them on pp. 149 and 169 (*OC*, 5:173, 422). He distinguishes project and sacrifice on pp. 136 and 149, and aligns poetry with sacrifice on pp. 135 and 149 (*OC*, 5:156, 172). He relates poetry and sacrifice in "La Notion de dépense," *OC*, 1:306. Also consider the following remark, "I'm just as opposed to poetic mysticism as Hegel is. Aesthetics and literature (literary dishonesty) depress me." *Guilty*, trans. Bruce Boone, introd. Denis Hollier (Venice, Cal.: Lapis Press, 1988), 99; *OC*, 5:344–45.

15.   In 1950 Blanchot published a new version of *Thomas l'obscur: a récit* rather than a *roman*. Only the *récit* has been translated into English. I reproduce here with slight modifications the passage in the novel translated in *Inner Experience*, 101–2. Bataille's text should be compared with *TO* (1), 14–15, and with *Thomas l'obscur: nouvelle version* (Paris: Gallimard, 1950), 17–18.

16. Blanchot, *Thomas the Obscure*, 98; *TO* (2), 114.

17. See Saint John of the Cross, "The Dark Night," in *The Collected Works of St. John of the Cross*, trans. Kieren Kavanaugh and Otilo Rodriguez (Washington, D.C.: ICS, 1979), 337.

18. See Blanchot, "The Two Versions of the Imaginary," *Space of Literature*, 255; *EL*, 343.

19. However, see Blanchot's remarks in "René Char and the Thought of the Neutral," *Infinite Conversation*, 300; *EI*, 442.

20. How Ignatius conceived the application of the senses in meditation is a complex and disputed issue. See his *Spiritual Exercises* §§ 69, 124 for instances of passing from the five senses to the spiritual senses. *The "Spiritual Exercises" and Selected Works*, ed. George E. Ganss et al., preface by John W. Padberg (New York: Paulist Press, 1991), 141, 151. Also see Hugo Rahner's discussion of the spiritual senses in his *Ignatius the Theologian*, trans. Michael Barry (New York: Herder and Herder, 1968), 198–206.

21. See Bataille, *Inner Experience*, 59, 119; *OC*, 5:74, 138. Note, though, that Bataille says that "My method is at the antipodes of 'Yoga.'" "Method of Meditation," *The Unfinished System of Nonknowledge*, 78; *OC*, 5:194. Also see Jean Bruno, "Les Techniques d'illumination chez Georges Bataille," *Critique* 195–96 (1963): 706–20.

22. Blanchot, *Writing of the Disaster*, 72; *ED*, 117; *The Instant of My Death*, bound with Jacques Derrida, *Demeure*, both trans. Elizabeth Rottenberg, dual language ed. (Stanford: Stanford University Press, 2000), 5. I discuss both incidents in the following chapter.

23. See Bataille, "Autobiographical Note," *My Mother, Madame Edwarda, The Dead Man*, trans. Austryn Wainhouse with essays by Yukio Mishima and Ken Hollings (London: Marion Boyars, 1989), 221; *OC*, 7:462. Also see *OC*, 5:421. Michel Fardoulis-Lagrange gives the flavor of those years in his *G.B. ou un ami présomptueux* (Paris: José Corti, 1996).

24. Bataille may have been echoing in his choice of title Ernst Jünger's *Der Kampf als inneres Erlebnis* (1922) to the extent that he prizes contestation as an endless struggle, although he would have had little sympathy with Jünger's cult of the virile hero.

25. Roger Caillois, *Man and the Sacred*, trans. Mary Barash (1959; rpt. Urbana: University of Illinois Press, 2001), 35. It should be noted that Bataille talks of "le crime d'*autorité* qu'il *expiera*" as early as "La Folie de Nietzsche" (1939), *OC*, 1:549.

26. Blanchot, "Inner Experience," *Faux Pas*, 37; *FP*, 48. Bataille will also say, "In a general way, religion *questions everything.*" *Guilty*, 79; *OC*, 5:321.

27. See Bataille's letter to Kojève in *Guilty*, 123–25; *OC*, 5:369–71.

28. See, for example, Saint Teresa of Jesus, *The Life of the Holy Mother Teresa of Jesus, The Complete Works*, trans. E. Allison Peers (London: Sheed and Ward, 1978), chap. 20.

29. See Bataille, *Inner Experience*, 42; *OC*, 5:55 and *Guilty*, 139; *OC*, 5:388.

30. A careful reading of Saint Teresa's account of rapture would lead one to modify Bataille's claim. See, for example, *The Life of the Holy Mother Teresa of Jesus*, chap. 20.

31. The books were *Oeuvres de Maître Eckhart: Sermons-traités*, trans. Paul Petit, Les classiques allemands (Paris: Gallimard, 1942), and *Maître Eckhart: Traité et sermons*, trans. F. A. and J. M., introd. Maurice de Gandillac, Philosophie de l'esprit (Aubier and Paris: Éditions Montaigne, 1942). It is worth noting that Bataille also speaks of "Eckhart's inner experience" in 1942. See "Nietzsche's Laughter," *The Unfinished System of Nonknowledge*, 19; *OC*, 6:308. Pierre Prévost

mentions conversations with Bataille about Eckhart after *Oeuvres de Maître Eckhart* appeared. See his *Rencontre Georges Bataille* (Paris: Jean-Michel Place, 1987), 100–101.

32. Blanchot, "Maître Eckhart," *Faux Pas*, 23; *FP*, 31.

33. The edition prefaced by Gandillac includes the sermon "In hoc apparuit caritas dei in nobis" in which Eckhart maintains that were life asked why it lives it would respond, "I live in order to live": "Vous demanderiez mille ans durant à la Vie: 'Pourquoi vis-tu?,' elle répondrait toujours: 'Je vis pour vivre.'" *Maître Eckhart: Traités et sermons*, 144.

34. The second text in Petit's translation is "Du détachement." Many years after reviewing the two books on Eckhart, in 1980, Blanchot will at once testify to his continued interest in the Meister and distance himself from his specific doctrine when writing, "Detached from everything, including detachment," *Writing of the Disaster*, 12; *ED*, 25.

35. The edition of Eckhart's work prefaced by Maurice de Gandillac contains "De l'homme noble."

36. Blanchot, "La Mystique d'Angelus Silesius," *Journal des Débats*, October 6, 1943, 3. The column is a review of *La Mystique d'Angelus Silesius*, ed. Henri Plard (Paris: Aubier-Montaigne, 1943).

37. Blanchot, "La Mystique d'Angelus Silesius," 3. In his "The Three Creations" Eckhart observes that God "dwells in the nothing-at-all that was prior to nothing," *The Works of Meister Eckhart*, ed. Franz Pfeiffer, reprint ed. (Kila, Mont.: Kessinger, n.d.), 387.

38. It should be noted that Blanchot does not maintain the distinction between God and the Godhead in his writings. In "The Most Profound Question," for example, he observes that "A being like God . . . could not put himself in question—he would not question; the word of God needs man to become the question of man." *Infinite Conversation*, 14; *EI*, 16–17. However, see his remarks on creation in "Affirmation (desire, affliction)," *Infinite Conversation*, 117; *EI*, 169–70.

39. Blanchot, "Maître Eckhart," *Faux Pas*, 27; *FP*, 36.

40. Blanchot, "Maître Eckhart," *Journal des Débats*, November 4, 1942, 3.

41. Blanchot, "Nicolas de Cues," *Journal des Débats*, January 6, 1943, 3. Blanchot's unease with respect to mystical transcendence is also indicated in "Les Plaintes de l'ombre," *Journal des Débats*, December 10, 1943, 1. It is worth noting that Bataille attended Alexandre Koyré's class on Cusanus in 1932–33. See Michel Surya, *Georges Bataille: An Intellectual Biography*, trans. Krzysztof Fijalkowski and Michael Richardson (London: Verso, 2002), 188.

42. Blanchot, "Reflections on the New Poetry," *Faux Pas*, 130; *FP*, 151.

43. Blanchot, "La Mystique d'Angelus Silesius," 3.

44. Blanchot, "La Poésie religieuse," *Journal des Débats*, June 9, 1943. Also see "Poetry and Language," *Faux Pas*, 137; *FP*, 159; "Claudel and the Infinite," *Book to Come*, 75; *LV*, 105; and "Prophetic Speech," *Book to Come*, 85; *LV*, 119.

45. Blanchot, "Reflections on the New Poetry," *Faux Pas*, 130; *FP*, 151.

46. For comments on the production of *Faux pas*, see *Pour l'amitié* (Paris: Fourbis, 1996), 10–12. The collection consists mainly of articles from the *Journal des Débats* but includes two pieces from *L'Insurgé*: "Le Monologue intérieur" (September 1, 1937) and "Le Temps et le roman" (September 29, 1937). Blanchot revised many pieces before

collecting them in *Faux pas*, and there is no reason to think that he did not order the pieces himself.

47. With Paul Claudel specifically in mind, however, Blanchot observes that the mystic turns from the world while the poet seeks to express and transform it. See "Études sur Paul Claudel," *Journal des Débats*, August 11, 1943, 3.

48. Blanchot, "On the Subject of *The Fruits of the Earth*," *Faux Pas*, 298; *FP*, 339. See André Gide's entry for July 22, 1922, in his *Journals*, trans. Justin O'Brien, 4 vols. (Urbana: University of Illinois Press, 2000), 2:306. Gide and Blanchot develop a more passionate version of a view about how writing changes one's mind or one's being that goes back to Saint Augustine. See his *The Trinity*, 3.1.

49. See Blanchot, "L'Étrange et l'étranger," *La Nouvelle NRF* 70 (1958), 674.

50. Bataille was converted to the Catholic faith (his father was irreligious, and his mother had no interest in religion) in 1914. He reports in the third person that in 1920 at Quarr Abbey he "suddenly loses his faith because his Catholicism has caused a woman he has loved to shed tears." "Autobiographical Note," 217; *OC*, 7:459. His friends found traces of that faith for the next year or two, however. Bataille then studied at the École Nationale des Chartes and became a librarian specializing in numismatics at the Bibliothèque Nationale. Interestingly, he appears briefly as a seminarian in Jean Renoir's film *Une Partie de campagne* (1935).

51. J.-P. Migne, ed., *Patrologiae Cursus Completus, Series Latina*, 180.255C, 182.1055.

52. On this issue see G. R. Evans, *Old Arts and New Theology: The Beginnings of Theology as an Academic Discipline* (Oxford: Clarendon Press, 1980), chap. 1.

53. An important moment in the relationship of Bataille and Daniélou occurred on March 5, 1944, when Daniélou offered a considered response to Bataille's lecture on sin. See "Father Daniélou's Presentation," *Unfinished System of Nonknowledge*, 34–40; *OC*, 6:322–27.

54. Quoted by Henri de Lubac, *At the Service of the Church: Henri de Lubac Reflects on the Circumstances That Occasioned His Writings*, trans. Anne Elizabeth Englund (San Francisco: Ignatius Press, 1993), 247. See Parente, "Nuove tendenz teologiche," *L'Osservatore romano*, February 9–10, 1942.

55. Lubac's work on the supernatural goes back to the early 1930s; it was not until *Surnaturel*, however, that his work attracted adverse attention in Rome.

56. Réginald Garrigou-Lagrange, "La Nouvelle Théologie où va-t-elle?" *Angelicum* 23, nos. 3–4 (1946): 126–45. The essay begins with a critical account of Henri Bouillard's *Conversion et grâce chez S. Thomas d'Aquin* (1944) and turns to Lubac's *Surnaturel* on p. 132. Blanchot published an essay on Lubac's account of atheism, though without using the expression "la nouvelle théologie," in early 1946. See "Du côté de Nietzsche," *L'Arche* 12 (December 1945–January 1946): 103–12. It should be noted that Pierre Klossowski, whose writing became important for Blanchot, was a student at Fourvière during the Occupation; before his time at Lyon he studied with the Dominicans at Saint-Maximin, and after he studied at the Institut catholique in Paris. He left the religious life in 1944 and married. See his *La Vocation suspendue* (Paris: Gallimard, 1950), and Alain Arnaud, *Pierre Klossowski* (Paris: Seuil, 1990), 186–87. Blanchot evokes "a new gnosis" with respect to Klossowski and speaks also of "theological debauchery" in his writing. See his essay "The

Laughter of the Gods" in *Friendship*, 170; *A*, 193. Certainly Klossowski makes use of notions drawn from the *Summa theologiae* such as *delectio morosa*—see *Sade mon prochain* (Paris: Éditions du Seuil, 1947), 119–20—and of the language of scholasticism in *Roberte ce soir* (Paris: Éditions de Minuit, 1953). Bataille's admiration for Klossowski's writing was muted: he reviewed *Sade mon prochain* negatively (see *OC*, 9:247–54), was less than enthusiastic about *Roberte ce soir* (see *OC*, 12:305–10), but published Klossowski's essays on Pierre-Jean Jouve, Kafka, Brice Parain, and Rilke in *Critique*. One can only speculate on whether Bataille would have claimed *Le Baphomet* (Paris: Éditions du Mercure de France, 1965) as a contribution to the *nouvelle théologie mystique*, had he lived and had he still been interested in the project.

57. Blanchot, "Thought and the Exigency of Discontinuity," *Infinite Conversation*, 3; *EI*, 1.

58. See Friedrich von Hügel, "Experience and Transcendence," *Dublin Review* 138 (1906): 357–79; George Tyrrell, *Through Scylla and Charybdis; Or, The Old Theology and the New* (London: Longman, Green, 1907), 374; and Alfred Loisy, *My Duel with the Vatican: The Autobiography of a Catholic Modernist*, trans. Richard Wilson Boynton, introd. E. Harold Smith (New York: Greenwood Press, 1968), 103, for his repudiation of supernaturalism, and *La Crise morale du temps présent et l'education humaine* (Paris: Libraire Émile Nourry, 1937), 242, for his late affirmation of God's transcendence.

59. See Bernard M. G. Reardon, *Roman Catholic Modernism* (Stanford: Stanford University Press, 1970), 10. Pius X had attacked modernism in the decree *Lamentabili sane exitu* that was promulgated on July 4, 1907. *Pascendi* is dated September 8, 1907.

60. Pius X, *Pascendi, The Papal Encyclicals, 1903–1937*, ed. Claudia Carlen (New York: McGraw, 1981), 72. Of course there were other significant modernists I have not named, Edouard Le Roy, Giovanni Semeria and Maude Petre among them.

61. See Carlo Sforza, *Makers of Modern Europe: Portraits and Personal Impressions and Recollections* (Indianapolis: Bobbs-Merrill, 1930), 136.

62. Pius X, *Pascendi*, 73.

63. Gary Lease goes so far as to argue that theological modernism is a consequence of cultural modernism, very broadly understood. See his *"Odd Fellows" in the Politics of Religion: Modernism, National Socialism, and German Judaism* (New York: Mouton de Gruyter, 1995), chap. 6, especially p. 126.

64. *Georges Bataille: Choix de lettres 1917–1962*, ed. Michel Surya (Paris: Gallimard, 1997), 392.

65. Bataille, "The Surrealist Religion," in *The Absence of Myth: Writings on Surrealism*, ed., trans., and introd. Michael Richardson (London: Verso, 1994), 75; *OC*, 7:386. Bataille anonymously contributed translations of several medieval poems to *La Révolution surréaliste* in 1925; he was attacked by Breton in *Deuxième manifeste du surréalisme* (1929) and replied in like manner with several other disaffected former surrealists in *Un Cadavre* (1930). Later, however, he contributed "L'Absence de mythe" to *Le Surréalisme en 1947*. In an interesting formulation dating from 1946 he observes, *"I situate my efforts beyond but alongside Surrealism."* "Method of Meditation," 77; *OC*, 5:193.

66. Bataille, "Maurice Blanchot . . . ," *Gramma* 3–4 (1976): 218. The essay is reproduced in Bataille's *Une Liberté souveraine*, ed. Michel Surya (Vendôme: Farrago, 2000), 67–73.

Bataille also speaks of "the two greatest minds Marcel Proust and Maurice Blanchot (who made derangement the result of the search for rules)." "Aphorisms for the 'System,'" *Unfinished System of Nonknowledge*, 162; *OC*, 8:570.

67. Bataille, "Surrealism," *Absence of Myth*, 55; *OC*, 11:313.

68. Bataille, "Surrealism and How It Differs from Existentialism," *Absence of Myth*, 66; *OC*, 11:81.

69. Blanchot, "Reflections on Surrealism," *Work of Fire*, 93; *PF*, 98.

70. See Henri de Lubac, *The Mystery of the Supernatural*, trans. Rosemary Sheed (London: Geoffrey Chapman, 1967), 185–93. I am indebted to Lubac's brief history of the progress of this doctrine.

71. See Henri de Lubac, *Surnaturel* (Paris: Aubier, 1946), 483, and *Mystery of the Supernatural*, 176–77.

72. Lubac, *At the Service of the Church*, 59.

73. Stephen J. Duffy, *The Graced Horizon: Nature and Grace in Modern Catholic Thought* (Collegeville, Mich.: Liturgical Press, 1992), 8.

74. In the foreword to the new edition of *Surnaturel* in 1964, Lubac included the following: "We must add, finally, that the 'traditional interpretation' of Saint Thomas, in the name of which some have reproached us for introducing a 'new theology,' is today held by no serious historian of Thomistic thought, while what was declared new is recognized by a certain number of these historians as the authentic thought of Saint Thomas." *At the Service of the Church*, 128–29.

75. Bataille, "The Psychological Structure of Fascism," *Visions of Excess: Selected Writings, 1927–1939*, ed. and introd. Allan Stoekl (Minneapolis: University of Minnesota Press, 1985), 153, trans. modified; *OC*, 1:361.

76. See Bataille, *Guilty*, 6; *OC*, 5:240. This God is "comic," Bataille says. See his interview with Marguerite Duras, "Bataille, Feydeau and Dieu," in her *Outside: Selected Writings*, trans. Arthur Goldhammer (Boston: Beacon Press, 1986), 14. The interview originally appeared in *France-Observateur* (1957).

77. See Bataille, "The Use Value of D. A. F. de Sade," *Visions of Excess*, 102 n. 2; *OC*, 2:62n. This is the basis of Bataille's differences with Durkheim, who observes, "The sacred thing is, par excellence, that which the profane must not and cannot touch with impunity." *Elementary Forms of Religious Life*, 38.

78. Bataille, *Theory of Religion*, trans. Robert Hurley (New York: Zone Books, 1989), 33; *OC*, 7:301.

79. Bataille, *Death and Sensuality*, 32; *OC*, 10:36.

80. *La Somme athéologique* eventually became three volumes. In the mid-1950s, however, Bataille intended to add two further volumes: *Le Pur Bonheur* and *Le Système inachevé du non-savoir*.

81. Bataille, *OC*, 3:491.

82. The second and third parts of the trilogy were to be *Ma Mère*, which was published in 1966, and *Charlotte d'Ingerville*, which was never completed.

83. Bataille, *My Mother, Madame Edwarda, The Dead Man*, 150; *OC*, 3:21. The association of the

abject and the divine is explored by Blanchot in his third and final novel, *Le Très-Haut* (1948), through the character of Henri Sorge. Blanchot testifies to the singularity of *Madame Edwarda* and to the impact it had on him in *Vicious Circles: Two Fictions and "After the Fact,"* trans. Paul Auster (Barrytown, N.Y.: Station Hill Press, 1985), 62–63; *Après coup, précédé par Le Ressassement éternel* (Paris: Éditions de Minuit, 1983), 90.

84. Bataille, "The Labyrinth" (1935–36), *Visions of Excess*, 172; *OC*, 1:434.

85. Bataille, *Visions of Excess*, 39; *OC*, 2:103.

86. Breton, "Second Manifesto of Surrealism," *Manifestoes of Surrealism*, trans. Richard Seaver and Helen R. Lane (Ann Arbor: University of Michigan Press, 1969), 123.

87. Bataille, *Literature and Evil*, trans. Alastair Hamilton (New York: Marion Boyars, 1985), 28; *OC*, 9:186. Also see Blanchot, "L'Étrange et l'étranger," 674.

88. Blanchot, "Reflections on Surrealism," *Work of Fire*, 93; *PF*, 98. Blanchot's admiration for surrealism can be seen also in his earlier piece, "Tradition et surréalisme," *Journal des Débats*, December 23, 1943, 3.

89. Blanchot, *Lautréamont et Sade* (Paris: Éditions de Minuit, 1963), 165. Also see "'Where Now? Who Now,'" *Book to Come*, 216; *LV*, 294.

90. See Blanchot, "Literature and the Original Experience," *Space of Literature*, 234–47; *EL*, 313–33.

91. Jean Paulhan, *Les Fleurs de Tarbes, ou la Terreur dans les lettres* (Paris: Gallimard, 1941).

92. Blanchot, "La Terreur dans les lettres," *Journal des Débats*, October 21, 1941, 3.

93. Two further installments of this review appeared in the November and December of 1941 and formed the basis for *Comment la littérature est-elle possible?* (Paris: José Corti, 1942). A shorter version of the study appeared in *Faux pas* (Paris: Gallimard, 1943), 92–101. Blanchot returned to the role of rules in literature in "Paradoxes sur le roman," *Journal des Débats*, December 30, 1941, 3, and reflected on the relations of eloquence and experience in "L'Éloquence et la littérature," *Journal des Débats*, April 28, 1943, 3.

94. On December 1, 1941, Paulhan wrote to Francis Ponge, "Mais vexé de n'avoir pas les 3 articles des *Débats* (!) sur les *Fleurs*, qu'on me dit bien meilleurs que les *Fleurs*." Jean Paulhan-Francis Ponge, *Correspondance 1923–1968*, ed. Claire Boaretto, 2 vols., vol. 1: *1923–1946* (Paris: Gallimard, 1986), 263. For Paulhan's private views of Blanchot's reading of *Les Fleurs de Tarbes*, see his letter to Julian Benda of April 1945, in *Choix de lettres*, ed. Dominique Aury et al. 3 vols. (Paris: Gallimard, 1992), vol. 2: *Traité des jours sombres*, 412.

95. See Mallarmé, "Le Mystère dans les lettres," *Oeuvres complètes*, ed. Henri Mondor and G. Jean-Aubry, Bibliothèque de la Pléiade (Paris: Gallimard, 1945), 385.

96. See E. D. James's chapters on Nicole's responses to mysticism and quietism in his *Pierre Nicole, Jansenist and Humanist* (The Hague: Martinus Nijhoff, 1972), part 3.

97. Quoted by Blanchot in "Mystery in Literature," *Work of Fire*, 58n; *PF*, 63n. The passage may be found in *Traité de la grâce générale*, 2 vols. (n.p., 1715), 1:96.

98. See Paulhan, *Les Fleurs de Tarbes*, 150–54.

99. Paulhan, *Le Clair et l'obscur*, preface by Philippe Jaccottet (Cognac: Le temps qu'il fait, 1983), 100. The essay first appeared in *La Nouvelle NRF* 64 and 66 (1958).

100. Paulhan, *Le Clair et l'obscur*, 116. Also see Paulhan's "Lettres à Madame ***": "Voici, pour l'essentiel: c'est qu'il est parfaitement chimérique de chercher à connaître Dieu directement. Ce qui se passe, il me semble, c'est qu'il arrive dans la vie à chacun de nous, dans certains instants privilégiés, de nous trouver au contact de ce qui passe nos calculs, nos réflexions, notre raison, bref du Divin." *La Nouvelle Revue Français* 228 (1971): 80.

101. In his inscription of Francis Ponge's copy of *Fleurs*, Paulhan quotes Augustine's remarks in *The Trinity* to the effect that whoever grasps a word before it is spoken and allowed to generate images begins to see the divine Word. See Paulhan-Ponge, *Correspondance*, 1:265. Paulhan asks Henri Pourrat in November 1941 if he knows the passage from Augustine. See *Choix de lettres*, 2:254.

102. I explore this and the following issues in more detail in "'The Experience of Nonexperience,'" *Mystics: Presence and Aporia*, ed. Michael Kessler and Chris Sheppard (Chicago: University of Chicago Press, 2003), 188–206.

103. Blanchot, "How Is Literature Possible?" *Faux Pas*, 80; *FP*, 96–97. The motif of the secret is important to Blanchot, especially in the period of *Faux pas*. See for example "Le Secret de J. K. Huysmans," *Journal des Débats*, November 18, 1941, 3; "L'Art d'André Dhotel," *Journal des Débats*, March 16, 1944, 2–3; "Les Secrets du rêve," *Journal des Débats*, April 6, 1944, 2–3; and "L'Accent du secret," *Journal des Débats*, May 25, 1944, 2–3.

104. "For verses are not, as people imagine, simply feelings (those one has early enough),—they are experiences [*Erfahrungen*]. For the same of a single verse, one must see many cities, men and things, one must know the animals, one must feel how the birds fly and know the gesture with which the little birds open in the morning." Rainer Maria Rilke, *The Notebooks of Malte Laurids Brigge*, trans. M. D. Herter Norton (New York: W. W. Norton, 1964), 26.

105. Blanchot, "On the Subject of *The Fruits of the Earth*," *Faux Pas*, 298; *FP*, 339.

106. In terms of Lubac's distinction, we might plausibly align Blanchot with a displaced mysticism of exegesis (that is, transposed into writing) and Bataille with a displaced mysticism of spirituality. See Lubac, *Medieval Exegesis*, 1:vi. It should also be kept in mind that the "primal scene" and the "execution scene," both of which I discuss in the next chapter, are akin to raptures but have no dimension of an active contestation. Blanchot makes a brief remark on mysticism and writing in "De Jean-Paul à Giraudoux," *Journal des Débats*, February 3, 1944, 2.

107. Hans Urs von Balthasar, *The Glory of the Lord: A Theological Aesthetics*, 7 vols., vol. 1: *Seeing the Form*, ed. Joseph Fessio SJ and John Riches, trans. Erasmo Leiva-Merikakis (San Francisco: Ignatius Press, 1982), 412. Also see Balthasar's essay "Experience God?" in his *New Elucidations*, trans. Sister Mary Theresilde Skerry (San Francisco: Ignatius Press, 1986).

108. Blanchot, "Mystery in Literature," *Work of Fire*, 57; *PF*, 63. It is worth recalling Thomas's words: "I brought her the one true mystery, which consisted of the absence of mystery, and which she could therefore do nothing but search for, eternally." *Thomas the Obscure*, 101; *TO* (2), 118. See also Blanchot's comments on mystery in "Histoire de fantôme," *Journal des Débats*, July 29, 1942, 3.

CHAPTER TWO

1. Blanchot, "Après le coup de force germanique," *Combat* 4 (1936): 59. A fuller account of this period is offered by Steven Ungar in *Scandal and Aftereffect: Blanchot and France since 1930* (Minneapolis: University of Minnesota Press, 1995).

2. Note, however, that earlier Blanchot spoke of Germany's policies as forming "l'apothéose mystique de la nation." "M. de Monzie, émule de Mussolini et de Hitler," *Le Rempart* 32 (May 23, 1933): 1–2.

3. On Blanchot's distaste for Léon Blum's government, one might cite the following: "Si être Français, c'est se sentir solidaire de Blum, nous ne sommes pas de bons Français." "Blum provoque à la guerre," *L'Insurgé* 12 (March 31, 1937): 4. Sharp as this is, far more extreme remarks were made by the ultra right-wing Comité Secret de l'Action Révolutionnaire, which was eventually suppressed by the Blum administration in 1937. In a letter to Roger Laporte dated December 24, 1992, Blanchot responds to an inquiry about Blanchot's column "La Politique de Sainte-Beuve," *Journal des Débats*, March 10, 1942, 1–2. Blanchot did not recall the piece, although when he read it he criticized it and himself in the strongest possible terms: "Let me go immediately to the worst. That in March 1942 one pronounces the name of Maurras (particularly when nothing in the context demands a name such as this) is detestable and inexcusable." "A Letter," trans. Leslie Hill, *Maurice Blanchot: The Demand of Writing*, ed. Carolyn Bailey Gill (London: Routledge, 1996), 210. The letter was read aloud at the conclusion of Jeffrey Mehlman's paper, "Pour Saint-Beuve: Maurice Blanchot, 10 March 1942," presented at the International Conference on Maurice Blanchot in London in January 1993. "Pour Saint-Beuve" is the concluding piece in Gill's collection. Mehlman had earlier interested himself in the possibility of Blanchot's collaboration in 1942. See his polemical essay "Blanchot at *Combat*: Of Literature and Terror," in *Legacies of Anti-Semitism in France* (Minneapolis: University of Minnesota Press, 1983). The essay partly relies on dubious testimony given by Paul Léautaud in his *Journal littéraire* for 1942 (Paris: Mercure de France, 1963), 237, 327–28. Blanchot rejects this testimony in a letter that is partly quoted by Mehlman in *Legacies*, 117, and Mehlman returns to the issue in "Pour Saint-Beuve," 213–14. An even, steady appraisal of Blanchot's writings before World War II is given by Leslie Hill in *Blanchot: Extreme Contemporary* (London: Routledge, 1997), 17–52.

4. See Blanchot, "Le Terrorisme, méthode de salut public," *Combat* 7 (1936): 106. Also see, by way of background to this theological language, Blanchot's direct response to Pius XI's disastrous arrangement with Germany in 1933, "Une Intervention du Pape," *Le Rempart* 54 (June 14, 1933): 2. The short text is subtitled "Offrande au paganisme hitlérien des sacrifices de la chrétienté."

5. Denis Hollier, ed., *The College of Sociology, 1937–39* (Minneapolis: University of Minnesota Press, 1988), xxiii.

6. Blanchot, *Vicious Circles: Two Fictions and "After the Fact,"* 60; *AC*, 86. On Blanchot's invisibility, see Georges Perros, *Papiers collés*, 3 vols. (Paris: Gallimard, 1978), 3:18–19.

7. As it happens, Blanchot's reflections on the "I" begin very early in his life as a critic. See for example "Le 'Je' littéraire," *Journal des Débats*, June 1, 1944, 2–3.

8. *Boswell's "Life of Johnson,"* ed. George Birkbeck Hill, rev. and enlarged by L. F. Powell, 6 vols. (Oxford: Clarendon Press, 1934–50), 1:471.

9. Blanchot, *Writing of the Disaster*, 72; *ED*, 117. This text was originally published as "Une Scène primitive" in *Le Nouveau Commerce* 39–40 (Spring 1978): 43. It begins, however, with the same lead line we find in the later publication, "(Une scène primitive?)."

10. Blanchot, *The Most High*, trans. and introd. Allan Stoekl (Lincoln: University of Nebraska Press, 1996), 23; *Le Très-Haut* (Paris: Gallimard, 1948), 29. Pierre Klossowski offers an interesting reading of the novel from a Heideggerian theological perspective in "Sur Maurice Blanchot," *Les Temps Modernes* 40 (1949): 298–314. A shorter version appears in *Un Si Funeste Désir* (Paris: Gallimard, 1963), 161–83.

11. Immanuel Kant, *The Critique of Judgement*, trans. James Creed Meredith (Oxford: Clarendon Press, 1952), § 25.

12. Robert Musil, "From the Posthumous Papers," trans. Burton Pike, in *The Man without Qualities*, 2 vols. (New York: Alfred A. Knopf, 1995), 2:1358. See Blanchot's "Musil" in his *The Book to Come*, 134–49; *LV*, 184–206.

13. Angela Richards, ed. *Case Histories*, vol. 2, The Pelican Freud Library, 15 vols., trans. James Strachey (Harmondsworth: Penguin, 1979), 9:259.

14. See Hélène Cixous, *Readings: The Poetics of Blanchot, Joyce, Kafka, Kleist, Lispector, and Tsvetayeva*, ed. and trans. Verena Andermatt Conley (Minneapolis: University of Minnesota Press, 1991), chap. 1.

15. Blanchot, *Writing of the Disaster*, 67; *ED*, 110. It should be recalled that Blanchot studied medicine in the early 1930s, specializing in neurology and psychiatry. See Christophe Bident, *Maurice Blanchot: Partenaire invisible* (Seyssel, Fr.: Champ Vallon, 1988), 49.

16. Donald W. Winnicott, "Fear of Breakdown," in *Psycho-Analytic Explorations*, ed. C. Winnicott, R. Shepherd, and M. Davis (London: Karnac Books, 1989), 90, 92. The paper first appeared, posthumously, in *International Review of Psycho-Analysis* 1, nos. 1–2 (1974): 103–7, and appears to have been written in 1963.

17. Serge Leclaire, *A Child Is Being Killed: On Primary Narcissism and the Death Drive*, trans. Marie-Claude Hays (Stanford: Stanford University Press, 1998), 2.

18. Blanchot, *The Step Not Beyond*, trans. Lycette Nelson (Albany: State University of New York Press, 1992), 2; *Le Pas au-delà* (Paris: Gallimard, 1973), 9. Bident phrases the matter carefully when he says that "(Une scène primitive?)" is "donnée comme autobiographique." *Maurice Blanchot*, 17. It should be noted that, in French psychoanalysis, *Moi* also means ego.

19. Blanchot, "Atheism and Writing, Humanism and the Cry," *Infinite Conversation*, 258; *EI*, 386. Charles Baudelaire, "Le Gouffre," *Les Fleurs du mal*, introd. Claude Pichois (Paris: Gallimard, 1978), 220; Lautréamont, *Maldoror and Poems*, trans. Paul Knight (Harmondsworth: Penguin, 1978), 77.

20. See, for example, Charles Kligerman, "A Psychoanalytic Study of the *Confessions* of St. Augustine," *Journal of the American Psychoanalytic Association* 5 (1957): 469–84, and Paul W.

Pruyser, "Psychological Examination: Augustine," *Journal for the Scientific Study of Religion* 5 (1966): 284–89.

21. I follow J. J. O'Donnell in his commentary on *Confessions* 9.10.24. See his edition, Augustine, *Confessions*, 3 vols., vol. 3: *Commentary on Books 8–13, Indexes* (Oxford: Clarendon Press, 1992), 133.

22. In his study of the origins of Christian mysticism, Andrew Louth devotes a substantial part of his chapter on Augustine to this very passage. See his *The Origins of the Christian Mystical Tradition: From Plato to Denys* (Oxford: Clarendon Press, 1981), 134–41. Also see the ascent described in *Confessions* 7.17.23, but, as Augustine himself says, this occurred when he was "cold, removed from the fire of the Spirit." *Confessions* 9.7.15. There has been considerable debate over whether or to what extent the vision at Ostia is mystical. Paul Henry argues that the experience is indeed mystical in his *The Path to Transcendence: From Philosophy to Mysticism in Saint Augustine*, trans. and introd. Francis F. Burch (Pittsburgh: Pickwick Press, 1981). The book appeared in French in 1938. In broad agreement with Henry, George St. Hilaire maintains that Augustine and Monica received infused grace and that they therefore had mystical ecstasy. "The Vision at Ostia: Acquired or Infused?" *Modern Schoolman* 35 (1958): 117–23. John Mourant, however, urges that the experience does not merit being described as "mystical" in his "Ostia Reexamined: A Study in the Concept of Mystical Experience," *International Journal for Philosophy of Religion* 1 (1970): 34–45. Wilma von Jess argues against Mourant in her "Augustine at Ostia: A Disputed Question," *Augustinian Studies* 4 (1973): 159–74, who defends himself in "A Reply to Dr von Jess' 'Augustine at Ostia: A Disputed Question,'" *Augustinian Studies* 4 (1973): 175–77.

23. Saint Augustine, *Confessions*, trans. Chadwick, 9.10.23–24.

24. On *idipsum*, the self-same, understood to be the highest good, which is God, see Augustine, *The Trinity*, 3.2.8.

25. Blanchot, "A Toute Extrémité," *La Nouvelle NRF* 26 (1955): 290–91.

26. It must be stressed that the sense of generosity explored by Guillaume Apollinaire in his lyric "Il y a" is completely foreign to the sense of the expression detailed by Lévinas and Blanchot.

27. The rejection of mysticism should be balanced with the fact that Blanchot's model of conversation derives from a Jewish idea of prayer. See chap. 7.

28. See, for example, Pierre Courcelle, *Recherches sur les Confessions de Saint-Augustin* (Paris: E. de Boccard, 1950), 222–26.

29. The line separating quotation and allusion in *Confessions* 9.10, as elsewhere in Augustine, is often far from clear. Appeals to Rom. 8:23, Matt. 25:21, and 1 Cor. 15:51 are made, and allusions are made to Phil. 3:13, John 14:6, Isa. 64:4, Pss. 35:10 (36:9) 79:2 (80:1), Ezek. 34:14, and Prov. 8:23–31, among other passages.

30. See Augustine, *Confessions*, 7.10.16 and 7.17.23.

31. Plotinus, *The Enneads*, trans. Stephen MacKenna, rev. B. S. Page, foreword by E. R. Dodds, introd. Paul Henry (London: Faber and Faber, 1962), 5.1.6.

32. If those lines have been drawn more sharply since, it is still difficult if not impossible to

separate Christianity from Philosophy, even in the modern sense of "philosophy." See Karl Barth, *The Göttingen Dogmatics: Instruction in the Christian Religion*, ed. Hannelotte Reiffen, trans. Geoffrey W. Bromiley, 2 vols. projected (Grand Rapids: William B. Eerdmans, 1991), 1:259.

33. In his commentary on the Ostia passage O'Donnell reminds us of Monica's role as *mulier sapiens* at Cassiciacum, and rightly observes, "M. represents an alternative path." Augustine, *Confessions*, 3.123. It should also be noted that the vision at Ostia is part of a short biography of Monica. The emphasis throughout is on the significance of the mother for the son.

34. See Martin Heidegger, *An Introduction to Metaphysics*, trans. Ralph Manheim (New York: Anchor Books, 1961), 6.

35. Blanchot, *Infinite Conversation*, xx; *EI*, xxi.

36. See David Hume, "Of Personal Identity," *A Treatise of Human Nature*, ed. L. A. Selby-Bigge (Oxford: Clarendon, 1896), 1.4.6.

37. Blanchot, *Step Not Beyond*, 19; *PAD*, 31.

38. Blanchot, "Literature and the Original Experience," *Space of Literature*, 243; *EL*, 326.

39. Nietzsche's first allusion to the vision is found in *The Gay Science: With a Prelude in Rhymes and an Appendix of Songs*, trans. and commentary by Walter Kaufmann (New York: Random House, 1974), § 341. The book first appeared in 1882. Also see Nietzsche's account of the idea of eternal recurrence as "the highest formula of affirmation that can possibly be attained" in *Ecce Homo: How One Becomes What One Is*, trans. R. J. Hollingdale, introd. Michael Tanner (1979; rpt. London: Penguin, 1992), 99.

40. Derrida draws attention to Blanchot's notion of an event that occurs but does not happen. See the brief discussion of *survenir* and *arriver* in his "A Witness Forever" in Hart, *Nowhere without No*, 42.

41. Augustine, *Confessions*, 10.17.26.

42. Blanchot, "The Outside, the Night," *Space of Literature*, 164; *EL*, 214.

43. Blanchot, *Writing of the Disaster*, 65, 91; *ED*, 108, 143. Cf. Blanchot's remarks on the word *God* in *Step Not Beyond*, 48; *PAD*, 69–70.

44. Saint Augustine, *The Literal Meaning of Genesis*, trans. John Hammond Taylor, 2 vols. (New York: Paulist Press, 1982), 1.4.3.8. Plotinus approaches the formulation when he writes ἦλθεν ὡς οὐκ ἐλθών: in *Enneads* 5.5.8.14. In the Loeb edition, A. H. Armstrong translates the expression as follows: "came as one who did not come." *Enneads*, 7 vols. (Cambridge: Harvard University Press, 1966).

45. Blanchot, "Literature and the Right to Death," *Work of Fire*, 340; *PF*, 327; "The Great Refusal," *Infinite Conversation*, 47; *EI*, 67; "The Relation of the Third Kind (*man without horizon*)," *Infinite Conversation*, 73; *EI*, 104. Also see Derrida, "Pas," *Parages* (Paris: Gallimard, 1986), 90–91.

46. On the nonoccurrence of the event, also see "Encountering the Imaginary," *Book to Come*, 9; *LV*, 18, and "The Fragment Word," *Infinite Conversation*, 310; *EI*, 455.

47. See Blanchot, "The Two Versions of the Imaginary," *Space of Literature*, 261; *EL*, 352.

48. Blanchot, "Literature and the Right to Death," *Work of Fire*, 301; *PF*, 294.

49. Ramon Fernandez, "The Method of Balzac" in *Messages: Literary Essays*, trans. Mont-

gomery Belgion (New York: Harcourt, Brace, 1927), 63. The essay, "La Méthode de Balzac," appeared in *Messages: première série* (Paris: Gallimard, 1926). Rather than use Belgion's word "recital" I have retained the original French "récit." Blanchot follows Fernandez's distinction in "The Enigma of the Novel," *Faux Pas*, 190; *FP*, 217.

50. See Blanchot's section, "The Interminable, the Incessant," in "The Essential Solitude," *Space of Literature*, 26–28; *EL*, 20–23.

51. Certainly Blanchot comes to be uneasy with the designation "récit" with regard to several of his own narratives. *La Folie du jour* was first entitled "Un récit" or "Un récit?" depending on whether one reads the cover of *Empédocle* 2 (May 1949) or the title of the text, and then the word was withdrawn. *L'Arrêt de mort* was marked as a récit, but the 1971 reedition of the work omitted the word. Similarly, *Le Dernier Homme* was first published as a récit and then, also in 1971, deprived of its generic designation. No such thing happened with either *Au moment voulu* or *Celui qui ne m'accompagnait pas*. Sarah Kofman suggests that Blanchot withdraws the word "récit" because of his conviction that after Auschwitz no story can be written. See *Smothered Words*, trans. Madeleine Dobie (Evanston: Northwestern University Press, 1998), 14–15.

52. Blanchot, "Encountering the Imaginary," *Book to Come*, 7; *LV*, 14. Also see Blanchot's comments on the récit in his review of Marcel Arland's *Zélie dans le désert: Récit* (Paris: Gallimard, 1944). I would especially like to draw attention to these lines, "Nous croyons à un événement qui s'est passé, et s'il est touchant, nous sommes émus. Mais nous aimons aussi croire ce qui n'a peut-être tout à fait réel, ce qui exprime une expérience sans la reproduire." "Récits," *Journal des Débats*, July 13–14, 1944, 2. Blanchot had discussed the récit earlier that year in "Contes et récits," *Journal des Débats*, March 3, 1942, 3, and he returns to the topic in "Nouvelles et récits," *Journal des Débats*, April 20, 1944, 2–3.

53. Blanchot, "The Speech of Analysis," *Infinite Conversation*, 231; *EI*, 345.

54. For Blanchot, however, to enter analysis is to begin to hear "what is unceasing and interminable: the eternal going over, and over and over again, whose exigency the patient has encountered but has arrested in fixed forms henceforth inscribed in his body, his conduct, and his language." "The Speech of Analysis," *Infinite Conversation*, 236; *EI*, 353.

55. Blanchot, "Where Now? Who Now," *Book to Come*, 213; *LV*, 290–91.

56. Blanchot, "Literature and the Original Experience," *Space of Literature*, 240–41; *EL*, 322–23.

57. See Blanchot, "The Work and Death's Space," *Space of Literature*, 96; *EL*, 119. The reflection first appears in a review of Paul-Louis Landsberg, *Essai sur l'experience de la mort suivi de problème moral du suicide* (Paris: Seuil, 1951), and Camille Schuwer, *La Signification métaphysique du suicide* (Paris: Aubier, 1949), *Critique* 62 (July 1952): 921.

58. Friedrich Nietzsche, *The Will to Power*, trans. Walter Kaufmann and R. J. Hollingdale (New York: Random House, 1968), § 853.

59. Nietzsche, *Gay Science*, § 107. It must be kept in mind that over the course of his long writing career Nietzsche vacillated on the question of the right relationship of art and truth. In 1873, for instance, we find him in a notebook counting art as one of the three "truest things in his world"—the others are love and religion—and observing that while love pen-

etrates to the core of the suffering individual, art "gives consolation for this suffering by telling stories about another world order and teaching us to disdain this one." *Unpublished Writings from the Period of "Unfashionable Observations,"* trans. and with an afterword by Richard T. Gray, *Complete Works of Friedrich Nietzsche,* vol. 11 (Stanford: Stanford University Press, 1999), 192.

60. Nietzsche, *Will to Power,* § 822. On Heidegger's understanding, "truth," here, means "the 'true world' of the supersensuous, which conceals in itself the danger that life may perish, 'life' in Nietzsche's sense always meaning 'life which is on the ascent.' The supersensuous lures life away from invigorating sensuality, drains life's forces, weakens it." *Nietzsche,* 4 vols., vol. 1: *The Will to Power as Art,* trans. David Farrell Krell (San Francisco: Harper and Row, 1979), 75.

61. Heidegger, "The Word of Nietzsche: 'God Is Dead,'" *The Question concerning Technology and Other Essays,* trans. and introd. William Lovitt (New York: Harper and Row, 1977), 93.

62. In "Parler de Blanchot," a discussion among Robert Antelme, Dionys Mascolo, and Maurice Nadeau, Mascolo suggests that "Le première apparition du mot 'désastre' chez Maurice Blanchot se trouve dans un texte anonyme de *Comité* (octobre 68)." Dionys Mascolo, *À la recherche d'un communisme de pensée* (Paris: Fourbis, 1993), 408. However, one hears the word in Blanchot's first essay on Kafka—"Kafka's narratives are among the darkest in literature, the most rooted in absolute disaster"—as early as 1945. See "Reading Kafka," *Work of Fire,* 10; *PF* 18. And the word can also be heard later but before 1968 ("Yes, we are tied to disaster"), *Space of Literature,* 244; *EL,* 327.

63. See Emmanuel Lévinas, "Reality and Its Shadow," *Collected Philosophical Papers,* trans. Alphonso Lingis (The Hague: Martinus Nijhoff, 1987), 5–8; *Les Imprévus de l'histoire,* preface by Pierre Hayat (Montpellier: Fata Morgana, 1994), 132–36. In his account of the image, Blanchot focuses on the cadaver resembling itself: see "The Two Versions of the Imaginary," *Space of Literature,* 254–63; *EL,* 341–55.

64. It is worth noting the difference between Blanchot's understanding of death and Cocteau's in his *Thomas l'imposteur,* a novel sometimes regarded as partly inspiring *Thomas l'obscur.* When Guillaume Thomas is hit by a bullet he says to himself, "*Je suis perdu si je ne fais pas semblant d'être mort,*" and the narrator observes, "Mais en lui, la fiction et la réalité ne formaient qu'un." *Thomas l'imposteur* (Paris: Gallimard, 1923), 174. For Blanchot, death is not the coinciding of image and reality; rather, dying approaches us when we recognize that reality is ontologically insecure.

65. Blanchot, "The Experience of Proust," *Book to Come,* 14; *LV,* 23.

66. Blanchot, "Literature and the Original Experience," *Space of Literature,* 223; *EL,* 297.

67. For an intriguing instance of this in Blanchot's narrative writing, see *When the Time Comes,* trans. Lydia Davis (Barrytown, N.Y.: Station Hill Press, 1985), 69–70; *Au moment voulu* (Paris: Gallimard, 1951), 157.

68. Blanchot notes that the question of literature is one that "a secular tradition of aestheticism has concealed, and continues to conceal." "Note," *Infinite Conversation,* xi; *EI,* vi.

69. On this theme see Alexandre Kojève, *Introduction à la lecture de Hegel: Leçons sur la 'Phénoménologie de l'esprit,' professées de 1933 à 1939 à l'École des Hautes Études,* ed. Raymond

Queneau (Paris: Gallimard, 1947), and Bataille's response to those lectures: "Hegel, Death, and Sacrifice," 9–28; *OC*, 12:326–45.

70. Martin Heidegger, *Being and Time*, trans. John Macquarrie and Edward Robinson (Oxford: Basil Blackwell, 1973), 294.

71. Lévinas, "Reality and Its Shadow," 11; *IH*, 143.

72. Augustine, *The City of God*, trans. Marcus Dods, introd. Thomas Merton (New York: Modern Library, 1950), 13.11.

73. John of Ford, on the other hand, takes Aminadab to be the bride's name for the Son. See the sixtieth sermon in his *Sermons on the Final Verses of the Song of Songs*, 7 vols. (Kalamazoo: Cistercian Publications, 1983), 4:193. Origen's famous commentary on the Canticle, as historically received, contains no comments on Cant. 6:12.

74. *Collected Works of St. John of the Cross*, 563. Roland E. Murphy indicates the mystic's use of the scriptural reference in his *The Song of Songs: A Commentary on the Book of Canticles or The Song of Songs*, ed. S. Dean McBride Jr. (Minneapolis: Fortress Press, 1990), 176.

75. See Bataille, *Guilty*, 81–82; *OC*, 5:323–25.

76. Blanchot, "The Work and Death's Space," *Space of Literature*, 99; *EL*, 225.

77. See Gerald L. Bruns's subtle reading of this passage in his *Maurice Blanchot: The Refusal of Philosophy* (Baltimore: Johns Hopkins University Press, 1997), 224–25.

78. Blanchot, *Instant of My Death*, 3; *L'Instant de ma mort*, dual language ed. (Stanford: Stanford University Press, 2000), 2. Blanchot does not call *L'Instant de ma mort* a récit, although it could be argued that it participates in that genre. Blanchot's narrative recalls a well-known passage in *The Idiot* where Prince Myshkin relates the story of a man reprieved from execution at the last moment. See Fyodor Dostoyevsky, *The Idiot*, trans. Anna Brailovsky et al., introd. Joseph Frank (New York: Modern Library, 2003), 63–65.

79. Blanchot, *Writing of the Disaster*, 83; *ED*, 132. The statement should be read alongside Blanchot's very early comment, made with Mahatma Gandhi in mind, "Toute révolution est spirituelle." "Mahatma Gandhi," *Les Cahiers mensuels*, 3rd ser., no. 7 (July 1931).

80. Quoted by Bernard-Henri Lévy, *Adventures on the Freedom Road: The French Intellectuals in the Twentieth-Century*, ed. and trans. Richard Veasey (London: Harvill Press, 1995), 318. It needs to be added that Blanchot condemned the "persécutions barbares contre les juifs" in "Des violences antisémites à l'apothéose du travail," *Le Rempart*, May 1, 1933, 37.

81. Blanchot, *The Madness of the Day*, trans. Lydia Davis, bilingual edition (Barrytown, N.Y.: Station Hill Press, 1981), 6. That the event is not a literary fiction is underscored by Jacques Derrida when he quotes a letter from Blanchot: "July 20. Fifty years ago, I knew the happiness of nearly being shot to death." Derrida, *Demeure*, 52. Maurice Nadeau reports in his literary memoir, "Durant la guerre, le révoltent les ignominies, d'Hitler d'abord, de Vichy ensuite, contre les juifs. Il est pris comme otage dans une ville du Midi où il séjourne, il va être fusillé, il échappe à la mort par miracle, dans des circonstances qu'il me décrit mais qu'il appartient à lui seul de révéler." *Grâces leur soient rendus* (Paris: Albin Michel, 1990), 71.

82. Blanchot, *Unavowable Community*, 18–19; *CI*, 36–37.

83. Blanchot quotes Bataille's remark, *Writing of the Disaster*, 90; *ED*, 142.

84. In this regard see *Writing of the Disaster*, 50; *ED*, 84. Also see "On Hindu Thought," *Faux Pas*, 33–36; *FP*, 42–46, and "Le Pèlerinage aux sources," *Journal des Débats*, January 13, 1944, 2–3. I would like to draw attention to an alternate account of this passage by Philippe Lacoue-Labarthe in his essay "The Contestation of Death," trans. Philip Anderson, in *The Power of Contestation: Perspectives on Maurice Blanchot*, ed. Kevin Hart and Geoffrey Hartman (Baltimore: Johns Hopkins University Press, 2004).

85. Leslie Hill proposes a fascinating reading of *Le Très-Haut* as offering "cogent expression" of Blanchot's "political opinions" in the years following World War II. See his *Bataille, Klossowski, Blanchot: Writing at the Limit* (Oxford: Oxford University Press, 2001), 181–206. I quote from 185 n. 8.

86. Blanchot, *Step Not Beyond*, 24; *PAD*, 38.

87. Blanchot, "On a Change of Epoch: The Exigency of Return," *Infinite Conversation*, 273; *EI*, 408. Blanchot has in mind Klossowski's *Nietzsche and the Vicious Circle*, trans. Daniel W. Smith (Chicago: University of Chicago Press, 1997), although his own meditation on the eternal lapping of the Outside in *The Space of Literature* is at least of equal importance here.

CHAPTER THREE

1. Maurice Blanchot, "The Great Refusal," *Infinite Conversation*, 37; *EI*, 52. In *L'Entretien infini* Blanchot makes a number of changes from the journal publication of his reviews, "Le Grand Refus" and "Comment découvrir l'obscur?" When revising the essays for inclusion in *L'Entretien infini* Blanchot introduced the notion of the neutral and placed "l'impossibilité" in quotation marks in order to resist any implication that one can have access to the impossible.

2. In the original review Blanchot testifies that Bonnefoy is a poet who is close to him. "Le Grand refus," *La Nouvelle Revue Française* 82 (October 1959), 678. The two never met face to face.

3. Yves Bonnefoy, "Critics—English and French, and the Distance between Them," *Encounter* 58 (1958): 44. Also see Alan Boase, "Critiques français, critiques anglais ce qui les divise. Réponse à Yves Bonnefoy," *Cahiers de l'Association Internationale des Études Française* 16 (1964): 157–65. Boase's remarks on Bonnefoy and Blanchot appear on pp. 163–64.

4. For another example of Blanchot's and Bonnefoy's contrary responses to a particular writer, see their discussions of Louis René des Forêts's *Le Bavard*. Blanchot's essay "Idle Speech" appears in *Friendship*, while Bonnefoy's study, "Une Écriture de notre temps," may be found in *La Vérité de parole* (Paris: Mercure de France, 1988). And for thoughts about Blanchot by a poet who is closer to him than Bonnefoy has been, see Jacques Dupin, "Maurice Blanchot and Poetry," trans. Lydia Davis, in Hart, *Nowhere without No*, 15–17.

5. Bonnefoy observes, "l'artiste veut se porter vers cet au-delà du représentable." "La Liberté de l'esprit," *Raymond Mason*, by Dominique Bozo et al. (Paris: Musée National d'Art, 1985), 11.

6. See Bonnefoy, "Le Temps et l'intemporel dans la peinture du Quattrocento," *L'Improbable et autre essais suivi de Un Rêve à Mantoue*, new ed. (Paris: Gallimard, 1992), 69. Bonnefoy declares that "La poésie est la mémoire d l'Un." "Poésie et Liberté," *Entretiens sur la poésie: 1972–1990* (Paris: Mercure de France, 1990), 328.

7. See Bonnefoy, "Quelques Notes sur Mondrian," *Le Nuage rouge: Essais sur la poétique*, rev. ed. (Paris: Mercure de France, 1992), 123.

8. See Blanchot, "Reflections on Surrealism," *Work of Fire*, 89; *PF*, 94. Also see Bonnefoy, "The Feeling of Transcendency," *Yale French Studies* 31 (1964): 135.

9. See Blanchot, "Penser l'Apocalypse," *Le Nouvel Observateur*, January 22–28, 1988, 45.

10. Bonnefoy, "Baudelaire Speaks to Mallarmé," *The Act and the Place of Poetry: Selected Essays*, ed. and introd. John T. Naughton, foreword by Joseph Frank (Chicago: University of Chicago Press, 1989), 58. When presented as a lecture in Geneva in 1967, the essay was originally entitled "L'Art et le sacré."

11. Bonnefoy's criticisms continue in "La Poétique de Mallarmé," *Le Nuage rouge*, especially p. 199. Note Bonnefoy's concession that "We are all, more or less, disciples of Mallarmé." "Baudelaire Speaks to Mallarmé," 65. Also see Bonnefoy's thoughts on "la 'notion pure,'" in "La Poétique de Mallarmé: Quelques remarques," *Lieux et destins de l'image: Un Cours de poétique au Collège de France, 1981–1993* (Paris: Seuil, 1999), 243–50.

12. Bonnefoy, "Baudelaire contre Rubens," *Le Nuage rouge*, 79.

13. Dante, *The Divine Comedy*, 3 vols., vol. 1: *Hell*, trans. Dorothy L. Sayers (Harmondsworth: Penguin, 1949), 3.60–61. Complete agreement as to the identity of this "coward spirit" is lacking among scholars of Dante. Pontius Pilate and Dioclitian have been proposed, alongside others, although most scholars favor Pietro di Murrone, not least of all because his resignation meant that it became possible for Cardinal Gaetani, Dante's enemy, to become pope.

14. Bonnefoy, "The Act and the Place of Poetry," *Act and the Place of Poetry*, 101. Bonnefoy speaks of the "refus moderne de l'être" in "Byzance," *L'Improbable*, 176. On Bonnefoy's attitude to Valéry, see Michel Jarrety, "Lire Valéry," *Magazine Littéraire* 421 (June 2003), 56–59.

15. Bonnefoy, "Les Tombeaux de Ravenne," *L'Improbable*, 13–14. Bonnefoy steadily maintains the idea throughout his writing life. See, for example, "Baudelaire Speaks to Mallarmé," 64.

16. See Bonnefoy, "Avant-propos," *Poésie et rhétorique: La conscience de soi de la poésie* (Paris: Lachenal and Ritter, 1997), 8, and *Remarques sur le regard* (Paris: Calmann-Lévy, 2002), 14.

17. See Bonnefoy, "The Act and the Place of Poetry," and "French Poetry and the Principle of Identity," both in *Act and the Place of Poetry*, 104, 122.

18. On this theme see Cyril O'Regan, *Gnostic Return in Modernity* (Albany: State University of New York Press, 2001).

19. Breton, *Manifestoes of Surrealism*, 123. For Bonnefoy's sense of Breton, see his *Breton à l'avant de soi* (Tours: Farrago, 2001).

20. Bonnefoy, *Le Cœur-espace 1945, 1961* (Tours: Farrago, 2001), 12. I translate as follows:

> I have seen the dogs of wind tearing the cliffs
> The heavy linen rolling in my throat (but I have lived in this porous house)
> I have seen the wind hollow out the girders at six o'clock the earth wandering in its tombs
>   of space
> There was a cemetery of nettles the heavy proofs of wind assembled round the stones
> I have seen the day crack I have lived the site's days of division.

21. Breton, *Manifestoes of Surrealism*, 304. Breton discusses Hegel in his "Surrealist Situation of the Object," 258–59.

22. See Bonnefoy, *Rimbaud*, trans. Paul Schmidt (New York: Harper and Row, 1973), 448–49. Also see *Remarques sur le regard*, 170–75, and the title essay of *Sous l'horizon du langage* (Paris: Mercure de France, 2002), 8.

23. Georges Bataille, *Guilty*, 139; *OC*, 5:388. Bataille's gnostic tendency, which is sometimes expressed in strong terms ("I've never found a way out of this disgusting world"), was suspended for a while by the "political ferment" of the Popular Front. See his 1957 interview with Marguerite Duras, "Bataille, Feydeau, and God," in Duras, *Outside*, 11–16.

24. See Bonnefoy, "The Origins and Development of My Concept of Poetry: An Interview with John E. Jackson," *Act and the Place of Poetry*, 149. One index of the importance of Chestov to Bonnefoy is that the poet contributed an introductory essay, "L'Obstination de Chestov," to *Athènes et Jérusalem: Un essai de philosophie religieuse*, trans. Boris de Schloezer (Paris: Flammarion, 1967). Also see Bonnefoy's 1996 paper "À l'impossible tenu: la liberté de Dieu et celle de l'écrivain dans la pensée de Chestov," *Yves Bonnefoy*, ed. Jacques Ravaud (Cognac: Le Temps qu'il fait, 1998).

25. Bataille translated, with T. Rageot-Chestov, one of Chestov's books. See *L'Idée de bien chez Tolstoï et Nietzsche (Philosophie et prédication)* (Paris: Éditions du Siècle, 1925). Bataille observes of Chestov, "je l'écoutai docilement lorsqu'il me guida avec beaucoup de sens dans la lecture de Platon." *OC*, 8:563. On the relationship of Bataille and Chestov, see Michel Surya, *Georges Bataille: La Mort à l'oeuvre* (Paris: Gallimard, 1992), 67–74. Also see Bonnefoy: "Qui demeure à côté de lui [Chestov] dans la conscience contemporaine—sinon Bataille, pour le comprehendre mais nullement pour le survive—quand il vient provoquer, comme par un second degré de la 'folie' paulinienne, ce Dieu absolument libre—prêcher ce Dieu inconnu?" "L'Obstination de Chestov," 13.

26. *The Collected Dialogues of Plato, Including the Letters*, ed. Edith Hamilton and Huntington Cairns, rev. ed. (Princeton: Princeton University Press, 1963).

27. Lev Chestov, *Potestas Clavium*, trans. Bernard Martin (Athens: Ohio University Press, 1968), 40.

28. Bonnefoy points out the ties between surrealism and Christianity in *Alberto Giacometti: A Biography of His Work*, trans. Jean Stewart (Paris: Flammarion, 1991), 182. Bataille wrote a notice about *Rupture inaugurale*, over the initials "N. L." (Noël Léon), in *Critique* 15–16 (1947). The piece is reproduced in Bataille's *Une Liberté souveraine*, 45–46.

29. See Chestov, *Les Révélations de la mort: Doestoëivsky-Tolstoi*, trans. Boris de Schloezer (Paris: Plon, 1923); *Kierkegaard et la philosophie existentielle: Vox clamantis in deserto*, trans. T. Rageot and B. de Schloezer (Paris: J. Vrin, 1972); and *Athènes et Jérusalem*. Also see Bonnefoy's essay "Boris de Schloezer," *Boris de Schloezer*, Cahiers pour un temps (Paris: Centre Georges Pompidou/Pandora Editions, 1981), 51–60.

30. Bonnefoy, *Dans le leurre du seuil* (Paris: Mercure de France, 1975), 234. In the English version of *Pierre écrite* and *Dans la leurre du seuil*, *Poems 1959–1975* (New York: Vintage, 1985), Richard Pevear translates the lines as follows:

> *And Boris de Schloezer, when he died*
> *Hearing music from the landing*
> *That his near ones could not hear (was it*

The flute of revealed deliverance already,
Or a last gift from the lost earth,
A "work," transfigured?)—left behind only
These waters burnt by the enigma.

. Bonnefoy mentions Bataille's essay in "'The Origins and Development of My Concept of Poetry," *Act and the Place of Poetry*, 145–46. Bataille's "Base Materialism and Gnosticism" appears in *Visions of Excess; OC*, 1:220–26.

32. Bonnefoy, *L'Arrière-pays* (Paris: Flammarion, 1982), 19–20. The book was first published by Editions d'Art Albert Skira in 1972. A sense of this exile can be found of course even in Bonnefoy's favorite poets. See his "'La Belle Dorothée,' or Poetry and Painting," trans. Jan Plug, in *Baudelaire and the Poetics of Modernity*, ed. Patricia A. Ward with the assistance of James S. Patty (Nashville: Vanderbilt University Press, 2001), 86.

33. Bonnefoy, "Sur la fonction du poème," *Le Nuage rouge*, 298.

34. See Bonnefoy, *Remarques sur le regard*, 16.

35. Bonnefoy, "Entretiens avec Bernard Falciola," *Entretiens sur la poésie*, 47. My translation.

36. Bonnefoy, "Baudelaire contre Rubens," 83.

37. See Nietzsche, *Twilight of the Idols and The Anti-Christ*, trans. R. J. Hollingdale (Harmondsworth: Penguin, 1968), 38; Ferdinand de Saussure, *A Course in General Linguistics*, ed. Charles Bally and Albert Sechehaye et al., trans. Roy Harris (La Salle, Ill.: Open Court, 1986).

38. Bonnefoy, "L'Origine de la parole," in *Rue Traversière et autre récits en rêve* (Paris: Gallimard, 1992), 147.

39. Hegel and Kojève as quoted by Bataille in "Hegel, Death and Sacrifice," 9, 10; *OC*, 12:326, 327.

40. Bonnefoy, "Les Fleurs du mal," *L'Improbable*, 34.

41. Bonnefoy, "The Act and the Place of Poetry," 114. In an essay in the same collection, "Baudelaire Speaks to Mallarmé," Bonnefoy modifies his view: "I used to think that words, desiccated by their conceptual use, failed to convey presence, were forever limited to a 'negative theology.' Now I sense that some sort of archeology is possible, which would reveal, piece by piece, the essential elements of our form" (63). Bonnefoy, however, continues to evoke "negative theology" in this context as recently as his "Entretien avec Fabio Scotto," *Europe* 890–91 (2003): 54. Philippe Jaccottet's warning about the use of technical expressions such as "negative theology" when discussing lyric poetry should be kept in mind. See Jaccottet, *Paysage avec figures absentes*, new ed. (Paris: Gallimard, 1976), 174–75.

42. Bonnefoy, "Critics—English and French," 45.

43. Bonnefoy, *Alberto Giacometti*, 176.

44. Bataille, *The Impossible*, trans. Robert Hurley (San Francisco: City Lights Books, 1991), 10; *OC*, 3:101.

45. Bataille, *Guilty*, 139; *OC*, 5:388.

46. G. W. F. Hegel, *The Phenomenology of Mind*, trans. and introd. J. B. Baillie (New York: Harper and Row, 1967), 93.

47. Blanchot published the essay over two numbers of *Critique* in 1947 and 1948. It was later reprinted as the final piece of *La Part du feu*.

260

48. Hegel, *Phenomenology of Mind*, 160.
49. Blanchot, "Literature and the Right to Death," trans. Lydia Davis, *Work of Fire*, 325; PF, 315.
50. See Mallarmé, "Crise de vers," *Oeuvres complètes*, 363–64.
51. See Roland Barthes, "The Death of the Author," *Image-Music-Text*, trans. Stephen Heath (New York: Hill and Wang, 1977), and Blanchot, "The Essential Solitude," *Space of Literature*, 23; *EL*, 16.
52. Bonnefoy, "Baudelaire contre Rubens," 67.
53. See Bonnefoy, "Peinture, poésie: Vertige, paix," *Le Nuage rouge*, 323.
54. Bonnefoy, "'Image and Presence,'" *Act and the Place of Poetry*, 170. Writing shortly after this comment about the image had been made, Jérome Thélot observed, "A l'époque de *Dans la leurre du seuil* le poète aurait pu dire: S'il n'y a pas de poésie sans discours, comment la sauver sinon en aggravant son mal . . . " To which Bonnefoy added by way of response, "Non pas en aggravant son mal, maintenant: mais en le décrispant. Passage de la 'théologie' négative à la théologie positive." *Poétique d'Yves Bonnefoy* (Geneva: Librairie Droz, 1983), 92, 258. Notice that shortly after making his remark on waging war against the image Bonnefoy adds, "having refused the Image, poetry accepts it in a kind of circle which constitutes its mystery." "'Image and Presence,'" 171.
55. Bonnefoy, *Poèmes* (Paris: Mercure de France, 1978), 221. Pevear translates as follows:

> *We no longer need*
> *Harrowing images in order to love.*
> *That tree over there is enough for us, loosed*
> *From itself by light, knowing nothing*
> *But the almost uttered name of an almost incarnate god.* (*Poems*, 53)

However, also see the lines, "Le désir déchira le voile de l'image / L'image donna vie à l'exsangue désir" (225). In Pevear's rendering, "Yearning tore the veil of the image, / The image gave bloodless yearning life" (57).
56. Bonnefoy, "Lettre à John E. Jackson," *Entretiens sur la poésie*, 107.
57. Bonnefoy, *Poèmes*, 295. Pevear renders the lines, "But always and distinctly I also see / The black stain in the image, I hear / The cry that pierces the music." *Poems*, 135.
58. Bonnefoy, "L'Imperfection est la cime," *Poèmes*, 117. Galway Kinnell and Richard Pevear translate the lyric as follows:

> *So one had to destroy and destroy and destroy,*
> *There was salvation only at that price.*
>
> *To ruin the naked face that rises in marble,*
> *To hammer down every form and beauty.*
>
> *To love perfection because it is the threshold,*
> *But deny it, once known, and forget it, dead.*
>
> *Imperfection is the summit.*

Bonnefoy, *Early Poems: 1947–1959*, trans. Galway Kinnell and Richard Pevear (Athens: Ohio University Press, 1991), 217.

59. See Jean-Luc Nancy, "The Sublime Offering," in *Of the Sublime: Presence in Question*, by Jean-François Courtine et al., trans. Jeffrey S. Librett (Albany: State University of New York Press, 1993), 25–53.

60. Bonnefoy, *Poèmes*, 211. In Pevear's rendition:

> *We no longer see each other in the same light,*
> *We no longer have the same eyes or the same hands.*
> *The tree is closer, the voice of the springs more lively,*
> *Our steps are deeper now, among the dead.*

> *God who are not, put your hand on our shoulder,*
> *Sketch out our body with the weight of your return,*
> *Complete the mixing of our souls with these stars,*
> *These woods, these bird-calls, these shadows, these days.*

> *Renounce yourself in us as a fruit bursts open,*
> *Blot us out in you. Unveil for us*
> *The mysterious meaning of what is all so simple*
> *And would have burnt darkly in loveless words. (Poems, 43)*

For later reflections on God, see Bonnefoy's poem "L'Encore aveugle," *Les Planches courbes* (Paris: Mercure de France, 2001), 107–12, and, more indirectly, "Les Noms divins," *Le Théâtre des enfants* (Périgueux: William Blake, 2001).

61. "Transcendence" here is used in a sense closer to Edmund Husserl's than to Karl Rahner's. The transcendent is what is outside consciousness—the body, the world—and is not linked to what Rahner calls "transcendental experience." See Husserl, *Ideas: General Introduction to Pure Phenomenology*, § 38, and Rahner, *Foundations of Christian Faith: An Introduction to the Idea of Christianity*, trans. William V. Dych (New York: Crossroad, 1982), 20.

62. Bonnefoy, "The Act and the Place of Poetry," 114.

63. Franz Kafka, "Reflections on Sin, Pain, Hope and the True Way," § 24, *The Great Wall of China*, trans. Willa Muir and Edwin Muir (New York: Schocken Books, 1970), 167.

64. Bonnefoy, "Il reste à faire le négatif . . . ," *Pouvoirs du négatif dans la psychanalyse et la culture*, by Yves Bonnefoy et al. (Seyssel, Fr.: Éditions Champ Vallon, 1988), 9. Also see *Alberto Giacometti*, 386.

65. Bonnefoy, "Lifting Our Eyes from the Page," trans. John Naughton, *Critical Inquiry* 16, no. 4 (1990): 198. The essay first appeared in 1988, in a special issue of the *Nouvelle Revue de Psychanalyse*. Also see Bonnefoy on Chagall: "Il s'identifie de la même façon, dans son avivement, son possible retour à la condition de lumière, avec cette *couleur* que Chagall tient que chaque homme a en lui comme sa plus élémentaire conscience, au point de profondeur où l'expérience sensible se raccorde avec l'absolu." *La Religion de Chagall* (Paris: Maeght, 1962), 18.

66. See Blanchot, "Interruption (as on a Riemann surface)," *Infinite Conversation*, 75–79; *EI*, 106–12.

67. Bataille, "Hegel, Death and Sacrifice," 18; *OC*, 12:335.

68. I have taken the translation from "The Great Refusal," *Infinite Conversation*, 36. Michael Hamburger's version runs, "But now day breaks! I waited and saw it come, / And what I saw, the hallowed, my word shall convey." See Friedrich Hölderlin, *Poems and Fragments*, trans., preface and notes by Michael Hamburger (London: Anvil Press, 1994), 395. The punctuation around "the hallowed" is an interpretation at odds with most recent Hölderlin scholarship.

69. M. B. Benn, *Hölderlin and Pindar* (The Hague: Mouton, 1962), 18.

70. Martin Heidegger, "'As When on a Holiday . . . ,'" *Elucidations of Hölderlin's Poetry*, trans. and introd. Keith Hoeller (Amherst: Humanity Books, 2000), 90.

71. Hölderlin, *Poems and Fragments*, 639. I have not quoted the final paragraph of the commentary. Hamburger translates Hölderlin's translation of Pindar as follows:

> *The law*
> *King of all, both mortals and*
> *Immortals; which for that very reason*
> *Compellingly guides*
> *The justest justice with a sovereign hand.*

72. This is not to say that "holy" and "sacred" are always synonymous. Lévinas, for instance, distinguishes them. See chapter 6.

73. Paul de Man points out with respect to Heidegger's reading of "Das Höchste" that while it is correct to say "that the immediate contains the possibility of the mediation of the mediate because it permits it in its being," it is incorrect to add that "the immediate is, therefore, itself the mediating intercession." "Heidegger's Exegeses of Hölderlin," *Blindness and Insight*, 260.

74. Yet Bonnefoy has never been as close to Heidegger as to other European philosophers. See Robert Kopp's interview with Bonnefoy, "'La seule réalité, c'est l'être humain engagé dans sa finitude,'" *Magazine Littéraire* 421 (2003): 24.

75. *Work of Fire*, 126; *PF*, 128.

76. Although Blanchot is not mentioned, Blanchot's reservations about Heidegger's reading of the hymn are underlined by Hans-Jost Frey in his *Studies in Poetic Discourse: Mallarmé, Baudelaire, Rimbaud, Hölderlin*, trans. William Whobrey (Stanford: Stanford University Press, 1996), 182–83.

77. It is worth noting that as late as November 10, 1987, in a letter to Catherine David, Blanchot retains the expression "langage sacré." The letter addresses the dossier opened by Victor Farias concerning Heidegger's association with the Nazi party. In a post scriptum to the letter he repeats what he said at the end of n. 4 to "Reflections on Nihilism," *Infinite Conversation*, 451; *EI*, 210. Then he adds, "Oui, le même langage sacré, peut-être un peu plus grossier, un peu plus emphatique, mais qui désormais se fera entendre jusque dans les commentaires sur Hölderlin et altérera ceux-ci, mais pour d'autres raisons

encore." "Penser l'Apocalypse," *Écrits politiques: Guerre d'Algérie, Mai 68, etc.* (Paris: Lignes, Éditions Léo Scheer, 2003), 163. Here, "langage sacré" applies to Heidegger's writing rather than Hölderlin's, although, to be sure, it is with the elucidations of Hölderlin's poems in prospect. What is curious is that, in 1987, the word *sacré* is not placed in quotation marks.

78. See Erich Przywara, "Um Hölderlin," *In und Gegen: Stellungnahmen zur Zeit* (Nuremberg: Glock und Lutz, 1955), 141.

79. A confusion arises in the English translation. The sentence that reads, "A little further on, Heidegger adds, 'Chaos is the Sacred in the self'" should have as the quotation from Heidegger, "Chaos is the Sacred itself" ("Das Chaos ist das Heilige selbst"). Blanchot's French runs, "le chaos est le Sacré en soi." "The 'Sacred' Speech of Hölderlin," *Work of Fire*, 120; *PF*, 123. I should add that Blanchot's distrust of the immediate should be read alongside his remarks on the aesthetic and the immediate in his "Kierkegaard et l'esthétique," *Journal des Débats*, July 13, 1943, 3.

80. Blanchot talks of the poet sacrificing himself or herself in the act of writing as early as "Oeuvres poétiques," *Journal des Débats*, December 9, 1942, 3.

81. Blanchot, "Madness par excellence," *The Blanchot Reader*, ed. Michael Holland (Oxford: Basil Blackwell, 1995), 124; "La Folie par excellence," *Critique* 45 (February 1951): 116.

82. Elsewhere Blanchot observes that with Heraclitus "Sacred discourse becomes a discourse of *physis*." "Heraclitus," *Infinite Conversation*, 86; *EI*, 121.

83. Blanchot, "The Beast of Lascaux," trans. Leslie Hill, *Oxford Literary Review* 22 (2000): 9; *La Bête de Lascaux* (Montpellier: Fata Morgana, 1982), 13. Blanchot makes the same point with respect to Simone Weil in "Affirmation (desire, affliction)," *Infinite Conversation*, 120; *EI*, 175.

84. Blanchot, "The Beast of Lascaux," 11; *BL*, 18. Also see "René Char," *Work of Fire*, 100; *PF*, 105.

85. René Char, "Partage formel," *Fureur et mystère*, preface by Yves Berger, Collection poésie (Paris: Gallimard, 1967), 73.

86. As we will see in chapters 6 and 7, Blanchot affirms the universalization of an ethics revealed in Jewish Scripture. There, however, the movement toward universalization is leagued with the thought of the neuter.

87. See Char's introduction to *Héraclite d'Éphèse*, trans. Yves Battistini (Paris: Éditions Cahiers d'Art, 1948), 11–15.

88. Blanchot, "René Char," *Work of Fire*, 104; *PF*, 108. The essay is a commentary on *Avez-vous lu Char?* by Georges Mounin. For Mounin's exasperated response see "Maurice Blanchot et la poésie toujours mal entendue de René Char," *La Communication poétique précédé de Avez-vous lu Char?* (Paris: Gallimard, 1969), 229–45.

89. Blanchot, "The Great Refusal," *Infinite Conversation*, 38; *EI*, 54. The discussion of Hölderlin's "Das Höchste," broached in the concluding essay in *L'Espace littéraire*, is found in *L'Entretien infini* but not in the original journal article. In the years separating the two versions of "Le Grand Refus" Blanchot would appear to have been influenced by Derrida's deconstruction of the metaphysics of presence, especially by those essays collected in *L'Écriture et la différence* (1968). On Blanchot's revisions of his

texts along "Derridian" lines, see Derrida's *Resistences of Psychoanalysis*, trans. Peggy Kamuf, Pascale-Anne Brault, and Michael Naas (Stanford: Stanford University Press, 1998), 61–62.

90. See Heidegger, *Elucidations of Hölderlin's Poetry,* 97; Blanchot, "The 'Sacred' Speech of Hölderlin," *Work of Fire*, 112; *PF,* 116. It should be noted that Blanchot changes his mind about the historicity of Hölderlin's turn. This can be seen in his response to the "turn" that literary historians believe was accomplished by Hölderlin in or around 1801. In "La Folie par excellence" (1951) Blanchot maintains that "there is no turning-point in the work of Hölderlin, but a continuous development." *Blanchot Reader,* 118. However, by the time he considers Beda Allemann's *Hölderlin und Heidegger* (1954) in "Le Tournant" (1955) he has come to accept that there was indeed a turn in the poet's development around the beginning of the nineteenth century. Even so, what the turn signifies—the double infidelity—marks poetry as such, Blanchot suggests, and is not restricted to the singularity of Hölderlin's historical situation. "Le Tournant" was retitled "L'Itinéraire de Hölderlin" and included in *L'Espace littéraire* (1955). See "Hölderlin's Itinerary," *Space of Literature,* 274; *EL,* 370–71.

91. Blanchot, "Hölderlin's Itinerary," 274; *EL,* 370–71.

92. Blanchot, "Prophetic Speech," *Book to Come,* 81; *LV,* 112. Also see "Le Bon Usage de la science-fiction," *La Nouvelle Revue Française* 73 (1959): 94.

93. See Blanchot, "Being Jewish," *Infinite Conversation,* 125; *EI,* 183.

94. Bonnefoy, "The Act and the Place of Poetry," 114.

95. Blanchot, *Most High,* 254, 1; *TH,* 243, 9.

96. On responding to the impossible and naming the possible, see "The Great Refusal," *Infinite Conversation,* 48; *EI,* 69, and "Le 'Discours Philosophique,'" *L'Arc* 46 (1971): 2. Blanchot also draws the distinction in a letter to Bataille on January 24, [1962]. See Georges Bataille, *Choix de lettres 1917–1962,* 596.

97. See Blanchot, *Writing of the Disaster,* 132; *ED,* 200. The lines are taken from Bonnefoy's *Poèmes,* 231. Once more I call upon Pevear:

> But no, once again
> Unfolding the wing of the impossible
> You awaken, with a cry,
> From the place which is only a dream . . . (Poems, 63)

98. Bonnefoy, "'Image and Presence,'" *The Act and the Place of Poetry,* 172.

99. Blanchot, "Literature and the Original Experience," *Space of Literature,* 233; *EL,* 310–11.

100. Blanchot develops his thoughts about magic in "The Two Versions of the Imaginary," *Space of Literature,* 262; *EL,* 352–53. Bonnefoy's unease with the imaginary could perhaps be traced by way of his strictures on the récit. See his *Breton à l'avant de soi* (Tours: Farrago/Éditions Léo Scheer, 2001), 37–38, 75–80.

101. Saint Theodore the Studite, *On the Holy Icons,* trans. Catharine P. Roth (1981; rpt. Crestwood, N.Y.: St. Vladimir's Seminary Press, 2001), 110.

102. Blanchot, "The Essential Solitude," *Space of Literature,* 32; *EL,* 30.

103. An alternate way of approaching the issue would be by way of what Jean-Luc Nancy calls "exscription." See the essay "Exscription" in his *The Birth to Presence*, trans. Brian Holmes et al. (Stanford: Stanford University Press, 1993), 319–40.

104. See Bonnefoy, "La Mort de peintre d'icônes," *Récits en rêve* (Paris: Mercure de France, 1987), 170–73.

105. Blanchot, "Note," *Infinite Conversation*, xii; *EI*, viii.

106. Blanchot, *Unavowable Community*, 2; *CI*, 11.

107. Bonnefoy, "Ronsard Today," *Theme and Version: Plath and Ronsard*, ed. Anthony Rudolf (London: Menard Press, 1995), 66.

CHAPTER FOUR

1. Blanchot, "Reflections on Hell," *Infinite Conversation*, 176; *EI*, 264.

2. Bataille, *Inner Experience*, 108; *OC*, 5:126.

3. Michel Foucault, "Maurice Blanchot: The Thought from Outside," trans. Brian Massumi, in *Foucault/Blanchot* (New York: Zone Books, 1990), 13. Foucault expresses his reservations about seeing negative theology as Blanchot's path to the outside on p. 16.

4. Gottfried Wilhelm Leibniz, *New Essays concerning Human Understanding*, trans. A. G. Langley (La Salle, Ill.: Open Court, 1949), 410.

5. See Immanuel Kant, *Critique of Pure Reason*, trans. Norman Kemp Smith (London: Macmillan, 1933), 337.

6. F. W. J. von Schelling, *On the History of Modern Philosophy*, trans. and introd. Andrew Bowie (Cambridge: Cambridge University Press, 1994), 47.

7. Honoré de Balzac, "Descartes," in *Oeuvres diverses*, 2 vols. (Paris: Gallimard, 1990), 1:573.

8. André Gide, *The Fruits of the Earth*, trans. Dorothy Bussy (New York: Alfred A. Knopf, 1949), 225. Gide also remarks with respect to the devil that "if we were more humble we should recognize him in the *Cogito ergo sum*. That ergo is the cloven hoof." *Journals*, vol. 2: *1914–1927*, 188–89.

9. Husserl, *Cartesian Meditations*, 24. Also see Husserl's *The Crisis of European Sciences and Transcendental Phenomenology*, trans. and introd. David Carr (Evanston: Northwestern University Press, 1970), 81–82.

10. Maurice Merleau-Ponty, *The Primacy of Perception: And Other Essays on Phenomenological Psychology, the Philosophy of Art, History and Politics*, ed. and introd. James M. Edie (Evanston: Northwestern University Press, 1964), 21–22. Merleau-Ponty's fullest remarks on the Cogito are to be found in his *Phenomenology of Perception*, trans. Colin Smith (London: Routledge and Kegan Paul, 1962), section 3, part 1.

11. See, for example, A. J. Ayer, "Cogito ergo sum," *Analysis* 14 (1953): 27–31; J. Hintikka, "Cogito ergo sum: Inference or Performance?" *Philosophical Review* 71 (1962): 3–32; and Martial Guéroult, *Descartes selon l'ordre des raisons*, 2 vols. (Paris: Aubier Montaigne, 1953), 2:308. Recent scientific accounts of the brain as a series of neural circuits arranged in parallel relays might lead one to say, with S. J. Singer, "I link, therefore I am." Some analytic philosophers have shown interest in this position, although of course one would not

expect Blanchot to comment on it. See Edward O. Wilson, *Consilience: The Unity of Knowledge* (New York: Alfred A. Knopf, 1998), 110.

12. See Blanchot, "Penser l'apocalypse," *EP*, 162–63. Also Blanchot's emphasis upon the "beginning" and the "beginning still more beginning" recalls Heidegger's stress on the *Anfang* or *Ursprung* in his winter semester 1934–35 lecture course on Hölderlin's "Germanien" and "Der Rhein." See *Hölderlins Hymnen "Germanien" und "Der Rhein," Gesamtausgabe*, series ed. Herman Heidegger, vol. 39 (Frankfurt: Klostermann, 1980), 3.

13. Heidegger underlines the point in *What Is a Thing?* trans. W. B. Barton Jr. and Vera Deutsch, analysis by Eugene T. Gendlin (Chicago: Henry Regnery, 1967), 110. Theodor W. Adorno observes in his 1965 lectures on metaphysics that, far from eliminating theological assumptions in his account of Dasein, Heidegger maintains them in a covert manner. See his *Metaphysics: Concept and Problems*, ed. Rolf Tiedemann, trans. Edmund Jephcott (Stanford: Stanford University Press, 2000), 107. I discuss the issue in chapter 7.

14. Heidegger, *The Basic Problems of Phenomenology*, trans., introd., and lexicon by Albert Hofstadter (Bloomington: Indiana University Press, 1982), 80. Heidegger returns to Suárez several times in this lecture series. See especially pp. 94–99. Also see the discussion of Suárez in *The Fundamental Concepts of Metaphysics: World, Finitude, Solitude*, trans. William McNeill and Nicholas Walker (Bloomington: Indiana University Press, 1995), § 14.

15. On Descartes's encounter at La Flèche with Suárez, "*la lumière de la théologie*," see Camille de Rochmonteix, *Un Collège de Jésuites aux XVIIe et XVIIIe siècles*, 4 vols. (Le Mans: Leguicheux, 1889), vol. 4: *Le Collège Henri IV*, 17. Descartes alludes to the *Disputationes metaphysicae* in his "Reply to the Fourth Set of Objections." See Descartes, *Philosophical Essays and Correspondence*, ed. and introd. Roger Ariew (Indianapolis: Hackett, 2000), 184. Descartes considers eternal truths in letters to Marin Mersenne on April 15, May 6, and May 27, 1630. Timothy J. Cronin argues that Descartes cites Suárez without naming him in that exchange. See his *Objective Being in Descartes and in Suárez* (Rome: Gregorian University Press, 1966), 241 n. 38. Also see Jean-François Courtine, *Suarez et le système de la métaphysique* (Paris: Presses Universitaires de France, 1990), 482–95.

16. Heidegger, *Being and Time*, 254.

17. Heidegger observes with respect to the signification of "being" in different ontic realms, "In working out this problem ontologically, Descartes is always far behind the Schoolmen; indeed, he evades the question." *Being and Time*, 126.

18. See Heidegger, *Seminare, Gesamtausgabe*, series ed. Herman Heidegger, vol. 15 (Frankfurt: Klostermann, 1986), 436–37.

19. See Gustav Siewerth, *Das Schicksal der Metaphysik von Thomas zu Heidegger* (Einseideln: Johannes Verlag, 1959), chap. 11, and Olivier Boulnois, *Être et représentation: Une généalogie de la métaphysique moderne à l'époque de Duns Scot (XIIIe–XIVe siècle)* (Paris: Presses Universitaires de France, 1999), 479–93.

20. Blanchot speaks of the "intellectual shock" that *Sein und Zeit* provoked in him in "Penser l'apocalypse," *EP*, 162.

21. Blanchot's testimony to the value of Heidegger's writing for regarding art may be found in "L'Ebauche d'un roman," *Aux Écoutes*, July 30, 1938, 31; and a violent putdown of Heidegger's thought appears in "Penser avec les mains," *L'Insurgé*, January 27, 1937, 5.

22. Heidegger, "Qu'est-ce que la métaphysique?" trans. H. Corbin-Petithenry and introd. Alexandre Koyré, *Bifur*, June 1931, 5–27. The translation was reproduced in *Questions*, 4 vols. (Paris: Gallimard, 1966–76), 1:47–84. As it happens, Koyré (1892–1964) was a Descartes scholar. See his *Essai sur l'idée de Dieu et les preuves de son existence chez Descartes* (Paris: Leroux, 1922); *Trois leçons sur Descartes* (Cairo: Impr. nationale, 1938); and *La Loi de la chute des corps: Descartes et Galilée* (Paris: Hermann, 1939). Koyré also attended Kojève's lectures on Hegel.

23. It would be a mistake to see Hegel as simply replacing Heidegger in Blanchot's world, not least of all because in "What Is Metaphysics?" Heidegger talks in Hegelian tones of Nothing as the negation (*Verneinung*) of what-is, and of raising Nothing into the higher category of the Negative (*Nichthaftes*). Nietzsche is plainly another vanishing point of Blanchot's world, though exactly when he encountered Nietzsche is hard to tell.

24. See Raymond Queneau, "Premières Confrontations avec Hegel," *Critique* 195–96 (1963): 694–700.

25. G. W. F. Hegel, *System of Ethical Life and First Philosophy of Spirit*, ed. and trans. H. S. Harris and T. M. Knox (Albany: State University of New York Press, 1979), 221–22. Blanchot quotes this passage in "Literature and the Right to Death," discussed later.

26. Blanchot, "Literature and the Right to Death," *Work of Fire*, 322; *PF*, 312. Hegel's argument was not only taken up by Kojève's circle; it is repeated by someone as unsympathetic to Blanchot as E. M. Cioran. See his *A Short History of Decay*, trans. Richard Howard (New York: Viking, 1975), 7. The French original of Cioran's book appeared in 1949.

27. Hegel, *Phenomenology of Mind*, 94.

28. For the observation about the demise of philosophy and the end of war, see Alexandre Kojève, *Introduction to the Reading of Hegel*, ed. Allan Bloom, trans. James H. Nichols Jr. (Ithaca: Cornell University Press, 1969), 159n. The English translation is not complete. Kojève adds, "La fin de l'Histoire est la mort de l'Homme proprement dit." *Introduction à la lecture de Hegel*, 388n.

29. Marcel Proust, *In Search of Lost Time*, trans. C. K. Scott-Moncrieff and Terrence Kilmartin, rev. D. J. Enright, 6 vols. (New York: Modern Library, 1992), vol. 2: *Within a Budding Grove*, 405–6. Blanchot discusses this passage in "The Experience of Proust," *Book to Come*, 18; *LV*, 30.

30. Bataille, *Guilty*, 139; *OC*, 5:388.

31. Bataille remembers, "Blanchot asked me: why not pursue my inner experience as if I were the *last man*?" *Inner Experience*, 61; *OC*, 5:76. In this connection see Bataille's remarks on the notion of the "last man" in his lecture of 1951 "Un-knowing and Its Consequences," *October* 36 (1986): 84; *OC*, 8:196. Blanchot's récit *Le Dernier Homme* was published in 1957. See *The Last Man*, trans. Lydia Davis (New York: Columbia University Press, 1987). Blanchot continues to insist on the importance of "the end of history," right up to *The Writing of the Disaster*, 73; *ED*, 118.

32. Blanchot, *Most High*, 153, 42; *TH*, 149, 47.

33. Blanchot, *The One Who Was Standing Apart from Me*, trans. Lydia Davis (Barrytown, N.Y.: Station Hill Press, 1993), 64; *Celui qui ne m'accompagnait pas* (Paris: Gallimard, 1953), 120.

34. I am using "unity" here to refer to the identity of the subject. Graham Bird points out that Kant uses "unity" ambiguously, meaning both "the identity of a person apperceiving different ideas" and "a person's apperceiving identical ideas." On Bird's analysis, Kant distinguishes between these two senses of "unity" while insisting on their close connection. See Bird, *Kant's Theory of Knowledge: An Outline of One Central Argument in the "Critique of Pure Reason"* (London: Routledge and Kegan Paul, 1962), 120–23.

35. See Kant, *Critique of Pure Reason*, A597/B625n.

36. See Aristotle, *Metaphysics*, 1048b.

37. Blanchot, "How to Discover the Obscure?" *Infinite Conversation*, 42; *EI*, 59. I should add that Blanchot's discussion of possibility comes considerably later than his discussion of the three systems of thought I go on to evoke.

38. Blanchot, "The Work and Death's Space," *Space of Literature*, 96; *EL*, 115.

39. Heidegger, *Being and Time*, 183.

40. Blanchot and Lévinas are very close here. Lévinas outlines his criticism of Heidegger in *Time and the Other*, trans. Richard A. Cohen (Pittsburgh: Duquesne University Press, 1987), 70–71; *Le Temps et l'autre* (1979; Paris: Quadrige/PUF, 1994), 57–58, and switches Heidegger's well-known formulation in *Totality and Infinity*, 235; *TI*, 262. Blanchot alludes to the difference between Heidegger and Lévinas in "Literature and the Original Experience," *Space of Literature*, 240; *EL*, 326.

41. One must distinguish "transcendence" as used by Husserl and as commonly used in theology. The latter is roughly a way of evoking the absolute alterity of God, while the former describes "all acts directed towards essences, or towards the intentional experiences of other Egos with other experience-streams; likewise all acts directed upon things, upon realities generally." Husserl, *Ideas: General Introduction to Pure Phenomenology*, § 38.

42. See Lévinas, *Existence and Existents*, 57–64; *EE*, 93–105. The book appeared in French in 1947. Blanchot had already explored the notion of being without beings in the opening pages of *Thomas l'obscur* (1941). Lévinas's remarks on the Cogito developed in *Existence and Existents* also converge with Blanchot's in *Thomas l'obscur*, as will become evident.

43. Heidegger, *Being and Time*, 72. The point is developed by Heidegger in his *What Is a Thing?* 104–5; "The Age of the World Picture," *Question Concerning Technology*, appendix 4, 140–41; and *Nietzsche*, 4 vols., vol. 4: *Nihilism*, ed. David Farrell Krell, trans. Frank A. Capuzzi (San Francisco: Harper and Row, 1982), chaps. 15–17.

44. Heidegger, *Being and Time*, 68.

45. See Heidegger, *Hegel's Concept of Experience*, no trans. (San Francisco: Harper and Row, 1970), 65–67.

46. See Diane Rubenstein, *What's Left? The Ecole Normale Supérieure and the Right* (Madison: University of Wisconsin Press, 1990), 39.

47. Blanchot, "Our Clandestine Companion," in *Face to Face with Lévinas*, ed. Richard A. Cohen (Albany: State University of New York Press, 1986), 42.

48. Lévinas, *Otherwise than Being or Beyond Essence*, trans. Alphonso Lingis (The Hague: Martinus Nijhoff, 1981), 170; *Autrement qu'être, ou Au-delà de l'essence* (1974; Paris: Kluwer Academic, 1990), 263. My emphasis.

49. See Blanchot, "Our Clandestine Companion," 47. Blanchot also draws attention to Lévinas's association of skepticism and language in *Writing of the Disaster*, 76–77, 110; *ED*, 123, 170.

50. Blanchot, "Une Vue de Descartes," *Journal des Débats*, August 11–12, 1941. Also see "Les Idoles hors la loi," *Journal des Débats*, March 9, 1944, 2–3.

51. *TO* (1), 48. I shall quote from Lamberton's translation and, where necessary, draw attention to differences between the "nouvelle version" and the "roman" version. The passage quoted appears in *Thomas the Obscure*, 36.

52. In the novel version the final sentence quoted reads, "C'est la propriété de ma pensée non pas de m'assurer de l'existence, comme toutes choses, comme la pierre, mais de m'assurer la permanence de ce *Je* dans le néant même et de me convier à n'être pas pour me fair sentir alors mon admirable absence." *TO* (1), 218.

53. J. G. Fichte, *Science of Knowledge*, ed. and trans. Peter Heath and John Lachs (Cambridge: Cambridge University Press, 1982), 100–101. Also see Hegel, *Lectures on the History of Philosophy*, trans. E. S. Haldane and Frances H. Simson, 3 vols. (1896; rpt. New York: Humanities Press, 1974), 3:229–30.

54. Hegel, *Phenomenology of Mind*, 780. My ellipsis.

55. Kojève, *Introduction to the Reading of Hegel*, 140–41. My ellipsis.

56. Blanchot, "Literature and the Right to Death," *Work of Fire*, 323; *PF*, 313. The entire discussion of the woman and death is haunted by Mallarmé's "Je dis: une fleur!, et hors de l'oubli où ma voix relègue aucun contour, et tant que quelque chose d'autre que les calices sus, musicalement se lève, idée même et suave absence de tout bouquet." *Oeuvres complètes*, 368. That Blanchot never swerved from maintaining a relation between language and death is evident from his very late remarks in "L'Écriture, entre la vie et la mort," in "Écrits pour Claude Lucas," *Rémanences* 8 (1998): 28.

57. Blanchot, *Thomas the Obscure*, 99–100; *TO* (1), 218.

58. See Heidegger, *On the Way to Language*, trans. Peter D. Hertz (New York: Harper and Row, 1982), 134.

59. Although a translation of this passage appears in *The Infinite Conversation*, I have preferred the version offered in *German Aesthetic and Literary Criticism: The Romantic Ironists and Goethe*, ed. Kathleen Wheeler (Cambridge: Cambridge University Press, 1984), 92–93.

60. Blanchot, "The Narrative Voice," *Infinite Conversation*, 380; *EI*, 557.

61. Blanchot, "The Atheneum," *Infinite Conversation*, 357; *EI*, 524. There is a good deal to unpack in this complex sentence, though its basis is perhaps best clarified by Husserl in his insistence that speech is in no sense a translation of concepts into words: "in speaking we are continually performing an internal act of meaning, which fuses with the words and, as it were, animates them. The effect of this animation is that the words and the entire locu-

tion, as it were, *embody* in themselves a meaning, and bear it embodied in them as their sense." *Formal and Transcendental Logic*, trans. Dorion Cairns (The Hague: Martinus Nijhoff, 1978), 22. Needless to say, the difference between speech and poetic speech, a topic Husserl does not touch, needs further justification.

62. Blanchot, *Writing of the Disaster*, 12; *ED*, 25.

63. Quoted by Wm. Actander O'Brien in his *Novalis: Signs of Revolution* (Durham: Duke University Press, 1995), 83–84. Translation modified. I am indebted to O'Brien's discussion of this passage.

64. Hegel, *Aesthetics: Lectures on Fine Art*, trans. T. M. Knox, 2 vols. (Oxford: Clarendon Press, 1975), 1:64.

65. Blanchot, *Writing of the Disaster*, 54; *ED*, 90–91. My ellipsis.

66. On the question whether geometrical truths are preserved only by inscription, see Jacques Derrida, *Edmund Husserl's "Origin of Geometry": An Introduction*, ed. David B. Allison, trans. John P. Leavey (Stony Brook, N.Y.: Nicolas Hays, 1978).

67. Blanchot, "Literature and the Right to Death," *Work of Fire*, 328; *PF*, 317.

68. Blanchot avoids the word *sublime* in order to escape all suggestion of aestheticism. See "Note," *Infinite Conversation*, xi; *EI*, vi.

69. Heidegger, *Being and Time*, 72.

70. A Kantian would have more reason for worry when confronted with Adorno's criticisms of the Kantian subject in his 1959 lectures on the first *Critique*. Adorno finds a contradiction "that, on the one hand, the concept of subjectivity cannot be conceived of without the personal subject from which it has been derived; but that, on the other hand, the personal subject has first to be constituted and so cannot be presupposed in advance." *Kant's Critique of Pure Reason*, ed. Rolf Tiedemann, trans. Rodney Lingstone (Stanford: Stanford University Press, 2001), 90.

71. See Maurice Merleau-Ponty, *The Visible and the Invisible*, ed. Claude Lefort, trans. Alphonso Lingis (Evanston: Northwestern University Press, 1968), passim but especially 201, 246. Merleau-Ponty is indebted to Husserl's analysis of anonymity in *The Crisis of European Sciences and Transcendental Phenomenology*, § 29. Also see Husserl's *Experience and Judgement: Investigations in a Genealogy of Logic*, rev. and ed. Ludwig Landgrebe, trans. James S. Churchill and Karl Ameriks (Evanston: Northwestern University Press, 1973), §§ 33–46.

72. See Blanchot, "The Speech of Analysis," *Infinite Conversation*, 230–37; *EI*, 343–54.

73. See Paul Ricoeur, *Oneself as Another*, trans. Kathleen Blamey (Chicago: University of Chicago Press, 1992). Also see "Emmanuel Lévinas: Thinker of Testimony," in his collection *Figuring the Sacred: Religion, Narrative, and Imagination*, ed. Mark I. Wallace, trans. David Pellauer (Minneapolis: Fortress Press, 1995).

74. Lévinas, *Outside the Subject*, trans. Michael B. Smith (Stanford: Stanford University Press, 1994), 35, 125; *Hors sujet* (Montpellier: Fata Morgana, 1987), 52, 187.

75. See Blanchot, "The Right to Insubordination (1960)," in Holland, *Blanchot Reader*, 197. The French original, "[Je voudrais dire d'abord . . .]," may be found in *EP*, 37–42.

76. Blanchot, *Writing of the Disaster*, 18; *ED*, 35.

77. Ibid., 19; 37.

78. Blanchot, "Reflections on Surrealism," *Work of Fire*, 86; *PF*, 91.

79. Blanchot, "Dreaming, Writing," in *Friendship*, 146; *A*, 169.

80. On this topic see Blanchot's *Writing of the Disaster*, 65–72; *ED*, 108–117.

81. For an early consideration of the relations between the "I" and the community, see Blanchot, "Le Souci de sincérité," *Journal des Débats*, August 3, 1944, 2–3.

82. For Blanchot's remarks on Kantian critique see "The Task of Criticism Today," trans. Leslie Hill, *Oxford Literary Review* 22 (2000): 23; *Lautréamont et Sade*, rev. ed. (Paris: Éditions de Minuit, 1963), 13.

83. Blanchot, "Literature and the Original Experience," *Space of Literature*, 244, my ellipsis; *EL*, 332.

84. Ibid., 244; 327.

85. Blanchot, *Step Not Beyond*, 76; *PAD*, 106.

86. Blanchot, "The Work and Death's Space," *Space of Literature*, 151; *EL*, 198. My ellipsis.

87. Blanchot, "How to Discover the Obscure?" *Infinite Conversation*, 45; *EI*, 64.

88. Blanchot, "The Limit-Experience," *Infinite Conversation*, 207, 210; *EI*, 307–11. My ellipsis. Cf. a later remark by Blanchot with respect to Bataille's "inner experience": "the *experience* could not take place for the single being because its characteristic is to break up the particularity of a particular person and to expose the latter to someone else." *Unavowable Community*, 21; *CI*, 41.

89. S. L. Frank, *The Unknowable: An Ontological Introduction to the Philosophy of Religion*, trans. Boris Jakim (Athens: Ohio University Press, 1983), 17.

90. Bataille, "Un-knowing: Laughter and Tears," *October* 36 (1986): 95; *OC*, 8:223.

91. Blanchot, "How to Discover the Obscure?" *Infinite Conversation*, 44; *EI*, 63.

92. Robert Antelme, *The Human Race*, trans. Jeffrey Haight and Annie Mahler (Malboro, Vt.: Malboro Press, 1992), 21. Blanchot discusses Antelme's book in "Humankind," *Infinite Conversation*, 130–35; *EI*, 191–200. It would be worthwhile comparing Antelme's narrative with Primo Levi's *If This Is a Man*. In his experience of Auschwitz Levi testifies to the Nazis' attempts to transform human beings into beasts and speaks of the prisoners' sense that "history has stopped." *If This Is a Man/The Truce*, trans. Stuart Wolf, introd. Paul Bailey (Harmondsworth: Penguin, 1979), 47, 112, 123.

93. Blanchot, "Humankind," *Infinite Conversation*, 130; *EI*, 191.

94. It needs to be recalled, however, that Blanchot's "L'Indestructible" appeared in *La Nouvelle Revue Française* 112 (April 1962) and was later divided into two texts: "Le Rapport du troisième genre (*homme sans horizon*)" and "L'Indestructible" in *L'Entretien infini*, 99–100, 102–3, and 191–200.

95. Blanchot to Bataille, August 8, [1960?], *Georges Bataille: Choix de lettres 1917–1962*, 592.

96. Blanchot, *Step Not Beyond*, 6; *PAD*, 15. Heidegger speaks of the "I" as a "non-committal formal indicator." *Being and Time*, 152.

97. Proust, *In Search of Lost Time*, vol. 5: *The Fugitive*, 660.

98. Blanchot, *Last Man*, 10–11; *Le Dernier Homme*, new ed. (1957; Paris: Gallimard, 1985), 22. Compare this passage with the following: *"And when we ask ourselves the question 'Who was the subject of this experience?' this question is perhaps already an answer if, even to him who led it, the experience asserted itself in this interrogative form, by substituting the openness of a*

'Who?' without answer for the closed and singular 'I'; not that this means that he had simply to ask himself 'What is this I that I am?' but much more radically to recover himself without reprieve, no longer as 'I' but as a 'Who?', the unknown and slippery being of an infinite 'Who?'" "Friendship," *Friendship*, 291; *A*, 328.

99. Heidegger, *Basic Problems of Phenomenology*, 120.

100. Heidegger, *Being and Time*, 150.

101. Blanchot, "Who?" in *Who Comes after the Subject?* ed. Eduardo Cadava, Peter Conner, and Jean-Luc Nancy (New York: Routledge, 1991), 59.

102. Blanchot, *The One Who Was Standing Apart from Me*, 65; *CQMP*, 122–23.

103. Blanchot discusses the founding of community in *Unavowable Community*, 9; *CI*, 22. See Blanchot's comments on May 1968 on pp. 29–31. According to Lévinas, Blanchot "experienced 1968 in an extraordinary manner. He always chose the least expected, most noble and difficult path. This moral elevation, this fundamentally aristocratic nature of thinking, is what counts the most and edifies." *Is It Righteous to Be? Interviews with Emmanuel Lévinas*, ed. Jill Robbins (Stanford: Stanford University Press, 2001), 29.

104. Blanchot, *Awaiting Oblivion*; trans. John Gregg (Lincoln: University of Nebraska Press, 1997), 16; *L'Attente l'oubli* (Paris: Gallimard, 1962), 34.

105. Blanchot, *Writing of the Disaster*, 37; *ED*, 65. It would be worthwhile to devote a patient analysis to Blanchot's remarks, as quoted, and the following observations by Merleau-Ponty: "We are not in some incomprehensible way an activity joined to a passivity, an automatism surmounted by a will, a perception surmounted by a judgment, but wholly active and wholly passive, because we are the upsurge of time." *Phenomenology of Perception*, 428.

106. Blanchot, "Reflections on Nihilism," *Infinite Conversation*, 152; *EI*, 228.

107. Blanchot, "The Ease of Dying," *Friendship*, 161; *A*, 184.

CHAPTER FIVE

1. Blanchot discusses behaviorism, however, in the context of Alain's writings. See "Vigiles de l'esprit," *Journal des Débats*, October 14, 1942, 3.

2. Blanchot, "De Jean-Paul à Giraudoux," *Journal des Débats*, February 3, 1944, 2. Certainly Blanchot distances himself from Jean-Paul's prizing of the "I."

3. Blanchot, "L'Expérience de Proust," *Journal des Débats*, May 12, 1943, 3; "L'Expérience magique d'Henri Michaux," *Journal des Débats*, August 17, 1944, 2–3; "Gide et la littérature d'expérience," *L'Arche* 23 (1947): 87–98; "L'Expérience de Lautréamont" appeared under that title in the revised edition of *Lautréamont et Sade* (Paris: Éditions de Minuit, 1963). Blanchot used the title "L'Expérience de Proust" again, this time to embrace two essays in *Le Livre à venir*. In the years to come Blanchot used the word in other titles, most notably in "L'Art, la littérature et l'expérience originelle" (1952), "Mallarmé et l'expérience littéraire" (1952), and "L'Expérience d'Igitur" (1953). He returned to consider Michaux and the theme of experience in "L'Honneur des poètes," *L'Arche* 18–19 (1946): 171–73.

4. Jean Pfeiffer, "L'Expérience de Maurice Blanchot," *Empédocle* 11 (1950): 55. Since the

French word *vécu* does not come up in this chapter, I will use the English word *experience* to translate "expérience." Pfeiffer wrote other pieces on Blanchot, most notably "La Passion de l'imaginaire," *Critique* 229 (1966): 571–78, and "Approche partielle de *L'Entretien infini,*" *Obliques* 2 (1972): 106–7, neither of which sees Blanchot in quite the Hegelian manner of his first essay. He returned to write on *L'Arrêt de mort* in "*L'Arrêt de mort* et le problème du récit," *Cahiers du Chemin* 24 (1975).

5. Husserl, *Logical Investigations*, trans. J. N. Findlay, 2 vols. (London: Routledge and Kegan Paul, 1970), 2:540.

6. Heidegger, *Zur Bestimmung der Philosophie*, ed. B. Heimbüchel, *Gesamtausgabe*, series ed. Herman Heidegger, vol. 56/57 (Frankfurt: Klostermann, 1987), 89, 117.

7. Michel Leiris comments on the word *expérience* in *Scratches*, trans. Lydia Davis (Baltimore: Johns Hopkins University Press, 1991), 97–98. That Leiris admired Bataille's *L'Expérience intérieure* is attested by Aliette Armel in her biography, *Michel Leiris* (Paris: Fayard, 1997), 434.

8. Bataille, *Inner Experience*, 7; *OC*, 5:19–20. *Anschauung* is best translated as "awareness," while *Intuition* denotes the reception of information.

9. Pfeiffer would surely be thinking, among other things, of his own work in the genre of the récit. Introducing his third book, he says it is not simply a journal, for "Elle ne sert pas à retracer ou à noter le développement d'une expérience, mais à la vivre." *Traité de l'aventure* (Paris: Éditions de Minuit, 1946), 8. This vitalism can be traced back to his poems, *La Vie exclusive* (Brussels: La Jeune Muse, 1938).

10. Bataille, *Inner Experience*, 7; *OC*, 5:19.

11. Blanchot, *Death Sentence*, 1; *AM*, 7.

12. Heidegger, "The Origin of the Work of Art," *Poetry, Language, Thought*, 72.

13. Hegel, *Phenomenology of Mind*, 160.

14. Kojève recasts Hegel's view in more dramatic terms when he observes that "*conceptual comprehension* (Begreifen) is equivalent to *murder.*" *Introduction à la lecture de Hegel*, 372.

15. Blanchot, "Literature and the Right to Death," *Work of Fire*, 323; *PF*, 313.

16. Ibid., 322; 312.

17. Blanchot, "Baudelaire's Failure," *Work of Fire*, 149; *PF*, 149.

18. See Hegel, *Phenomenology of Mind*, 96, 142–43.

19. Blanchot, *Lautréamont et Sade*, 90. The significance of the passage for Blanchot is attested by the fact that it appeared the year before in "Lautréamont ou l'espérance d'une tête," *Cahiers d'art* 1, no. 1 (1948): 70.

20. Hegel, *Phenomenology of Mind*, 801.

21. Blanchot, "Gazes from Beyond the Grave," *Work of Fire*, 244; *PF*, 238.

22. See Blanchot, "Literature and the Right to Death," 301; *PF*, 294.

23. Blanchot, "Gide and the Literature of Experience," *Work of Fire*, 224; *PF*, 220. Cf. Blanchot's remarks on experience in Gide in "On the Subject of *The Fruits of the Earth,*" *Faux Pas*, 298; *FP*, 339.

24. Blanchot, "Reflections on Surrealism," *Work of Fire*, 89; *PF*, 94.

25. See Michel Foucault, *The Order of Things: An Archeology of the Human Sciences*, no trans.

(London: Tavistock, 1970), 383–84. Deleuze clearly points out the main lines of influence running from Blanchot to Foucault in his *Negotiations 1972–1990*, trans. Martin Joughin (New York: Columbia University Press, 1995), 97. Also see his *Foucault*, trans. Seán Hand (London: Athlone Press, 1988), 14, 87.

26. See Foucault, "Maurice Blanchot: The Thought from Outside," in *Foucault/Blanchot*, trans. Jeffrey Mehlman and Brian Mussumi (New York: Zone Books, 1999), 9–19.

27. Pseudo-Dionysius Areopagite, *The Divine Names and Mystical Theology*, trans. John D. Jones (Milwaukee: Marquette University Press, 1980), 649A.

28. Blanchot, "The Experience of Proust," *Book to Come*, 14; *LV*, 23.

29. Saint Augustine, *Of True Religion*, 29.72, in *Augustine: Earlier Writings*, ed. John H. S. Burleigh, Library of Christian Classics (London: SCM Press, 1953), 262.

30. Husserl, *Cartesian Meditations*, 157.

31. See Blanchot, "Atheism and Writing, Humanism and the Cry," *Infinite Conversation*, especially 252–53; *EI*, 377–79.

32. Blanchot would also be critical of a later scenario, aptly summed up by Henri Bergson. "The philosopher," Bergson says, "may hypostatize the unity of nature, or, what comes to the same thing, the unity of science, in a being who is nothing since he does nothing, an ineffectual God who simply sums up in himself all the given; or in an eternal Matter from whose womb has been poured out the properties of things and the laws of nature; or, again, in a pure Form which endeavors to seize an unseizable multiplicity, and which is, as we will, the form of nature or the form of thought." *Creative Evolution*, trans. Arthur Mitchell (1911; rpt. Boston: University Press of America, 1983), 196–97.

33. See Plotinus, *Enneads*, 5.4, and Proclus, *The Platonic Theology*, trans. Thomas Taylor, preface by R. Baine Harris, 2 vols. (Kew Gardens, N.Y.: Selene Books, 1985), vol. 1, book 3, chap. 3. Hans Urs von Balthasar observes, "the concept of unity, which everyone takes for granted as something well known and transparently obvious, is at bottom as full of mystery as all the other fundamental concepts pertaining to being. We do not know what unity is in truth." *Theo-Logic: Theological Logical Theory*, 3 vols., vol. 1: *Truth of the Word*, trans. Adrian J. Walker (San Francisco: Ignatius Press, 2000), 157.

34. See Irenaeus, *Adversus Haereses*, 2.1.5.

35. See Aquinas, *Summa theologiae*, 1a, 2, 2 ad. 1.

36. Aquinas notes that "there is nothing to stop a man accepting on faith some truth which he personally cannot demonstrate, even if that truth in itself is such that demonstration could make it evident." *Summa theologiae*, 1a, 2, 2, ad. 1.

37. See Aquinas, *Summa contra gentiles*, 5 vols., trans. and introd. Anton C. Pegis (Notre Dame: University of Notre Dame Press, 1975), I, 42, 1.

38. See *Proclus' Commentary on Plato's "Parmenides*," trans. Glenn R. Morrow and John M. Dillon, introd. and notes by John M. Dillon (Princeton: Princeton University Press, 1987), 557–78.

39. Proclus, *Alcibiades I*, trans. and commentary by William O'Neill (The Hague: Martinus Nijhoff, 1965), 162. Also see his "On Providence, Fate and That Which Is within Our Power," in *Essays and Fragments of Proclus the Platonic Successor*, trans. Thomas Taylor (1788–1825; rpt. Frome: Prometheus Trust, 1999), §§ 19, 24.

40. Doubtless Blanchot would agree with Heidegger that there are complex links between the philosophy of subjectivity and the Christian era. Unlike him, though, he does not urge a methodological atheism in order to release thought into its own possibilities or to render human being open to God. On the connections of atheism and subjectivity according to Heidegger, see Laurence Paul Hemming, *Heidegger's Atheism: The Refusal of a Theological Voice* (Notre Dame: University of Notre Dame Press, 2002), 173–77.

41. See Martin Jay's intriguing essay "Experience without a Subject: Walter Benjamin and the Novel," *Cultural Semantics: Keywords of Our Time* (Amherst: University of Massachusetts Press, 1998), 47–61.

42. Foucault, *Order of Things*, xiv.

43. Blanchot, "Atheism and Writing," *Infinite Conversation*, 250; *EI*, 374.

44. Blanchot, *Space of Literature*, 238, 75, 31, 242–43; *EL*, 318, 89, 27, 326.

45. Foucault, "Maurice Blanchot," 54.

46. See Deleuze, *Foucault*, 93. Also see *Foucault*, 87, and *Negotiations*, 110.

47. Blanchot, "À toute extrémité," *La Nouvelle NRF* 26 (1955): 299. All further references to this essay will be incorporated into the text. Blanchot cannibalized this essay for passages in *L'Espace littéraire*, 101–6, and *Le Livre à venir*, 147–48, but never reprinted the passage from which I have quoted. Also see Blanchot's remarks on experience and literature in the closing sentences of "L'Étranger et l'étranger," 682–83. Earlier in that article, it should be noted, Blanchot had pointed out, "La pensée est elle-même et pour elle-même son expérience" (674).

48. Proust, *In Search of Lost Time*, vol. 4: *Sodom and Gomorrah*, 434.

49. With respect to Simone Weil, Blanchot construes mystical experience as "The experience of what cannot be grasped through experience," a formulation that could encompass both mystical and limit-experience. See "Affirmation (desire, affliction)," *Infinite Conversation*, 107; *EI*, 154. It should be noted that Lévinas also entertains the notion of an "absolute experience." See *Totality and Infinity*, 65–66; *TI*, 61.

50. Blanchot, "The Experience of Proust," *Faux Pas*, 42; *FP*, 53.

51. Blanchot, "The Pursuit of the Zero Point," trans. Ian Maclachlan, in *Blanchot Reader*, 149; *LV*, 284.

52. Blanchot, "The Experience of Proust," *Book to Come*, 14; *LV*, 23.

53. A recent translation of Verlaine's influential and much-quoted poem runs as follows:

> *Let your verse be aimless chance, delighting*
> *In good-omened fortune, sprinkled over*
> *Dawn's wind, bristling scents of mint, thyme, clover . . .*
> *All the rest is nothing more than writing.*

One Hundred and One Poems by Paul Verlaine, Norman R. Shapiro, trans. (Chicago: University of Chicago Press, 1999), 129.

54. Blanchot, *The One Who Was Standing Apart from Me*, 89, 90; *CQMP*, 167, 168–69. Let me add that Derrida's comments on Blanchot's lack of morbidity are exemplary: "Maurice Blanchot loved, affirmed, only life and living, and the light of appearing. We have a thousand

indications of this, both in his texts and in the way he held on to life, in the way he *preferred* life, until the end. With, dare I say it, a singular gaiety, the gaiety of affirmation and of 'yes,' a different gaiety from that of *gai savoir*, less cruel perhaps, but a gaiety, the joy itself of happiness which even mildly sharp ears couldn't fail to perceive." "A Witness Forever," trans. Charlotte Mandell, in Hart, *Nowhere without No*, 39.

55. See *Selected Letters of Stéphane Mallarmé*, ed. and trans. Rosemary Lloyd (Chicago: University of Chicago Press, 1988), 60.

56. Blanchot, *Space of Literature*, 38; *EL*, 37.

57. Blanchot, "Hölderlin's Itinerary," *Space of Literature*, 275; *EL*, 372.

58. Blanchot, *Space of Literature*, 38; *EL*, 38.

59. Blanchot, "The Great Refusal," *Infinite Conversation*, 42; *EI*, 59.

60. Kant, *Critique of Pure Reason*, A218/B265.

61. Blanchot, "How to Discover the Obscure," *Infinite Conversation*, 42; *EI*, 59.

62. Blanchot, "The Two Versions of the Imaginary," *Space of Literature*, 260; *EL*, 350.

63. Ibid., 258; 347.

64. Heidegger, *Being and Time*, 281, 238.

65. See Blanchot, "Friendship," *Friendship*, 292; *A*, 330. Also see Blanchot's moving response to the death of Robert Antelme, "Dans la nuit surveillée," in Robert Antelme, *Textes inédites sur "L'Espèce humaine": Essais et Témoignages* (Paris: Gallimard, 1996), 71–72.

66. Heidegger, *Being and Time*, 88, 61. Heidegger introduces the notion of obtrusiveness on 103, 73.

67. Such is Aquinas's view. See his *Summa theologiae*, 2a2æ. q.175 art. 4.

68. Karl Barth, *Church Dogmatics*, 4 vols., I.ii, ed. G. W. Bromiley and T. F. Torrance, trans. G. T. Thomson and Harold Knight (Edinburgh: T. and T. Clark, 1956), 532.

69. See Karl Rahner, "The 'Spiritual Senses' according to Origen," *Theological Investigations*, vol. 16: *Experience of the Spirit: Source of Theology*, trans. David Morland (London: Darton, Longman and Todd, 1979), 81–134. Also see Jacopone di Todi, *Le Laude*, ed. Luigi Fallacara (Florence: Libreria Editrice Fiorentina, 1955), 356.

70. Friedrich Schleiermacher, *On Religion: Speeches to Its Cultured Despisers*, trans. John Oman, introd. Rudolf Otto (New York: Harper and Row, 1958), 43.

71. Rahner, *Foundations of Christian Faith: An Introduction to the Idea of Christianity*, trans. William V. Dych (New York: Seabury Press, 1978), 20–21.

72. Eberhard Jüngel, *God as the Mystery of the World: On the Foundation of the Theology of the Crucified One in the Dispute between Theism and Atheism*, trans. Darrell L. Guder (Grand Rapids: William B. Eerdmans, 1983), 32. Jüngel refers to Heidegger's account of *Angst* though he makes no reference to Heidegger's early use of the expression "experience of experience" ("Erleben des Erlebens").

73. Hegel, *Lectures on the Philosophy of Religion*, ed. Peter C. Hodgson, trans. R. F. Brown et al., 3 vols. (Los Angeles: University of California Press, 1984–85), 1:227. In 1824 Hegel speaks instead of a "*counterthrust*" (1:322).

74. Also see Hegel, *Phenomenology of Mind*, 800.

75. Blanchot, "The Great Refusal," *Infinite Conversation*, 45; *EI*, 64. *Writing of the Disaster*, 15: *ED*, 30.

76. See Jean-Luc Marion, *Being Given: Toward a Phenomenology of Givenness*, trans. Jeffrey L. Kosky (Stanford: Stanford University Press, 2002), 114.

77. Blanchot, "The Limit-Experience," *Infinite Conversation*, 207; *EI*, 308.

78. Deleuze, *Foucault*, 7.

79. Foucault, "The Order of Discourse," trans. Ian McLeod, in *Untying the Text: A Post-Structuralist Reader*, ed. and introd. Robert Young (London: Routledge and Kegan Paul, 1981), 51; "What Is an Author?" in *Language, Counter-Memory, Practice: Selected Essays and Interviews*, ed. and introd. Donald F. Bouchard, trans. Donald F. Bouchard and Sherry Simon (Ithaca: Cornell University Press, 1977), 138.

80. Adam Zagajewski, *Another Beauty*, trans. Clare Cavanagh (New York: Farrar, Straus and Giroux, 1998), 28.

81. Blanchot, "Ars Nova," *Infinite Conversation*, 348; *EI*, 511. My emphases.

82. Blanchot, "Note," *Infinite Conversation*, xii; *EI*, viii. It should be underlined, however, that no community is meant to survive. See Blanchot, *Unavowable Community*, 30, 32; *CI*, 52, 56.

83. Blanchot, *Step Not Beyond*, 49; *PAD*, 71.

84. For Blanchot's response to *Ostinato*, see "Le blanc Le noir," *Une Voix venue d'ailleurs: Sur les poèmes de Louis-René des Forêts* (Dijon: Ulysse Fin de Siècle, 1992), 21–24.

85. Adorno, *Philosophy of Modern Music*, trans. Anne G. Mitchell and Wesley V. Blomster (New York: Seabury Press, 1973), 181.

86. Walter Benjamin, "The Task of the Translator," *Selected Writings*, gen. ed. Michael W. Jennings, 3 vols., vol. 1: 1913–1926, ed. Marcus Bullock and Michael W. Jennings (Cambridge: Belknap Press of Harvard University Press, 1996), 260.

87. See Friedrich Schlegel, *Philosophical Fragments*, trans. Peter Firchow, foreword by Rodolphe Gasché (Minneapolis: University of Minnesota Press, 1991), especially ix, xxvii. Also see Philippe Lacoue-Labarthe and Jean-Luc Nancy, *The Literary Absolute: The Theory of Literature in German Romanticism*, trans. Philip Barnard and Cheryl Lester (Albany: State University of New York Press, 1988), chap. 1.

88. Blanchot, "Translating," *Friendship*, 61; *A*, 73.

89. Benjamin, *The Origin of German Tragic Drama*, trans. John Osborne (London: NLB, 1977), 29.

90. Franz Rosenzweig, *The Star of Redemption*, trans. William W. Hallo (Notre Dame: University of Notre Dame Press, 1985), 12.

91. Simone Weil, *Notebooks*, trans. Arthur Wills, 2 vols. (London: Routledge and Kegan Paul, 1976), 2:417.

92. See, for example, David Tracy, "Fragments: The Spiritual Situation of Our Times," in *God, the Gift, and Postmodernism*, ed. John D. Caputo and Michael J. Scanlon (Bloomington: Indiana University Press, 1999), especially 178–81.

93. See Jean-Louis Chrétien, *The Unforgettable and the Unhoped For*, trans. Jeffrey Bloechl (New York: Fordham University Press, 2002), 121–22.

94. Blanchot, *Writing of the Disaster*, 20: *ED*, 38.
95. Gilles Deleuze and Félix Guattari, *Anti-Oedipus: Capitalism and Schizophrenia*, trans. Robert Hurley, Mark Seem, and Helen R. Lane (New York: Viking, 1977), 42.
96. See Deleuze and Guattari, *A Thousand Plateaus: Capitalism and Schizophrenia*, trans. and foreword by Brian Massumi (Minneapolis: University of Minnesota Press, 1987), 265.
97. Blanchot, "Michel Foucault As I Imagine Him," *Foucault/Blanchot*, 76–77; *Michel Foucault tel que je l'imagine* (Montpellier: Fata Morgana, 1986), 29. My emphasis.
98. Blanchot, "Atheism and Writing, Humanism and the Cry," *Infinite Conversation*, 251; *EI*, 375. Blanchot could have deduced the same consequence from Derrida's early writing.
99. Blanchot, "The Great Refusal," *Infinite Conversation*, 44; *EI*, 62.
100. Heidegger's fullest remarks on attunements are given in his *The Fundamental Concepts of Metaphysics: World, Finitude, Solitude*, trans. William McNeill and Nicholas Walker (Bloomington: Indiana University Press, 1995), part 1.
101. Blanchot, "Everyday Speech," *Infinite Conversation*, 240; *EI*, 357.
102. See ibid., §§ 19–38.
103. Blanchot, "Hölderlin's Itinerary," *Space of Literature*, 275; *EL*, 372.
104. Durkheim, *Elementary Forms of Religious Life*, 208.
105. Blanchot, *Infinite Conversation*, xii; *EI*, vii.
106. Blanchot, "How to Discover the Obscure," *Infinite Conversation*, 45; *EI*, 63.
107. Roberto Juarroz, *Vertical Poetry*, trans. W. S. Merwin (San Francisco: North Point Press, 1988), 136.
108. Blanchot, "The Limit-Experience," *Infinite Conversation*, 207; *EI*, 307–8.
109. Blanchot, "Mystery in Literature," *Work of Fire*, 57; *PF*, 63.

CHAPTER SIX

1. Blanchot, "Paix, paix au lointain et au proche," *De la Bible à nos jours: 3000 ans d'art* (Paris: Société des Artistes Indépendants, 1985), 53. My translation. The first part of this essay was reprinted in *Le Nouvel Observateur*, 31 May–6 June 1985, 79.
2. Blanchot, *Step Not Beyond*, 15; *PAD*, 26.
3. See Franz Rosenzweig, "'The Eternal': Mendelssohn and the Name of God," in Martin Buber and Franz Rosenzweig's *Scripture and Translation*, trans. Lawrence Rosenwald with Everett Fox (Bloomington: Indiana University Press, 1994), 99–113.
4. Blanchot, "The Most Profound Question," *Infinite Conversation*, 14; *EI*, 17.
5. Yet see Blanchot's remarks on symbolic readings of the Bible in "Prophetic Speech," *Book to Come*, 84; *LV*, 117.
6. Some of Blanchot's strongest fiction involves a reflection of the failure of allegory. *L'Arrêt de mort*, for instance, could be read as a contestation of the very allegory—the parallel between J. and France—that generates it.
7. Blanchot, "The Essential Solitude," *Space of Literature*, 23; *EL*, 17. On the question of translating Scripture, see Blanchot, "Les Quatre Évangiles," *Journal des Débats*, January 27,

1944, 2–3. And for Blanchot's admiration for the Jerusalem Bible, see "Prophetic Speech," *Book to Come*, 257 n 14; *LV*, 119 n 1.

8. Blanchot, "Reading," *Space of Literature*, 195; *EL*, 256.

9. Unlike the description "Hebrew Bible," the acronym Tanakh—Torah, Neviim and Ketuvim—has the virtue of not erasing the Aramaic passages in Jewish Scripture. Blanchot, however, like most Jews, uses the word "Bible" when speaking of the Law, the Prophets, and the Writings.

10. Blanchot, "Paix, paix au lointain et au proche," 53.

11. Blanchot, *Writing of the Disaster*, 141; *ED*, 214.

12. Blanchot, "The Great Refusal," *Infinite Conversation*, 40, 39; *EI*, 56, 55. In the French original, Blanchot quotes Hölderlin in French translation.

13. I am alluding to Blanchot's essay "The 'Sacred' Speech of Hölderlin," in his *The Work of Fire*, discussed in chapter 3.

14. Christopher Fynsk, "Foreword" to *The Station Hill Blanchot Reader: Fiction and Literary Essays*, ed. George Quasha, trans. Lydia Davis et al. (Barrytown, N.Y.: Station Hill Press, 1999), xix.

15. George Quasha and Charles Stein, "Afterword," *Station Hill Blanchot Reader*, 523.

16. Scholars knew from Hippolytus that there had been a Gospel of Thomas. See Hippolytus, Bishop of Portus, *The Refutation of All Heresies*, trans. J. H. MacMahon, The Ante-Nicene Christian Library, 10 vols. (1994; rpt. Edinburgh: T. and T. Clark, 1886), vol. 5: *The Refutation of All Heresies*, book 5, chap. 2, p. 48. Fragments of the Greek version of the Gospel were discovered at the beginning of the twentieth century in the Oxyrhynchus Papyri, but they were identified as part of the Gospel only after the findings at Nag Hammadi. Blanchot might have encountered the apocryphal *Acts of Thomas*, in which Thomas is presented as Jesus's twin, and he might have known the Infancy Gospel of Thomas, but no evidence of either is apparent. What is important is that "Thomas" is a Semitic word for twin.

17. Blanchot, *Most High*, 136; *TH*, 133. For a consideration of the apocalypse and politics, also see Blanchot, "Une Étude sur l'apocalypse," *Journal des Débats*, November 3, 1943, 3.

18. See Mark Brett's discussion of this point in his *Genesis: Procreation and the Politics of Identity* (London: Routledge, 2000), 55.

19. Michel Foucault's argument that "Sorge wears a mask from Greek tragedy" is important here. See Foucault and Blanchot's joint volume, *Foucault/Blanchot*, 39–40. Blanchot himself indicates the pertinence of Antigone in his sleevenote for the 1988 reedition of *Le Très-Haut*.

20. There is considerable doubt that "Amminadib" is indeed a proper name in Cant. 6:12. More likely than not, two Hebrew words—*ammi* (my people) and *nadib* (prince)—have been run together. The most thoughtful work on the significance of the novel's title is Michael Holland's essay "Qui est l'Aminadab de Blanchot?" *Revue des Sciences Humaines* 253 (1999): 21–42.

21. In "The Birth Mark" Nathaniel Hawthorne depicts a man called Aminadab who is the servant of Aylmer. Aminadab is characterized as "a man of low stature, but bulky frame, with

shaggy hair hanging about his visage, which was grimed with the vapors of the furnace . . .
he seemed to represent man's physical nature; while Aylmer's slender figure, and pale, intellectual face, were no less apt a type of the spiritual element." *Mosses from an Old Manse,*
Centenary Edition of the Works of Nathaniel Hawthorne, 23 vols. (Columbus: Ohio State
University Press, 1974), 10:43.

22. Marie-Anne Lescourret, *Emmanuel Lévinas* (Paris: Flammarion, 1994), 68.

23. Blanchot, *Aminadab,* 186; *Am.,* 213. Any reader of Kafka is likely to think of his story "Before the Law," although it seems that Blanchot had not read Kafka at this time.

24. Blanchot, *When the Time Comes,* 65; *AMV,* 147. The story of Abraham and Isaac is also considered, and from the same perspective, in "Kafka and Literature," *Work of Fire,* 14–15; *PF,*
22. Also see the reference to Isaac in *Thomas the Obscure,* 94; *TO* (2), 107.

25. The debate is reviewed by Gary D. Mole in his "Blanchot's *Au moment voulu* and the Silence of Abraham," *Australian Journal of French Studies* 32, no. 1 (1995): 58–63.

26. See Michel, *Maurice Blanchot et le déplacement d'Orphée,* 151–58.

27. Blanchot, "Reading," *Space of Literature,* 195; *EL,* 257.

28. Blanchot, "Literature and the Right to Death," *Work of Fire,* 327; *PF,* 316.

29. Ibid., 326; *PF,* 315–16. Hegel remarks, "Der erste Act, wodurch Adam seine Herrschafft
über die Thiere constitutiert hat, ist, daß er ihnen Nahmen gab, d.h. sie als seiende ver-
nichtete, und sie zu für sich ideellen macht . . . Im Nahmen ist die für sich seyende Real-
ität des Zeichens vernichtet." *Jenaer Systementwürfe,* vol. 1, ed. K. Düsing and H. Kim-
merle, *Gesammelte Werke* (Hamburg: Felix Meiner, 1975), 6:20.

30. Hegel, *Phenomenology of Mind,* 160.

31. See Jean Hyppolite, "The Ineffable," in his *Logic and Existence,* trans. Leonard Lawlor and
Amit Sen (Albany: State University of New York Press, 1997). The original French volume
appeared in 1953, several years after the first publication of Blanchot's "La Littérature et
le droit à la mort." Later, Blanchot thinks the Other by way of God. See "Being Jewish,"
Infinite Conversation, 129; *EI,* 188.

32. Blanchot, *Thomas the Obscure,* 89; *TO* (2), 100.

33. A summary of patristic commentary on the passage is given by Saint Thomas Aquinas in
the *Catena Aurea,* 4 vols. (Albany: Preserving Christian Publications, Inc., 1999), vol. 2:
St Mark, 97–104.

34. See Gospel of Nicodemus, or Acts of Pilate, 7, in *The Apocryphal New Testament,* trans.
and notes by M. R. James (Oxford: Clarendon Press, 1924). The woman's name is
Beronice in Coptic and Veronica in Latin. In view of the tradition of Veronica's image of
Jesus, the chances are that the name occurs as a corruption of *vera icon,* "true image."
Also see Macarius Magnes, *Apocriticus,* trans. T. W. Crafter (New York: Macmillan,
1919), 1:31.

35. Leslie Hill develops an intriguing political reading of the dates in *L'Arrêt de mort* in *Blanchot: Extreme Contemporary,* 145–47. His reading and mine are not mutually exclusive.

36. Blanchot, "The Great Refusal," *Infinite Conversation,* 36; *EI,* 50.

37. Blanchot, "Literature and the Right to Death," *Work of Fire,* 328; *PF,* 317.

38. Blanchot, "Glances from beyond the Grave," *Work of Fire,* 255; *PF,* 248.

39. Blanchot, "Pascal's Hand," *Work of Fire*, 263; *PF*, 255.

40. Blanchot, *Awaiting Oblivion*, 28; *AO*, 56.

41. Jacques Derrida argues that the récit does not take the Gospel as a paradigm but rather is a "seriality without paradigm." See his "Living On: Border Lines," trans. James Hulbert, *Deconstruction and Criticism*, ed. Geoffrey Hartman (London: Routledge and Kegan Paul, 1979), 130. For Derrida, J.'s revival is a "resurrection." See "Living On," 117, 125, 149.

42. Blanchot, *The One Who Was Standing Apart from Me*, 43; *CQMP*, 83. Also see the comments on mystery in *Awaiting Oblivion*, 56; *AO*, 108.

43. See Blanchot's author's note at the beginning of *The Space of Literature* and also his letter to Evelyn Londyn quoted in her "L'Orphique chez Blanchot: voir et dire," *French Forum* 3, no. 3 (1980): 261–67.

44. See Blanchot, "Rilke and Death's Demand," *Space of Literature*, 157; *EL*, 206. A quite different reading of the rose, based on Paulhan's *Les Fleurs de Tarbes*, is offered by Jeffrey Mehlman in "Iphigenia 38: Deconstruction, History, and the Case of *L'Arrêt de mort*," *Genealogies of the Text: Literature, Psychoanalysis, and Politics in Modern France* (Cambridge: Cambridge University Press, 1995), 82–96. Also see Alain P. Toumayan's account of the rose in his *Encountering the Other: The Artwork and the Problem of Difference in Blanchot and Levinas* (Pittsburgh: Duquesne University Press, 2004), 79–80.

45. Blanchot, "Gazes from beyond the Grave," *Work of Fire*, 253; *PF*, 247. Blanchot misquotes the verse so that it reads, "love stronger than death" ("l'amour plus fort que la mort"). La Bible de Jérusalem renders the verse as follows: "Car l'amour est fort comme la Mort." Also see Blanchot's *Unavowable Community*, 45; *CI*, 75.

46. Blanchot, "The Great Refusal," *Infinite Conversation*, 33; *EI*, 46.

47. See Ernst Robert Curtius, *European Literature and the Latin Middle Ages*, trans. Willard R. Trask (New York: Harper and Row, 1953), 310–11.

48. Friedrich Schlegel, "Ideas," § 95, in *Philosophical Fragments*, trans. Peter Firchow, foreword by Rodolphe Gasché (Minneapolis: University of Minnesota Press, 1991), 102. On the absolute book see Blanchot, "The Book to Come," *Book to Come*, 228; *LV*, 309.

49. See Hegel, *Lectures on the Philosophy of Religion*, vol. 3: *The Consummate Religion*, 257–60.

50. In "Lautréamont" Blanchot detects in *Maldoror* a "hidden effort toward a kind of pure book." See *Faux Pas*, 172; *FP*, 197. Blanchot devotes a rich and exacting study to Mallarmé's *Le Livre* and *Un Coup des dés* in the title essay of *The Book to Come*. His interest in the latter, as well as in the figure of the book, can be traced back to "Le Livre," *Journal des Débats*, January 20, 1943, 3.

51. The Greek τὰ βιβλία was translated by the Latin *biblia*, a neuter plural noun, but in late Latin *biblia*, a feminine singular noun, meant "the book," and this lexical misidentification came to hold sway in vernacular translations of *biblia*. Robert Alter testifies to the "extreme heterogeneity" of the Tanakh and then concedes that "the retrospective act of canonization has created a unity among the disparate texts that we as later readers can scarcely ignore; and this unity in turn reflects, though with a pronounced element of exaggeration, an intrinsic feature of the original texts—their powerfully allusive character." *The Literary Guide to the Bible*, ed. Robert Alter and Frank Kermode (London:

Collins, 1987), 12–13. The same point is made with respect to the Christian Bible by Northrop Frye. See his *The Great Code: The Bible and Literature* (New York: Harcourt Brace Jovanovich, 1982), xii–xiii.

52. See Tertullian, *Adversus Marcionem*, ed. and trans. Ernest Evans, 2 vols. (Oxford: Clarendon Press, 1972), vol. 2; Saint Irenaeus, *Proof of the Apostolic Preaching*, trans. and annotated by Joseph P. Smith (Westminster: Newman, 1952), section C; and Origen, *On First Principles*, ed., trans., and notes by G. W. Butterworth, introd. Henri de Lubac (Gloucester, Mass.: Peter Smith, 1973), 6. It is Origen in the passage cited who supplies the first rationale for what has become known as "systematic theology."

53. Blanchot, "Atheism and Writing, Humanism and the Cry," *Infinite Conversation*, 262; *EI*, 392.

54. The matter is considered in detail by Jacob Neusner in his *What, Exactly, Did the Rabbinic Sages Mean by "The Oral Torah"? An Inductive Answer to the Question of Rabbinic Judaism* (Atlanta: Scholars Press, 1998).

55. See Rabbi Isaac the Blind of Provence, "The Mystical Torah—Kabbalistic Creation," *The Early Kabbalah*, ed. and introd. Joseph Dan, trans. Ronald C. Kiener, preface by Moshe Idel (New York: Paulist Press, 1986), 75–76.

56. Blanchot, "The Absence of the Book," *Infinite Conversation*, 430; *EI*, 631.

57. See Blanchot's remarks on Kabbalah in "Gog and Magog," *Friendship*, 230–32; *A*, 261–64. Blanchot concedes that Abraham ben Samuel Abulafia testified to certain experiences, principally for pedagogic reasons. Other exceptions include Rabbi Joseph Karo and Rabbi Hayyim Vital. See *Jewish Mystical Autobiographies*, trans. and introd. Morris M. Faierstein, preface by Moshe Idel (New York: Paulist Press, 1999).

58. See Blanchot, "Thanks (Be Given) to Jacques Derrida," trans. Leslie Hill, *Blanchot Reader*, 321. In this essay Blanchot reflects further on the distinction between oral and written Torah.

59. Blanchot, "The Absence of the Book," *Infinite Conversation*, 433; *EI*, 635.

60. It is likely that Blanchot draws the idea from Meister Eckhart. See his comments on Eckhart in *Faux Pas*, 26; *FP*, 34–35.

61. See Moses Maimonides, *The Guide for the Perplexed*, trans. M. Friedländer, 2nd ed. (London: George Routledge and Sons, 1904), part 2, chap. 1.

62. Blanchot shows little or no interest in historical understandings of "being Jewish." There is no discussion, for instance, of the Jews as those descendants of Abraham who lived in the kingdom of Judah and no distinction drawn between "Hebrew" and "Jew." He declares that the Jews were "constituted as a people by the revelation at Sinai." "Paix, paix au lointain et au proche," 51. For the dubious historicity of Blanchot's claim see Gerhard von Rad, *Old Testament Theology*, trans. D. M. G. Stalker, 2 vols. (London: SCM Press, 1975), 1:6.

63. Blanchot, "Kafka and the Work's Demand," *Space of Literature*, 83; *EL*, 101.

64. Blanchot, "Being Jewish," *Infinite Conversation*, 127–28; *EI*, 187.

65. See Martin Buber, "Spinoza, Sabbatai Zvi, and the Baal-Shem," in his *The Origin and Meaning of Hasidism*, ed. and trans. Maurice Friedman (New York: Harper Torchbooks, 1966), 93. Also see Blanchot, "Prophetic Speech," *Book to Come*, 82; *LV*, 114; "The Pain of

Dialogue," *Book to Come*, 153, 156, 158; *LV*, 212, 215, 217–18. Blanchot is also indebted to André Neher's discussion of prophecy and dialogue in the introduction to *L'Essence du prophetisme* (Paris: Presses Universitaires de France, 1955).

66. See, for example, Buber, *Moses: The Revelation and the Covenant*, no trans. (New York: Harper Torchbooks, 1958), 9–10, and *Two Types of Faith: A Study of the Interpenetration of Judaism and Christianity*, trans. Norman P. Goldhawk (New York: Harper Torchbooks, 1961), 130.

67. Blanchot, "Gog and Magog," *Friendship*, 231; *A*, 263. For a quite different view of dialogue with God, see Karl Rahner, "Dialogue with God," *Theological Investigations*, vol. 18: *God and Revelation*, trans. Edward Quinn (New York: Crossroad, 1983), 122–31. Blanchot makes little here of the role of silence in prophetic speech. Neher talks of "a 'hiding of God's face' because of the sin or the guilt of the enquirer. Sin prevents, as it were, the possibility of a relationship between God and man." *Speech and "Silence" in Prophecy* (Jerusalem: Department for Education and Culture in the Diaspora of the World Zionist Organization and the World Jewish Bible Society, 1969), 6.

68. See Eberhard Jüngel, *Paulus und Jesus: Eine Untersuchung zur Präzisierung der Frage nach dem Ursprung der Christologie* (1962; rpt. Tübingen: J. C. B. Mohr [Paul Siebeck], 1986), 135, thesis 2.

69. Blanchot, "Paix, paix au lointain et au proche," 51. On the theme of a "Jewishness beyond all Judaism" also see Derrida, *Archive Fever: A Freudian Impression*, trans. Eric Prenowitz (Chicago: University of Chicago Press, 1996), 74.

70. Blanchot, "Do Not Forget," trans. Michael Holland, *Blanchot Reader*, 245. In a homage to Edmond Jabès, Blanchot returns to the theme of forgetting and remembering with respect to Exod. 17:14 and Deut. 25:19 in "L'Écriture consacrée au silence," *L'Œil de Bœuf* 14/15 (1998): 81–83.

71. Blanchot, "Paix, paix au lointain et au proche," 51.

72. See Lévinas, *Of God Who Comes to Mind*, trans. Bettina Bergo (Stanford: Stanford University Press, 1998), 68; *De Dieu qui vient à l'idée*, pocket ed. (1982; rpt. Paris: J. Vrin, 1992), 113.

73. Emmanuel Lévinas, "Judaism and the Present," *Difficult Freedom: Essays on Judaism*, trans. Séan Hand (Baltimore: Johns Hopkins University Press, 1990), 211; *Difficile Liberté: essais sur le Judaïsme*, 3rd ed. (Paris: A. Michel, 1983), 295.

74. Lévinas, "Meaning and Sense," *Collected Philosophical Papers*, trans. Alphonso Lingis (The Hague: Martinus Nijhoff, 1987), 92; "La Signification et le sens," *Humanisme de l'autre homme* (Montpellier: Fata Morgana, 1972), 45.

75. Ibid., 89; 40.

76. René Descartes, "Discourse on Method," in *Philosophical Works of Descartes*, trans. Elizabeth S. Haldane and G. R. T. Ross, 2 vols. (Cambridge: Cambridge University Press, 1972), 1:17.

77. Lévinas, "Language and Proximity," *Collected Philosophical Papers*, 122; *En découvrant l'existence avec Husserl et Heidegger*, expanded ed. (Paris: J. Vrin, 1994), 232.

78. Robert Antelme, *Human Race*, 219. The point is usually associated with Herder, though in

a different context. Elsewhere, Blanchot admits the possibility of a "union that does not make a unity," though it is unclear what this would be. See his *Le Dernier à parler* (Montpellier: Fata Morgana, 1984), 11. Sarah Kofman points out that Antelme's "fierce affirmation of the unity of the species does not amount to the denial of differences or, indeed, oppositions. On the contrary, it is because no community is possible with the SS that there is also the strongest community, the community (of those) without community." *Smothered Words*, 70.

79. Lévinas, "The Vocation of the Other," *Is It Righteous to Be?* 113.
80. Blanchot, "The Absence of the Book," *Infinite Conversation*, 433; *EI*, 635.
81. See Blanchot, "Paix, paix au lointain et au proche," 53, and *Unavowable Community*, 56; *CI*, 91–92.
82. Blanchot, "Being Jewish," *Infinite Conversation*, 125; *EI*, 182.
83. A sympathetic though nonetheless reserved discussion along these lines is provided by Eberhard Jüngel in his essay "The Dogmatic Significance of the Question of the Historical Jesus," *Theological Essays*, 2 vols., vol. 2, ed. and introd. J. B. Webster, trans. Arnold Neufeldt-Fast and J. B. Webster (Edinburgh: T. and T. Clark, 1995), 97–99.
84. Lévinas, *Nine Talmudic Readings*, trans. Annette Aronowicz (Bloomington: Indiana University Press, 1990), 93; *Du sacré au saint: Cinq nouvelles lectures talmudiques* (Paris: Éditions de Minuit, 1997), 10. Lévinas admits that "the sacred is the ambience in which holiness often dwells." Raoul Mortley, "Emmanuel Lévinas," *French Philosophers Talking* (London: Routledge, 1991), 17. Also see *Nine Talmudic Readings*, 145, 17; *DSS*, 96, *Quatre Lectures talmudiques* (Paris: Éditions de Minuit, 1968), 39.
85. See Blanchot, "On a Change of Epoch: The Exigency of Return," *Infinite Conversation*, 279; *EI*, 417. Blanchot places scare quotes around "ethical."
86. Blanchot, "Do Not Forget," 245.
87. Blanchot, "Being Jewish," *Infinite Conversation*, 124; *EI*, 181. Students of English literature will recall a not dissimilar argument in Matthew Arnold's *Literature and Dogma* and F. H. Bradley's sharp reply to his reasoning there in his *Ethical Studies*, 2nd ed. (Oxford: Clarendon Press, 1927), 318 n. 2.
88. Rosenzweig, *Star of Redemption*, 409.
89. André Neher, *Moses and the Vocation of the Jewish People*, trans. Irene Marinoff (New York: Harper, 1959), 162. The book first appeared in French in 1956.
90. Hans Urs von Balthasar quotes from Heinrich Schlier's "Das Mysterium Israels," *Die Zeit der Kirche: Exegetische Aufsätz und Vorträge* (Freiburg: Herder, 1966), 232–33. See his *Theo-Drama: Theological Dramatic Theory*, 5 vols., vol. 3: *Dramatis Personae: Persons in Christ*, trans. Graham Harrison (San Francisco: Ignatius Press, 1992), 372. I am indebted to Balthasar's volume for the reference to Schlier's study and for his discussion of it.
91. Lévinas quotes a letter to that effect from Blanchot in "Judaism and Revolution," *Nine Talmudic Readings*, 115–16; *DSS*, 48–49. The paper was first presented at the 1969 Colloque des Intellectuels Juifs de langue française. Lévinas does not name Blanchot although there can be no doubt that the letter is his.

92. The first quotation is taken from a passage of a letter to Roger Laporte that Leslie Hill cites in his introduction to Gill, *Maurice Blanchot: The Demand of Writing*, 10. The second quotation is taken from Blanchot, "Traces," *Friendship*, 223; *A*, 252.

93. Lévinas, "Interview with Salomon Malka," *Is It Righteous to Be?* 97. Blanchot alludes to this statement in a footnote to his letter to Malka. Also see, in this regard, Dionys Mascolo's remarks on the metaphysical status of the Jews in his recollections of working for the Resistance in Robert Antelme, *Textes inédits*, 265–66.

94. See Aquinas, *Faith, Reason and Theology*, q. III, art. 1.

95. Without quite endorsing Blanchot's phrasing, Edmond Jabès is sympathetic to Blanchot's remarks on exodus and exile. See his *From the Desert to the Book: Dialogues with Marcel Cohen*, trans. Pierre Joris (Barrytown, N.Y.: Station Hill Press, 1990), 68.

96. See Blanchot, *Writing of the Disaster*, 64; *ED*, 106.

97. Blanchot, "Knowledge of the Unknown," *Infinite Conversation*, 56; *EI*, 80. It should be noted that Lévinas credits the view to Plato, not to the Bible: "Discourse is discourse with God and not with equals, according to the distinction established by Plato in the *Phaedrus*." *Totality and Infinity*, 297; *TI*, 330.

98. Blanchot, "Keeping to Words," *Infinite Conversation*, 61; *EI*, 86.

99. Buber, *I and Thou*, trans. Ronald Gregor Smith, 2nd ed. (Edinburgh: T. and T. Clark, 1958), 99.

CHAPTER SEVEN

1. Blanchot, "Keeping to Words," *Infinite Conversation*, 59; *EI*, 84.

2. Blanchot, "Reading," *Space of Literature*, 193; *EL*, 254.

3. Also see Blanchot's remarks on reading in "Vast as the Night," *Infinite Conversation*, 320, 328; *EI*, 468–69, 481. Later still, Blanchot ventures to say "Reading is anguish," by which he means that no text has any ground. See *Writing of the Disaster*, 10; *ED*, 23.

4. Blanchot, "Communication," *Space of Literature*, 199; *EL*, 264. See Heidegger's comments on dialogue as a revelation of the essence of language in *Hölderlins Hymnen "Germanien" und "Der Rhein,"* *Gesamtausgabe*, 39:68–69. Also see Jean-Luc Nancy, *Le Partage des voix* (Paris: Galilée, 1982), 87–90.

5. See Walter J. Ong, *Ramus, Method, and the Decay of Dialogue* (Cambridge: Harvard University Press, 1958), 9, 287.

6. See Blanchot, "Communication," 204; *EL*, 271–72.

7. Michael Hamburger renders the lines as follows: "Much, from the morning onwards, / Since we have been a discourse and have heard from one another, / Has human kind learnt; but soon we shall be song." Hölderlin, *Poems and Fragments*, 461.

8. Blanchot, *Unavowable Community*, 2; *CI*, 10.

9. See Blanchot, "Marx's Three Voices," *Friendship*, 98–100; *A*, 115–17; and *Unavowable Community*, 2; *CI*, 10.

10. "Connaissance de l'inconnu" appeared in *Nouvelle Revue Française* 108 (December 1961): 1081–94; "Tenir parole" followed in *Nouvelle Revue Française* 110 (February 1962): 290–98; and a third dialogue, "L'Indestructible," concluded the series in *Nouvelle Revue*

Française 112 (April 1962): 671–80. This third dialogue was recast as "Le Rapport du troisième genre (*homme sans horizon*)" and "L'indestructible" in *L'Entretien infini*.

11. See Blanchot, "From Anguish to Language," *Faux Pas*, 1–16; *FP*, 9–23; "How Is Literature Possible?" 76–77; *FP*, 92–93; "Le Terrorisme, méthode de salut public," *Combat* 7 (July 1936): 106.

12. Augustine, *Enarrationes in Psalmes*, 62.16. Speaking of God, Augustine says, "semper enim ille maior est."

13. Lévinas, "God and Philosophy," *Of God Who Comes to Mind*, 69; *DVI*, 115.

14. The distinction between the immediate and the nonmediate is often missed by commentators on Blanchot. See, for example, Ullrich Haase and William Large, *Maurice Blanchot* (London: Routledge, 2001), 100.

15. See John Henry Newman, *An Essay in Aid of a Grammar of Assent*, introd. Nicholas Lash (Notre Dame: University of Notre Dame Press, 1979), 36.

16. Blanchot, "How to Discover the Obscure?" *Infinite Conversation*, 42; *EI*, 59.

17. See, for example, Plotinus, *Enneads*, 5.3.15.33–35.

18. According to this way of thinking, miracles are to be explained by way of *potentia absoluta* understood as *potentia extraordinaria*.

19. Leibniz, *Discourse on Metaphysics, Correspondence with Arnaud, Monadology*, 2nd ed., introd. Paul Janet (La Salle, Ill.: Open Court, 1973), "Monadology," § 45. In a well-known passage Kant rejected Leibniz's argument in his *Critique of Pure Reason*, A602/B630.

20. Heidegger, *Being and Time*, 183.

21. See, in particular, "As something possible, it is to show as little as possible of its possibility. On the other hand, if Being-towards-death has to disclose understandingly the possibility which we have characterized, and if it is to disclose it *as a possibility*, then in such Being-towards-death this possibility must not be weakened: it must be understood *as a possibility*, it must be cultivated *as a possibility*, and we must *put up with* it *as a possibility*, in the way we comport ourselves towards it." *Being and Time*, 306.

22. Adorno, *Metaphysics*, 107.

23. For a defense of the possible as a category unable to be subsumed by onto-theology, see Richard Kearney, *The God Who May Be* (Bloomington: Indiana University Press, 2001), especially chap. 5.

24. Derrida notes, and is rightly critical of, the elision of "community" and "fraternity" in Blanchot. See his *Politics of Friendship*, trans. George Collins (London: Verso, 1997), 48.

25. See Blanchot's discussion of Musil, "The Experience of 'the Other State,'" *Book to Come*, 141–49; *LV*, 193–206.

26. Musil, *Man without Qualities*, 2:828.

27. Blanchot, "Le Communisme sans héritage," *Comité* 1 (1968): 14; *EP*, 115. None of the texts now believed to be by Blanchot are signed. See his "Sur les Comités d'action," *Les Lettres Nouvelles* 109–9 (1969): 184–88, and "Lettres à Christian Limousin," *Gramma* 3–4 (1975), especially the letter of July 28, 1975.

28. See Blanchot, *Unavowable Community*, 30, 32; *CI*, 52, 56.

29. See Blanchot, "Affirmer la rupture," *Comité* 1 (1968): 4–5; *EP*, 104–6. In one sense, as

Blanchot acknowledges, what he proposes must fall under the sign of theory. Yet no panoptic vision of politics is thereby supposed.

30. Blanchot, "The Wooden Bridge (repetition, the neutral)," *Infinite Conversation*, 392; *EI*, 575.

31. *Midrash Rabbah*, trans. and notes by Rabbi Dr. H. Freedman and Maurice Simon, foreword by Rabbi Dr. I. Epstein, 10 vols. (London: Soncino Press, 1939), vol. 1: *Genesis*, 1:1. Philo relates the same story in "On the Account of the World's Creation" but significantly talks of "Divine Reason" rather than Torah. See *Philo*, trans. F. H. Colson and G. H. Whitaker, 10 vols. (Cambridge: Harvard University Press, 1929–62), 1:17–20.

32. *The Babylonian Talmud*, trans. Rabbi Dr. I. Epstein (London: Soncino Press, 1938), vol. 2: *Shabbath* 88b. Cf. vol. 6: *Sukkah* 55b.

33. Roger Laporte notes that Blanchot uses the phrase "l'ancien l'effroyablement ancien" "at least seven times" over the course of his writing life. See his essay "'L'Ancien, l'effroyablement ancien,'" *Études* (Paris: P. O. L., 1990), 17. For a more general consideration of fear in Blanchot and Lévinas, see Françoise Collin, "La Peur: Emmanuel Lévinas et Maurice Blanchot," *Cahier de l'Herne: Emmanuel Lévinas*, ed. Catherine Chalier and Miguel Abensour (Paris: Éditions de l'Herne, 1991), 334–56.

34. Blanchot, *The One Who Would Not Accompany Me*, 23–24; *CQMP*, 47–48.

35. Blanchot, "Literature and the Original Experience," *Space of Literature*, 229; *EL*, 305.

36. Hegel, *Aesthetics: Lectures on Fine Art*, 1:11.

37. Blanchot, *Step Not Beyond*, 14; *PAD*, 24. The expression "ancient fear" is found on pp. 1, 133, and 134; *PAD*, 8, 182.

38. See Blanchot, "Traces," *Friendship*, 220; *A*, 249.

39. See Blanchot, *Writing of the Disaster*, 51; *ED*, 85. Also see "The Two Versions of the Imaginary," *Space of Literature*, 262; *EL*, 353.

40. Proust, *In Search of Lost Time*, vol. 6: *Time Regained*, 264.

41. Blanchot, *Step Not Beyond*, 1; *PAD*, 8.

42. Blanchot, *Writing of the Disaster*, 72; *ED*, 117. My emphasis.

43. Blanchot, *Writing of the Disaster*, 137; *ED*, 208.

44. See Bataille and Leiris's notes on Laure's notion of the sacred in Laure, *Collected Writings*, 87. See Bataille, *Inner Experience*, 81; *OC*, 5:96; and *On Nietzsche*, trans. Bruce Boone, introd. Sylvère Lotringer (New York: Paragon House, 1992), 19; *OC*, 6:44. Blanchot alludes to Laure in his comments on the secret in *The Unavowable Community*, 20; *CI*, 39. Bataille and Laure play a variation on a well-known theme of Christian spirituality. Consider the following: "To lose yourself, as if you no longer existed, to cease completely to experience yourself, to reduce yourself to nothing is not a human sentiment but a divine experience." Bernard of Clairvaux, *On Loving God* (Kalamazoo: Cistercian Publications, 1973), 10:27.

45. See Blanchot, "The Detour toward Simplicity," *Friendship*, 193; *A*, 220. Also see chapter 3, "The Impossible."

46. Blanchot, "Mystery in Letters," *Work of Fire*, 57; *PF*, 63.

47. Blanchot, *The One Who Would Not Accompany Me*, 43; *CQMP*, 83.

48. The expression occurs several times in the récit. See Blanchot, *The One Who would not*

Accompany Me, 69, 74, 92; *CQMP*, 129, 139, 172. Hegel evokes "a depth which is empty" in his *Phenomenology of Mind*, 74.

49. L.-F. Fogel and D. Rondeau, eds., *Pourquoi écrivez-vous? 400 écrivains répondent* (Paris: Libération, 1985), 188. My translation.

50. Blanchot, *Most High*, 23; *TH*, 29.

51. Blanchot, *The One Who Would Not Accompany Me*, 72; *CQMP*, 136. There are no quotation marks around *dehors* in the French text.

52. Blanchot, "On One Approach to Communism," *Friendship*, 95; *A*, 112.

53. The verb *entretenir* does not presume the priority of constituted subjects in quite the way that "to converse" does in English.

54. Blanchot, *Space of Literature*, 275; *EL*, 373.

55. *Philosophical Works of Descartes*, 1:166.

56. See ibid., vol. 2, passim.

57. Lévinas, *Totality and Infinity*, 49; *TI*, 41. Translation slightly modified.

58. Lévinas speaks of the "false and cruel transcendence" of the pagan gods in his 1976 essay "Secularization and Hunger," trans. Bettina Bergo, *Graduate Faculty Philosophy Journal* 20, no. 2, and 21, no. 1 (1998): 9.

59. Blanchot, "Connaissance de l'inconnu," *Infinite Conversation*, 53; *EI*, 76.

60. Lévinas maintains the formality of the *vous* form in *Totalité et infini* but in "Phénomène et énigme" has recourse to the *tu* form. I quote the relevant passage later in this chapter. For the *vous* form, see *Totality and Infinity*, 75; *TI*, 73.

61. One of the speakers in "Humankind" paraphrases Antelme, "'To live,' as he more or less says, 'is then all that is sacred.'" *Infinite Conversation*, 133; *EI*, 196. On the fascination of the sacred, see Otto, *Idea of the Holy*, chap. 6. I have already noted that, in his consideration of the sacred, Blanchot pays no attention to the profane as a distinct category; and it should be added that whereas in religion an experience of the sacred usually involves a sense of profound diminishment of the "I," for Blanchot fascination results in a shift from the "I" to "one."

62. Jean Paulhan, "The Marquis de Sade and His Accomplice," in Marquis de Sade, *Justine, Philosophy in the Bedroom, and Other Writings* (New York: Grove, Weidenfeld, 1990), 10.

63. Blanchot, *Lautréamont et Sade*, 35.

64. See the Marquis de Sade, *La Philosophie dans le boudoir* (Paris: U. G. E., 1991), 40–44.

65. See Lévinas, *Existence and Existents*, 93–94; *EE*, 159–61; *Time and the Other*, 51–57; *TA*, 31; and *Ethics and Infinity: Conversations with Philippe Nemo*, trans. Richard A. Cohen (Pittsburgh: Duquesne University Press, 1985), 51–52; *Éthique et infini: Dialogues avec Philippe Nemo* (Paris: Fayard, 1982), 42–43.

66. Lévinas, "The Poet's Vision," *Proper Names*, 137; *SMB*, 23.

67. Blanchot, "On One Approach to Communism," 97; *A*, 114.

68. Lévinas, *Totality and Infinity*, 80; *TI*, 78–79.

69. Lévinas, "Enigma and Phenomenon," *Collected Philosophical Papers*, 73; *DEHH*, 216. Also see with respect to this passage, "The Name of God According to a Few Talmudic Texts," *Beyond the Verse: Talmudic Readings and Lectures*, trans. Gary D. Mole (Bloomington: Indiana Uni-

versity Press, 1994), 127–28; *L'Au-delà du verset: Lectures et discours talmudiques* (Paris: Éditions de Minuit, 1982), 157; and *Otherwise Than Being or Beyond Essence*, 185; *AQE*, 281.

70. See Lévinas's essay "A Religion for Adults," *Difficult Freedom*, 11–23; *DL*, 24–42.

71. Lévinas, "The Trace of the Other," *Deconstruction in Context: Literature and Philosophy*, ed. Mark C. Taylor (Chicago: University of Chicago Press, 1986), 359.

72. Kant, *Religion within the Limits of Reason Alone*, trans., introd., and notes by Theodore M. Greene and Hoyt H. Hudson (New York: Harper and Row, 1960), 5.

73. Lévinas, *Totality and Infinity*, 40; *TI*, 30.

74. Blanchot, *Writing of the Disaster*, 64; *ED*, 106.

75. Lévinas, *Totality and Infinity*, 297; *TI*, 330. Also see III. B.7, "The Asymmetry of the Interpersonal." Later, in *Pour l'amitié* (1996), Blanchot rephrases Lévinas's statement in order to speak of "the Good" rather than "God." See *Pour l'amitié*, 35.

76. Lévinas, *Totality and Infinity*, 291; *TI*, 324.

77. Blanchot, *Infinite Conversation*, 70; *EI*, 100.

78. Ibid., 56; *EI*, 80. For Blanchot's retraction, see 441 n. 2; *EI*, 80.

79. Lévinas, *Totality and Infinity*, 95; *TI*, 96.

80. Blanchot, "Humankind," *Infinite Conversation*, 130; *EI*, 191.

81. Under the influence of Lévinas's *Autrement qu'être* Blanchot will speak in his later writings of *Dire* rather than *parler*.

82. Antelme, *Human Race*, 3.

83. Blanchot, "The Limit-Experience," *Infinite Conversation*, 212; *EI*, 315.

84. The dialogue was renamed "Parler, ce n'est pas voir" before it was included in *L'Entretien infini*.

85. Heidegger, "A Dialogue on Language," *On the Way to Language*, trans. Peter D. Hertz (New York: Harper and Row, 1971), 13.

86. See Blanchot, "Knowledge of the Unknown," *Infinite Conversation*, 57; *EI*, 82.

87. See Nancy, *The Inoperative Community*, ed. Peter Connor, trans. Peter Connor et al., foreword by Christopher Fynsk (Minneapolis: University of Minnesota Press, 1991), 14–15. The first part of Blanchot's *La Communauté inavouable* is in part a response to the first chapter of Nancy's study. Also see Jorge Semprun's comments on death as the substance of brotherhood in Buchenwald, *L'Écriture ou la vie* (Paris: Gallimard, 1994), 34.

88. Blanchot, *Death Sentence*, 20; *AM*, 36.

89. Blanchot, "Our Responsibility," trans. Franklin Philip, *For Nelson Mandela*, ed. Jacques Derrida and Mustapha Tlili (New York: Henry Holt, 1987), 250. The French original, *Pour Nelson Mandela*, appeared with Gallimard in 1986.

90. Raymond Carpentier, "L'Échec de la communication," in Jean Lacroix, ed., *Les Hommes devant l'échec* (Paris: Presses Universitaires de France, 1968), 20. I have quoted David Maisel's translation, as given in André Neher, *The Exile of the Word: From the Silence of the Bible to the Silence of Auschwitz* (Philadelphia: Jewish Publication Society of America, 1981), 48. Carpentier goes on to say, "Le vrai dialogue est sacrifice" (20). Also note Neher's remark about the Maharal de Prague, "Le face-à-face organique des hommes ne peut être qu'une discorde. La forme ontologique de la communication c'est la *concurrence.*" *Le Puits*

de l'exil: La théologie dialectique du Maharal de Prague (1512–1609) (Paris: Éditions Albin Michel, 1966), 180.

91. Blanchot, *Writing of the Disaster*, 34; *ED*, 59–60.

92. On this theme see Jean-Michel Besnier, *La Politique de l'impossible: L'Intellectuel en révolte et engagement* (Paris: La Découverte, 1988). Without subscribing to Blanchot's sense of the impossible, Luce Irigaray sees herself as "a political militant for the impossible, which is not to say a utopian. Rather, I want what is yet to be as the only possibility of a future." *I Love to You: Sketch of a Possible Felicity in History*, trans. Alison Martin (London: Routledge, 1996), 10. See Penelope Deutscher, "Luce Irigaray and Her 'Politics of the Impossible,'" *Forms of Commitment: Intellectuals in Contemporary France*, ed. Brian Nelson, Monash Romance Studies 1 (1995), 141–56, especially 147. Derrida has also come to talk of politics and the impossible. See my essay "Impossible Marx," *Arena Journal* 5 (1995): 185–208.

93. Lévinas, *Otherwise Than Being*, 183; *AQE*, 281. The expressions "the kingdom of God" and "the kingdom of the LORD" are not first heard in the New Testament but are Targumic in origin. See Bruce Chilton, *God in Strength: Jesus' Announcement of the Kingdom* (Sheffield: J. S. O. T. Press, 1987).

94. Blanchot, *Unavowable Community*, 25; *CI*, 46. For friendship as neutral and associated with the unknown, also see Robert Antelme's comments as quoted by Dionys Mascolo, *Autour d'un effort de mémoire* (Paris: Éditions Maurice Nadeau, 1987), 23–24.

95. Blanchot, "For Friendship," trans. Leslie Hill, *Oxford Literary Review* 22 (2001): 35; *PA*, 35.

96. Blanchot, *Unavowable Community*, 40; *CI*, 68. Lévinas hesitates about using the word *love* with regard to ethics. He remains wary of the romantic implication of fusion. See, for example, Richard Kearney's interview, "Ethics of the Infinite," *Dialogues with Contemporary Continental Thinkers: The Phenomenological Heritage* (Manchester: Manchester University Press, 1984), 66.

97. For the hint of catastrophe in "far off . . . near," see Jan L. Koole, *Isaiah III*, 3 vols. (Leuven: Peeters, 2001), vol. 3: *Isaiah Chapters 56–66*, 110.

98. Blanchot observes in a letter to Bataille, January 6, [1962], "J'ajoute que l'amitié est aussi la vérité du désastre." *Georges Bataille, Choix de letters: 1917–1962*, 595.

99. Blanchot, *Friendship*, 291; *A*, 328. I take it that Blanchot requires the end of the final sentence to read "but abides in the movement of understanding . . . " It is worth comparing Blanchot's insight with the lines of the unidentified guest in one of T. S. Eliot's plays: "We must also remember / That at every meeting we are meeting a stranger." T. S. Eliot, *The Cocktail Party* (London: Faber and Faber, 1950), 63.

100. Blanchot held a similar view about May 1968 which, be believed, opened a space of friendship: one should not write *about* it. See the unsigned text "Tracts, affiches, bulletins," *Comité* 1 (1968): 16; *EP*, 118.

101. On this notion see Jean-Luc Marion, "In the Name: How to Avoid Speaking of It," *In Excess: Studies of Saturated Phenomena*, trans. Robyn Horner and Vincent Berraud (New York: Fordham University Press, 2002), 157.

102. Blanchot, "The Limit-Experience," *Infinite Conversation*, 211; *EI*, 313.

CONCLUSION

1. Bataille, *Inner Experience*, 102; *OC*, 5:120.
2. Blanchot, "Master Eckhart," *Faux Pas*, 23; *FP*, 31.
3. Blanchot, "L'Étrange et l'étranger," *La Nouvelle Revue Française* 70 (1958): 675.
4. Blanchot, "The Relation of the Third Kind (*Man without Horizon*)," *Infinite Conversation*, 72; *EI*, 102.
5. Tzvetan Todorov claims, without citing evidence, that Blanchot endorsed the anti-Semitism of Action Française and calls for an acknowledgment of his past blindness. See his *Face à l'extrême* (Paris: Éditions du Seuil, 1991), 128–29. Blanchot's letter to Roger Laporte of December 24, 1992, discussed in chapter 2 n. 3, could perhaps be construed as a response to Todorov's criticism.
6. See Karl Rahner, "Anonymous Christians," *Theological Investigations*, vol. 6: *Concerning Vatican II*, trans. Karl-H. Kruger and Bonniface Kruger (London: Darton, Longman and Todd, 1969), and "Anonymous and Explicit Faith," *Theological Investigations*, vol. 16: *Experience of the Spirit: Source of Theology*, trans. David Morland (New York: Crossroad, 1979).
7. For a close engagement with the issue, see Eberhard Jüngel, "*Extra Christum nulla salus—* A Principle of Natural Theology? Protestant Reflections on the 'Anonymity' of the Christian," *Theological Essays*, trans. and introd. J. B. Webster (Edinburgh: T. and T. Clark, 1989), 173–88.
8. Blanchot, "Being Jewish," *Infinite Conversation*, 125; *EI*, 183.
9. Theodor Adorno, "Reason and Revelation," *Critical Models: Interventions and Catchwords*, trans. and preface by Henry W. Pickford (New York: Cornell University Press, 1998), 139.
10. Blanchot, "Literature and the Original Experience," *Space of Literature*, 233; *EL*, 311.
11. Blanchot, "Note," *Infinite Conversation*, xii; *EI*, viii.
12. See, for instance, Tzvetan Todorov, *Critique de la critique: Un roman d'apprentissage* (Paris: Éditions du Seuil, 1984), 73–74.
13. Blanchot, "L'Inquisition a détruit la religion catholique . . . " (206).
14. Blanchot cites Bousquet on counterwriting in his review of *Traduit du silence* (1941) in *Faux pas*. "Contre-écrire," Bousquet writes, "C'est une operation que je me promets de pratiquer. Elle consiste à dégager toujours, sous la forme d'une vérité très simple, ce qui va consacrer l'inutilité du plus grand nombre de paroles. On appelle cela arriver à l'expression definitive." Joë Bousquet, *Traduit du silence* (1941; Paris: Gallimard, 1968), 36. Also see Pierre Klossowski, *Les Lois de l'hospitalité* (Paris: Gallimard, 1965), 131–32, and Jacques Derrida, "Following Theory," *Life after Theory*, ed. Michael Payne and John Schad (New York: Continuum, 2003), 10.
15. William Wordsworth, essay II, "Essays on Epitaphs," in *The Prose Works of William Wordsworth*, ed. W. J. B. Owen and Jane Worthington Smyser, 3 vols. (Oxford: Clarendon Press, 1974), 2:84–85.
16. Blanchot, *Writing of the Disaster*, 142; *ED*, 215.

17. See Theodor Adorno, *Negative Dialectics*, trans. E. B. Ashton (London: Routledge and Kegan Paul, 1973), 141.

18. See Heidegger, *Phenomenology of the Religious Life*, trans. Matthias Fritsch and Jennifer Anna Gosetti (Bloomington: Indiana University Press, 2004), and, for example, Oscar Cullmann, *Christ and Time: The Primitive Christian Conception of Time and History*, rev. ed. (Philadelphia: Westminster Press, 1964).

19. As indicated in chapter 6, Blanchot's ideas on prophecy partly derive from his reading of Neher, *L'Essence du prophétisme* (Paris: Presses Universitaires de France, 1955). André Neher's volume appeared the same year as *L'Espace littéraire*. It is worth noting that, although he does not affirm the Outside, Lévinas seeks to rethink spirituality by way of the exteriority of the other person. See his "Amour et révélation," *La Charité aujourd'hui: Colloque de théologiens organisé par l'Association pour la Fondation Jean-Rodhain* (Paris: Éditions S. O. S., 1981), 135.

20. For Fichte, "spirit" is "the ability of the productive imagination to convert feelings into representations." See J. G. Fichte, "Second Lecture concerning the Difference between the Spirit and the Letter," *Early Philosophical Writings*, ed. and trans. Daniel Breazeale (Ithaca: Cornell University Press, 1988), 199. Blanchot would respond by saying that counterspirit contests that ability and seeks to pass beyond representation to the Outside.

21. Geoffrey Hartman, *Scars of the Spirit: The Struggle against Inauthenticity* (New York: Palgrave Macmillan, 2002), 107. Hartman speaks of "counter-spirit" in his "Maurice Blanchot: The Spirit of Language after the Holocaust," in Hart and Hartman, *The Power of Contestation: Perspectives on Maurice Blanchot*.

22. Blanchot, "Prophetic Speech," *Book to Come*, 83; *LV*, 115.

INDEX

Adorno, Theodor W., 6, 155–56, 198, 226, 267n13, 271n70
allegory, 163, 165, 180–81, 209
Angela of Foligno, 23–24
Angelus Silesius, 31, 34
Antelme, Robert, 127–29, 185, 194, 215–16
Aristotle, 111, 134, 197
art, 108, 123, 136–37, 210, 224; and the Cogito, 126; and the impossible, 65–67, 76–77, 148; and the mystical, 22–23; and the Outside, 154–55, 227; and the sacred, 101, 224; spiritual needs, 202–3
atheism, 3, 10, 59, 83, 184, 230; and the absence of God, 4–6; and counter-spirituality, 20–21; and "I," 6, 141, 143, 147, 160; and nonexperience, 160; as protest, 143; and the sacred, 3–4, 10
Augustine, Saint, 3, 9, 15–16, 24, 252n22; *Confessions*, 55–61, 202; *On Christian Teaching*, 67–68; *On True Religion*, 141
Auschwitz, 70–72, 74
autobiography, 55, 59, 70
Autrui, 128–29, 179, 188–99, 207–8, 213–15, 225

Balthasar, Hans Urs von, 10, 48, 275n33
Barth, Karl, 195
Barthes, Roland, 87
Bataille, Georges, 4–5, 11, 35, 106, 110, 121, 126, 205, 223, 240n78; *L'Expérience intérieure*, 23–25, 27–28, 30, 33, 35, 74, 80, 133, 242n14; and Hegel, 91; *Madame Edwarda*, 4, 42–43; and the mystical, 9; and poetry, 84–85; and religion without religion, 11; and the

sacred, 16–17, and transcendence, 38–45
Baudelaire, Charles, 22, 79
Beckett, Samuel, 64, 103
Benjamin, Walter, 156
Bernard of Clairvaux, Saint, 36, 288n44
Bible, 15, 162–90 *passim*, 226; Torah, 164, 176, 180, 199–200
Blanchot, Maurice: *Aminadab*, 12, 68–70, 136, 166; *L'Arrêt de mort*, 13, 62, 136, 169–74, 231, 254n51; *Celui qui m'accompaignait pas*, 111, 130, 200, 231; *Le Dernier Homme*, 129, 254n51; *La Folie du jour*, 72, 238n66; *L'Instant de ma mort*, 20, 71–75; *Au moment voulu*, 166–67; "Une scène primitive," 51–75 *passim*, 160; *Thomas l'obscur*, 3, 11–13, 24–29, 44, 62, 106, 114–15, 117–19, 121, 135–36, 149, 164–65, 231; *Le Très-Haut*, 52, 99, 110–11, 136, 165, 205
Bonaventure, Saint, 15
Bonnefoy, Yves, 76–104 *passim*
book, 45, 64, 69, 175–78; absence of, 1; secret, 45–46, 48–49
Breton, André, 43, 63, 80–82, 123
Bruno, Giordano, 2, 228, 233n4
Buber, Martin, 179–80, 190

Caillois, Roger, 5, 11, 28
Cajetan, Tommaso, 40, 43
Campanella, Tommaso, 2
Camus, Albert, 105–6
Char, René, 4, 10, 96–98, 103–14, 164
Chestov, Lev, 81–82
Chrétien, Jean-Louis, 157
Cixous, Hélène, 53
Cogito, 15, 26, 40, 105–26 *passim*, 200. *See also* "I"

communication, 16, 39, 61, 113, 185, 218, 224; and community, 194–194; and death, 81, 85; and the impossible, 126; and the sacred, 4–5, 93, 204–5; and the self, 121; and surrealism, 39; and the unknown, 30, 110

communism, 194, 210, 227–28; and affirmation, 155; communism beyond communism, 129, 175, 214; and community, 199, 205

community, 63, 193, 205, 221, 228, 231; and death, 218–219; and ethics, 214–15; and the "I," 124, 129–31; and sacred, 5, 9, 11, 17, 28, 39; unavowable, 103

contestation, 6, 19, 29, 33–34, 36, 44, 64, 90, 223; and experience, 47, 161; and language, 90; and selfhood, 201, 218–19; and the social, 155; and the sublime, 120; and words, 23

Dante, 2, 13, 78

dark gaze, 8, 11–14, 20, 23, 27, 40, 66, 98, 102, 118, 144, 160, 171, 193, 218, 224

Dasein, 129, 150, 159; and death, 67, 112–13, 154, 182, 198

death: approach of, 112; of author, 23, 51, 87, 168, 210; as dying, 67–68, 75, 86, 95, 109, 130, 171–74; "I am dead," 22–23, 29, 32, 59, 124; as impossible, 54, 67, 87, 109, 114, 125, 130; and love, 26, 174; and philosophy, 81; as possible, 54, 65, 67, 87, 112, 130, 147–48; and speech, 83; work of, 54, 112, 172

Deleuze, Gilles, 154, 157

Denys the Areopagite, 30, 90, 140, 142, 223

Derrida, Jacques, 45, 154, 214

Descartes, René, 10, 112, 123, 130, 185, 192; and the Cogito, 15, 105–8, 114–15, 123; and God, 207–8

dialogue, 75, 190, 216–17, 219, 225; and Israel, 179; as response, 192–93

disaster, 13, 16, 221, 231; and art, 65; and community, 214; and fall, 126, 203; and Freud, 52–53; and the Holocaust, 70; and the loss of the divine, 59; and totality, 18

Duns Scotus, Johannes, 10, 224, 236n40

duplex ordo, 41–42, 48–49

Durkheim, Émile, 4–5, 11, 16–17, 160

Eckhart, Meister, 31–34, 142, 223–24, 227

Einstein, Albert, 6–7, 18

Éluard, Paul, 80–81

ethics, 9, 175, 213–14, 218, 220; and "I," 122, 124; and Judaism, 180–82, 186–87; and Outside, 209–10; and religion without religion, 11; and unity, 189

everyday, 48, 106, 145–45, 154, 158–61

excarnation, 79, 81, 89, 102

existentialism, 39, 43

experience, 20, 28, 33, 46, 61, 125, 133–61 passim; and counter-experience, 153; of death, 111, 137, 173; as Erfahrung, 5, 47, 134–35, 137–38, 152, 155, 203; as Erlebnis, 47, 134, 152, 203, 224; of experience, 27, 134, 152; of image, 145, 149–50; inner, 23, 27–35, 43, 61, 74, 81, 96, 135, 221–22; limit, 5, 23, 29, 53, 117, 194, 200, 202–3, 205; and literature, 12, 35, 46–47, 61, 125, 133–34, 138–39, 144–45, 149; of nonexperience, 9, 20, 47–48, 57, 61, 74, 126–27, 145, 160, 203; original, 41, 44, 64, 125–26, 146–47, 153, 158, 202; of strangeness, 187–88, 208, 226; of subjectivity, 139

Faith, 169, 189, 224–25; and Eckhart, 31; and Judaism, 189; profession of, 142; and religion, 16 fascination, 57, 70, 113, 126, 152, 159; and the gaze, 13, 66; and literature, 86; and the *mysterium tremendum*, 208; and writing, 146

fear, 195–96, 202

Fernandez, Roman, 62, 73

Fichte, J. G., 115, 119, 122

Foucault, Michel, 106, 139, 141, 143–44, 154, 158–59

fragmentary, 17, 155–57, 175

Freud, Sigmund, 52–53, 63, 121–22

friendship, 220–22

Garrigou-Lagrange, Réginald, 37–38

gaze, 14–15, 17, 150, 214, 218; of Orpheus, 13, 16–17; phenomenological, 14–15. *See also* dark gaze

Gide, André, 35, 107, 139, 144

gnosticism, 10, 87, 102, 125, 142; and Heidegger, 94; and kabbalah, 90; and surrealists, 79–82

God, 1–2, 32, 195–96, 221; absence of, 3, 5, 20, 55, 64, 146–47; death of, 17, 78, 89, 183; experience of, 151–52; and Godhead, 31–32, 89, 224; *imago dei*, 151; and possibility, 148; and transcendence, 5, 9, 40–41, 61, 89, 141–42

Hartman, Geoffrey, 229

Hegel, G. W. F., 11, 32, 77, 90, 115–18, 168, 175, 229; and aesthetics, 201–2; and death, 65, 67, 85–86, 172; and Kojève, 29; 83; *Lectures on the Philosophy of Religion*, 152–53; *Phenomenology of Spirit*, 77, 136–39; and selfhood, 109–12; and Spirit, 19

Heidegger, Martin, 10–11, 29, 77–78, 93–96, 127, 148–51; and art, 136, 209; "Aus einem Gespracht von der Sprache," 216–18; and Dasein, 112–13, 129, 182; and death, 65, 67; and looking, 14–15; *Sein und Zeit*,

107–9; "Was ist Metaphysik?" 144–45, 158–59

Heraclitus, 10, 95, 97

history, 29, 111, 155–56, 165, 180, 184, 188

Hölderlin, Friedrich, 17, 99–101, 147, 156, 164, 224, 227, 265n90; and community, 193; and the holy, 91–95; and the withdrawal of the gods, 204, 206

Holocaust, 70. *See also* Auschwitz

human relation. *See* relation without relation

Hume, David, 60, 142, 216

Husserl, Edmund, 14–15, 139, 141, 143, 146, 214; and epistemology, 112; and experience, 134–35; and intentionality, 158, 160

"I," 2, 55, 128–29, 154, 157–58, 174; and God, 141–42, 147–48; and Hegel, 110–11, 116; and Kant, 121; and literature, 51; "me," 122–23, 128, 130; and poet, 95; and selfhood, 59–60. *See also* Cogito

icon, 102–3

Ignatius Loyola, Saint, 27

il y a, 37, 57, 59, 61, 195, 201, 209

image, 12, 27, 51, 114, 145; and event, 57, 61; and icon, 102–3; and negation, 148–51; and negativity, 65–66; and the Outside, 140; and poetry, 87–88; and the Turin Shroud, 170; and unknown, 27

imaginary, 66, 77, 145, 148–49, 229

imagination, 97

immediate, 92–93, 205

incarnation, 82, 89. *See also* excarnation

infinite/infinity, 2, 225, 231; and desire, 209; as divine predicate, 179; and God, 206–7; and Judaism, 181; and the neutral, 75

interruption, 10, 87, 91, 186, 218

Irenaeus, Saint, 176

Isaac the Blind, Rabbi, 176

Jaspers, Karl, 31, 114, 198
Jean-Paul, 133
Jews, 161, 177–90 *passim*, 225–26
John of the Cross, Saint, 30, 34, 48,
  69–70, 223
Jouhandeau, Marcel, 12
Juarroz, Roberto, 10, 160
Jüngel, Eberhard, 152, 230

Kabbalah, 90, 176–77
Kafka, Franz, 10, 55, 140, 154; and Judaism, 199–200; and the negative, 90
Kant, Immanuel, 44, 91, 111–12, 142,
  149, 152–53, 199; and the Cogito, 107,
  121, 124–25, and experience, 9, 46;
  and religion, 11, 184, 212; and the
  subject, 130; and the sublime, 88
Kierkegaard, Søren, 31, 41, 196, 210,
  240n85
Klossowski, Pierre, 3, 75, 209, 228,
  245n56
Kojève, Alexandre, 29, 83, 85, 115–17

Lactantius, 16
Lautréamont, Comte de, 55, 133, 138,
  175
learned ignorance, 32–33
Leclaire, Serge, 54
Leibniz, Gottfried, 107, 198
Leiris, Michel, 124, 135, 139
Leo XIII, Pope, 38, 40
Lévinas, Emmanuel, 10, 15, 66–67, 103,
  166, 203, 218, 220; and *Autrui*,
  128–29; and ethics, 122; 181–90 *passim*; and God, 206–15 *passim*, 225; and
  language, 113, 120; and religion without religion, 4, 11
literature, 1, 44, 50, 64–65, 145; and
  Cogito, 120; and consciousness, 2–3,
  6, 11; and criticism, 46–47, 97, 125;
  and death, 85–86; and deceit, 61, 139;
  enabling condition, 44; and experience, 12, 35, 61, 133–34, 139–40,

144–45, 149; and language, 87; mystery in, 45, 48; and the Outside, 103;
  possibility of, 44–47, 86, 125; quest
  for origin, 126; and the singular, 168;
  space of, 8, 108, 145. *See also* poetry
Louis XVI, 3–4
Lubac, Henri de, 37, 41, 43, 48, 155,
  249n106
Luther, Martin, 204–5

Maimonides, Moses, 177
Mallarmé, Stéphane, 19, 50, 60, 64, 78,
  87, 109, 116, 175; and death, 22–23,
  29; "Les Fenêtres," 48, 55; and the
  now, 98; and the void, 146–47
Mann, Thomas, 155
Marion, Jean-Luc, 10, 153
Mauras, Charles, 50
Mauss, Marcel, 5, 11, 16, 205
Mendelssohn, Moses, 162
Merleau-Ponty, Maurice, 107, 121
messiah, 164, 228–29
metaphysics, 97, 108, 110, 112
Michelet, Jules, 4
Milton, John, 117
Musil, Robert, 52, 199
mystery, 5, 7, 174
mysticism, 46, 52, 73, 137, 140, 160; and
  art, 22–23; and atheism, 59; Christian,
  25, 48, 55–59, 73; ecstasy, 29–30, 43,
  57, 72–74; of exegesis, 9–10; and inner experience, 24–25, 30, 32–34;
  mystic marriage, 69–70; and philosophy, 46; of spirituality, 9; of writing, 10

Nancy, Jean-Luc, 88, 266n103
negativity, 29, 109–10, 137; and death,
  117, 172–73; and Hegel, 85–87; and
  image, 65–55
neuter, philosophy of, 10, 97, 108,
  224–25, 230
neutral, 10–11, 121, 161, 204; and Augustine, 68, 75; experience of, 113;

and Heraclitus, 97; and language, 117; and mystery, 208; as origin, 126, as outside dialectic, 91; and reading, 193

Newman, John Henry, 197

Nicholas of Cusa, 32–33, 198

Nicole, Pierre, 45

Nietzsche, Friedrich, 6, 19, 112, 131, 147–48; and art, 65, 67; and eternal return, 60, 75, 224; and God, 83, 89, 183

night, 12, 25–26, 40, 83; *other* night, 17, 26, 60–61

nihilism, 17–18, 227, 230–31

nonknowledge, 33–34, 39, 141, 204, 223

Novalis, 118–20, 175

One, 8, 154, 161; and God, 141–42; and Plotinus, 197; and poetry, 82–83, 90

Origen, 151, 163, 176, 283n52

Outside, 4, 18, 20, 23, 63, 96, 178, 201, 209; approach of, 20, 202; and art, 67; and being, 10; and experience, 144–45, 151, 159; Foucault on, 144, 154, 159; and God, 9–10, 140; and *il y a*, 57; and light, 15; and literature, 103, 231; and origin, 60–61; and otherness, 189; and responsibility, 196, 210; and sacred, 9, 18, 99, 103, 204, 206, 210; and writing, 203. *See also* neutral

Parmenides, 10, 14, 195, 207

Pascal, Blaise, 2, 41, 220

Paulhan, Jean, 44–46, 57, 86

Pfeiffer, Jean, 133–38

Pius X, Pope Saint, 38–39

Pius XII, Pope, 37

Plato, 18, 177, 198; *Parmenides*, 207; *Phaedrus*, 95; *Timaeus*, 145, 195

Plotinus, 58, 140–41, 197

poetry, 104, 146; and absence of God, 64; and desire, 96; and dying, 77, 95, 146; and finitude, 79; hatred of, 84–85; and inner experience, 34–35; and mystical,

25; and the One, 90; and prophecy, 98–100; religious, 34–35; and sacred, 36, 76, 93–96, 98, 147, 196, 224–25; and salvation, 79, 90; and unity, 183–85 possible, 33, 106, 123, 160; attunement to, 159, 199, human relation with, 148; impossible, 29, 77, 126, 204; and Kant, 153; and neutral, 97–98; and Outside, 67; and Plotinus, 197–98; and poetry, 85, 87, 94, 98–99, 100; and the self, 111–12, 131

Poulet, Georges, 1–6, 11, 20

prayer, 6, 20, 56, 58–59, 93–94, 103, 225

Proclus, 140–42

prophecy, 11, 95–96, 102, 104, 225

Proust, Marcel, 2, 35, 48, 140, 145, 203; *À la recherche du temps perdu*, 110, 129

Przywara, Erich, 94

psychoanalysis, 52–55, 63–64, 121

Rahner, Karl, 152, 226, 230, 262n61

reading, 167, 192–93

récit, 61–64, 73

relation without relation, 139, 211–12; and Heidegger, 136; and the impossible, 153; and neutral, 61

relativity, 6–8

religion, 5, 16, 20, 42, 211, 213; without religion, 4, 11, 98, 179, 186, 212, 230

resemblance, 66–67, 148–49

resurrection, 168, 172–74, 198

revelation, 11, 51–52, 60, 188, 225; and the Bible, 164, 176; and Hölderlin, 214; and human relation, 194; and Lévinas, 184, 186, 212; and Nietzsche, 162; and the poet, 98

revolution, French, 3–4, 86; Kantian, 46

Ricoeur, Paul, 122

Riemann, Georg, 7

Rilke, Rainer Maria, 10, 12, 35, 47–48, 126; "Nirgents ohne Nicht," 19–20, 102, 159

Rimbaud, Arthur, 35, 81, 138

romanticism, 76, 118, 126, 132–33, 156

Rosenzweig, Franz, 156

Sacred (holy), 4, 20, 128, 224–25; anteriority of, 17; and art, 23, 101; and cosmos, 18; Durkheim on, 4; and ethics, 186; and Hades, 10; and Heidegger, 93; and immediate, 87–88, 90, 92–94, 98, 100; and inner experience, 28; and Israel, 178; and Lévinas, 186; and neutral, 160, 204; and Outside, 206, 210, 227; and profane, 4–5, 16, 41–42; without the sacred, 9, 11, 100; and sacrifice, 16–17; and speech, 9, 25, 93–96, 136, 164, 168

sacrifice, 16, 23, 35–36, 91, 95–96

Sade, Marquis de, 3, 209

Sartre, Jean-Paul, 14, 39

saying/said, 120, 184–85

Schlegel, Friedrich, 175

Schleiermacher, Friedrich, 152

secret, 52, 61, 81, 204–5; secret book, 45–46, 48–49

Shekinah, 187

Shroud of Turin, 169–70

skepticism, 42, 113–14, 120

Sophocles, 17, 221

speech, 109, 118–19, 128, 209, 215; infinite, 129, 216; plural, 154, 178; poetic, 90, 118; as promised land, 180; sacred, 9, 25, 93, 136, 164, 168. *See also* sacred

spirit, 19–20, 91; counterspirit, 19–21, 228–31

Suárez, Francesco, 10, 40, 43, 108, 224, 267n15

sublime, 52, 88–89, 120, 229

suffering, 127–28, 130, 158–59, 173

supernatural, 41

surrealism, 39–40, 43–44, 77, 80, 123, 134–35, 139

Talmud, 176–77

terrorism, 44–47, 50, 84, 216

Theodore the Studite, Saint, 102–3

theology, 36, 137, 184; of earth, 82, 87; of light, 14–16, 144; negative theology, 84, 87–88, 90, 97, 99, 106, 201; new theology, 9, 24, 27–28, 30, 36, 50, 106; noncorrelational, 184, 212; *nouvelle théologie*, 9–10, 36–39, 41; positive theology, 79, 198; theological antimodernism, 40–41; theological modernism, 37–39, 134

Thomas Aquinas, Saint, 15, 38, 40, 42–43, 142

time, 145–47, 159; and eternity, 183; and literature, 152–53; messianic, 229–30; "other time," 102–3; without present, 75; of prophecy, 99

trace, 182–83, 185, 212

Traherne, Thomas, 2

transcendence, 55, 161, 207–8; and atheism, 43; and Eckhart, 31; and ethics, 185, 189–90, 195, 208, 212; of France, 50; as gnostic, 89; and God, 5, 9, 40–41, 61, 141–42, 195; and immanence, 38, 41, 43; and the negative, 61; neoplatonic, 142; phenomenological, 100, 112, 127, 207; and sacred, 100; self-transcendence, 35, 57–58; and theological modernism, 38

transgression, 16, 30–31, 40, 42–43, 55, 74–75

Union, 70

unity, 3, 161, 183, 191; and cosmology, 6–7; and God, 140–42, 177, 179; of Godhead and soul, 31; Greek heritage of, 18; pre-theoretical, 185–86; and the subject, 158

universe, 1–2, 7–8

unknown, 23, 25, 27–28, 97, 106, 126–27, 221; and God, 25

Urban II, Pope, 91

Valéry, Paul, 114

Verlaine, Paul, 146

Weil, Simone, 156, 238n55

Whitehead, Alfred North, 7

Winnicot, Donald, 54

Wordsworth, William, 89, 202, 228–29

writing, 8, 64, 83, 139, 154; and counter-writing, 228; and dark gaze, 12; and dying, 147; and experience, 47; first and second, 177, 180, 200; and "I," 129; and nonexperience, 47; and Outside, 203–4; as response to Cogito, 120; and selfhood, 131; and transcendental disunity, 111; and unwriting, 83. *See also* literature